COGNITIVE NEUROSCIENCE

EDITED BY
MICHAEL D. RUGG
UNIVERSITY OF ST ANDREWS

Psychology Press
a member of the Taylor & Francis group

Psychology Press, Publishers
Taylor and Francis
27 Church Road
Hove East Sussex, BN3 2FA
UK

British Library Cataloguing in Publication Data
A catalogue record for this book is available from the British Library.

ISBNs: 0-86377-489-X HB
        0-86377-490-3 PB

Cover painting *Sculptured head* (Tempra) by Ian Hopton

Printed and bound in the United Kingdom by Biddles Ltd,
Guildford and King's Lynn.

Contents

3. Neural coding schemes for sensory representation: theoretical proposals and empirical evidence 47
David K. Fotheringhame & Malcolm P. Young

4. Learning and memory: computational principles and neural mechanisms 77
Matthew L. Shapiro & Howard Eichenbaum

Contributors

Anders M. Dale, Department of Radiology, Harvard Medical School and MGH NMR Center, Charlestown, MA 02114, USA.

Howard Eichenbaum, Laboratory of Cognitive Neurobiology, Department of Psychology, Boston University, 64 Cummington Street, Boston MA 02215, USA.

David K. Fotheringhame, University Laboratory of Physiology, Parks Road, Oxford OX1 3PT, UK.

Karl J. Friston, Wellcome Department of Cognitive Neurology, Institute of Neurology, 12 Queen Square, London WC1N 3BG, UK.

Christopher D. Frith, Wellcome Department of Cognitive Neurology, Institute of Neurology, 12 Queen Square, London WC1N 3BG, UK.

Apostolos P. Georgopoulos, Brain Sciences Center, Veterans Affairs Medical Center and Departments of Physiology, Neurology and Psychiatry, University of Minnesota Medical School, Minneapolis, MN 55417, USA.

David Howard, Department of Speech, University of Newcastle-upon-Tyne, Newcastle-upon-Tyne NE1 7RU, UK.

John Jonides, Department of Psychology, University of Michigan, 525 E. University St., Ann Arbor, MI 48109-1109, USA.

Stefan Köhler, Rotman Research Institute of Baycrest Centre for Geriatric Care, 3560 Bathurst Street, North York, Ontario, Canada M6A 2E1.

Marta Kutas, Departments of Cognitive Science and Neurosciences, University of California, San Diego, La Jolla, CA 92093-0515, USA.

Morris Moscovitch, Department of Psychology, Erindale Campus, University of Toronto, Mississauga, Ontario, Canada L5L 1C6; Rotman Research Institute and Department of Psychology of Baycrest Centre, North York, Ontario, Canada M6A 2E1.

William A. Phillips, Centre for Cognitive and Computational Neuro-science, Department of Psychology, University of Stirling, Stirling FK9 4LA, UK.

Michael D. Rugg, Wellcome Brain Research Group, School of Psychology, University of St Andrews, St Andrews, Fife KY16 9JU, UK.

Matthew L. Shapiro, Department of Psychology, McGill University, Montreal, Quebec, Canada H3A 1B1.

Edward E. Smith, Department of Psychology, University of Michigan, 525 E. University St., Ann Arbor, MI 48109-1109, USA.

Malcolm P. Young, Neural Systems Group, Department of Psychology, University of Newcastle-upon-Tyne, Ridley Building, Claremont Place, Newcastle-upon-Tyne NE1 7RU, UK.

Series preface

Over the past 20 years enormous advances have been made in our understanding of basic cognitive processes concerning issues such as: what are the basic modules of the cognitive system? How can these modules be modelled? How are the modules implemented in the brain. The book series *Studies in Cognition* seeks to provide state-of-the-art summaries of this research, bringing together work on experimental psychology with that on computational modelling and cognitive neuroscience. Each book contains chapters written by leading figures in the field, which aim to provide comprehensive summaries of current research. The books should be both accessible and scholarly and be relevant to undergraduates, postgraduates and research workers alike.

Glyn Humphreys
27 May 1997

Studies in Cognition

Editor: Glyn Humphreys
University of Birmingham

CHAPTER 1

Introduction

Michael D. Rugg

Cognitive neuroscience aims to understand how cognitive functions, and their manifestations in behaviour and subjective experience, arise from the activity of the brain. It is a hybrid of several historically distinct disciplines, among which there was until recently little interchange of methods and ideas. These disciplines include those, such as cognitive psychology, that are concerned primarily with the investigation of human cognition and behaviour at a purely functional level;[1] others, such as clinical neuropsychology, that study the consequences of damage to the human brain; and the fields of physiological psychology and neurophysiology, which until recently were primarily concerned with the neural bases of basic sensory, motor and motivational processes in animal subjects.

No single factor has caused the convergence of these different subjects to form cognitive neuroscience. Rather, it is the outcome of a series of different developments over the past twenty or so years, some of which are highlighted below.

First, there has been an increasingly close interaction between cognitive psychology and clinical neuropsychology. For well over a hundred years research has been conducted on the cognitive impairments caused by brain injury, and much of this research has been directed towards identifying the brain regions and their interconnections that support the cognitive processes responsible for complex behaviours such as language. For most of this time, research was hampered by a

1

lack of well-articulated models of normal function, necessary both to guide empirical questions and to provide a framework within which to interpret results. The emergence of cognitive psychology during the 1960s, with its focus on the development of functional models of normal cognitive processing, and of experimental methods for testing such models, provided neuropsychology with a much-needed conceptual framework. Now securely embedded within this framework, studies of the effects of brain lesions in humans remain central to the aim of understanding the relationship between the brain and cognition. For instance, they play a key role in determining whether a given brain region or structure is necessary for a particular cognitive process to proceed normally.

Lesion studies also provide important information about cognition at the functional level. Studies of cognitive impairment following brain damage and, in particular, of patterns of dissociations between impaired and unimpaired functions, can provide powerful constraints on functional models (Shallice 1988). For example, the proposal that "implicit" and "explicit" memory rely on functionally distinct processes receives much of its support from the finding that amnesic patients, in whom explicit memory for all types of new information is grossly impaired, exhibit normal implicit memory in a wide range of circumstances (Moscovitch et al. 1993; see also Ch. 4).

A second factor in the emergence of cognitive neuroscience has been the application of invasive methods in experimental animals to the study of "higher" cognitive functions. The most prominent of these methods is the recording of the activity of single neurons from awake animals as they perform experimental tasks. This method has been employed to study such functions as face recognition (e.g. Perrett et al. 1992; see also Ch. 3), attention (e.g. Moran & Desimone 1985), and working memory (e.g. Funahashi et al. 1993; see also Ch. 8), each of which is also the object of intensive research in human subjects. The findings from such studies provide otherwise unobtainable data about how information is physically represented and manipulated by the brain. Together with studies employing the much older, but still important, method of investigating the effects of brain lesions in experimental animals, single neuron recording gives information about the structures and circuits that participate in different cognitive functions. Equally important, single neuron recording provides knowledge about *how* neurons implement these functions. This knowledge is essential if our understanding of the neural basis of human cognition is to extend beyond the localization of the brain regions that support different cognitive processes to include a specification of how neurons perform the computations that are manifest as those processes.

A third component in the evolution of cognitive neuroscience has been the development of methods that allow the structure and function of the human brain to be investigated *in vivo*. Until the early 1970s, it was rarely possible to localize with accuracy lesions or other brain abnormalities in a living person. Up until this time, reliable information about the localization of brain lesions came almost exclusively from the relatively few cases in which a post-mortem investigation was possible. With the introduction first of computed tomography (CT), and then the more sensitive technique of magnetic resonance imaging (MRI), it became possible to obtain accurate information about lesion localization in living subjects. As MRI, unlike CT, does not depend on the use of ionizing radiation, it can also be used to perform research on the brains of healthy individuals, allowing a search for relationships between structural measures, such as the volume of a given structure, and cognitive function (e.g. Golomb et al. 1994).

More profound still has been the advent of techniques that permit not just the structure but also the *functions* of the brain to be imaged non-invasively (Posner & Raichle 1994). The most prominent of these techniques are positron emission tomography (PET) and functional magnetic resonance imaging (fMRI), both of which are able to localize precisely the changes in cerebral blood flow that accompany local variations in neural activity (see Ch. 6), albeit at a temporal resolution far removed from the time-course of the activity itself. Other techniques, based on recording from the scalp the electromagnetic fields that are generated by synchronous neural activity, allow the neural correlates of the processing of discrete stimuli to be tracked in real time, albeit at a spatial resolution much coarser than that possible with blood flow measures (see Ch. 7). While by no means free from methodological and conceptual difficulties (Rugg & Coles 1995), these metabolic and electromagnetic imaging methods provide a way to investigate the activity of the brain in healthy subjects while they undertake experimental tasks. Among their other uses, these methods are an important tool with which to test and refine functional models of cognition, providing a means to separate and identify different cognitive functions in terms of their differing neurophysiological correlates.

Functional neuroimaging methods are also an important complement to studies of the effects of brain lesions, in that they permit hypotheses derived from such studies to be tested in normal subjects. They also extend the lesion method in two important respects. First, they can identify brain regions that, while not necessary for the performance of a cognitive task, are nonetheless engaged during its performance. Such regions cannot be detected by the lesion method. Secondly, functional neuroimaging permits investigation of the function of regions, such as the anterior cingulate cortex, that are rarely damaged selectively in humans, and about which little has been learned from lesion studies.

Finally, functional neuroimaging has an important role to play in establishing the generality of findings from invasive studies of animals to the human brain. For example, findings from PET and fMRI experiments strongly suggest that the pattern of regional and functional specificity found in the different cortical areas of the primate visual system largely holds true for the human visual cortex (e.g. Lueck et al. 1988, Watson et al. 1993, Sereno et al. 1995). Such findings are important because existing functional neuroimaging techniques provide only crude information about the neurophysiological properties of the neural activity that they detect, and give no information at all about the dynamics of the activity of individual or small populations of neurons. It is therefore necessary to rely on the results of invasive studies in animals to obtain knowledge about what neurons are actually doing when they engage in information processing. The closer the functional correspondence between the brain of another species and the human brain at the regional level, the more likely it is that there will be a close functional correspondence at the cellular level too.

The fourth factor to contribute to the emergence of cognitive neuroscience has been the development of computational models of cognitive function employing "parallel distributed" or "connectionist" architectures (Rumelhart & McClelland 1986). This general approach, based on highly abstracted model neural networks (of varying degrees of biological plausibility), represents a radical departure from earlier "symbol based" approaches to modelling cognition (Newell et al. 1989). The connectionist approach gains much of its appeal for two reasons. First, the architecture of the models is intrinsically "brain like", and is thus well suited to modelling functions thought to be implemented by the brain. Secondly, the models are often implemented in computer software, allowing their functional properties to be tested empirically. Computational models based on connectionist networks are now routinely employed to develop and test hypotheses about how information is acquired, represented and modified by populations of real neurons (e.g. Zipser & Andersen 1988; see also Chs 1, 4 and 5); to construct functional models of cognitive processes (e.g. Seidenberg & McClelland 1989); and to model the effects of brain lesions (e.g. Plaut & Shallice 1993).

In light of this brief survey, one might ask whether cognitive neuroscience is anything more than a collection of methods. Given its relatively short history, it would not be surprising if there was rather little that distinguished it as a scientific discipline in its own right. It is arguable, however, that in at least one respect cognitive neuroscience is distinct from the disciplines from which it derives. The distinctiveness arises from a lack of commitment to a single "level" of explanation, and the resulting tendency for explanatory models to combine functional and physiological concepts. A good example of this explanatory approach is given in Chapter 8 of the present volume by Jonides and Smith. They argue that because spatial and verbal working memory tasks are associated with different patterns of brain activation, as measured by PET, these two forms of working memory are functionally distinct. Thus, they argue, the PET findings support models of working memory, derived from behavioural and neuropsychological evidence, that propose separate systems for the storage and rehearsal of spatial and verbal material. On the basis of the PET results, they further argue that the processes underlying memory for spatial and verbal memory rely largely on the posterior cortex of the right and left hemispheres, respectively.

This account stands in marked contrast to the explanations historically favoured in cognitive psychology and cognitive science, where the emphasis is placed on models of cognitive function that make no reference to their possible biological substrates, and the idea that biological data might constrain or inform functional models is treated with scepticism (e.g. Mehler et al. 1984). Accounts such as that of Jonides and Smith, typical within cognitive neuroscience, do not merely reflect a change of explanatory style from the one favoured in the past. They are predicated on an important assumption, which is at the heart of contemporary cognitive neuroscience. This is that the mapping between physical activity in the brain and its functional state is such that when two experimental conditions are associated with different patterns of neural activity, it can be assumed that they have engaged distinct cognitive functions.

While this assumption may at first glance appear to be no more than a corollary of materialism (i.e. that mental (cognitive) phenomena are caused exclusively by the physical activity of the nervous system), this is not in fact the case (Rugg & Coles 1995). Implicit in the assumption is the notion that a one-to-one mapping exists between a given pattern of neural activity and a specific cognitive function. The idea that multiple cognitive functions can be associated with the same pattern of brain activity is obviously incompatible with materialism. This is not the case, however, for the idea that the same cognitive function can be implemented by more than one pattern of brain activity; this idea is wholly compatible with a materialist position. Nevertheless, if it is correct (and it has been seriously advanced as a reason why physiological data are irrelevant to functional models of cognition (Mehler et al. 1984)), it would undermine the rationale for many of the present-day approaches to interrelating brain and cognition. In fact, there is little evidence at present to suggest that it is true. Thus there is no reason to question the assumption that, however complex the mapping might be between cognition and its biological substrate (see Mesulam (1990), for discussion of this issue), it is invariant. This is fortunate, as it is this assumption that opens the way for physiological data to play a role in the development of functional models of cognition, and for such models to provide the framework within which to interpret physiological findings. It is as well to remember, however, that, in principle at least, the assumption is open to empirical refutation.

1.1 THIS BOOK

It would be impossible in a book of this size to deal with the range of topics falling within the scope of cognitive neuroscience or, for any given topic, to cover all of the different ways it could be approached empirically and theoretically (diversities well illustrated by the extensive collection of papers in Gazzaniga (1995)). The chapters that follow do, however, cover a representative sample of the major topic areas of cognitive neuroscience, and range across the diverse empirical and conceptual approaches that are typical of the discipline.

The contributions fall into four groups. Chapters 2 (Phillips) and 3 (Fotheringhame and Young) address fundamental questions about the ways in which neurons encode, transform and transmit information. In the first of these chapters, emphasis is placed on how computer simulations of idealized neural networks, when subjected to appropriate biological constraints, can be used to gain an understanding of how networks of real neurons might work. The subsequent chapter deals with how information might be represented in the brain by single or relatively small numbers of neurons. It discusses the long-standing question of how information about a single concept is distributed across a population of neurons, as well as the relatively neglected topic of whether, and if so how, temporal coding is employed to represent information in the central nervous system.

Chapters 4 (Shapiro and Eichenbaum) and 5 (Georgopoulos) have as their topics learning and memory, and voluntary movement, respectively. The first of these chapters focuses on why memories for certain classes of event depend critically upon the hippocampus, and what this structure does to give it such a pivotal role in memory. Chapter 5 describes some of the basic properties of skilled movements, and discusses in detail the role played by neurons in the motor cortex in the programming of directional movement. Both of these contributions draw mainly upon evidence obtained from animal studies to address questions about how information is processed and represented by local populations of neurons, and to develop empirically constrained computational models of these operations. The chapters provide good examples of a level of analysis of brain function that, for the foreseeable future, is unlikely to be directly possible in human subjects.

For reasons that have already been discussed, functional neuroimaging of the brain in healthy human subjects plays a major role in cognitive neuroscience, so much so that it is already difficult to follow key developments in several subject areas without some understanding of the most commonly used methods. Chapters 6 (Frith and Friston) and 7 (Kutas and Dale) cover the two most important classes of methods for the non-invasive measurement of human brain activity: the functional neuroimaging of cerebral blood flow with PET and fMRI (Ch. 6), and the recording of time-locked electrical and magnetic fields from the surface of the scalp (Ch. 7). The chapters give accessible and up-to-date descriptions of these different techniques. Chapter 6 goes beyond an account of the methodology of PET and fMRI to discuss how these techniques can contribute to the study of interactions between different functionally specialized brain regions. Chapter 7 includes a historically based review of research employing event-related brain potentials, providing a gateway to a large and sometimes rather intimidating literature extending back more than thirty years.

The final three chapters are concerned with different topics in human cognition. In Chapter 8, Jonides and Smith draw on cognitive studies in humans, experimental data from PET, and single neuron data from animal studies, in order to develop a combined functional and neurobiological model of human working memory. Howard (Ch. 9) reviews the representation of language processes in the brain, criticizing the "classical" view handed down from the nineteenth century, and revising it in light of data derived from modern structural and functional neuroimaging methods. In the final chapter, Köhler and Moscovitch review neuropsychological evidence for dissociations between performance on visual tasks and conscious appreciation of the stimuli on which the performance is based. They address the question of whether these disorders of visual awareness can be accommodated within a single explanatory framework, and discuss their implications for understanding perhaps the most difficult of all questions confronting cognitive neuroscience: how the brain gives rise to conscious experience.

ACKNOWLEDGEMENTS

I am grateful to L. Annlo-Vento, D. I. Donaldson and A. D. Milner for their comments on a draft version of this chapter.

NOTE

1. By this is meant the development of theories of cognitive function framed in terms of abstact information processing operations, without reference to their physiological basis.

REFERENCES

Funahashi, S., M. V. Chafee, P. S. Goldman-Rakic 1993. Prefrontal neuronal activity in rhesus monkeys performing a delayed anti-saccade task. *Nature* **365**, 753–6.

Gazzaniga, M. S. 1995. *The cognitive neurosciences*. Cambridge, MA: MIT Press.

Golomb, J., A. Kluger, M. J. de Leon, S. H. Ferris, A. Convit, M. S. Mittelman, J. Cohen et al. 1994. Hippocampal formation size in normal human aging: a correlate of delayed secondary memory performance. *Learning and Memory* **1**, 45–54.

Lueck, C. J., S. Zeki, K. J. Friston, M -P. Deiber, P. Cope, V. J. Cunningham, A. A. Lammerstsma et al. 1988. The colour centre in the cerebral cortex of man. *Nature* **340**, 386–9.

Mehler, J., J. Morton, P. W. Jusczyk 1984. On reducing language to biology. *Cognitive Neuropsychology* **1**, 83–116.

Mesulam, M. M. 1990. Large-scale neurocognitive networks and distributed processing for attention, language, and memory. *Annals of Neurology* **28**, 597–613.

Moran, J. & R. Desimone 1985. Selective attention gates visual processing in the extrastriate cortex. *Science* **229**, 782–4.

Moscovitch, M., E. Vriezin, Y. Goshen-Gottstein 1993. Implicit tests of memory in patients with focal lesions or degenerative brain disorders. In *Handbook of neuropsychology*, vol. 8, F. Boller & J. Grafman (eds), 133–73. Amsterdam: Elsevier.

Newell, A., P. S. Rosenbloom, J. E. Laird 1989. Symbolic architectures for cognition. In *Foundations of cognitive science*, M. I. Posner (ed.), 93–132. Cambridge, MA: MIT Press.

Perrett, D. I., J. K. Hietanen, M. W. Oram, P. J. Benson 1992. Organisation and functions of cells responsive to faces in the temporal cortex. *Philosophical Transactions of the Royal Society of London, Series B* **335**, 23–30.

Plaut, D. C. & T. Shallice 1993. Deep dyslexia – a case study of connectionist neuropsychology. *Cognitive Neuropsychology* **10**, 377–500.

Posner, M. I. & M. E. Raichle 1994. *Images of mind*. New York: Scientific American Library.

Rugg, M. D. & M. G. H. Coles 1995. The ERP and cognitive psychology: conceptual issues. In *Electrophysiology of mind: event-related brain potentials and cognition*, M. D. Rugg & M. G. H. Coles (eds), 27–39. Oxford: Oxford University Press.

Rumelhart, D. G. & J. L. McClelland 1986. *Parallel distributed processing: explorations in the microstructure of cognition,* 2 vols. Cambridge, MA: MIT Press.

Seidenberg, M. S. & J. L. McClelland 1989. A distributed developmental model of word recognition and naming. *Psychological Review* **96**, 523–68.

Sereno, M. I., A. M. Dale, J. B. Reppas, K. K. Kwong, J. W. Belliveau, T. J. Brady, B. R. Rosen et al. 1995. Borders of multiple visual areas in humans revealed by functional magnetic resonance imaging. *Science* **268**, 889–93.

Shallice, T. 1988. *From neuropsychology to mental structure*. Cambridge: Cambridge University Press.

Watson, J. D. G., R. Myers, R. S. J. Frackowiak, J. V. Hajnal, R. P. Woods, J. C. Mazziotta, S. Shipp et al. 1993. Area V5 of the human brain: evidence from a combined study using positron emission tomography and magnetic resonance imaging. *Cerebral Cortex* **3**, 79–94.

Zipser, D. & R. A. Andersen 1988. A back-propagation programmed network that simulates response properties of a subset of posterior parietal neurons. *Nature* **331**, 679–84.

CHAPTER 2

Theories of cortical computation

William A. Phillips

2.1 INTRODUCTION

If we are ever to understand how the mammalian cerebral cortex works then we will have to understand the work that it does. Theories of cortical computation must therefore play a crucial role in cortical neurobiology and neuropsychology. Many such theories have been proposed, and although none has gained general acceptance, many may have useful insights to offer. Just a few are outlined here. For other views on these issues see Abeles (1991), Arbib (1995), Gluck & Rumelhart (1990), Schwartz (1990), Churchland & Sejnowski (1992) and Koch & Davis (1994). By "computation" I simply mean any procedure for transmitting, recoding, combining, storing or using information, where "information" is defined as in the very general conception provided by Shannon & Weaver (1949). Variablity and uncertainty are at the heart of this conception. Information in this sense is anything that reduces uncertainty about things that vary.

Sections 2.2 and 2.3 of this chapter are concerned with general strategic issues. Section 2.4 asks "What basic computational capabilities do the various cognitive subsystems require?", and "What cortical circuitry is available to provide those capabilities?". The focus there, and throughout the chapter as a whole, is upon capabilities and mechanisms that are common to many different regions of cortex. Section 2.5 gives a brief overview of the elements of computation in neural systems, i.e. the local processing units, the architectures, the relation between knowledge and processing, and the procedures for learning. The remaining five sections then outline five different hypotheses concerning the basic goals of cortical computation. These theories are not necessarily incompatible, and all may have something to contribute to a more complete theory of how the cortex computes.

2.2   VARIETIES AND USES OF COMPUTATIONAL THEORY

2.2.1   Three levels of description

Marr (1982) distinguished three levels at which any information processing system can be understood: (a) computational theory; (b) representation and algorithm; and (c) hardware implementation. What Marr calls the level of "computational" theory is the most abstract. It is concerned with describing the underlying information processing task to be performed, and with making clear why it is useful and how, in principle, it is possible. "Representation" is concerned with the format in which information is presented, and "algorithm" is concerned with the detailed operations performed upon that information. To illustrate these distinctions he uses the example of addition. Numbers can be given in many different formats, Arabic numerals and Roman numerals for example. The detailed operations required to achieve addition are different in these two systems because representation and algorithm are highly interdependent. Arithmetic is much more difficult using Roman numerals, and that is one reason why Arabic numerals are now more widely used. The goal of addition and the underlying mathematical theory is identical in the two cases, however. Hardware implementation is concerned with how the representations and algorithms are actually realized in a physical system. This can be done in many different ways, just as many different representations and algorithms can be used to achieve the same underlying goals. Thus what Marr calls the level of computational theory is the most general, and the level of hardware implementation is the most specific.

Attempts to describe the underlying computational capabilities of cortex are a major focus of this chapter, but the phrase "computational theory" is used in a broader way than by Marr, so as to include any theory of how the system computes, whether that theory is abstract and general or detailed and specific.

2.2.2   Simplifying theories and detailed models

Sejnowski et al. (1988) distinguish between simplifying models and realistic models. The former emphasizes underlying capabilities or principles of organization so as to show clearly what they are, why they work and why they are useful. The latter aims to replicate known anatomical structures and physiological process as accurately as possible within a working simulation. An essential difference between them thus concerns the amount of detail that is relevant. For simplifying theories the less detail the better; for realistic models the more detail the better.

One way to see this difference is to imagine that visiting scientists from some alien culture with no prior knowledge of flight or aeroplanes discover a jumbo jet sitting on a beach, and try to discover what it does and how it works. The simplifying approach would try to find some fundamental capabilities and principles of operation. If they realized that flight was an essential underlying capability they might eventually think about propulsion, lift and aerodynamics. This might lead them to explore computer models of a single simplified wing in an air current. The detailed modelling approach, by contrast, would be concerned with simulating part or all of the jumbo, including possibly the internal seating, the navigation and communication equipment, etc., in as much detail as possible, to explore their properties. Eventually the two approaches might be combined by applying the principles of aerodynamics and air-flow studies to the jumbo's wing simulated in detail.

Sejnowski et al. (1988) note that the detailed modelling approach needs a large amount of empirical data, because it is unlikely to be of use to build a model with much more detail in it than is known about the system it attempts to model. Complex models that fix the values of many free parameters just to explain a few empirical phenomena are not satisfactory, because theories are of most value when they use a little to explain a lot. Sejnowski et al. (1988) also note that the goals of simplification and detailed modelling may be better seen as end-points on a continuum, and that any given theory may be simplifying in relation to some aspects and detailed in relation to others.

2.2.3 Primal theories and formal theories

It is important to realize that theories of cortical computation cannot be identified with computer programs that deal with some aspect of the brain. If the program deals only with aspects little related to computational function, then it would not constitute a theory of cortical computation even though it was a program. Furthermore, not all theories of cortical computation need be expressed as computer programs. They could simply be expressed formally, and studied by techniques of mathematical analysis that do not use computer simulations, as done for example in many sections of the book by Amit (1989) on the modelling of brain functions. Furthermore, a theory could be proposed in terms that are neither formalized nor simulated, but are approximate, vague or crude conceptions of possible computational principles. Valentino Braitenberg (personal communication) calls these "primal theories", and he thinks them valuable because they usually precede and give direction to the more precise formulations. Others may refer to them as "frameworks" to distinguish them from formal theories and detailed models. One role of cognitive psychology and neuropsychology is therefore to help us form the right primal theories. This role may be crucial because it is all too easy to spend a lot of time and effort studying some formalizable approach that implies implausible psychological assumptions.

2.2.4 Uses of computational theories and simulations
Computational theories have various uses:

(a) The main use of simplifying theories is to show how complex behaviour can arise from the interaction of elements with simple properties, and thus to aid comprehension of a complex mass of data by revealing underlying commonalities or principles that run through and unite many diverse findings.

(b) Abstract theories of the job to be done may suggest ways in which it could be done, and some brain theories begin with a thorough job specification and then derive the theory from that (e.g. Intrator & Cooper 1992).

(c) Important roles for formal theories are to demonstrate that some conception of cortical function is internally coherent, and to show why the capabilities that it delivers would be useful. In addition, formalization may aid comparisons between informal theories that are expressed in terms which on the face of it are different (Grossberg 1990). Formalizing the theories will help show whether any differences are fundamental or terminological.

(d) Another role for computational theories is to show that the conceptions of cortical function upon which they are based do not depend upon implicit but unintended assumptions. A theory stated in less precise terms may depend upon some construct, such as a homunculus, that may be neither intended nor made explicit. Simulations showing that the explicitly stated components of the theory are adequate for the task for which they are designed helps reduce this difficulty.

(e) Theories suggest new experiments together with the reasons for doing them.

(f) An important role for simulations is to determine whether the operations required by the theory are feasible within given constraints on such things as processing time and information storage capacity.

(g) Simulations can also be used to perform experiments that cannot be performed on animals or humans for either practical or ethical reasons.

(h) Simulations are often used to derive predictions from theories the implications of which are otherwise unclear.

(i) Finally, theories of cortical computation, and of neural computation in general, can be used to help design information processing systems that can be applied to technological problems that have not been adequately solved within the conceptual framework of conventional computing (e.g. Hecht-Nielsen 1990, Haykin 1994).

2.3 LEVELS OF ORGANIZATION AT WHICH COGNITION AND CORTEX MAY BE COMPREHENSIBLY RELATED

There are various levels of organization at which cortex and cognition can be studied (Shepherd 1990b; Churchland et al. 1990). At the lowest level that is relevant to the analysis of cortical computation there are the molecules that make up the cells and the neurotransmitters, etc. through which they communicate. Progressively larger structures are built from these, e.g.: the cell membranes together with their specialized synapses; microcircuits that process and communicate information between local regions of the dendritic trees of neurons (Shepherd 1990b); whole neurons; local cortical circuits that are made up of neurons all located within some tiny region of cortex; cortical regions or maps; systems composed of many cortical regions and the pathways connecting them; and, finally, the central nervous system as a whole. It may be supposed that we should try to relate cognitive processes only to the higher of these levels of cortical organization. In my opinion this is not so. Cognition and cortex may be comprehensibly related at all these levels. Some cognitive phenomena, such as the effects of certain drugs, pathologies or altered states of consciousness, may be best understood by using knowledge of how specific substances, such as neurotransmitters or neuromodulators, affect processing at the subcellular level. For a detailed example that relates schizophrenic disturbances to molecular processes via a model of cortical computation see Cohen & Servan-Schreiber (1992). Another, and much simpler, example is that the spectral-sensitivity function that is measured psychophysically for dark-adapted vision is directly comparable to the absorption spectrum of retinal rhodopsin to light of different wavelengths. The working assumption that I derive from these and many other examples is that possibilities for comprehensible relations between cortex and cognition exist at all levels of organization.

2.4 ASPECTS OF COGNITIVE AND CORTICAL ORGANIZATION

Various computational functions are performed at each level of organization. Theories should therefore be clear about the particular functions with which they are concerned. No theory that attempts to explain the whole of cognition on the basis of just a few cortical principles is likely to be successful. This can easily be seen in our analogy of aliens studying the jumbo jet, because no amount of insight into aerodynamics will help them understand how the plane maintains communication with control towers. Different subsystems may well interact with and constrain each other, but that doesn't invalidate the view that different subsystems play different roles in the system as a whole, and solve essentially distinct problems. This section therefore outlines some relevant aspects of the organization of cognition and cortex. In particular, we are concerned with computational capabilities that are required by many different cognitive subsystems, and with any intrinsic neural circuitry and processes that may be common to different cortical regions. More information on these issues can be found in other chapters of this book. They are discussed here to make clear what the focus of this chapter is, and how it relates to other issues.

2.4.1 Specialized cognitive functions
and their common computational requirements

Functional specialization is a central feature of cognitive organization. This has been shown by many studies of both normal and brain-damaged subjects, and it is most firmly established for basic perceptual and motor functions. The existence of functional specialization within the highest level functions such as strategic control is controversial, but there is evidence for it even there (Shallice 1991).

One major distinction is that between long-term memory (LTM) and working memory. The latter plays a central role in human thought and voluntary problem-solving, and is discussed elsewhere in this book (see Ch. 8). Here we focus on theories of basic cortical functions that do not depend in any essential way upon the voluntary thought processes of working memory.

Even within LTM there is good evidence for fundamental distinctions (Tulving 1985, Schacter 1987, Squire 1992). One major distinction is that between acquired skills and knowledge of specific unique events.

The skills may be sensorimotor, perceptual or conceptual, and the internal knowledge upon which they depend is often referred to as procedural memory. Knowledge of specific events is often referred to as episodic memory. The status of semantic memory, i.e. general knowledge that has been gradually acquired and which can be explicitly reported, remains unclear. Whatever the status of semantic memory, however, it is clear that episodic and procedural memories are fundamentally distinct. One clear difference is that episodic memory depends upon the hippocampus, whereas procedural memory does not (Squire 1992; Ch. 4). A crucial difference from the computational point of view is that procedural memory acquires knowledge of the general statistical structure of inputs and outputs, whereas episodic memory is concerned with particulars rather than generalities. Procedural memory must therefore combine knowledge gained from similar events that occur at different times, whereas episodic memory must not combine information from events that occur at different times, but must keep them distinct even if they are similar.

The remainder of this chapter focuses on theories that are concerned with the acquisition and use of skills. For a detailed computational theory of possible relations between episodic and procedural memories see McClelland et al. (1995). My working assumption is that enhanced corticohippocampal interactions in higher species improves their episodic memory capabilities, and in a way that depends upon the basic capabilities of the cortex.

It is likely that evolution has enhanced the basic capabilities in other ways, and in particular in relation to language, thought, long-range strategic planning and intentionality (i.e. relating and distinguishing between representations and referents). If so, an understanding of such functions may not follow simply from an understanding of the basic cortical capabilities with which we are concerned in this chapter.

It may seem that if we do not include thought, episodic memory, language, intentionality and planning in our focus of interest then we will leave little of concern to psychologists. This is not so, however, because much behaviour depends upon the basic processes with which we are concerned. For an example from the study of animal behaviour consider MacPhail's (1987) search for differences in the basic learning abilities of different species. This led him to the hypothesis that all the learning and "problem-solving" abilities of non-human animals depend upon a basic associative process that learns the statistical contingencies between events, and that there are no essential differences in "intelligence" between non-human animals. This hypothesis may seem implausible but it is not easily disproved, and it may rightly emphasize how much is achieved by common basic processes. For an example from the study of human cognition consider the theories of functional specialization proposed by cognitive neuropsychologists to explain face perception or the recognition and reproduction of spoken and written words. These are the focus of much research within experimental psychology and neuropsychology, and they are good examples of procedural skills. Finally, a focus on such basic processes is in keeping with an argument presented by Marr & Nishihara (1978). They suggest that we should first try to understand the operations that humans perform well, reliably and fluently. These may not be the tasks that we understand well intellectually, such as mental arithmetic, because we usually perform such tasks poorly, which suggests that they are not the tasks to which our basic computational capabilities are well suited. An adequate understanding of the limitations and capabilities of the more basic functions may eventually make some contribution to our understanding of the higher cognitive functions that are built upon them, by showing why those higher functions are necessary and upon what foundations they are built.

Along with most cognitive neuropsychologists I assume that procedural knowledge is organized into many different subsystems, and a primary goal of neuropsychology has been to map this architecture, i.e. to determine what things there are specialized subsystems for and by what routes they are connected. These theories usually distinguish different subsystems by the contents with which they are concerned, such as the auditory forms of familiar words, or the visual forms of facial expressions. To the extent that they do so they suggest that these subsystems differ primarily in what it is that they operate upon, rather than in the operations performed. Mapping the cognitive architecture is a complex and important task, but the detailed accuracy of these maps is not necessarily crucial to the attempt to determine what operations these subsystems perform. Adding or deleting subsystems or routes between them will only be crucial to that issue to the extent that it changes the set of basic computational capabilities required. Neuropsychologists do try to explore what individual subsystems do, but this has not been their primary concern. A central issue for cognitive neuropsychology therefore concerns the basic computational capabilities required by the various cognitive subsystems that it proposes. If there are any common computational requirements then it is those that we should seek to explain in terms of neural structures and processes common to different regions of cortex.

2.4.2 Specialized cortical regions and their common intrinsic organization

It is now well established that cortex contains many specialized regions. The number varies with species, rising to more than a hundred in

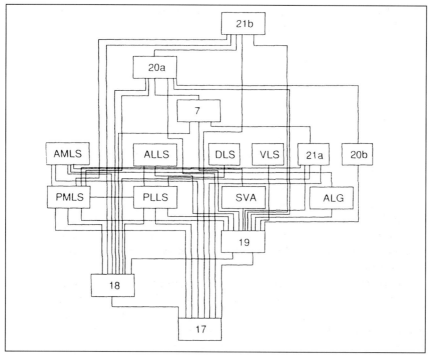

FIG. 2.1.   A hierarchy of visual areas in cat cerebral cortex. There are 16 areas, or regions, arranged in 8 hierarchical levels and connected by 62 pathways. Most connections between areas are reciprocal, with approximately as many descending fibres as ascending. Ascending and descending pathways are not distinguished in this figure. In macaque monkeys there are 32 areas, arranged in 10 cortical levels, connected by 305 pathways, and organized in an analogous hierarchical fashion to that shown here. The numbers refer to cortical areas distinguished using Brodmann's criteria. The additional areas are: ALG, anterolateral gyrus; ALLS, anterolateral lateral suprasylvian; ALMS, anteromedial alteral suprasylvian; DLS, dorsolateral suprasylvian; PLLS, posterlateral lateral suprasylvian; PMLS, posteromedial lateral suprasylvian; SVA, splenial visual area; VLS, ventrolateral suprasylvian. Reproduced from Felleman & Van Essen (1991).

humans. Felleman & Van Essen (1991) distinguish 16 regions in the visual system of the cat, and 32 in the visual system of the monkey, for example. The visual regions in the cat and the connections between them are shown in Figure 2.1. In addition, Felleman & Van Essen (1991) propose that the pathways that connect cortical regions can be divided into feedforward, feedback, and horizontal on the basis of the cortical layers from which they arise and to which they project.

A central issue therefore concerns the intrinsic organization within the various regions. In what ways is it common, and in what ways does it vary from region to region? Although there are differences in internal structure there is a widespread belief in commonalities:

> It is easy to recognize a histological (e.g. Golgi) preparation as being cortex rather than cerebellum or tectum. It is much more difficult to tell whether it is human or bovine, motor, sensory, or associative cortex. (Braitenberg 1978: 444)

> Despite the many detailed properties that can be used to differentiate among the various cortical areas, the common properties of all the cortical areas are overwhelming. The same cell types, the same types of connections, and the same distributions of cells and connections across the cortical depth are found in all parts of the isocortex. These properties of the cortex are markedly different from those found in the other parts of the brain. (Abeles 1991: 33)

Generalities such as these are often thought to imply common information processing operations, for example: "The typical wiring of the cortex, which is invariant irrespective of local functional specialization, must be the substrate of a special kind of operation which is typical for the cortical level." (Braitenberg 1978: 444); "It is taken as an article of faith that there is an information processing algorithm unique to cortex that is a product of the regularities of its architecture." (Stryker 1988: 133); "For many anatomists, it seems perverse to regard the visual cortex as an *ad hoc* collection of specialist circuits, rather than a set of basic circuits adapted to perform many different tasks ... For the neocortex, an unconventional class of models needs to be developed – models that are neural networks, but based directly on the biology; derived from visual cortex, but not designed to solve a particular problem in visual processing." (Douglas & Martin 1991: 291–2).

Although these arguments for commonalities have some force, they are still far from being conclusive, and some researchers are sceptical of the existence of any common cortical circuit or computational design. Nevertheless, if there are computationally relevant aspects of intrinsic organization that are common then it is clearly crucial to determine what they are, and to determine whether or not the capabilities to which they give rise are the same as the capabilities identified as being required by the various cognitive subsystems.

Outlines of a basic or canonical cortical circuit are given by Shepherd & Koch (1990), Douglas & Martin (1990) and White (1989). Shepherd (1990b) proposes the basic cortical circuit outlined in Figure 2.2. Some generalizations concerning cortical circuitry are summarized in the following list, compiled from Edelman & Mountcastle (1978), Rakic & Singer (1988), White (1989), Shepherd (1990a), Braitenberg & Schüz (1991) and Abeles (1991). Any theory of cortical computation that denies

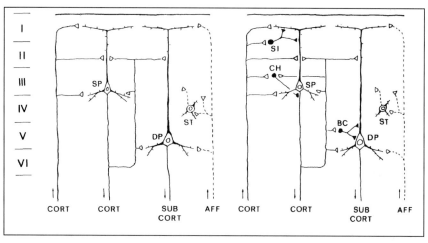

FIG. 2.2.   The basic cortical circuit and its excitatory and inhibitory components in the mammalian neocortex. This circuit is replicated many thousands of times within each of the cortical areas shown in Figure 2.1. The cortical layers (I–VI) are indicated on the far left. On the left are shown excitatory subcircuits. Inputs from other cortical areas are shown as CORT; thalamocortical afferents are shown as AFF in dashed lines. SP, superficial pyramidal neuron; DP, deep pyramidal neuron; ST, stellate cell. On the right, several of the main types of inhibitory neurons have been included, together with some suggested possible circuits: feedforward inhibitory connections through superficial inhibitory neurons (SI) and chandelier cells (CH), and feedback through basket cells (BC). Reproduced from Shepherd (1990b).

such generalizations should be able to justify doing so, and the more that are incorporated within any theory the more convincing it will be.

(a) Projections between regions are localized, and in part preserve neighbourhood relationships.
(b) Feedforward input projects most densely to layer IV. Pyramidal cells in higher layers predominantly provide feedforward output to further cortical regions, whereas those in lower layers predominantly provide feedback to earlier stages and projections to subcortical centres.
(c) Approximately 80% of all cells are pyramidal cells, they are all excitatory and provide all the long-range projections. The remainder are local circuit neurons, divided roughly equally between those that are excitatory and those that are inhibitory.
(d) Pyramidal and local circuit neurons receive collaterals from distant pyramidal cells within the same cortical region.
(e) Most pyramidal cells receive specific input directly from outside their region. Thus signals can traverse a region via just one synapse. In the primary visual cortex (V1), for example, complex

cells in layers II and III receive direct input from the lateral geniculate nucleus (LGN) as well as input from nearby simple cells and from local-circuit neurons.

(f) All pyramidal cells receive input from diffuse arousal systems.

(g) A 0.03mm diameter column through the cortex has approximately 110 cells (except only for V1 in primates, which has nearly twice as many).

(h) Within cortical columns there are positive feedback loops between pyramidal cells in the deep and superficial layers. This reduces their dependence on the absolute strength of their input. The potential tonic overexcitation is controlled by inhibitory local circuit neurons that are activated by the extrinsic input and by connections from the local pyramidal cells. The time-courses of excitation and inhibition produce characteristic effects upon the time-courses of pyramidal cell response to inputs from outside the region.

(i) A large proportion of the inputs to pyramidal cells is via spines on their dendrites, usually with one excitatory input per spine.

(j) There are a few thousand synaptic inputs per pyramidal cell, e.g. about 8000 in the mouse cortex.

(k) The majority of inputs, about 75%, are directly from other pyramids, usually with just one synapse between any connected pair. Each pyramid therefore projects to a few thousand others, but to each via just a single synapse.

(l) All inputs to the soma and to the initial segment of the axon are inhibitory. Thus, inhibitory inputs, although fewer, are better placed to have large effects on output.

(m) Excitatory receptor channels at the synapses are of two types: those that produce conventional summative post-synaptic effects; and those that depend upon the post-synaptic voltage, e.g. N-methyl-D-asparate NMDA receptor channels, such that their effects are greater the more depolarized the cell. Both types are widely distributed throughout cortex.

(n) Average spike rates vary greatly. They are usually highest in primary sensorimotor regions, and do not often exceed 50 spikes per second in other regions.

(o) The excitatory post-synaptic potentials (EPSPs) produced by spikes decay within a few milliseconds. The EPSPs produced via a single synapse receiving inputs at rates of 50 spikes per second or less will therefore not summate very effectively with each other.

(p) The number of excitatory synaptic inputs that must be summed to produce an output spike varies, but will rarely be less than ten or more than a few hundred.

(q) The cortex matures slowly and shows prolonged plasticity. Synapses at spines seem to be particularly involved in plasticity. They are distributed throughout cortex and predominantly mediate excitatory connections between pyramidal cells.

2.5 THE ELEMENTS OF NEURAL COMPUTATION

The study of computation in neural systems has a long history, and major advances in formalization were provided by McCulloch and Pitts in the 1940s. Much work was done in the 1950s and 1960s, but interest then declined. It has risen steeply since the mid-1980s (see Haykin (1994) and Arbib (1995) for reviews). One of the reasons for this is that research in artificial intelligence during the 1970s and 1980s made it clear that, although classical symbolic von Neumann computation is well suited to the high-level intellectual tasks for which humans use voluntary thought processes, it is poorly suited to those tasks that we perform automatically and efficiently. Thus it is unlikely to help us understand those capabilities that we share with other species, and which support most of our daily activities. Another reason for the current interest in neural computation is that there have been conceptual advances showing how it can, in principle, provide the kind of computation that our basic everyday activities seem to require. These advances include the development of a powerful learning algorithm for neural nets with multiple stages of processing, and the use of concepts from statistical physics to show how the dynamics of nets with reciprocal connections can be thought of as retrieving "concepts". Some of the simplest of these ideas are outlined below, but the field is now far too big to be covered in a single chapter or a single book. More extensive reviews are provided by Arbib (1995), Grossberg (1988), Carpenter (1989), Abeles (1991), Rumelhart & McClelland (1986), Hertz et al. (1991) and Haykin (1994).

2.5.1 The processing elements

Figure 2.3a shows a simple processing unit that can be used to build systems that compute in a neural style. To a first approximation it can be thought of as being analogous to a single neuron. This processing unit receives inputs from many other units via connections, or synapses, with varying strengths. The strengths on these connections are often referred to as "weights", e.g. w_{ix}, where the first subscript shows which unit the signal is going to, and the second shows which it is coming from. The input signals O_x are multiplied by the strength of their particular connection and then summed to determine the state of

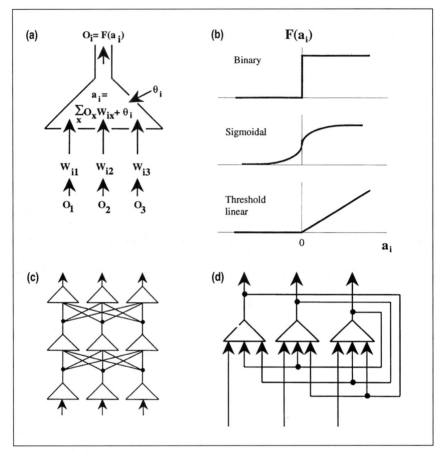

FIG. 2.3. (a) A simple processing element that transforms inputs O_1, etc., into an output O_i via weights w_{i1}, etc., that are associated with each input, and a threshold or bias value, θ. (b) Examples of functions $F(a_i)$ that are used to translate internal activation a_i into output. (c) A fully connected feedforward net. (d) A recurrent associative net of the sort used for content-addressable memory.

internal activation a_i of the unit. A threshold term is also usually included, shown in Figure 2.3a by the symbol θ. The signal O_i to be transmitted to other units is then specified as some function F of a_i. Various functions have been used, three of which are shown in Figure 2.3b.

A major reason for the utility of this processing element is that it operates as a filter that performs a matching operation between the current input and the vector of values stored in its weights. The better that match the stronger its internal state of activation will be. The element can therefore operate as a filter that responds much better to some inputs than to others. If the weights can somehow be usefully adapted to the patterns of input received then we have an adaptive filter from which many different computing systems can be built (Carpenter 1989). In general the weights should not be set so that the unit never responds, nor such that it always responds, because in either case the unit would then transmit no information. The weights need to be set so that the unit makes discriminations that are useful in relation to the inputs that it receives.

The simple processing unit just described is sometimes called a "point neuron" (Abeles 1991) because it ignores the complex morphology of real neurons, such as that of their dendritic trees. This subcellular level of complexity may provide a far greater capacity for processing than simply weighting and summing inputs. Some approaches to computation in the cortex therefore emphasize this subcellular level and model it by using theories that describe the flow of current within electrical cables, and by dividing the cell into a number of separate compartments that are treated as being electrically homogeneous and which are interconnected via ohmic resistances (e.g. Koch 1990). To what extent the details of subcellular structure are crucial to an understanding of cortical computation is not known. It may be that they are crucial to some computational capacities but not others.

2.5.2 Network architectures

Connectivity in the cortex results from interactions between pre-specification and learning in ways that remain to be determined. In the first instance, pre-specification can be thought of as giving a network architecture within which processes of learning then operate. Many different neural network architectures are found in biological nervous systems, and most seem to be designed for very specific roles. Much of the theoretical work on neural computation has focused on a few multipurpose architectures, however. They have not usually been explicitly designed as models of specifically cortical processing, but the general utility of their design makes them relevant candidates for this role. Architectures that are used in the theories to be discussed below include layered feedforward nets (Fig. 2.3c), recurrent nets in which all or many of the units are reciprocally interconnected (Fig. 2.3d), layered feedforward nets with specialized lateral connections within layers, layered nets with feedback connections between layers, and layered nets with local rather than full connectivity between layers.

2.5.3 Short-term dynamics and long-term weight change

Processing within a neural network is carried out by the short-term dynamics that change the internal state of activation. This might be a simple flow of activation through the net as in a strictly feedforward architecture, or it might involve a complex pattern of change over time as can happen in a net with many reciprocal connections. What the net brings to this process of interaction with its inputs is the information or "knowledge" stored within its weighted synaptic connections. Changes in these weights constitute learning. Thus, as the weights form an integral part of the processing, new knowledge in the system can be thought of as being stored through changes in the processors. This contrasts with computation in conventional von Neumann computers, the processors in which have a fixed set of operations and store knowledge in a way that is quite separate from those operations.

Note that a short-term change in the weights could also be part of the processing, and it is just such a possibility that is emphasized by the "dynamic link" approach advocated by von der Malsburg & Schneider (1986) and by Bienenstock & Doursat (1991).

2.5.4 Learning algorithms

Learning plays a central role in modern theories of neural computation, just as it does in the cerebral cortex. Many different learning algorithms have been studied. Some of the more prominent ones are outlined here. The simplest is based on Hebb's proposal in 1949 that connections between a pair of cells should strengthen if the pre-synaptic cell repeatedly or persistently takes place in firing the post-synaptic cell. This is usually extended to include weakening of the connection when one cell fires and the other does not. A version of this rule can be expressed as changing the strength of the connection in direct proportion to the product of pre-synaptic and post-synaptic activity. The advantage of this simple rule is that the weight then reflects the correlation or the covariance between pre-synaptic and post-synaptic activity. This rule is therefore often referred to as a "covariance rule". Some neurophysiologists think that it is a good description of the nature of synaptic plasticity, and they summarize it by saying that cells that fire together wire together.

The previous rules are often referred to as being "unsupervised" in that they depend only on pre-synaptic and post-synaptic activity without making any reference to what the post-synaptic output "should be". For supervised learning rules some additional source is assumed to provide information during training about what the output activity should be, and this is known as the target or desired output. These learning rules are also known as "error correcting" because they are designed to change the weights in such a way as to reduce the difference between the output that the net does produce on that trial and what it should produce. When formulated for units that produce binary outputs this rule is known as the "perceptron learning rule", and when it is formulated for units producing continuous outputs it is known as the "delta rule". It can be shown formally that when implemented in a network with a single layer of weights both versions will reduce the error to zero if a set of correct weights exists within this network given the data on which it is trained. For an outline of the proof see Haykin (1994). Figure 2.4 illustrates the error-correcting process as applied to the weights into the final output layer. A major difference between error-correcting learning rules and the covariance or "Hebbian" learning rules is that error-correcting rules can do more than simply learn correlations. Given an input with some large correlations but also some reliable exceptions to those correlations, the error-correcting rules can learn the exceptions as well as the correlations. This gives them abilities that transcend those of the Hebbian covariance rules, which are completely dominated by pairwise correlations between inputs and outputs. Hancock et al. (1991) have shown that an error-correcting rule with capabilities comparable to the delta rule results from a form of synaptic plasticity that has been observed in slices of adult rat cortex.

Elementary processing units of the kind shown in Figure 2.3a just compute weighted linear sums of their inputs. Thus a feedforward net with just one stage of weighted connections can only produce mappings that can be generated by these simple calculations. Minsky & Papert (1969) showed formally that this greatly limits the capabilities of such nets. This is true no matter which learning rule they use. However, if the net has more than one stage of weights mediating between input

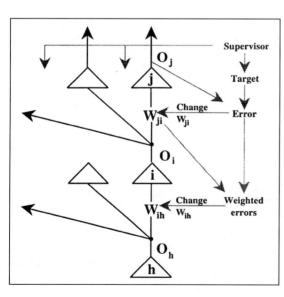

FIG. 2.4.   A simplified sketch of the procedure for learning by back-propagating errors. The error is the difference between the output produced and what the supervisor says it should be. Weighted errors are all the errors at the output to which each hidden unit sends signals weighted by the strength of its connection to those units. The sketch shows the computation of just one of those weighted errors for just one hidden unit.

and output then it can, in principle, compute any mapping. The units in the intermediate layers within such nets are called "hidden units", and it was the invention of the "back-propagation" algorithm (Rumelhart et al. 1986) for training such units that was a major reason for the great growth of work on neural computation in the mid-1980s. A sketch of this algorithm is shown in Figure 2.4, which shows it to be a generalization of the delta rule. The back-propagation learning algorithm requires the transfer function of the processing units to be differentiable, i.e. to change smoothly as input changes, and to ensure this the sigmoidal (or logistic) output function shown in Figure 2.3b is normally used. Zipser & Rumelhart (1990: 194) summarize back-propagation as follows:

> The basic learning procedure is a two stage process. First, an input is applied to the network, then, after the system has processed for some time, certain units of the network are informed of the values they ought to have at this time. If they have attained the desired values, the weights are unchanged. If the unit's values differ from the target values, then the weights are changed according to the difference between the actual values the units have attained and the targets for those units. This difference becomes an error signal. This error signal must then be sent back to those units that impinged on the output units. Each such unit receives an error measure, which is equal to the error in all of the units to which it connects multiplied by the weight connecting it to the output unit. Then, based on this error the weights into these "second layer" units are modified, after which the error is passed back another layer. This process continues until the error signal reaches the input units or until it has passed back for a fixed number of times. Then a new input is presented and the process repeats.

This learning algorithm is computationally powerful and has served as the basis for many theories and technological applications. Its possible relevance to cortical computation is discussed in the following section.

2.6 THE ACQUISITION AND RETRIEVAL OF MAPPINGS IN FEEDFORWARD NETS

2.6.1 Examples of theories that use feedforward nets

It is clear that the cortex transmits information from input to output through multiple stages of internal processing. One of the simplest architectures that can be imagined for doing this is a feedforward network with no connections either within layers or descending from higher layers back down to lower layers (Fig. 2.3c). The output generated by such a network depends upon the strengths of all the internal connections, and this output can be calculated using just one set of summations per layer. The connection strengths may be genetically prespecified, may be learned, or may arise through some combination of the two. The theories discussed here all use back-propagation learning. Many of these theories are primarily related to processes studied by cognitive psychologists and neuropsychologists, e.g. word recognition and naming in reading (Seidenberg & McClelland 1989) or learning the past tense of English verbs (Rumelhart & McClelland 1986). Here we focus on theories that have been related in detail to cortical neurobiology.

Zipser & Andersen (1988) used a feedforward net trained by back-propagation to throw light on the complex response properties of a subset of neurons in the posterior parietal cortex of monkeys. When orienting to or reaching for a visually perceived object, information about the position of the eyes in the head must somehow be combined with information about the retinal position of the image of the object on the retina, and the posterior parietal cortex is known to play a major role in this kind of visual-motor integration. One useful thing to do would be to combine information about eye position with information about retinal position so as to signal the position of the object relative to the head. Cells in the relevant part of parietal cortex, area 7a, were therefore studied to see whether they signalled position relative to the head (Andersen et al. 1985). Some cells in area 7a are sensitive only to retinal position, some only to eye position, and some to both, so it is the latter that are good candidates for computing head-centred position. This was not what Andersen et al. found, however. The cells that were sensitive to both retinal and eye position combined them in a more complex way. The interaction was multiplicative such that the output of the cells could be described as a gain that was a function of eye position, multiplied by the response profile of the retinal receptive field. These cells do not directly signal head-centred position, and none that did was discovered. Interpretation of these results is difficult, because these cells are in an area known to be concerned with the appropriate functions. They combine the appropriate inputs, but they do not seem to combine them in the appropriate way.

The results obtained by Zipser & Andersen (1988) using a three-layer feedforward net trained by back-propagation may help solve this puzzle. The input layer had 96 units, 64 signalling the position of the stimulus on the retina and 32 signalling the position of the eyes. The number of units in the hidden layer varied from 9 to 36. The output layer was used to code head-centred position in one of a number of different formats. After training for about a 1000 trials with a supervisor telling the output layer the correct head position for each input, the net was then able to carry out the required computation of head-centred position given just the retinal position and eye position inputs. The central finding was that when they analysed the responses of the hidden units to different inputs they found that they were very similar to those that had been observed by Andersen et al. (1985) in the parietal cells that combine information about retinal and eye position. The network simulation therefore shows that these response properties can provide an intermediate step in the computation of information about head-centred position.

For further discussion and more examples of the use of such nets in relation to cortical neurobiology see Zipser (1990), Lehky & Sejnowski (1988), Mazzoni et al. (1991) and Abeles (1991).

One important message from this work concerns the transmission of information through a population of cells. The response profiles of individual cells in monkey cortex and of the hidden units in the simulations are complex and very difficult to interpret intuitively. They transmit the necessary information, but they do so in the combined responses of a large population of cells. This suggests that we should be very wary of our natural inclination to interpret the activity of single cells as embodiments of our intuitive concepts.

Another message is that the details of the response profiles observed in the hidden layers of such nets change considerably from simulation to simulation as a function of various things such as the initial values given to the weights and the exact sequence of inputs given during training. This illustrates the fact that there are many different sets of weights within the network that can achieve the required goal, and different solutions are found in different cases. There is also considerable variance in the detailed response profiles of cells both within and across individual animals, so this is in keeping with the results obtained from the simulations. A corollary to this is that, as the genome cannot know exactly what role individual cells will acquire, the initial patterns of cortical connectivity cannot be too specific, and indeed they are not.

Finally, note that hidden units are not necessary for the computation of head position from retinal and eye position. These require just a simple linear summation, which could be achieved by a direct mapping from input to output. Why the cortex seems to engage in more complex operations in this case is not clear, but these results suggest that multiple stages of processing in the cortex do not necessarily imply that they are there to compute high-order non-linear functions.

2.6.2 Feedforward networks in the cortex?

Anatomy clearly shows that the cortex is much more than a simple multistage feedforward net, but the question is whether it includes such an architecture as a crucial part of its computational design. Two simple observations suggesting that it might are the speed of cortical processing, and the nature of receptive field selectivity. Cells deep in the system can respond selectively to external stimulation in less than a 100ms (Oram & Perrett 1992), and highly selective overt responses can occur in less than 300ms. The processing that achieves this selectivity cannot involve repeated reciprocal interactions between cells because they do not respond sufficiently quickly. This suggests, therefore, that the fast initial responses to stimulation may be based upon a simple feedforward architecture. Furthermore, the time constraints may be so tight that initially each stage of processing may be able to make use of no more than just one or two spikes per synaptic input (Oram & Perrett 1992). In broad outline the receptive field selectivity that is observed within the cortex also fits a feedforward view because it can be seen as evidence for a sequential hierarchy that progressively computes more abstract properties.

One modification that can easily be made to the simple feedforward architecture and which would make it more relevant to cortex is to allow layers to receive inputs not just from the immediately preceding layer but also from earlier layers. For example, pyramidal cells in the superficial cortical layers provide the main feedforward projections to other cortical regions. They receive input from outside their region via cells in layer 4, but they also receive it directly. Thus they receive ascending input from layer 4 cells, but also directly from the cells in other regions that provide input to the layer 4 cells. This possibility is allowed for in a generalized feedforward architecture that allows connections from more than just the immediately preceding layer. At the systems level of analysis it is also clear that regions usually receive input not just from immediately preceding regions, but also directly from regions that are earlier than that in the processing hierarchy (Felleman & Van Essen 1991), as shown in Figure 2.1. Another simple modification that makes feedforward nets more similar to cortex is to restrict the connectivity such that each unit in any layer projects to just a small subset of units in the following layers.

In sum, cortical computation probably includes a feedforward style of processing, but the profusion of recurrent lateral and feedback connections shows that there must be more to it than that.

2.6.3 Back-propagation of errors in the cortex?

The biological plausibility of back-propagation has been much debated (Grossberg 1987, Crick 1989, Zipser 1990, Zipser & Rumelhart 1990, Bienenstock & Doursat 1991, Becker & Hinton 1992). One problem is that special mechanisms for transmitting the weighted error back through the net are required, and these must know the strengths of all the appropriate feedforward connections. Other problems are that the errors can be either positive or negative, and that the synapses in the feedforward net are assumed to be able to change sign. Possible answers to these problems are suggested by Zipser & Rumelhart (1990), but there are yet further problems. These include: slow learning in many cases, and particularly when there are more than just one or two intermediate layers; the "curse of dimensionality" (Bienenstock & Doursat 1991), which is that when the inputs have as many dimensions as natural stimuli then it is impossible in any realistic time-scale to give examples that densely cover the whole input space, with the consequence that there will be large regions of input space in which the net has no experience to guide it; an artificial separation between trials on which the desired outputs are assumed to be fully known and others on which they are assumed to be completely unknown; the use of signals that affect changes in synaptic strength without at the same time affecting post-synaptic activity; and, finally, the assumption of a supervisor that knows which internal states are desired.

In sum, back-propagation is of great value to the study of coding in feedforward nets, but as a theory of learning in the cortex it leaves much to be desired.

2.7 THE ACQUISITION AND RETRIEVAL OF ATTRACTOR STATES IN RECURRENT NETS

2.7.1 The complex short-term dynamics of recurrent nets

In a recurrent network there are reciprocal connections between units, as shown in Figure 2.3d. Activity does not just flow through the network, but flows "around" the network. This activity is not just a simple reverberation of whatever input is received from outside the net, however, because it will depend also upon the strengths of the internal connections between the units. If the feedback mediated by these connections tends to cause each unit to behave in the same way as the external input did then such reverberation could occur. Otherwise this feedback can cause the units to produce an output that differs from that produced by the external input alone. This will then change the feedback within the net which may again change the output, and so on. The sequence of changes in activity that this produces can be of great complexity, and it provides a rich source of opportunities for the application of non-linear mathematics and chaotic systems analysis (e.g. Skarda & Freeman 1987). Recurrent nets that stabilize in one of a number of different states are often assumed to retrieve specific concepts by reaching that state, and it is these that we are concerned with in this section. Others do not stabilize in a specific state, however, and may go through an indefinitely long sequence of states. It is possible that the latter are used to store and recreate temporal sequences of activity.

One reason for the interest of mathematicians in recurrent nets is that, despite their potential complexity, certain properties of the nets become analytically tractable given some simplifying assumptions. Furthermore, these properties provide the net with useful computational capabilities, and in particular with content-addressable memory. That is, given memories stored in the weights on the feedback connections the net can, under specifiable conditions, retrieve those memories from any retrieval cues that are sufficient to distinguish it from the other stored memories. This ability was studied formally by Amari (1977), who proposed it as a possible basis for high-level associative brain functions, including concept formation. Other examples are reviewed by Grossberg (1990) within a general mathematical framework for content addressable memory.

Hopfield (1982) saw an analogy between recurrent nets and the interactions of magnetic spins in a large population of atoms. He then used the mathematics that physicists had developed to describe the interactions of spins to clarify the dynamics of recurrent nets. This involved the concept of an "energy function", which describes the extent to which the current state of the system is in disagreement with the forces acting upon it. The energy is high when the disagreement is high. The forces will therefore tend to change the state of the system so as to reduce this disagreement. Within a recurrent net the internal weights will tend to change the output state so as to increase its agreement with those weights. All possible outputs of the net can therefore be thought of as lying on an energy surface showing the amount of disagreement. When placed in any one of these states the output will change so as to reduce the energy, i.e. it will move downhill on this surface. When it reaches a point where all the neighbouring states have higher energy it will remain in that state. This state is therefore called an "attractor", and all states leading to it are called its "attractor basin". Memories within the net can therefore be thought of as the attractor states, and the attractor basins specify the set of input cues from which they can be retrieved. Such memories are a property of the whole population of units, not of any single one, and they are robust in the face of noisy inputs or partial damage within the net. The memories, or attractors, that are formed will depend upon the learning algorithm used to determine the weights. Hopfield showed that if a Hebbian covariance rule is used in a net with symmetric weights between each pair of units, then the net can learn and retrieve up to about $0.144N$ orthogonal memory states with little interference, where N is the total number of units.

The possibility that attractors in neural nets could serve as the embodiment of concept acquisition and retrieval has aroused a great deal of interest, and Amit (1989), for example, bases his whole analysis of brain function on it. Other uses of this idea for analysing cognitive function and dysfunction have been developed by Plaut & Shallice (1993), who have shown how the functions can be combined with feed-forward nets to explain various neuropsychological symptoms.

2.7.2 Recurrent nets in the cortex?

After a comprehensive review of cortical anatomy Braitenberg & Schüz (1991: 195) concluded that the cortex is essentially a huge recurrent memory, and that this distinguishes cortex from other systems: "While in the cerebrum the 'skeleton cortex' of pyramidal cells impresses us with its massive positive feedback, there is not one positive re-entrant loop in the cerebellar cortex: all feedback circuits there involve inhibitory synapses." Their use of the term "cerebrum" should be taken to include the hippocampus, which is also likely to include recurrent connectivity. A detailed review of olfactory cortex also led Haberly (1990) to the conclusion that it is a good example of such a net, and detailed computational models have been built on this assumption (e.g. Granger et al. 1988, Wilson & Bower 1992). Finally, Abeles (1991) considered this issue in relation to what is known about various aspects of intracellular processing, and concluded that none of these detailed considerations provides grounds for rejecting recurrent nets as theories of cortical processing.

The above considerations thus support the use of recurrent nets in computational theories of the cortex, but important issues remain to be resolved. These include the following:

(a) Most concept retrieval occurs too rapidly to be based on a long sequence of internal state changes due to recurrent connections. Thought takes time, but much behaviour is not based on thought but on a rapid response to the prevailing situation.

(b) The output of an associative memory is completely ambiguous in terms of the origin of the information that it transmits. Whether it comes from memory or external input is unspecified. Although the use of memory to augment input is of great value, much of our behaviour must be adapted to the world as it currently is, not just as we remember it to be. Memory in the service of perception and motor control may therefore differ in crucial ways from memory in the service of cued concept retrieval.

(c) Although the anatomical evidence for recurrent connections is clear, the synaptic physiology of these connections is not yet fully established. For example, knowing that they are excitatory does not tell us how their input depends on the current state of depolarization of the cell. If they mainly use voltage-dependent synaptic channels (Fox et al. 1990), for example, then they will act mainly as gain controllers rather than as primary driving inputs, and this will greatly alter their effects upon the short-term dynamics.

2.8 MAXIMIZING INFORMATION TRANSMISSION AND RECODING TO REDUCE REDUNDANCY

Barlow (1961) hypothesized that a major goal of cortical processing is recoding to reduce redundancy, i.e. sensory messages are recoded so that their redundancy is reduced but comparatively little information is lost. This and other closely related ideas are still undergoing vigorous development (Linsker 1988, Barlow 1989, Barlow & Foldiak 1989, Daugman 1990, Foldiak 1990, Baddeley & Hancock 1991, Atick & Redlich 1993, Redlich 1993, Li & Atick 1994). The basic idea is that the flood of data to be processed can be reduced to more manageable amounts by using the statistical structure within the data as a whole to recode the information that it contains into a more efficient form. For example, patterns, features or objects that frequently recur in the raw data can be translated into summary descriptors that require the transmission of much less data than the patterns themselves. Recoding to reduce redundancy may then be seen as including the goal of feature discovery. If we distinguish between a population of data points and the total information contained in their joint distribution then we can see the task as that of data compression combined with information preservation. One reason why this is useful is that compressing the information in the sensory input into a smaller amount of data may help overcome the "curse of dimensionality" and make it much easier to discover new associations (Barlow 1989).

A neural net that reduces redundancy by using lateral connections within a sensory processing layer was designed by Foldiak (1990). The role of the lateral connections was to ensure that the units that they connect become sensitive to inputs that are not correlated. The feedforward connections between layers learned by a normal Hebbian rule, but the lateral decorrelating connections within layers learned through an anti-Hebbian rule, i.e. weights changed in *inverse* proportion to the conjunction of pre-synaptic and post-synaptic activity, which had the effect of driving their receptive field sensitivities apart. In addition, the net was designed to provide a sparse coding such that only a few units became active for any input, as is thought to be the case in cortex.

Linsker (1988: 113) proposed a closely related principle, called "infomax", described as follows: "Given a layer L of cells, and the stationary ensemble statistical properties of the signal activity values in the layer, and given that layer L is to provide input to another cell layer M, the transformation of activity values from L to M is to be chosen such that the rate R of information transmission from L to M is maximized, subject to constraints and/or additional cost terms." The constraints include the presence of noise, and only partial connectivity between layers. He showed that, given noise, this principle requires outputs with some redundancy, and the more noise the more redundancy is required to maximize information transmission. His simulations also showed how a multilayered net that learned by local Hebbian rules designed to meet the goal of infomax could generate a sequence of layers with receptive field sensitivities closely resembling those observed in the mammalian visual system. Furthermore, this occurred even when the activity on the sensory surface was just random activity! It is therefore possible that the oriented receptive fields of cells in the primary visual cortex of newborn animals could result from activity-dependent learning processes that operate upon the activity which is transmitted from retina to cortex in the embryo. Finally, Linsker pointed out the close relationship between this approach and that of statistical techniques, such as principal component analysis, for describing large amounts of data.

Infomax and the reduction of redundancy provide valuable perspectives from which to view sensory processing. They can be specified and analysed formally, and in addition their essence is simple enough to be understandable without that formalization. The extent to which they can predict many details of receptive field selectivity is impressive, and this is strengthened by showing that these selectivities are well adapted to the statistical structure of natural images. Whether these principles have relevance beyond the sensory systems remains to be determined, however. Furthermore, it would probably be a serious mistake to take the reduction of redundancy to the extreme of supposing that the goal of cortical processing as a whole is to produce a population of statistically independent signals. How far the principle should be taken is therefore a crucial issue for this theory. Finally, this principle does not imply codes at the single-unit level that match our intuitive concepts, and indeed the codes that have so far been derived from natural inputs by nets designed to reduce redundancy are far from being codes for things that are obvious to our intuition. In my opinion this latter aspect strengthens their biological plausibility because the receptive fields of cortical cells rarely, if ever, match our intuitive concepts.

2.9 DYNAMIC GROUPING THROUGH THE FORMATION OF SYNCHRONIZED POPULATION CODES

The activity relevant to individual objects and actions is widely distributed across cortex. Given the presence of many different things the question arises as to how the distributed activity is grouped into the appropriate subsets. This is often referred to as "the binding problem". The possibility on which we focus here is that the activity of subsets of cells is grouped by the synchronization of their spike trains to within a few milliseconds, with different groups being desynchronized so that they tend to fire at different times. This idea has long been advocated by Abeles on biophysical grounds and by von der Malsburg on theoretical grounds. Direct physiological evidence for this idea has now brought it into higher prominence. For reviews see Abeles (1991), Engel et al. (1992), Bienenstock & Doursat (1991) and Singer (1990, 1993, 1995).

Synchronization would be an effective signal for grouping because it ensures that the spikes will arrive at a cell's synapses within the integration time for post-synaptic signals (see points (n)–(p) in Section 2.4.2). Their combined effect upon the cell will therefore be greater than the sum of the effects that they would have separately. This signal for grouping is inherently relational, because it depends upon the temporal relations between inputs from different sources, and, unlike the more commonly studied rate and place codes, it is undefined on the signals transmitted by single cells. The use of synchronization as a code is compatible with an oscillatory or semi-periodic pattern of single cell activity, but it does not require it. Synchronization and oscillation can each occur without the other. There is evidence that the appropriate grouping is achieved at least in part by specialized synchronizing connections that are included in the long-range horizontal connections within regions and in the descending connections from higher regions (Singer 1993, 1995). These connections help determine exactly when a cell will fire, and are distinct from the receptive field inputs which provide the primary drive.

Thus synchronized population coding is the transmission of information through the combined activity of a set of cells that all send action potentials down their axons at the same time. The composition of this set is determined dynamically in a context-dependent manner (Singer 1993, 1995). Synchronized population codes have important advantages: (a) they are flexible because they are created dynamically; (b) they have a very high capacity because each cell can be part of many different groupings; (c) they are fast because in the limit all that needs to be synchronized is a single spike from each cell in the group; (d) they do not compromise the meaning of the individual signals in the group; and (e) they can produce long sequences of events with relative timing between the events that is precise to within a few milliseconds, i.e. the synfire chain (Abeles 1991).

Synchronized population codes have been used in many different computational theories, and they have been applied to a wide variety of tasks, e.g.: the cocktail-party problem (von der Malsburg & Schneider 1986); perceptual grouping within and between multiple visual feature domains (Wang et al. 1990, Eckhorn et al. 1991, Tononi et al. 1992a,b, Schillen & König 1994); object recognition (Hummel & Biederman 1992, Neven & Aertsen 1992); and the binding of events across widely distributed cortical zones (Damasio 1989). They have even been used in speculations concerning reasoning (Shastri & Ajjanagadde 1993) and consciousness (Crick & Koch 1990).

For extensive discussions of the anatomical and physiological evidence see the reviews cited above. One limitation of the theory is that synchronization cannot act as a code for a hierarchy of groupings (Hummel & Holyoak 1993). A hierarchy can be given by the anatomy, with different levels occupying different regions, for example, but synchronization cannot be used to group entities that are themselves dynamically created groups from within the same subset of cells. If A, B, C and D are elements to be grouped then the groups (AB) and (CD) can be dynamically created and distinguished, but the hierarchical grouping ((AB)(CD)) cannot then be formed because synchronization of the whole would destroy the distinction between the two component subgroups. This raises difficulties for theories that try to explain higher cognitive functions such as reasoning directly in terms of such codes.

2.10 DISCOVERING AND USING KNOWLEDGE OF PREDICTIVE RELATIONSHIPS BETWEEN DIVERSE DATA SETS

Information about important environmental variables and relationships is spread across various subsets of the many diverse inputs to the cortex. Consider, for example, what we see and hear when we look at someone talking to us. The mouth movements will be related to the words that we hear, the facial expression will be related to the tone of voice, etc. These relations will not be between elements of the raw data, however, but between higher order variables that can be computed from those elements. This also applies within modalities. Information about surface depth, for example, may be spread across many different parts of the image which have only their depth in common. The ability to acquire and use knowledge of the predictive relationships between diverse data sets would therefore be of great use to any system that receives information about a multitude of different but related, and possibly previously unknown, things.

Becker & Hinton (1992) show how such an ability could be used to discover stereo depth in images without any need for a supervisor that already knows about depth. In their algorithm the predictive relationships across data sets were used only to guide learning, however, and were not used to guide processing. Kay & Phillips (1994) and Phillips et al. (1995a,b) have developed a similar but broader framework in which these relationships are used to guide both learning and processing. Local processors are assumed to receive two classes of input: receptive field input, which provides the primary drive; and local modulatory contextual field input, which arises from the specific context to which the receptive field input is to be related. Giving local processors, the contextual field input enables them preferentially to discover those receptive field variables that are predictably related to the context within which they occur, and to use the contextual predictions to emphasize coherent subsets of data during processing. Different processors have different receptive fields and contextual fields, depending upon the network architecture, and the connections mediating both kinds of inputs undergo activity-dependent self-organization. The synchronizing connections discussed in the preceding section are assumed to be an example of contextual field input. They influence the probability that the post-synaptic cell will fire, but they do not change the information that is conveyed by that activity about the receptive field. That is, they help determine whether a signal is sent but do not change what it means. Phillips et al. (1995b) show formally that this is possible if cells are treated as transmitting probabilistic binary signals. Contextual input can then change the probability, confidence or emphasis given to a decision, without changing the decision. This approach includes recoding to reduce redundancy as a special case, but differs in that each local processor can select those variables that are relevant to its role in the system as a whole. Phillips et al. (1995a,b) call this ability "coherent infomax", and they use information theory to describe it precisely, and simulations to study its computational feasibility.

Neuropsychological evidence for this theory is discussed in Phillips et al. (1995a). Anatomical and physiological evidence includes the following:

(a) Voltage-dependent synaptic receptor channels are common throughout cortex and act as gain controllers (Fox et al. 1990), so they could provide a mechanism for contextual modulation.

(b) Long-range horizontal collaterals within regions are also common (Gilbert 1992) and could provide some of the contextual input.

(c) The synchronized activity of cells with non-overlapping receptive fields (Singer 1993, 1995) is evidence that context guides processing, and helps form synchronized population codes.

(d) There is evidence that the long-range horizontal connections can learn (Löwel & Singer 1992, Hirsch & Gilbert 1993).

(e) There is evidence that the long-range horizontal collaterals in V1 have a voltage-dependent modulating synaptic physiology (Hirsch & Gilbert 1991), which indicates that they act as gain-controllers rather than as primary drivers.

This general approach has been developed in various ways (Phillips & Singer 1997). For example, in relation to short-term processing, Tononi et al. (1992a,b), have shown how re-entrant, or contextual, connections can be used to explain many perceptual phenomena. In relation to learning, Becker (1996) has shown how the maximization of mutual information between distinct streams of processing can be used as a basis for self-organization, such as in learning to recognize phonemes. Important issues remain resolved nevertheless. For example, within nets such as those studied by Phillips et al. (1995a,b) it is not clear how feedback from higher stages can enable the net to discover non-linear functions such as the exclusive–or. Whether this difficulty needs to be overcome is not clear, because we do not yet know whether or not the cortex is, in general, proficient at discovering solutions to such problems. This is therefore a crucial unresolved issue for all theories of cortical computation.

2.11 CONCLUDING COMMENTS

The cognitive capacities that are most distinctively human, e.g. referential representation, planning and language, are built on the computational capabilities of the cerebral cortex. The fundamental capabilities of cortex are not distinctively human, however, but are shared with mammals in general. It is therefore essential for any theory of cortical computation to be clear about whether it is trying to explain the fundamental shared capabilities or the higher capabilities that are built upon them. Cognitive psychology and neuropsychology show that there are major divisions of cognitive function, but exactly what these divisions imply about the underlying computations is not yet clear. A major task for theories of cortical computation is therefore to help us find out what the fundamental capabilities of cortex are and to show what they can and cannot achieve. That will help us understand why the higher cognitive capabilities are needed, and upon what foundations they are built.

These tasks require theories that provide co-ordinated accounts of learning and processing using known neural structures to provide computational capabilities with demonstrable relevance to cognitive functions. They must show how information is coded in neural activity, and make clear which operations are performed upon that information. It is my opinion that, for the fundamental capabilities of cortex, information theory and multivariate statistical data analysis provide useful frameworks within which to develop such theories. Coherent infomax (Kay & Phillips 1994, Phillips et al. 1995a,b, Phillips & Singer 1997) exemplifies such an approach: it provides an integrated account of learning and processing within a delimited cognitive domain; it combines a hypothesis concerning the way in which information is coded, i.e. synchronized population codes (Singer 1995), with a hypothesis concerning the operations that local cortical processors must perform, i.e. select and recode that information in the receptive field input that is predictably related to the context within which it occurs, and it shows how useful network properties result from the local operations. These specific hypotheses may prove inadequate, either in whole or in part, but I think that they tackle crucial questions in appropriate terms. I expect that within the next few decades computational theories such as this will become even more closely related to the biological and psychological evidence and will make major contributions to our understanding of how cognitive capabilities arise from neural activity.

ACKNOWLEDGEMENTS

Preparation of this chapter was supported in part by a Network grant from the Human Capital and Mobility Programme of the European Community. I thank Charles Garcia-Tobin, Debbie Goacher, Pamela Harris, Orion Hodson, Mick Rugg and Nick Wilson for their comments on an earlier draft. I also thank Kevin Swingler for help in producing the figures.

REFERENCES

Abeles, M. 1991. *Corticonics*. Cambridge: Cambridge University Press.

Amari, S.-I. 1977. Neural theory of association and concept formation. *Biological Cybernetics* **26**,175–85.

Amit, D. J. 1989. *Modeling brain function*. Cambridge: Cambridge University Press.

Andersen, R.A., G. K. Essick, R. M. Siegel 1985. Encoding of spatial location by posterior parietal neurons. *Science* **230**, 546–8.

Arbib, M. A. (ed.) 1995. *The handbook of brain theory and neural networks*. Cambridge, MA: MIT Press.

Atick, J. J. & A. N. Redlich 1993. Convergent algorithm for sensory receptive field development. *Neural Computation* **5**, 45–60.

Baddeley, R. J. & P. J. B. Hancock 1991. A statistical analysis of natural images matches psychophysically derived orientation tuning curves. *Proceedings of the Royal Society of London, Series B* **246**, 219–23.

Barlow H. B. 1961. Possible principles underlying the transformations of sensory messages. In *Sensory communication*, W. A. Rosenblith (ed.), 217–34. Cambridge, MA: MIT Press.

Barlow, H. B. 1989. Unsupervised learning. *Neural Computation* **1**, 295–311.

Barlow, H. B. & P. Foldiak 1989. Adaptation and decorrelation in the cortex. In *The computing neuron*, R. Durbin & C. Miall (eds), 54–72. New York: Addison-Wesley.

Becker, S. 1996. Mutual information maximization: models of cortical self-organization. *Network* **7**, 7–31.

Becker S. & G. E. Hinton 1992. Self-organizing neural network that discovers surfaces in random-dot stereograms. *Nature* **355**, 161–3.

Bienenstock, E. & R. Doursat 1991. Issues of representation in neural networks. In *Representations of vision*, A. Gorea (ed.), 47–67. Cambridge: Cambridge University Press.

Braitenberg, V. 1978. Cortical architectonics: general and areal. In *Architectonics of the cerebral cortex*, M. A. B. Brazier & H. Petsch (eds), 443–65. New York: Raven Press.

Braitenberg, V. & A. Schüz 1991. *Anatomy of the cortex*. Berlin: Springer-Verlag.

Carpenter, G.A. 1989. Neural network models for pattern recognition and associative memory. *Neural Networks* **2**, 243–57.

Churchland, P. S. & T. J. Sejnowski 1992. *The computational brain*. Cambridge, MA: MIT Press.

Churchland, P. S., C. Koch., T. J. Sejnowski 1990. What is computational neuroscience? In *Computational neuroscience*, E. L. Schwartz (ed.), 46–55. Cambridge, MA: MIT Press.

Cohen, J. D. & D. Servan-Schreiber 1992. Context, cortex, and dopamine: a connectionist approach to behaviour and biology in schizophrenia. *Psychological Review* **99**, 45–77.

Crick, F. 1989. The recent excitement about neural networks. *Nature* **337**, 129–32.

Crick, F. & C. Koch 1990. Towards a neurobiological theory of consciousness. *Seminars in the Neurosciences* **2**, 263–75.

Damasio, A. R. 1989. The brain binds entities and events by multiregional activity from convergence zones. *Neural Computation* **1**, 123–32.

Daugman, J. G. 1990. An information-theoretic view of analog representation in striate cortex. In *Computational neuroscience*, E. L. Schwartz (ed.), 403–23. Cambridge, MA: MIT Press.

Douglas, R. J. & K. A. C. Martin 1990. Neocortex. In *The synaptic organization of the brain*, G. M. Shepherd (ed.), 389–438. Oxford: Oxford University Press.

Douglas, R. J. & K. A. C. Martin 1991. Opening the grey box. *Trends in the Neurosciences* **14**, 286–93.

Eckhorn, R., P. Dicke, M. Arndt, H. Reitboeck 1991. Flexible linking of visual features by stimulus-related synchronizations of model neurons. In *Induced rhythms in the brain*, E. Basar & T. H. Bullock (eds), 397–416. Boston, MA: Birkhauser.

Edelman, G. M. & V. B. Mountcastle 1978. *The mindful brain*. Cambridge, MA: MIT Press.

Engel, A. K., P. König, A. K. Kreiter, T. B. Schillen, W. Singer 1992. Temporal coding in the visual cortex: new vistas on integration in the nervous system. *Trends in the Neurosciences* **15**, 218–26.

Felleman, D. J. & D. C. Van Essen 1991. Distributed hierachical processing in the primate cerebral cortex. *Cerebral Cortex* **1**, 1–47.

Foldiak, P. 1990. Forming sparse representations by local anti-Hebbian learning. *Biological Cybernetics* **64**, 165–170.

Fox, K., H. Sato, N. Daw 1990. The effect of varying stimulus intensity on NMDA-receptor activity in cat visual cortex. *Journal of Neurophysiology* **64**, 1413–28.

Gilbert, C. D. 1992. Horizontal integration and cortical dynamics. *Neuron* **9**, 1–13.

Gluck, M. A. & D. E. Rumelhart (eds) 1990. *Neuroscience and connectionist theory*. London: Erlbaum.

Granger, R., J. Ambros-Ingerson, G. Lynch 1988. Derivation of encoding characteristics of layer II cerebral cortex. *Journal of Cognitive Neuroscience* **1**, 61–87.

Grossberg, S. 1987. Competitive learning: from interactive activation to adaptive resonance. *Cognitive Science* **11**, 23–63.

Grossberg, S. 1988. *Neural networks and natural intelligence*. Cambridge, MA: MIT Press.

Grossberg, S. 1990. Content-addressable memory storage by neural networks: a general model and global Liapunov method. In *Computational neuroscience*, E. L. Schwartz (ed.), 56–65. Cambridge, MA: MIT Press.

Haberly, L. B. 1990. Olfactory cortex. In *The synaptic organization of the brain*, G. M. Shepherd (ed.), 317–45. Oxford: Oxford University Press.

Hancock, P. J. B., L. S. Smith, W. A. Phillips 1991. A biologically supported error-correcting learning rule. *Neural Computation* **3**, 201–12.

Haykin, S. 1994. *Neural networks: a comprehensive foundation*. New York: Macmillan.

Hecht-Nielsen, R. 1990. *Neurocomputing*. New York: Addison-Wesley.

Hertz, J., A. Krogh, R. G. Palmer 1991. *Introduction to the theory of neural computation*. New York: Addison-Wesley.

Hirsch, J. A. & C. D. Gilbert 1991. Synaptic physiology of horizontal connections in cat's visual cortex. *Journal of Neuroscience* **11**, 1800–9.

Hirsch, J. A. & C. D. Gilbert 1993. Long-term changes in synaptic strength along specific intrinsic pathways in the cat visual cortex. *Journal of Physiology* **461**, 247–62.

Hopfield, J. J. 1982. Neural networks and physical systems with emergent collective computational capabilities. *Proceedings of the National Academy of Sciences USA* **79**, 2554–8.

Hummel, J. E. & I. Biederman 1992. Dynamic binding in a neural network for shape recognition. *Psychological Review* **99**, 480–517.

Hummel, J. E. & K. J. Holyoak 1993. Distributing structure over time. *Behavioral and Brain Sciences* **16**, 464.

Intrator, N. & L. N. Cooper 1992. Objective function formulation of the BCM theory of visual cortical plasticity: statistical connections, stability conditions. *Neural Networks* **5**, 3–17.

Kay, J. & W. A. Phillips 1994. *Activation functions, computational goals and learning rules for local processors with contextual guidance*. Technical Report CCCN–15, University of Stirling, Centre for Cognitive and Computational Neuroscience, Stirling, UK.

Koch, C. 1990. The biophysics of computation: toward the mechanisms underlying information processing in single neurones. In *Computational neuroscience*, E. L. Schwartz (ed.), 97–113. Cambridge, MA: MIT Press.

Koch, C. & J. L. Davis 1994. *Large-scale neuronal theories of the brain*. Cambridge, MA: MIT Press.

Lehky, S. R. & T. J. Sejnowski 1988. Network model of shape-from-shading: neural function arises from both receptive and projective fields. *Nature* **333**, 452–4.

Li, Z. & J. J. Atick 1994. Efficient stereo coding in the multiscale representation. *Network* **5**, 157–74.

Linsker, R. 1988. Self-organization in a perceptual network. *Computer* **21**, 105–17.

Löwel, S. & W. Singer 1992. Selection of intrinsic horizontal connections in the visual cortex by correlated neuronal activity. *Science* **255**, 209–12.

Macphail, E. M. 1987. The comparative psychology of intelligence. *Behavioral and Brain Sciences* **10**, 645–95.

Marr, D. 1982. *Vision*. San Francisco, CA: Freeman.

Marr, D. & H. K. Nishihara 1978. Visual information processing: artificial intelligence and the sensorium of sight. *Technology Review* **81**, 2–23.

Mazzoni, P., R. A. Andersen, M. I. Jordan 1991. A more biologically plausible learning rule for neural networks. *Proceedings of the National Academy of Sciences USA* **88**, 4433–7.

McClelland, J. L., B. L. McNaughton, R. C. O'Reilly 1995. Why there are complementary learning systems in the hippocampus and neocortex: insights from the successes and failures of connectionist models of learning and memory. *Psychological Review* **102**, 419–57.

Minsky, M. L. & S. A. Papert 1969. *Perceptrons*. Cambridge, MA: MIT Press.

Neven, H. & A. Aertsen 1992. Rate coherence and event coherence in the visual cortex: a neuronal model of object recognition. *Biological Cybernetics* **67**, 309–22.

Oram, M. W. & D. I. Perrett 1992. Time course of neural responses discriminating different views of the face and head. *Journal of Neurophysiology* **68**, 70–84.

Phillips, W. A., J. Kay, D. Smyth 1995a. How local cortical processors that maximise coherent variation could lay foundations for representation proper. In *Neural computation and psychology*, L. S. Smith & P. J. B. Hancock (eds), 117–33. Berlin: Springer-Verlag.

Phillips, W. A. & W. Singer 1997. In search of common foundations for cortical computation. *Behavioral & Brain Sciences*, in press.

Phillips, W. A., J. Kay, D. Smyth 1995b. The discovery of structure by multi-stream networks of local processors with contextual guidance. *Network* **6**, 225–46.

Plaut, D. C. & T. Shallice 1993. Deep dyslexia: a case study of connectionist neuropsychology. *Cognitive Neuropsychology* **10**, 377–500.

Rakic, P. & W. Singer (eds) 1988. *Neurobiology of neocortex.* New York: Wiley.

Redlich, A. N. 1993. Redundancy reduction as a strategy for unsupervised learning. *Neural Computation* **5**, 289–304.

Rumelhart, D. E. & J. L. McClelland 1986. *Parallel distributed processing: explorations in the microstucture of cognition*, 2 vols. Cambridge, MA: MIT Press.

Rumelhart, D. E., G. E. Hinton, R. J. Williams 1986. Learning internal representations by back-propagating errors. *Nature* **323**, 533–6.

Schacter, D. L. 1987. Implicit memory: history and current status. *Journal of Experimental Psychology: Learning, Memory, and Cognition* **13**, 501–18.

Schillen, T. B. & P. König 1994. Binding by temporal structure in multiple feature domains of an oscillatory neuronal network. *Biological Cybernetics* **70**, 397–405.

Schwartz, E. L. (ed.) 1990. *Computational neuroscience.* Cambridge, MA: MIT Press.

Seidenberg, M. & J. L. McClelland 1989. A distributed, developmental model of word recognition and naming. *Psychological Review* **96**, 523–68.

Sejnowski, T. J., C. Koch, P. S. Curchland 1988. Computational neuroscience. *Science* **241**, 1299–306.

Shallice, T. 1991. Precis of From Neuropsychology to Mental Structure. *Behavioral and Brain Sciences* **14**, 429–69.

Shannon, C. E. & W. Weaver 1949. *The mathematical theory of communication.* Illinois: University of Illinois Press.

Shastri, L. & V. Ajjanagadde 1993. From simple associations to systematic reasoning: a connectionist representation of rules, variables and dynamic bindings using temporal synchrony. *Behavioral and Brain Sciences* **16**, 417–94.

Shepherd, G. M. (ed.) 1990a. *The synaptic organization of the brain.* Oxford: Oxford University Press.

Shepherd, G. M. 1990b. The significance of real neuron architectures for neural network simulations. In *Computational neuroscience*, E. L. Schwartz (ed.), 82–96. Cambridge, MA: MIT Press.

Shepherd, G. M. & C. Koch 1990. Introduction to synaptic circuits. In *The synaptic organization of the brain*, G. M. Shepherd (ed.), 3–31. Oxford: Oxford University Press.

Singer, W. 1990. Search for coherence: a basic principle of cortical self-organization. *Concepts in Neuroscience* **1**, 1–26.

Singer, W. 1993. Synchronization of cortical activity and its putative role in information processing and learning. *Annual Review of Physiology* **55**, 349–74.

Singer, W. 1995. Development and plasticity of cortical processing architectures. *Science* **270**, 758–64.

Skarda, C. A. & W. J. Freeman 1987. How brains make chaos in order to make sense of the world. *Behavioural and Brain Sciences* **10**, 161–95.

Squire, L. R. 1992. Memory and the hippocampus: a synthesis from findings with rats, monkeys, and humans. *Psychological Review* **99**, 195–231.

Stryker, M. P. 1988. Group report. Principles of cortical self-organization. In *Neurobiology of neocortex*, P. Rakic & W. Singer (eds), 115–36. New York: Wiley.

Tononi, G., O. Sporns, G. M. Edelman 1992a. The problem of neuronal integration: induced rhythms and short-term correlations. In *Induced rhythms in the brain*, E. Basar & T. H. Bullock (eds), 367–95. New York: Birkhauser.

Tononi, G., O. Sporns, G. M. Edelman 1992b. Reentry and the problem of integrating multiple cortical areas: simulation of dynamic integration in the visual system. *Cerebral Cortex* **2**, 310–35.

Tulving, E. 1985. How many memory systems are there? *American Psychologist* **40**, 385–98.

von der Malsburg, C. & Schneider, W. 1986. A neural cocktail-party processor. *Biological Cybernetics* **54**, 29–40.

Wang, D., J. Buhmann, C. von der Malsburg 1990. Pattern segmentation in associative memory. *Neural Computation* **2**, 94–106.

White, E. L. 1989. *Cortical circuits: synaptic organization of the cerebral cortex. Structure, function and theory*. New York: Birkhauser.

Wilson, M. A. & J. M. Bower 1992. Cortical oscillations and temporal interactions in a computer simulation of piriform cortex. *Journal of Neurophysiology* **67**, 981–95.

Zipser, D. 1990. Modelling cortical computation with backpropagation. In *Neuroscience and connectionist theory*, M.A. Gluck & D. E. Rumelhart (eds), 355–83. London: Erlbaum.

Zipser, D. & R. A. Andersen 1988. A back-propagation programmed network that simulates response properties of a subset of posterior parietal neurons. *Nature* **331**, 679–84.

Zipser, D. & D. E. Rumelhart 1990. The neurobiological significance of the new learning models. In *Computational neuroscience*, E. L. Schwartz (ed.), 192–200. Cambridge, MA: MIT Press.

CHAPTER 3

Neural coding schemes for sensory representation: theoretical proposals and empirical evidence[1]

David K. Fotheringhame & Malcolm P. Young

3.1 INTRODUCTION

It is widely, though not universally, believed among neuroscientists that states of an animal's environment are represented by states of its brain. Understanding how the environment is represented in the firing patterns of neurons has long been one of the central goals in the study of central nervous system function. This enterprise has been characterized in general by theoretical and experimental attempts to specify the neural "code" by which neurons represent behaviourally important events. The exact nature of the relationship between sensory stimulation, motor output and neural activity has been the subject of a large number of different proposals. Many electrophysiological experiments have been undertaken to test these proposals, and interpretations of the outcome of these experiments remain vigorously debated. Sensory information has variously been suggested to be coded, for example, by the activity of single cells, each of which would be capable of signalling sophisticated information, by the pattern of activity distributed across large populations of cells, each cell of which would only broadly discriminate the represented stimuli, or by patterns in the timing of neuronal firing. Experimental support can be adduced in favour of any and all of these proposals, and for most combinations of them. In this chapter, we elaborate some experimental findings in this area, selected from a very extensive literature, and discuss how they might distinguish between different theoretically possible neural coding schemes.

Theoretical investigations of the nature of neural coding have a long history (see, for example, Moore et al. (1966) for a review of early work). One of the first experimental demonstrations of the existence of a neural code, however, showed a relationship between the frequency of firing of peripheral sensory neurons and the intensity of an applied stimulus (Adrian & Zotterman 1926). The success of this approach lay in the experimenters' plausibly connecting a conception of the information being carried with a parameter of the neurons' physiological activity. This reflected, and reflects, a *sine qua non* for this area; insight into what information the system represents is required for an investigation of its means of information carriage. For neurons close to the sensory or motor periphery, reasonable assumptions could be made as to what was being represented by them, based on some knowledge of the sensory sheet or muscle to which they were connected. Co-variation between this conception of what was being represented—i.e. stimulus intensity and firing rate—suggested that rate coding was responsible for information carriage in this part of the system. Central neurons, however, presented a more difficult problem, since only cruder guesses could be made concerning the information being represented by them. This difficulty was circumvented by electrophysiologists who wished to investigate the cortex by the simple assumption that what could be concluded for peripheral neurons could be concluded for neurons everywhere in the nervous system; and the most influential conclusion from the periphery was that information was represented by firing frequency, or rate coding, in "labelled lines" (e.g. Adrian 1926).

Rate coding implies that a neuron signals changes in the information it represents by changes in the number of impulses it produces in a period of time. The concept of the "labelled line" encompasses the idea that a single neuron codes for a single pre-determined dimension. The measure of the success of these early insights is their remaining influence today. This influence is visible in the greater caution that often meets models or data that challenge the hegemony of these ideas, when compared with those that may be accommodated within the paradigm. Nonetheless, many variations and alternatives to the traditional ideas on neuronal coding have been proposed and investigated, and these approaches can be subdivided by their emphasis on spatial or temporal aspects of the suggested code. We have followed this subdivision in what follows, beginning by treating spatial aspects of coding, then treating temporal aspects of coding, and ending by examining possible relations between the two aspects of coding.

A caveat that affects all aspects of work on neural coding concerns "information". We face a problem of confusion of specialist vocabularies. "Information" has a specialist meaning derived from its use in Information Theory (Shannon & Weaver 1949, Abramson 1963, Gallager 1968). According to theory, information is a measure of the reduction in uncertainty in a communication channel attending receipt of a signal by a receiver. This use of "information" allows precise quantification and analysis. The usage of "information" made by neurophysiologists, however, is much less well defined. Although the two senses are related, they are certainly not interchangeable, and so confusion may arise from the use of the term. There is no reasonable alternative, however, and the sense of information used here is the ill-defined neurophysiological one, rather than the strict Information-Theoretic one.

3.2 SPATIAL ASPECTS OF CODING:
SINGLE CELLS, OR PATTERNS OF ACTIVITY IN POPULATIONS OF CELLS?

One of the principal issues in current debates about coding relates to the question of how many neurons are used to represent information, or to how *sparse* the neural code might be. One way to approach the issue of the sparseness of the representational code is first to describe positions reflecting the two extrema of this dimension.

In the now classical "grandmother cell" coding scheme, the firing of a single neuron exclusively signals a single event or concept, such as the appearance of one's grandmother. There are conceptual difficulties in specifying precisely what one "event" might mean in this context, and greater difficulties arising from the properties of any such code. The representational capacity of a very sparse code is very low: the code can represent only as many events as there are neurons available. The number of neurons available is far too low, even when the number of cells is as high as that in the primate nervous system: the number of discriminable events in a lifetime of sensory experience greatly exceeds the number of neurons. A grandmother cell code allows no generalization from old representations to new ones. The lack of generalization is a fundamental problem, since the system will almost never be presented with precisely the same stimulation more than once. A grandmother cell code, however, also has some desirable properties. It is straightforward to form associations between represented events and outputs from the system. Any output association can be learnt in a single trial by strengthening connections between the active representation neuron and the active output neurons using, for example, Hebb's learning rule (see Ch. 1). A grandmother cell code is effectively a "look-up table" in which there is no interference between the representations of different events, and learning information about a new event need not interfere with old representations, as long as there are sufficient neurons to represent the new state. A grandmother cell code might, therefore, be useful in an artificial computing device, but it is unlikely that this mode of coding is employed in the mammalian brain (Foldiak & Young 1995).

In a population code, each event is represented by the pattern of activity distributed across a population of neurons. If the code is far from sparse, little information about any real-world event would be available from sampling the output of the individual neurons in a population code. Population codes can represent a very high number ($\sim 2^N$, where N is the number of neurons) of different events by using the neurons in combination. This great representational power is largely superfluous, however, as the number of experienced events would not nearly approach this capacity. A population code pays for the potentially high representational capacity by a poor capacity to store different events. The number of events that an associative memory using a very dense or distributed population code can store may be lower than would be necessary biologically (Foldiak & Young 1995). The mapping between a population representation and an output can also be complex, and difficult to learn. Population representations ensure automatic generalization from older to newer representations (Hinton et al. 1986), but this sometimes manifests itself as undesirable interference between the representations of different events.

3.2.1 Inferotemporal cortex as an example of some issues in spatial coding

Whether the sensory hierarchies use a very sparse code or a very distributed one remains an actively debated issue in cortical neurophysiology. While very few researchers endorse either of the extreme positions identified above, many different conceptions of the sparsity of neural codes are informed by neurophysiological data. Sparse coding theories suppose that individual cells should show notable specificity for behaviourally relevant stimuli (Konorski 1967, Barlow 1972, 1985), while "population" theories expect cells to exhibit broadly graded responses (Freeman 1975, Georgopoulos et al. 1982, Lehky & Sejnowski 1990). In this context, reports of neurons in the inferotemporal cortex (IT) with specificity for faces or other complex stimuli (e.g. Gross et al. 1972, Perrett et al. 1982, Miyashita 1988, Miyashita & Chang 1988), and reports of striking correspondences between the properties of cells elsewhere in the cortical visual system and the properties of behaviour, have, understandably, been interpreted by some as strong support for sparse coding theories. On the other hand, while highly selective neurons may be quite sharply tuned to a *class* of stimuli, their firing is affected by more than one stimulus and they tend to be broadly tuned to stimuli within the category (Baylis et al. 1985). This feature of their responses could be consistent with population coding if the responses to suboptimal stimuli are systematically graded and not "noise".

The relation of the properties of these cells to neural codes of different sparsity was investigated explicitly by Young & Yamane (1992, 1993). In these reports, Young & Yamane examined 850 unit recordings in the inferotemporal gyrus and in the anterior superior temporal sulcus of macaque monkeys made while the monkeys performed a face discrimination task (Yamane et al. 1988). The face discrimination task required the monkey to make one type of response to three of 30 faces, and a different response to the remaining 27 faces. The monkeys responded at greater than 90% correct performance in this task. The results suggested that neurons in the inferotemporal cortex uses a sparse population code to represent faces. First, the redundancy of the coding characteristics of the neurons, which would not be expected in a very sparse code, suggested that individual cells do not respond independently but exhibit shared dimensions of specificity. It was evident from the breadth of tuning of the cells that it was not the case that each cell responded to only a limited range of these shared dimensions, as would be required for a grandmother cell code. Secondly, population responses were statistically related to identifiable dimensions of the face stimuli. This implied that there was information encoded at the population level, which again would not be the expected result if all information transfer were at the level of the single cell. This is illustrated in Figure 3.1. Thirdly, neurons responsive to faces exhibited systematically graded responses with respect to the face stimuli. Hence each cell would systematically participate in the representation of many faces, a feature that straightforwardly implies a population code. For these data, however, only a few tens of cells were capable of generating a code almost as precise as behaviour. The implication of this latter finding was that, while the representation certainly involved patterns of activity spread across the population, it was a sparse population code (Young & Yamane 1992, 1993, Young 1995).

The type of sparse population code described in these and other empirical studies (e.g. McNaughton & Morris 1987, Rolls & Treves 1990, Rolls & O'Mara 1993) was anticipated to be a likely solution for the brain on theoretical grounds. A sparse population code promises to combine the best properties of very sparse and very distributed codes, while avoiding most of their problems. Codes which involve relatively small proportions of the available neurons being active in the representation of any one event can possess a high representational capacity,

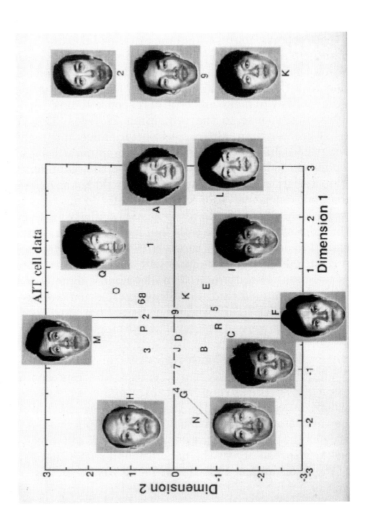

(a)

52

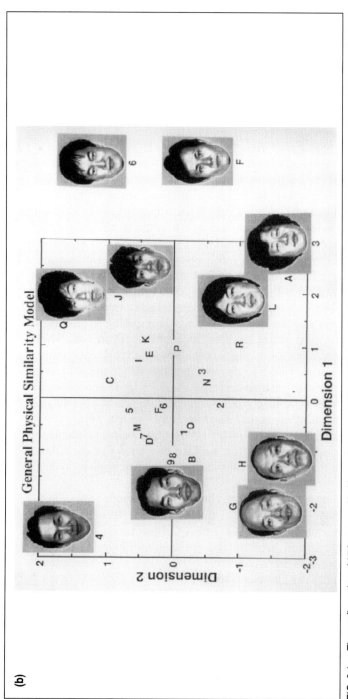

FIG. 3.1. The configuration of 27 faces used by Young & Yamane (1992, 1993), based on (a) their similarity on physical measurements, and (b) the similarity of the neural population responses to them. The configuration in (a) was derived from measurements of the distances between the faces' features which were then submitted to multidimensional scaling (Young & Yamane 1992, 1993). The two dimensions of this configuration preserved 94% of the variability in the original 29 different measurements. An arbitrary selection of faces are plotted at the position of their corresponding point in the diagram. The configuration represents round faces and faces with much hair at bottom right, less hirsute faces at bottom left and long faces toward the top of the figure. The configuration in (b) represents the neuronal population response to the face stimuli for a small population (40) of Anterior Inferotemporal (AIT) cells. Its two dimensions preserved 70% of the variability in the 40 cells' responses. Faces which evoked a similar response across the population of cells are plotted close together, while faces which evoked a very different population response are far apart. The configuration in (b), derived from the physiological selectivities of a population of cells in AIR, was statistically significantly related to the physical similarity model in (a). Identifiable information about the physical properties of the face stimuli was therefore coded by the population, which, because the number of cells in the sample of the population was small, implies that a sparse population code is employed in the anterior inferotemporal cortex. Reprinted with permission from Young & Yamane 1993.

although one that will be smaller than that of more distributed codes. Sparse population coding can store many more events than distributed population coding, and it is easier for a network with this type of coding to learn. Generalization in a sparse code might take place only between overlapping patterns, and new associations would not generally interfere with previous representations. The intermediate case of sparse population coding therefore has numerous advantages that might make it an adaptive choice for implementation by biological systems (Foldiak & Young 1995).

These considerations, however, are naturally dependent on assumptions related to the information being carried by the neurons under study, and it is instructive to consider further what information inferotemporal cells might carry. Cells with apparent selectivity for faces, could, on the one hand, signal information about the full configural and textural information present in a preferred face, or, on the other hand, be triggered simply by the presence of two horizontally arranged blobs (most faces have two eyes). There is evidence that the selectivities of some face cells reflect complex configural information (e.g. Yamane et al. 1988, Young & Yamane 1992, 1993), but there is also evidence that most cells in the inferotempral cortex, probably including face cells, prefer stimuli that are simpler than real-world objects. There are different consequences for coding of these two contrary conclusions about the information carried by inferotemporal cells. In general, cells with selectivity for simple patterns, rather than for more complex pattern information, would be likely to represent real-world objects in a more distributed population code (Stryker 1992, Young 1993, 1995). What it is that inferotemporal cells signal therefore bears on the issue of coding in the inferotemporal cortex, and we now turn to a consideration of the evidence for more distributed coding in that region.

3.2.2 The simplification approach to the stimulus preferences of inferotemporal cells

An approach to understanding the role of inferotemporal cells in information representation, which has long been employed (e.g. Gross et al. 1972), but which has more recently been applied as systematically as possible by Tanaka (Tanaka et al. 1991, Fujita et al. 1992), is to try to determine the cell's preferred features by simplifying the stimuli by which it is excited. This method begins by isolating and recording from a neuron, while presenting many visual objects to the animal, in order to find objects that excite the cell. The component features (as interpreted by the experimenters) of the exciting stimuli are then presented again singly or in combination. By monitoring the cell's firing rate during presentation of each of the real and simplified stimuli, the protocol attempts to find the simplest combination of features that maximally excites the neuron.

This approach suffers from the problem that even very simple visual objects contain a rich set of possible component features, not all of which need be apparent to the experimenters. Most visual objects, for example, have elements of luminance, contrast, colour, shape, orientation, depth, curvature, motion and texture, and often show shading or specular reflections. Elements in any of these domains, and any combination of the elements, may excite the cell. Hence, there is a vast number (greater than the factorial of the number of elementary features) of possible combinations of the elementary features of any object, which together constitute a huge search space which cannot be searched comprehensively. All possible feature combinations cannot therefore be presented systematically, and the simplified stimuli that are actually presented are a very small subset of the possible combinations, selected according to the intuition of the experimenters. Consequently, it is not possible to conclude that the best simplified stimulus found using this method is the optimal one for the cell. It cannot even be assumed that the cell codes only one optimal set of features, since it is possible that the cell could be excited by quite different feature combinations (Young 1993, 1995).

According to the results of this method, cells in the inferotemporal cortex show preferences for patterns that are most often simpler than real visual objects. An interpretation of these results is that cells in the inferotemporal cortex might together constitute a "visual alphabet" (Stryker 1992), in which each cell signals the presence of a particular pattern "partial", whenever it is present, and the whole pattern of activation across IT represents the particular real-world object. The idea is that the number of "partials" is small by comparison with the number of possible visual patterns that can be recognized, but the possible combinations offered by this alphabet is very large. These combinations of "partials" could signal an almost unbounded set of visual patterns in the same way that the number of words that can be constructed from an alphabet is very large. The representation of a real visual object is therefore conceived of as being carried in a distributed population code.

The idea, however, that an inferotemporal cell will reliably signal the presence of the particular pattern "partial" seems not to be supported by the results of Tanaka et al. (1991). This study showed that the presence of other visual features can disrupt the response of a cell to its "partial", a result that is not expected under the visual alphabet conception of the inferotemporal cortex. An example, from Tanaka et al. (1991), is shown in Figure 3.2. For this cell, the simplification protocol

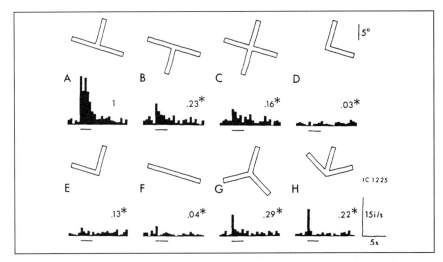

FIG. 3.2.   An experimental test of the assumption underlying the visual alphabet conception of cod-ing in the inferotemporal cortex. The simplification protocol converged here on an inverted "T" shape (a) as the preferred pattern "partial" for this cell. The assumption underlying the visual alphabet idea is that the cell would respond well to any more complex object that contains this "partial". A more com-plex object containing this "partial" is shown at (c). The response of the cell to this slightly more complex object is very small, despite the fact that the preferred pattern "partial" is still present. This implies that coding in this part of the brain is not undertaken in the way assumed by the visual alpha-bet idea. Reprinted with permission from Tanaka et al. 1991.

determined an inverted "T" shape as the preferred pattern "partial". On the visual alphabet model, any more complex object that contains this pattern "partial" should evoke strong firing as the cell informs others that its "partial" is present. Such a more complex object is also shown in Figure 3.2, together with the response of the cell to it. The cell did not respond to a "+" shape, in which the preferred "partial" is still present, in concert with a vertical bar below its centre. Hence, the presence of other visual features in this case disrupts the response of a cell to its "partial", a result which is quite the opposite of that assumed in the visual alphabet conception of coding in the inferotemporal cortex.

These considerations suggest that, at present, the characterization of the preferences of the cells as signalling pattern "partials" (Stryker 1992) appears not to anticipate the more complex informational inter-actions between inferotemporal cells that take place during the repre-sentation of visual objects. At the moment, then, the simplification approach seems not to capture either necessary or sufficient descrip-tions of the behaviour of inferotemporal cells during recognition (Young 1995), and consequently does not yet present a clear message on the sparseness of representation.

3.2.3 Other aspects of the issue of sparseness in neuronal coding

Sparseness in neural coding may be quantified by measuring the proportion of cells that is active in the representation of an event, the "activity ratio" (Foldiak & Young 1995). One direct approach to this issue that suggests itself is simply to record from a behaving animal in as natural a setting as possible. Such an approach could then follow that of a study of mathematically characterized oriented filters, which were used to model the responses of neurons in the primary visual cortex (Field 1994). This study examined the outputs of these oriented filters when presented with natural images. The outputs were considered to correspond to idealized cortical cell responses. The results showed that, for any natural image, most filters have responses near zero, and only a relatively small proportion of the filters give a large response, there being a different set of active filters for each image (Field 1994). By analogy, an examination of real neurons' activities might assess the frequency with which neurons in a given population show a response above background level. This could allow the response distribution of the data to be calculated, and the activity ratio to be inferred from it. There would, however, be some problems of sampling bias in applying this approach to the real brain, since sampling would occur from a particularly responsive subpopulation of the cells, i.e. those units that permit clean isolation from other units during electrode recording.

The degree of correlation between neural responses is another aspect of neural activity that bears on the nature of the distribution of information among neurons. It is often tacitly assumed that each neuron signals a unique and independent message. But neighbouring neurons frequently show highly correlated response patterns, as has been shown clearly for cells in the primate middle temporal visual area (MT) (e.g. Britten et al. 1992). There are several possible reasons for this seemingly inefficient and redundant arrangement, as discussed by Hurlbert & Derrington (1993). It is apparent, however, that the degree of correlation between neighbouring neurons is different in different parts of the brain. Gawne & Richmond (1993), for example, have shown that the firing of adjacent neurons in the inferotemporal cortex is more independent than that of cells in MT. This difference between regions might reflect very different roles of these two areas in the information processing economy of the brain, and serves as a caution against the supposition that a single method of neural coding pertains throughout.

A further issue in the spatial aspects of neuronal coding concerns how many dimensions the activity of a single neuron might represent. One neuron can certainly be involved in representing several features at once. In the primary visual cortex, for example, neurons can be selective for both spatial frequency and orientation (e.g. De Valois et al. 1982). Selectivity for more than one stimulus dimension abounds in the cortex, and this feature of cortical processing may have functional consequences for coding. Zohary (1992) suggests that neuronal tuning for multiple dimensions is an adaptation which could help in the "binding problem", namely the necessity for recombining information on different attributes to assign them to particular external objects. An impracticably large number of connections between neurons separately representing different stimulus dimensions would be required to produce a unitary representation of an object. Representing large numbers of stimulus dimensions in single neurons, however, might be inefficient, since there may be a trade-off between the number of dimensions to which a neuron is selective and the total number of such neurons required to represent all the dimensions to a given resolution (Zohary 1992).

3.3 TEMPORAL ENCODING: REPRESENTING INFORMATION IN THE TEMPORAL PATTERN OF FIRING

Almost every conclusion about information representation in the nervous system has come from work based on traditional assumptions about coding; namely that signals are carried by the firing rate of neurons, whether the neurons in question be few or many. One could infer from this either that ideas about more elaborate styles of coding are of limited significance for experimental scientists, or that there is a potentially rich source of information lying untapped in electrophysiologists' data files.

In what way could the presence of temporal encoding, and the assumption of its absence, have misled thinking about neural coding? It is possible, first, that the quantity of information conveyed by active neurons may have been underestimated. This might mean, for example, that orientation-selective neurons in striate cortex could be more sharply tuned than previously thought, when temporal information is taken into account. It is also possible that temporal encoding might reveal the representation of qualitatively different information by cells, such as coding for unsuspected multiple stimulus dimensions. This might mean, for example, that in higher sensory brain areas early sections of a spike train could reflect primarily the perceptual properties of a stimulus, while later sections could code mostly associative, mnemonic properties of the stimulus. It is not, however, of great interest to show that neurons might theoretically carry more information in a temporal code. It would be of interest to demonstrate that a particular code could be used by reading it, and relating the neural messages to external events, using the model of the influential work on frequency coding by Adrian (1926). This latter enterprise has proven quite difficult, except for the simplest possible temporal codes.

3.3.1 Temporal coding in the auditory system

The possibilities afforded by temporal encoding have been studied in the context of auditory processing in more detail than elsewhere in the nervous system. The physiology and anatomy of the mammalian peripheral auditory system have been investigated particularly intensively. One remarkable observation in the auditory system is that of 'phase locking', in which primary auditory fibres fire only at particular points in the cycle of a tone stimulus. This behaviour has been observed with tones as high as 8kHz (Kiang et al. 1965, Rose et al. 1967, Johnson 1980), and may be the most robust empirical example of temporal coding. The auditory system possesses some other properties that are difficult to account for in traditional rate coding terms. Psychophysical experiments, for example, show that human observers can detect a difference in the timing of arrival of sound at the two ears of as little as 10µs (Buser & Imbert 1992). In other auditory tasks, the minimum integration times can likewise be very short: 2–3ms in gap detection or amplitude-modulated noise paradigms (Green 1985), and 0.5ms when discriminating time-reversed stimuli (Henning & Gaskell 1981).

The question arises of how the auditory system can accommodate information at this fine temporal scale. The physiology and microanatomy of the first synapses in the auditory pathway may be revealing. Primary auditory fibres in the eighth nerve terminate in the cochlear nuclei. The physiology and morphology of cells in these nuclei have been examined simultaneously (Rhode et al. 1983, Smith & Rhode 1985). There are several different cell types in the cochlear nuclei, each characterized on the basis of their different responses to stimulus tones (Pfeiffer 1966). One of the cell types, called "primary-like", share many properties of primary auditory neurons. It is thought that these cells may act as simple relay neurons to higher auditory structures which require the preservation of precise timing information, perhaps for sound localization. Other cell types called, "pauser", "build-up", "onset" and "chopper", show more complex response properties and may process spatial or spectral information.

It is interesting that these different physiological properties are associated with different morphological cell types. The physiologically defined primary-like cells appear to correspond to morphologically defined bushy cells, characterized by a single dendritic trunk, short, thin and profusely branching beaded dendrites (see Fig. 3.3). These

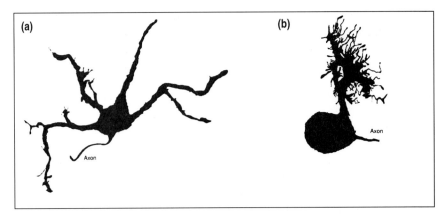

FIG. 3.3.   A small part of the variety of different cell types in the nervous system. (a) A stellate cell with several long spindly dendrites; it receives many small input synapses on its dendrites. (b) A shows a bushy cell, which has one large dendrite and receives input from a few large synapses called end bulbs. The radically different morphologies and connectivities of the cells can give rise to radically different outputs from essentially the same input (see text). Reprinted with permission from Oertel et al. (1988).

cells receive input from some of the most substantial endings from the auditory nerve, the end bulbs, which synapse on the soma. Electrical recordings show that single post-synaptic potentials on these cells are sufficient to raise a bushy cell's membrane potential above threshold for firing (Pfeiffer 1966, Romand 1978). Rhode et al. (1983) remark that "... these cells are well suited to maintain and convey pattern information from auditory nerve fibres ... The presumed synaptic potentials are so brief that phase-locking is maintained to tones of 1200 Hz. These cells therefore, can transmit information with a precision of less than 1 ms."

The other cell types which did not have the ability to convey precise temporal information also had different morphologies. The choppers are stellate cells with long branched dendrites, while the onset cells were either stellate or octopus cells (characterized by cell bodies covered with large spines and thick dendrites). Stellate cells receive smaller bouton terminals from the auditory nerve fibres, mostly made with their dendrites (except for onset-chopper cells). A quantitative approach to relating the morphology and physiology of these cells has been used by White et al. (1994) and Hewitt et al. (1992). Data on dendritic size and number, cell body size and various electronic properties of these cells can be used to construct computational models which allow their physiological responses to be predicted. These models show that the features of chopper response patterns such as poor phase locking above a few hundred hertz, regular interspike intervals, and precisely timed first spikes are consequences of the structure of stellate cells. The major difference between cells with onset-chopper responses (which show phase locking to high frequencies) and sustained-chopper cells is that the former have substantial input onto their somata whereas the latter have little or none. Hence, the carriage of fine temporal information may be achieved by bypassing the low-pass filtering action of cells' dendritic arbours, and it is apparent that, when temporal aspects of a representation are vital, the nervous system can support high-resolution temporal codes.

3.3.2 Temporal coding in other systems

Temporal coding is not limited to the auditory system. An example of such coding is that of the signalling of high-frequency vibratory touch sensations (Ferrington et al. 1987a,b). These sensations arise from Pacinian corpuscles in the skin, which make their first synapse on neurons in the dorsal column nuclei. The features of the interactions between the primary sensory neurons and their target dorsal column nuclei neurons are somewhat similar to those just described for the auditory system. Each impulse in a primary fibre can produce suprathreshold responses in one or more dorsal column nuclei neurons. Dorsal column nuclei neurons can show phase-locked responses to vibrations up to 500 Hz. Amplification of the primary input occurs by single input spikes producing bursts of output spikes in dorsal column nuclei neurons, and by single primary fibres activating multiple dorsal column nuclei neurons.

These rather specialized features characterize a type of secure transmission link from primary sensory neuron to the next neuron in the pathway. This type of linkage is found in many other systems, such as the spinal dorsal horn (P. B. Brown et al. 1973), the spinocervical tract (Hongo & Koike 1975, A. G. Brown et al. 1984), and some neurons of the lateral geniculate nucleus in the visual pathway (Bishop et al. 1958, Cleland et al. 1971). The detection of temporal variations in the ambient electric field by electrosensory neurons in electric fish may also be an example of this type of transmission. The electrosensory neurons project to the torus semicircularis (Heiligenberg 1991), where temporal modulations in the electric field around the fish are represented differently by neurons within the torus (Rose and Call 1993). The processing of temporal information in the torus is again most clearly explained in terms of the specialized morphology of, and interactions between, the participating neurons.

These aspects of processing at links in the neural pathways illustrate a number of points. First, where temporal coding is called for biologically, advantageous neuronal specializations can develop to mediate it. Secondly, neighbouring cells receiving input from the same neurons can represent quite different aspects of the incoming information, apparently using different codes. Thirdly, the carriage of temporally coded information in these parts of the system appears to require rather specific microanatomy and physiology, which may be unlike that elsewhere in the nervous system. Fourthly, following from this, neuronal coding mechanisms operating in one part of the nervous system do not have to operate throughout its extent, since there may be different biological constraints on different components of the system, and different biological specializations may consequently exist in these components.

3.3.3 The temporal properties of neurons

Do neurons in the general case possess the properties necessary to implement a temporal coding scheme? There is a substantial literature on the temporal integrative properties of single neurons (for an introduction see e.g. Shepherd and Koch (1990)). The factors affecting the temporal properties of neurons can be broken into different groups. The first concerns factors arising from the passive electrotonic properties of neurons, the second from factors due to the different molecular mechanisms of synaptic transmission, the third from factors due to the active properties of the dendritic and somatic membrane, and the fourth from factors due to the morphology of axonal trees. We will consider only the passive electrotonic properties of neurons here, but useful reviews of these and other factors can be found in Hartzell (1981), Llinás (1988) and Swadlow et al. (1980).

Rapid changes in current across the neuronal membrane charge or discharge the intrinsic membrane capacitance. Synaptic currents therefore have a delayed effect on the membrane potential. The degree to which the voltage change is delayed is determined by the membrane time constant. Traditional passive cable models of the neuron predict that the time-course of a synaptic input as measured at the soma is more rapid the closer the synapse is to the soma. This suggests that inputs to the distal dendrites could not be represented at high temporal resolution by the neuron's spike output. Various specializations make it possible for a neuron to counteract to a large degree this low-pass filtering of distal inputs (Shepherd & Koch 1990). Input directly onto the soma, however, bypassing the dendrites, may have a more rapid time-course and hence a greater frequency-following capacity, as noted for synapses in the peripheral auditory system.

A cell's membrane time constant thus seems to be an important factor in determining whether or how a cell might participate in a temporal coding scheme (see also Maffei & Rizzolatti 1967). There are, however, large variations, and some uncertainties, in reported values for cells' membrane time constants. Bernander et al. (1991) suggest that the level of background synaptic activity markedly influences the temporal integration properties of neurons, and showed that incorporating realistic levels of background activity into a model of a cortical pyramidal cell changed the value of its membrane time constants from 80 to 7ms. It is possible, therefore, that activity in other cells in a network may change the temporal properties of a neuron. Published values for the membrane time constant might best be considered with this in mind, but it is nonetheless interesting to note a possible relationship between the membrane time constant and the likely type of coding used by a cell. The hair cell of the inner ear, for example, which should be specialized for a high frequency-following capacity, is reported to possess a membrane time constant in the range 2.5–3.1ms (Preyer et al. 1994). This is to be compared with values for cerebellar Purkinje cells of 50ms (Rapp et al. 1994), cortical pyramidal cells of 12.0–19.5ms (Mason & Larkman 1990) and hippocampal cells of 28–66ms (Spruston & Johnston 1992).

3.3.4 Temporal encoding at the cortical level
These considerations of the temporal properties of neurons have some consequences for the likelihood of temporal encoding in cortical neurons which we will leave implicit for the moment. But it is at the cortical level that the present debate about the status of temporal coding sharpens, and it is to cortical processing that we now turn. As in our discussion of spatial aspects of neural coding, the issues can be illustrated by presenting two extreme positions.

A possible extreme temporal coding scheme, sometimes called "interval coding", is characterized by information being carried in the precise time of occurrence of each action potential. The limiting resolution of this code is determined by the biophysics of the spike-generating mechanism. MacKay and McCulloch (1952) estimate that "in the worst case, an imprecision ... of 0.3ms had to be accepted". They found that a code which used this precise timing information carried at least 2–3 times as much information as a code that did not. Rapoport & Horvath (1960) showed that, with a minimum discriminable time interval of 5µs, a model neuron could transmit information at 4000bit/s! Clearly, taking account of the time of occurrence of spikes as well as the number of spikes in a given interval gives, in theory, additional information. However, these theoretical calculations are unrealistic when confronted with the noisy nature of cortical neural transmission (see Stevens 1994, Shadlen & Newsome 1994, Softky 1995). Synaptic unreliability means that much less than 100% of impulses arriving at a synapse produce a post-synaptic response. This aspect of synaptic transmission is much more damaging to a code that is dependent on the precise timing of spikes than one dependent on their number in some broader time window. Single post-synaptic potentials caused by a pre-synaptic neuron cannot reliably produce single spikes in a post-synaptic neuron. This is because approximately 10–40 excitatory inputs are required to take a cortical neuron from resting potential to its firing threshold (Stevens 1994), and because the 10^4 or so other cells contacting each neocortical neuron interfere with the signal: the spontaneous discharges from the large number of input synapses will provide an unstable baseline from which to detect a synaptic event on a single input line. As we have seen above, the membrane of the post-synaptic cell's dendritic arbour effectively low-pass filters incoming signals. This means that any effective event will influence the cell over a duration determined by the membrane time constant. During this time, the signal will inevitably summate with other excitatory and inhibitory post-synaptic potentials, a feature that has consequences for coding schemes, as discussed by McKean et al. (1970). Furthermore, each neuron that is to read a high-resolution temporal code would require complex decoding mechanisms to extract the information so coded (see below).

The other extreme of the temporal coding spectrum is characterized by the idea that only the rate of firing in a broad time window carries information. The intervals between discharges in such a frequency code are assumed to be distributed independently, according, perhaps, to a Poisson or gamma distribution (Fitzhugh 1958, Shadlen & Newsome 1994). The interspike intervals will be random, bearing no relationship to any message carried. To estimate the rate at which a neuron fires, its output must be summed over time. The time-course of this summation, the integration interval, is usually taken to be of the order of tenths of a second in very many electrophysiological experiments on cortical neurons. From a theoretical viewpoint, longer integration intervals mean more accurate estimates of spike rate, and consequently a more robust code in the face of the transmission noise problems described above. However, from the post-synaptic neuron's point of view there must be an upper limit to the integration interval in order for it to be able to produce its own output response. Large intervals are unrealistic for various reasons. Once the integration interval is longer than the membrane time constant, some special mechanism must be invoked to store the summated input. External variables such as those relating to movement should be signalled with high time resolution, and this will be difficult to implement if all neurons work on timescales of tenths of a second. Finally, averaging across a large interval obviously loses any information carried in the finer temporal structure of spike trains, and therefore reduces the capacity of the code relative to a temporal encoding scheme (see Stein 1967).

Since neither extreme appears biologically attractive, the question arises of how temporal a cortical code might be. It is possible to conceive of a continuum of intermediate codes. As the integration interval is reduced, the ability to code information in changes in spike rate over time is gained. As a spike train is broken into increasingly shorter time segments, the timing of each spike becomes increasingly relevant to the code. Biological plausibility again settles on the membrane time constant as a critical variable, which sets an upper limit to the resolution of any temporal code. Signals in frequency ranges higher than the low pass imposed by the post-synaptic membrane will not carry useful information.

What experimental evidence bears on these issues? Krüger & Becker (1991) and Geisler et al. (1991) present experimental evidence that the temporal distribution of spikes codes for "objective meaning". Increasing the width of the spike bins (i.e. increasing the coarseness of the temporal code) eventually leads to a reduction in the degree to which neurons can discriminate different stimuli. Recent studies using multivariate statistics and information theory have presented evidence for temporal encoding in the lateral geniculate nucleus, primary visual cortex and inferotemporal cortex of behaving monkeys (Optican & Richmond 1987, Richmond & Optican 1990). In a particularly enlightening work, Miller et al. (1993) examined quantitatively the coding proposals of Richmond & Optican, together with two other proposals. They examined a simple spike rate code with spikes integrated over 225 ms, a temporal code based on that used by Richmond & Optican, again using data over a 225 ms response interval, and an intermediate temporal code, in which the response interval was divided into three 75 ms intervals and the number of spikes in each interval summed. The cut-off frequency of the latter code, according to sampling theory, was equivalent to about 7 Hz. Miller and colleagues found that the Richmond & Optican code carried more information than the rate code, but that the intermediate temporal code was "slightly but significantly" better than that of Richmond & Optican. Comparing the two temporal codes in part assesses the consequences of low-pass filtering with ~14 Hz (for Richmond & Optican's code) or 7 Hz cut-offs. Apparently, the removal of more of the higher frequencies does not degrade, but slightly enhances, the carriage of information. The comparison, however, is not a simple one because the Richmond & Optican code incorporates the additional processing of a principal components analysis which may have complex consequences (Fotheringhame & Young, 1997).

These results imply that a low frequency temporal code outperforms a spike rate code, and that it may be no worse than a higher frequency temporal code. The coding principle that might be taken to emerge is what some call "temporal coding", others "rate modulation", and still others "multivariate spike rate". This intermediate temporal code may overcome most of the problems associated with each of the two extreme positions outlined above, and might present an adaptive solution for biological implementation. Rate modulation has certainly proven a successful model for many parts of the nervous system. Muscle tension can be correlated very well with the instantaneous spike rate of motor neurons, and the short-term discharge rate of retinal ganglion cells correlates well with log light contrast (Hartline 1940). In these examples, it is critical that the rate signal be capable of rapid change.

It is interesting also to consider the constraints that are imposed in the more general case by the necessity to process information quickly. The response latencies of higher order cortical neurons and knowledge of the shortest routes by which sensory information could reach them may allow an estimate of the processing time available at each neuronal link before information is passed on. This notional processing time is quite short, and bears on the issue of how long a sample of a spike train could be used to transmit a message. Tovée et al. (1993) propose 15–20ms at each stage of the cortical pathway to the inferotemporal cortex. Dinse & Krüger (1994) estimate 5–15ms for the cat visual system. It is not likely, however, that processing is a simple sequential scheme, in which each stage of a pathway performs its computations and then passes out the results in the form of its spike train to the next stage. Dinse & Kruger (1994), for example, showed that processing at the various stages of the cat visual system is notably concurrent. Their data showed that 97% of area 18 and 74% of area 17 cells are active at the same time as all the cells at the thalamic relay stage are active. These data imply a different model of cortical processing, one perhaps more like the cascade model of McClelland (1979). This type of model might suggest that longer processing times are available than in a strictly sequential scheme. On the other hand, since Oram & Perrett (1992) showed that neurons in the inferotemporal cortex can discriminate well on the basis of the first 5ms of their spike train, one can wonder what the extra processing time might be used for. In this context, Rolls & Tovée (1994) have shown that when a picture of a face is presented for just 16ms, cells in the inferotemporal cortex respond for 200–300ms. This persistent activity, they suggest, is due to the operation of a short-term memory system, and they show that memory, but not recognition performance, can be abolished by presenting a masking stimulus a few tens of milliseconds after the face stimulus. Only

20–30ms of signalling are suggested to be required for inferotemporal cortex cells to mediate the recognition of a face (Rolls & Tovée 1994).

3.3.5 Decoding temporal information

Any useful neural code must be readable. Reading a code could be as simple as integrating spike inputs according to the passive properties of the post-synaptic membrane, such as may occur at the neuromuscular junction. More complex codes, however, will require more complex decoding schemes. Bialek and colleagues (Bialek et al. 1991, de Ruyter et al. 1988) have described a decoding mechanism that allows the reconstruction of high-resolution temporal information from real spike trains in real time. It uses simple analogue filtering of a kind that could be implemented by neurons. The principal advances of this approach are that it approaches the problem of neural decoding from the point of view of real neurons performing plausible functions. The scheme suggested by these authors is robust to noise in the timing of spikes, and to the addition or removal of spikes. A particular attraction is that the optimal filtering for decoding temporal messages resembles that performed by real synapses.

The temporal code proposed by Richmond & Optican (1987) requires a much more complex decoding scheme, because several tenths of second of spike input must be received before decoding can proceed. This presents problems in meeting the constraints, outlined above, in relation to speed of processing. There is also the problem that the filters required are complex (see Gawne et al. 1991). One mitigating suggestion is that decoding could be achieved in part by passing the temporal signal to many neurons, which would use elaborate cortical circuitry to extract the message (see also Jeffress 1948). This scheme has the disadvantage that it requires a large number of neurons to read reliably the output of a single neuron, and would appear to require an explosive increase in the number of neurons at higher levels in a pathway, which is not observed. Another proposal is that the distribution of inputs on a post-synaptic cell, precise patterns of axonal and dendritic morphology, and multiple transmitter systems could perform the complex decoding required (Gawne et al. 1991).

3.4 INTERACTIONS BETWEEN SPATIAL AND TEMPORAL ASPECTS OF NEURONAL CODING

The peripheral and central nervous systems differ in their neural architectures, development and phylogeny, and in their functions. One emphasis in the preceding discussion has been on the role of biological constraints in determining the nature of the neural codes used by parts of the system. Different biological constraints operate in different components of the nervous system, and we have suggested that different coding specializations may follow these constraints. A general consequence may be that different coding strategies are employed in the central and peripheral nervous systems. If this is the case, are there recoding mechanisms that facilitate the communication of information between the two?

The issue of recoding may be illustrated by insights from auditory physiology. Single auditory nerve fibres can signal sound intensity changes over a range of 20–50dB, while the auditory system as a whole, as in psychophysical experiments, works over a range of 120dB. The proposed solutions to this problem provide a variety of indications of the ways different types of neural code might interact in performing a single task. A partial solution to the problem is to return to the specification of labelled lines – a spatial code – at higher levels of the system, whereby different fibres signal different ranges of sound intensity. This mechanism could increase the dynamic range signalled within the auditory system far above that capable of being signalled by a single neuron, by distributing the information across a population. This kind of recoding, however, would also blur any information carried by the precise timing of signals in primary and some secondary fibres, lowering the temporal resolution of the peripheral code towards that for a rate code.

In this context, Feng et al. (1990) reported that the temporal resolution of responses to sounds that varied in volume over time decreased at increasingly higher levels of the auditory system. This means there is a reduced capacity to carry information in the temporal pattern of spikes at higher stages. Rose & Capranica (1985) also showed that auditory information on the loudness of sounds is recoded as it is passed up the auditory pathway. The code appears to change from one using high-resolution temporal synchrony to one using a simple average firing rate code. Higher level neurons in the midbrain, which were sharply tuned to the frequency of amplitude-modulated sounds, often showed little or no temporal synchronization to the stimulus waveform. Recoding information that can be carried temporally in the periphery, such as the frequency of amplitude-modulated sounds, may also use the temporal filtering properties of specialized neurons at early stages in the pathway. Cells in the dorsal medullary nucleus show a variety of frequency selectivities including low-pass, band-pass and all-pass types (Hall & Feng 1991). Selective connections from cells of this type to neurons coding by rate at higher levels might provide a basis for the latter cells' frequency selectivity.

The primate visual system shows evidence for a similar decrease in frequency-following capacity at higher stages. The lateral geniculate nucleus may act as a low-pass integrating device for the output of retinal ganglion cells (Bishop et al. 1953, Maffei & Rizzolatti 1967). Foster et al. (1985) showed that cells in cortical areas V1 and V2 responded best to grating patterns with temporal frequencies of 3–8 Hz. At the lower stage of the lateral geniculate nucleus, the peak temporal frequencies for both parvocellular and magnocellular neurons is higher at 10–20 Hz (Hicks et al. 1983). Psychophysical studies also provide evidence that central mechanisms low-pass filter the signals from the periphery. By comparing the flicker fusion frequency for human observers with the maximum frequency of luminance modulation at which geniculate cells respond, Kremers et al. (1993) showed that later stages of the visual pathway must low-pass filter the temporal information conveyed by ganglion cells.

The somatosensory system provides further indirect evidence for the presence of recoding mechanisms. Humans can sense the vibratory nature of stimuli applied to the skin up to 800–1000 Hz (Goff 1967), while neurons of the dorsal column nuclei cannot phase-lock their responses to this high a frequency. The discrimination must use information from separate channels, but, as very few central neurons can fire at the frequencies required, there must be some recoding of the signal from the phase-locked temporal code in the dorsal column nuclei for neurons higher in the pathway which are responsible for the observed psychophysical performance.

Cortical magnification may play a role in recoding information. Magnification relates to the fact that there are many cortical cells for each afferent sensory fibre. In the primate visual system, for example, there are 150–200 cortical neurons to each optic nerve fibre (Tolhurst & Ling 1988), while in the rat barrel field cortex there are 15 cortical cells to each sensory vibrissal fibre (Lee & Woolsey 1975). It has been thought that the increase in the number of cells processing the same sensory input was due to an increase in the elaboration of processing of incoming information. This elaboration leads to different aspects of the raw sensory data being processed separately at later stages. It is also possible that magnification is required to recode information into a form required for neurons that cannot support a fine temporal code. The format, or the dimensions, by which stimulus information is encoded by the sense organs and periphery is often not suited ideally to the higher level goals of cortical processing, such as object identification. Cortical neurons consequently need integrative properties very different from neurons in the periphery to perform their computations. We have suggested that these differences are likely to be manifest in different coding strategies, and that neurons at higher levels are less likely to use coding that involves high frequency temporal signalling. Wholesale loss of temporally coded information as it enters the central nervous system appears unlikely, since the higher frequency peripheral mechanisms could not in this case have been selected by evolution for their contributions to the whole animal's adaptivity. The reduced capacity of cortical cells to process temporal information must then be compensated for. This may be achieved by using more central cells to represent incoming information than coded it in the periphery.

The possible differences in processing emphases between the peripheral and the central nervous systems provide illustrations of recoding. But we envisage that recoding is a widespread phenomenon throughout the nervous system, which occurs between different areas of the brain and between neighbouring neurons when their coding strategies differ, and they are required to interact to generate adaptive behaviour.

3.5 CONCLUDING REMARKS

The area of neural coding schemes and their relation to the representation of behavioural events abounds with experimentally tractable, unanswered or further questions. How fine are the temporal codes in various parts of the system? How distributed are they? Does the later epoch of a neuronal spike train response contain qualitatively different information to that in the earlier transient epoch? Is the coding in different parts of the brain of the same kind? Do all neurons speak and understand the same language? What are the precise limits placed on the information content of a spike train by coding and decoding mechanisms? What are these mechanisms, precisely? Pessimists might conclude that these many questions are the result of an enterprise similar to trying to understand the workings of a telephone exchange armed with a voltmeter and no knowledge of the English language. Optimists might note the remarkable progress made on these very complex issues, and the excitement of an advancing and fundamental area.

We have suggested that examples of temporal coding are likely to reside in neurons close to the periphery, where the information being signalled contains inherently temporal characteristics, and where specialized adaptations may exist to support the temporal representation of this information. High-resolution temporal codes seem less likely to be implemented centrally, where computational and other biological demands suggest different coding strategies. Our framework has reflected the view that a profitable way to address questions of spatial and temporal coding in the nervous system is to consider (a) the structure of the neurons and their interactions, and (b) the biological constraints on the information they represent and their roles in the information processing economy of the system, particularly in the light of the biological problems the animal is trying to solve. We believe that these considerations are some of the keys to understanding coding and recoding strategies in the nervous system.

ACKNOWLEDGEMENT

D.F. was supported by a Wellcome Trust Prize Studentship.

NOTE

1. This chapter was written at the end of 1994 and was based on a review of work published at that time. It is not intended to be "encyclopaedic"; it contains a discussion of some of the main interesting issues in the field at that time.

REFERENCES

Abramson, N. 1963. *Information theory and coding*. New York: McGraw-Hill.

Adrian, E. D. 1926. The impulses produced by sensory nerve endings. Part I. *Journal of Physiology (London)* **61**, 49–72.

Adrian, E. D. & Y. Zotterman 1926. The impulses produced by sensory nerve-endings: Part 2. The response of a single end-organ. *Journal of Physiology (London)* **61**, 151–71.

Barlow, H. B. 1963. The information capacity of nervous transmission. *Kybernetik* **2**, 1.

Barlow, H. B. 1972. Single units and perception: a neuron doctrine for perceptual psychology? *Perception* **1**, 371–94.

Barlow H. B. 1985. The role of single neurons in the psychology of perception. *Quarterly Journal of Experimental Psychiatry* **37A**, 121–45.

Baylis G. C., E. T. Rolls, C. M. Leonard 1985. Selectivity between faces in the responses of a population of neurons in the cortex of the superior temporal sulcus of the monkey. *Brain Research* **342**, 91–102.

Bernander, O., R. J. Douglas, K. A. C. Martin, C. Koch 1991. Synaptic background activity influences spatiotemporal integration in single pyramidal cells. *Proceedings of the National Academy of Science USA* **88**, 11569–73.

Bialek, W., F. Rieke, R. R. de Ruyter van Steveninck, D. Warland 1991. Reading a neural code. *Science* **252**, 1854–7.

Bishop, P. O., D. Jeremy, J. G. McLeod 1953. Phenomenon of repetitive firing in lateral geniculate of cat. *Journal of Neurophysiology* **16**, 437.

Bishop, P. O., W. Burke, R. Davis 1958. Synapse discharge by single fibre in mammalian visual system. *Nature* **182**, 728–30.

Britten, K. H., M. N. Shadlen, W. T. Newsome, J.A. Movshon 1992. The analysis of visual motion. *Journal of Neuroscience* **12**, 4745–65.

Brown, A. G., H. R. Koerber, R. Noble, P. K. Rose, P. J. Snow 1984. Effect of single hair follicle afferent fiber discharge on spinocervical tract (SCT) fiber cells in the cat. *Journal of Physiology (London)* **346**, 50P.

Brown, P. B., H. Moraff, D. N. Tapper 1973. Functional organization of the cat's dorsal horn: spontaneous activity and central cell responses to single impulses in single type I fibers. *Journal of Neurophysiology* **36**, 827–39.

Burke, R. E. & P. G. Nelson 1966. Synaptic activity of motoneurons during natural stimulation of muscle spindles. *Science* **151**, 1088–91.

Buser P. & M. Imbert 1992. *Audition*, R. M. Kay (trans.). Cambridge, MA: MIT Press.

Cleland, B. G., M. W. Dubin, W. R. Levick 1971. Simultaneous recording of input and output of lateral geniculate neurons. *Nature* **231**, 191–2.

de Ruyter van Steveninck, R. R. & W. Bialek 1988. Real time performance of a movement sensitive neuron in the blowfly visual system: coding and information transfer in short spike sequences. *Proceedings of the Royal Society London, series B* **234**, 379–414.

De Valois, R. L., D. G. Albrecht, L. G. Thorell 1982. Spatial frequency selectivity of cells in macaque visual cortex. *Vision Research* **22**, 545–59.

Dinse, H. R. & K. Krüger 1994. The timing of processing along the visual pathway in the cat. *NeuroReport* **5**, 893–7.

Feng, A. S., J. C. Hall, D. M. Gooler 1990. Neural basis of sound pattern recognition in anurans. *Progress in Neurobiology* **34**, 313–29.

Ferrington, D. G., M. J. Rowe, R. P. C. Tarvin 1987a. Actions of single sensory fibres on cat dorsal column neurons: vibratory signalling in a one-to-one linkage. *Journal of Physiology (London)* **386**, 293–309.

Ferrington, D. G., M. J. Rowe, R. P. C. Tarvin 1987b. Integrative processing of vibratory information in cat dorsal column nuclei neurons driven by identified sensory fibers. *Journal of Physiology (London)* **386**, 311–31.

Field, D. 1994. What is the goal of sensory coding?, *Neural Computation* **6**, 559–601.

Fitzhugh, R. 1958. A statistical analyser for optic nerve messages. *Journal of General Physiology* **41**(4), 675–92.

Foldiak, P. & M. P. Young 1995. Sparse coding in primate cortex. In *Handbook of brain theory and neural networks*, M. J. Arbib (ed.). Cambridge, MA: MIT Press.

Foster, K. H., J. P. Gaska, M. Nagler, D. A. Pollen 1985. Spatial and temporal frequency selectivity of neurons in visual cortical areas V1 and V2 of the Macaque monkey. *Journal of Physiology (London)* **365**, 331–63.

Fotheringhame, D. K. & M. P. Young 1997. Is temporally coded information in spike trains due to the signal or the noise?, submitted.

Freeman, W. J. 1975. *Mass action in the nervous system*. New York: Academic Press.

Fujita I., K. Tanaka, M. Ito, K. Cheng 1992. Columns for visual features of objects in monkey inferotemporal cortex. *Nature* **360**, 343–6.

Gallager, R. G. 1968. *Information theory and reliable communication*. New York: Wiley.

Gawne, T. J. & B. J. Richmond 1993. How independent are the messages carried by adjacent cortical neurons? *Journal of Neuroscience* **13**, 2758–71.

Gawne, T. J., J. W. McClurkin, B. J. Richmond, L. M. Optican 1991. Lateral geniculate neurons in behaving primates III. Response predictions of a channel model with multiple spatial-to-temporal filters. *Journal of Neurophysiology* **66**(3), 809–23.

Geisler, W. S., D. G. Albrecht, R. J. Salvi, S. S. Saunders 1991. Discrimination performance of single neurons: rate and temporal-pattern information. *Journal of Neurophysiology* **66**(1), 334–62.

Georgopoulos A. P., J. F. Kalaska, R. Caminiti, J. T. Massey 1982. On the relations between the direction of two-dimensional arm movements and cell discharge in primate motor cortex. *Journal of Neuroscience* **2**, 1527–37.

Goff, G. D. 1967. Differential discrimination of frequency of cutaneous mechanical vibration. *Journal of Experimental Psychology* **74**, 294–9.

Green, D. M. 1985. *Temporal factors in psychoacoustics in time resolution in auditory systems*, A. Michelsen (ed.), 122–40. Berlin: Springer-Verlag.

Gross C. G., C. E. Rocha-Miranda, D. B. Bender 1972. Visual properties of neurons in the inferotemporal cortex of the macaque. *Journal of Neurophysiology* **35**, 96–111.

Hall, J. C. & A. S. Feng 1991. Temporal processing in the dorsal medullary nucleus of the northern leopard frog (Rana pipiens pipiens). *Journal of Neurophysiology* **66**(3), 955–73.

Hartline. H. K. 1940. The nerve messages in the fibres of the visual pathway. *Journal of th Optical Society of America* **30**, 239–47.

Hartzell, H. C. 1981. Mechanisms of slow postsynaptic potentials. *Nature* **291**, 539–44.

Heiligenberg, W. 1991. *Neural nets in electric fish*. Cambridge, MA: MIT Press.

Henning, G. B. & H. Gaskell 1981. Monaural phase sensitivity with Ronken's Paradigm. *Journal of the Acoustical Society of America* **70**, 1669–73.

Hewitt, M. J., R. Meddis, T. M. Shackleton 1992. A computer model of a cochlear-nucleus stellate cell: responses to amplitude-modulated and pure-tone stimuli. *Journal of Acoustical Society of America* **91**(4), 2096–109.

Hicks, T. P., B. B. Lee, T. R. Vidyasagar 1983. The responses of cells in the macaque lateral geniculate nucleus to sinusoidal gratings. *Journal of Physiology (London)* **337**, 183–200.

Hinton, G. E., J. L. McClelland, D. E. Rumelhart, 1986. Distributed representations. In *Parallel distributed processing*, vol. 1, D. E. Rumelhart & J. L. McClelland (eds), 77–109. Cambridge, MA: MIT Press.

Hongo, T. & H. Koike 1975. Some aspects of synaptic organizations in the spinocervical tract cell in the cat. In *The somatosensory system*, H. H. Kornhuber (ed.), 218–26. Stuttgart: Georg Thieme.

Hurlbert, A. C. & A. M. Derrington 1993. How many neurons does it take to see? *Current Biology* **3**, 510–12.

Jeffress, L. A. 1948. A place theory of sound localization. *Journal of Comparative Physiology and Psychology* **41**, 35–9.

Johnson, D. H. 1980. The relationship between spike rate and synchrony in responses of auditory nerve fibers to single tones. *Journal of the Acoustical Society of America* **68**, 1115–22.

Kiang, N. Y. S., T. Watanabe, E. C. Thomas, L. F. Clark 1965. *Discharge patterns of single fibers in the cat's auditory nerve*. Cambridge, MA: MIT Press.

Konorski, J. 1967. *Integrative activity of the brain: an interdisciplinary approach*. Chicago, Il: University of Chicago Press.

Kremers, J., B. B. Lee, J. Pokorny, V. C. Smith 1993. Responses of macaque ganglion cells and human observers to compound periodic waveforms. *Vision Research* **33**, 1997–2011.

Krüger, J. & J. D. Becker 1991. Recognizing the visual stimulus from neuronal discharges. *TINS* **14**(7), 282–6.

Lee, K. J. & T. A. Woolsey 1975. A proportional relationship between peripheral innervation density and cortical neuron number in the somatosensory system of the mouse. *Brain Research* **99**, 349–53.

Lehky S. R. & T. J. Sejnowski 1990. Neural model of stereoacuity and depth interpolation based on a distributed representation of stereo disparity. *Journal of Neuroscience* **10**(7), 2281–99.

Llinás, R. 1988. The intrinsic electrophysiological properties of mammalian neurons: insights into central nervous system function. *Science* **242**, 1654–64.

MacKay, D. M. & W. S. McCulloch 1952. The limiting information capacity of a neuronal link. *Bulletin of Mathematical Biophysics* **14**, 127–35.

Maffei, L. & G. Rizzolatti 1967. Transfer properties of the lateral geniculate body. *Journal of Neurophysiology* **30**, 333–40.

Mason, A. & A. Larkman 1990. Correlations between morphology and electrophysiology of pyramidal neurons in slices of rat visual cortex. II. Electrophysiology. *Journal of Neuroscience* **10**(5), 1415–28.

McClelland, J. L. 1979. On the time-relations of mental processes: an examination of systems of processes in cascade. *Psychological Review* **86**, 287–330.

McKean, T. A., R. E. Poppele, N. P. Rosenthal, C. A. Terzuolo 1970. The biologically relevant parameter in nerve impulse trains. *Kybernetik* **6**, 168–70.

McNaughton, B. L. & R. G. M. Morris 1987. Hippocampal synaptic enhancement and information storage within a distributed memory system. *TINS* **10**(10), 408–15.

Miller, E. K., L. Li, R. Desimone 1993. Activity of neurons in anterior inferior temporal cortex during a short-term memory task. *Journal of Neuroscience* **13**(4), 1460–78.

Miyashita, Y. 1988. Neuronal correlate of visual associative long-term memory in the primate temporal cortex. *Nature* **335**, 817–20.

Miyashita, Y. & H. S. Chang 1988. Neuronal correlate of pictorial short-term memory in the primate temporal cortex. *Nature* **331**, 68–70.

Moore, G. P., D. H. Perkel, J. P. Segundo 1966. Statistical analysis and functional interpretation of neuronal spike data. *Annual Review of Physiology* **28**, 493–522.

Oertel, D., S. H. Wu, J. A. Hirsch 1988. Electrical characteristics of cells and neuronal circuitry in the cochlear nuclei studied with intracellular recordings from brain slices. In *Auditory function: Neurobiological basis of hearing*, G. M. Edelman, W. E. Gall, W. M. Cowan (eds), 313–36. New York: Wiley.

Optican, L. M. & B. J. Richmond 1987. Temporal encoding of two-dimensional patterns by single units in primate inferior temporal cortex. III. Information theoretic analysis. *Journal of Neurophysiology* **57**(1), 162–78.

Oram, M. W. & D. I. Perrett 1992. Time course of neural responses discriminating different views of the face and head. *Journal of Neurophysiology* **68**(1), 70–84.

Perrett, D. I., E. T. Rolls, W. Caan 1982. Visual neurons responsive to faces in the monkey temporal cortex. *Experimental Brain Research* **47**, 329–42.

Pfeiffer, R. R. 1966. Classification of response patterns of spike discharges for units in the cochlear nucleus: tone burst stimulation. *Experimental Brain Research* **1**, 220–35.

Preyer, S., W. Hemmert, M. Pfister, H. P. Zenner, A. W. Gummer 1994. Frequency response of mature guinea-pig outer hair cells to stereociliary displacement. *Hearing Research* **77**, 116–24.

Rapoport, A. & W. Horvath 1960. The theoretical channel capacity of a single neuron as determined by various coding systems. *Information Control* **3**, 335–50.

Rapp, M., I. Segev, Y. Yarom 1994. Physiology, morphology and passive models of guinea-pig cerebellar Purkinje cells. *Journal of Physiology (London)* **474**, 101–18.

Redman, S. & B. Walmsley 1982. The time course of synaptic potentials evoked in cat spinal motoneurons at identified group Ia synapses. *Journal of Physiology* (London) **343**, 117–33.

Rhode, W. S., D. Oertel, P. H. Smith 1983. Physiological response properties of cells labelled intracellularly with horseradish peroxidase in cat ventral cochlear nucleus. *Journal of Comparative Neurology* **213**, 448-63.

Richmond, B. J. & L. M. Optican 1990. Temporal encoding of two-dimensional patterns by single units in primate primary visual cortex II. Information transmission. *Journal of Neurophysiology* **64**(2), 370–80.

Richmond, B. J., L. M. Optican, M. Podell, H. Spitzer 1987. Temporal encoding of two-dimensional patterns by single units in primate inferior temporal cortex. I. Response characteristics. *Journal of Neurophysiology* **57**(1), 132–46.

Rolls, E. T. & S. M. O'Mara 1993. Neurophysiological and theoretical analysis of how the primate hippocampus functions in memory. In *Brain mechanisms of perception: from neuron to behavior*, T. Ono, L. R. Squire, M. E. Raichle, D. I. Perrett, M. Fukada (eds), 276–300. New York: Oxford University Press.

Rolls, E. T. & M. J. Tovée 1994. Processing speed in the cerebral cortex and the neurophysiology of visual masking. *Proceedings of the Royal Society of London, series B* **257**, 9–15.

Rolls, E. T. & A. Treves 1990. The relative advantages of sparse versus distributed encoding for associative neuronal networks in the brain. *Network* **1**, 407–21.

Romand, R. 1978. Survey of intracellular recording in the cochlear nucleus of the cat. *Brain Research* **148**, 43–65.

Rose, G. J. & S. J. Call 1993. Temporal filtering properties of midbrain neurons in an electric fish: implications for the function of dendritic spines. *Journal of Neuroscience* **13**(3), 1178–89.

Rose, G. J. & R. P. Capranica 1985. Sensitivity to amplitude modulated sounds in the anuran auditory nervous system. *Journal of Neurophysiology* **53**(2), 446–65.

Rose, J. E., J. F. Brugg, D. J. Anderson, J. E. Hird 1967. Phase-locked responses to low-frequency tones in single auditory nerve fibers of the squirrel monkey. *Journal of Neurophysiology*. **30**, 769–93.

Shadlen, M. N. & W. T. Newsome 1994. Noise, neural codes and cortical organization. *Current Opinions of Neurobiology* **4**, 569–79.

Shannon, C. E. & W. Weaver 1949. *The mathematical theory of communication*. Urbana, Il: University of Illinois Press.

Shepherd, G. M. & C. Koch 1990. Introduction to synaptic circuits (pp 3–31), Appendix: Dendritic electrotonus and synaptic integration (pp 439–74). In *The synaptic organization of the brain,* G. M. Shepherd (ed.). Oxford: Oxford University Press.

Smith, P. H. & W. S. Rhode 1985. Electron microscopic features of physiologically characterized, HRP-labeled fusiform cells in the cat dorsal cochlear nucleus. *Journal of Comparative Neurology* **237**, 127–43.

Softky, W. R. 1995. Simple codes versus efficient codes. *Current Opinion in Neurobiology* **5**, 239–47.

Spruston, N. & D. Johnston 1992. Perforated patch clamp analysis of the passive membrane properties of three classes of hippocampal neurons. *Journal of Neurophysiology* **67**, 508–29.

Stein, R. B. 1967. The information capacity of nerve cells using a frequency code. *Biophysical Journal* **7**, 797–826.

Stevens, C. F. 1994. Cooperativity of unreliable neurons. *Current Biology* **4**, 268–9.

Stryker, M. P. 1992. Elements of visual perception. *Nature* **360**, 301–2.

Swadlow, H. A., J. D. Kocsis, S. G. Waxman 1980. Modulation of impulse conduction along the axonal tree. *Annual Review Biophysics and Bioengineering* **9**, 143–79.

Tanaka, K., H. Fukada, Y. Saito, M. Moriya 1991. Coding visual images of objects in the inferotemporal cortex of the macaque monkey. *Journal of Neuroscience* **6**, 134–44.

Tolhurst, D. J. & L. Ling 1988. Magnification factors and the organization of the human striate cortex. *Human Neurobiology* **6**(4), 247–54.

Tovée, M. J., E. T. Rolls, A. Treves, R. P. Bellis 1993. Information encoding and the responses of single neurons in the primate temporal visual cortex. *Journal of Neurophysiology* **70**(2), 640–54.

White, J. A., E. D. Young, P. B. Manis 1994. The electrotonic structure of regular-spiking neurons in the ventral cochlear nucleus may determine their response properties. *Journal of Neurophysiology* **71**(5), 1774–86.

Yamane, S., S. Kaji, K. Kawano 1988. What facial features activate face neurons in the inferotemporal cortex of the monkey? *Experimental Brain Research* **73**, 209–14.

Young, M. P. 1993. Visual cortex: modules for pattern recognition. *Current Biology* **3**, 44–6.

Young, M. P. 1995. Open questions about the neural mechanisms of visual pattern recognition. In *The cognitive neurosciences*, M. S. Gazzaniga (ed.), 463–74. Cambridge MA: MIT Press.

Young, M. P. & S. Yamane 1992. Sparse population coding of faces in the inferotemporal cortex. *Science* **256**, 1327–31.

Young M. P., & S. Yamane 1993. An analysis at the population level of the processing of faces in the inferotemporal cortex. In *Brain mechanisms of perception and memory: from neuron to behavior*, T. Ono, L. R. Squire, D. I. Perrett, M. Fukuda (eds). Oxford: Oxford University Press.

Zohary, E. 1992. Population coding of visual stimuli by cortical neurons tuned to more than one dimension *Biological Cybernetics* **66**, 265–72.

CHAPTER 4

Learning and memory: computational principles and neural mechanisms

Matthew L. Shapiro & Howard Eichenbaum

4.1 INTRODUCTION

Memory is typically described in terms of information storage and retrieval, and more rarely in terms of its the functional purpose: rapid behavioural adaptation. Memory provides the basis for expectancy, anticipatory adaptive responses and planning, as well as an ongoing record of events or personal history. This record includes recognition of familiar particulars, such as places, people and other individuals (specific animals, cars), as well as the individuation and contents of specific episodes. People and animals must remember many different types of information to solve problems and survive. Although one general-purpose memory system could in principle handle all types of memory, in fact several special-purpose memory systems have evolved to acquire and store different types of information (Schacter & Tulving 1994). Moreover, each of these memory systems is distinguished by a different set of anatomical pathways and operating principles. Thus, simple reflex conditioning requires cerebellar circuitry and not the forebrain (e.g. Thompson 1986); conditioned emotional responses require amygdaloid circuitry (e.g. Phillips & LeDoux 1992); simple stimulus–response learning requires the striatum (e.g. Packard et al. 1989); cognitive or relational learning requires hippocampal circuitry (e.g. Morris et al. 1982); and working memory requires prefrontal–cortical circuits (Goldman-Rakic et al. 1984, Goldman-Rakic 1995; see also Ch. 8).

These and other learning abilities can be multiply dissociated, which suggests that the different brain systems for memory can operate in parallel and independently (Sherry & Schachter 1987, Kesner et al. 1993, McDonald & White 1993).

Memory, in the common sense of the word, is more than the persistence of acquired adaptations, because it permits, to a greater or lesser degree of clarity, a re-presentation of the occurrence and contents of past events. In this chapter, "memory" will be used in this narrow and common sense of the word, referring to our ability to recall everyday facts and events, to bring memories to conscious recollection in ways that are subject to verbal or other explicit means of expression. This type of memory has been called "declarative" or "explicit" memory, to distinguish it from the acquisition of habitual routines and preferences that can occur unconsciously and are revealed in implicit changes in performance speed or bias. A wealth of evidence now indicates that declarative–explicit memory is mediated by the hippocampus and related structures, together with their interactions with the cerebral cortex.

The goal of this chapter is to review efforts to construct computational models of the hippocampal system that may help explain various aspects of declarative–explicit memory. Towards that end, in the first section of the chapter we attempt to characterize declarative memory primarily by describing the aspects of memory that break down in amnesia. Secondly, we summarize the known physiological and anatomical attributes of the brain regions and pathways critical to this type of memory. Finally, we describe how the cognitive and neural constraints have been combined by reviewing several computational models of hippocampal function as it relates to memory.

4.2 COGNITIVE CONSTRAINTS ON THE DEVELOPMENT OF MODELS OF HIPPOCAMPAL SYSTEM FUNCTION

The first requirement in developing a model of memory is to define its characteristics. Many of the properties now understood about the cognitive neuroscience of memory have come, somewhat paradoxically, from patients who lack memory. The abilities lost in amnesia have revealed fundamental properties of declarative memory and the central role of medial temporal lobe structures, including primarily the hippocampus and adjacent cortex, in mediating this kind of memory. Therefore, we briefly summarize recent findings on human amnesia, and then focus on studies of animal models of amnesia, with an emphasis on the common fundamental qualities of memory dependent on hippocampal function across species.

4.2.1 Human amnesia

Much of the current understanding of hippocampal function in humans comes from extensive studies on one particular patient who is known by his initials H.M. (Scoville & Milner 1957, for reviews see Corkin 1984, Cohen 1984, Squire 1992). After removal of most of the hippocampal formation, H.M. had a profound impairment in new learning in nearly every learning and memory test that could be devised for him, including recall or recognition of a wide variety of materials and regardless of the modality of their presentation. Early work with H.M. and other human amnesics emphasized the global extent of memory impairment, the selectivity of the deficit to memory functions, and the sparing of other perceptual, motor and cognitive capacities.

These same early studies also indicated that the hippocampus was important to only certain aspects of memory. H.M. and other amnesics show normal retention for much of the autobiographical memories acquired years prior to hippocampal damage. In addition, H.M. and other amnesics have intact immediate memory, such as the ability to retain the digits comprising a telephone number. Thus both short-term memory and retention of memories acquired prior to loss of hippocampal function are intact. These intact abilities suggest that the hippocampus is not needed for the early processing of items to be remembered, is not the final repository of memories, but is required to mediate the permanent consolidation of memories in a form by which they can be retrieved from long-term memory.

More recent work with amnesic patients has demonstrated that only certain aspects of new learning or of long-term memory are impaired after hippocampal system damage. This research has revealed that many learning and memory capacities are preserved in amnesia, and has led most investigators to think now in terms of separate domains of long-term memory that are either dependent upon or independent of the hippocampal system. Thus, despite the profound impairment in explicit remembering of learning materials and experiences, the performance of amnesics is influenced by these same learning experiences as revealed by implicit changes in their performance speed or bias. Thus motor, perceptual and cognitive skill learning, sensory adaptations and "priming" of perceptual and lexical stimuli are preserved in amnesia (for reviews of the set of preserved capacities see Cohen 1984, Shimamura 1986, Schacter 1987, Squire 1987, 1992, Tulving & Schacter 1990). For example, perceptual skills associated with reading mirror-reversed text (Cohen & Squire 1980) and motor skills associated with drawing using only a mirror view of one's hand (Corkin 1968) are spared in amnesia. In addition, after exposure to pictorial or verbal material, amnesic patients show normal facilitation in identification or biasing of response choices toward the previously studied items. Such priming effects occur in the absence of signs that the patients can recall or recognize that the materials were familiar (e.g. Warrington and Weiskrantz 1970, Graf et al. 1984). Impairment or sparing can be observed with the identical learning materials, depending upon exactly what the subject is instructed to do or chooses to do with the materials. For example, amnesic patients showed either impaired or intact ability to complete the "stem" (first three letters) of recently experienced words depending, respectively, on whether they were instructed to use the word stems as recall cues or simply asked to report "the first word that comes to mind" that completes each stem (Graf et al. 1984). The first of these strategies requires the subject to search his memory explicitly for representations of recent experiences of words, while the second strategy seems merely to re-engage processing of the familiar words unconsciously or implicitly. These findings suggested that the hippocampus plays a critical role in "declarative" or "explicit" memory characterized as the record of everyday facts and events that can be brought to conscious recollection and, typically, is subject to verbal reflection or other explicit means of expression (Graf & Schacter 1985). By contrast, the set of preserved learning and memory capacities in amnesia have been referred to collectively as "procedural" or "implicit" memory characterized as the non-conscious acquisition of a bias or adaptation that is typically revealed only by implicit measures of performance (Cohen & Squire 1980).

4.2.2 Animal models of amnesia

The characteristics of declarative memory in humans present a formidable challenge for the study of such memory in animals. We do not have the means for monitoring conscious recollection in animals; indeed, the very existence of consciousness in animals is debated (for an extended discussion of this point see Eichenbaum et al. 1992). An assessment of verbal reflection is impossible, and it is not otherwise obvious how to assess "explicit" memory expression in animals. However, the latter may be possible if we consider further distinctions between declarative and procedural memory. To the extent that these descriptions do not rely on consciousness or verbal expression, they might be operationalized for experimental analysis in animals.

Towards this goal, Cohen (1984) suggested that "a declarative code permits the ability to *compare and contrast* information from different processes or processing systems; and it enables the ability to *make inferences* from and generalizations across facts derived from multiple processing sources. Such a common declarative code thereby provides the basis for access to facts acquired during the course of experiences

4. LEARNING AND MEMORY 81

and for conscious recollection of the learning experiences themselves" (Cohen 1984: 97, italics added). Conversely, procedural learning was characterized as the acquisition of specific skills, adaptations and biases and that such "... procedural knowledge is tied to and expressible only through activation of the particular processing structures or procedures engaged by the learning tasks" (Cohen 1984: 96). These distinctions have helped develop assessments of declarative and procedural memory that may be applicable to animal studies. Thus declarative memory is first distinguished by its role in comparing and contrasting items in memory; procedural memory involves the facilitation of particular routines for which no such comparisons are executed. Declarative memory is also distinguished by its capacity to support inferential use of memories in novel situations; procedural memory only supports alterations in performance that can be characterized as re-running more smoothly the neural processes in which they were acquired.

Based on this general aspect of hippocampal-dependent memory, the hippocampal system appears to support a *relational representation* of items in memory (Eichenbaum et al. 1992, Shapiro & Olton 1994). Furthermore, a critical property of the hippocampal-dependent memory system is its *representational flexibility*, a quality that permits inferential use of memories in novel situations. According to this view, the hippocampal system mediates the organization of memories into what may be considered a multidimensional memory "space" with particular items in memory as informational "nodes" in the space and the relevant relations between the items as "connectives" between informational nodes. In such a memory space, activation of one node would result in activation of all sufficiently strongly associated connectives and, consequently, other informational nodes including ones never directly associated with the originally activated element. Such a process would support the recovery of memories in a variety of contexts outside the learning situation and would permit the expression of memories via various pathways of behavioural output. The combination of relational representation, a consequence of processing comparisons among items in memory, and representational flexibility, a quality of relational representation that permits inferential expression of memories, suggests an information processing scheme that might underlie declarative memory in humans and, indeed, in animals as well.

Conversely, hippocampal-independent memories can be construed as involving *individual representations*; such memories are isolated in that they are encoded only within the brain modules in which perceptual or motor processing is engaged during learning. These individual representations are *inflexible* in that they can be revealed only through reactivation of those modules within the restrictive range of stimuli and situations in which the original learning occurred. One might expect individual representations to support the acquisition of task procedures that are performed habitually across training trials; individual representations should also support the acquisition of specific information that does not require comparison and consequent relational representation.

Our work illustrates how the distinction between relational and individual representation is reflected in experiment studies on animals. These investigations have exploited the excellent learning and memory capacities of rats in odour discrimination learning (Eichenbaum et al. 1986a, 1988a,b, 1989a). The learning ability of intact rats was compared with that of rats with transection of the fornix, a fibre bundle supporting critical connections of the hippocampus with subcortical structures. In one series of studies learning was evaluated in variations of an odour discrimination task that assessed the capacity for relational representation by manipulating the demand for comparison and representation of relations among identical odour cues (Eichenbaum et al. 1988a)(Fig. 4.1). In a simultaneous discrimination task, two odour cues were presented at the same time and in close spatial juxtaposition; the discriminative response required a comparison of odours and a selection between equivalent left and right choices. Under these training conditions, rats with fornix lesions were severely and persistently impaired on a series of different odour discrimination problems. Alternatively, in a successive discrimination task, odours were presented separately across trials, hindering comparison among items, and the response required only completing or discontinuing the stimulus sampling behaviour, thus eliminating the response choice. In striking contrast to the preceding results, under these training conditions, rats with fornix lesions were *superior* to normal rats in acquiring the same series of discrimination problems that they had failed to learn under other task demands (see also Staubli et al. 1984, Eichenbaum et al. 1986a, Otto et al. 1991). Our interpretation of these findings is that severe impairment, transient impairment, or even facilitation may be observed under different task demands, even with the identical stimulus materials. Moreover, the differences in performance by rats with hippocampal system damage can be related to the demand for stimulus and response comparison.

To assess the capacity for representational flexibility in normal rats and rats with hippocampal system damage, a follow-up experiment on the simultaneous discrimination task was pursued (Eichenbaum et al. 1989a).

The investigation exploited a surprising finding in the results from that training condition; although rats were generally impaired on this

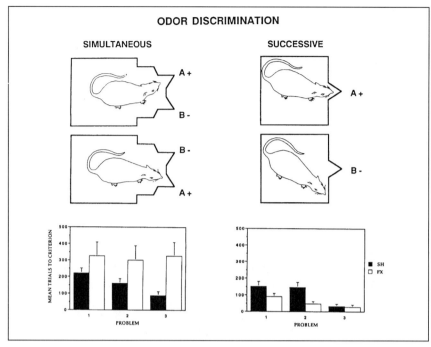

FIG. 4.1.   Assessment of learning on two variants of the odour discrimination paradigm. (Top) Schematic diagrams and trial examples showing both configurations of odour presentation used in each task variant and a rat executing the appropriate response: A+, rewarded odour; B−, non-rewarded odour. (Bottom) Performance on these tasks (±SE) by sham-operated rats (SH) and rats with bilateral fimbria–fornix transection (FX). Rats with fornix lesions are severely and persistently impaired on simultaneous discrimination but not impaired on successive discrimination involving the same odour pairs. From Eichenbaum et al. (1988b).

task, they succeeded in learning some of the discrimination problems at least as rapidly as normal animals. To understand why they occasionally succeeded and to explore the nature of memory representation when they did succeed, yoked pairs of normal rats and rats with fornix lesions were trained on a series of simultaneous odour discrimination problems until the rat with the fornix lesion in each pair had acquired two problems within the normal range of scores. According to our notion of relational representation, normal animals encode all the odour stimuli presented both within and across trials using an organized scheme that would support comparisons among odours not previously experienced together. Conversely, the representation of rats with hippocampal system damage was not expected to support recognition of the separate elements within each compound. To test these predictions, intermixed within a series of trials on two different instruction prob-

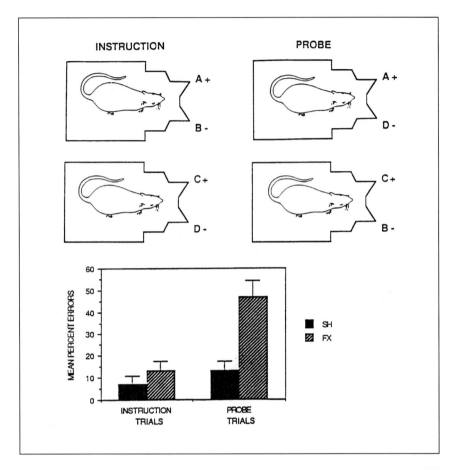

FIG. 4.2.   Assessment of flexible use of odour memory representations in sham-operated rats (SH) and rats with a fimbria–fornix transection (FX). (Top) Schematic diagrams of the odours presented on instruction and probe trials. (Bottom) SH and FX rats perform equivalently well in overtraining on instruction trials. SH rats continue to perform well on probe trials made up of mispairings of odour cues form the instruction trials, but FX rats made as many errors as would be predicted by chance. Data from Eichenbaum et al. (1989a).

lems were occasional probe trials composed of a mispaired rewarded odour from one problem and the non-rewarded odour from the other. Both normal rats and rats with fornix lesions continued to perform well on the trials composed of the odour pairings used on instruction trials. Normal rats also performed accurately on the probe trials, but, in striking contrast, rats with fornix lesions performed at chance levels on the probe trials when they were introduced, as if presented with novel stimuli (Fig. 4.2).

4.3 ANATOMY OF THE HIPPOCAMPAL SYSTEM

The existing detailed knowledge about hippocampal anatomy should constrain and inform any realistic model of hippocampal function. What follows is a brief review of the neuroanatomical literature on rats and primates aimed at providing a framework for constructing more or less detailed functional models. Detailed reviews are available from several sources (e.g. Amaral & Witter 1989, Squire et al. 1989, Witter 1989, Eichenbaum & Buckingham 1991).

The main pathways of information flow between the hippocampus and cortex can be divided into three basic components: the cortical systems afferent to the hippocampal region, the parahippocampal gyrus, and the hippocampal formation (Fig. 4.3). In addition, areas within the hippocampus receive important inputs from, and send projections to, subcortical nuclei via the fornix. Cortical afferent systems are composed of multiple successive stages of cortical processing including, at the lowest levels, the primary thalamocortical projection from the specific sensoria (Jones & Powell 1970). At the highest levels are so-called association areas that, in the posterior neocortex, receive multimodal sensory inputs and, in the anterior neocortex, receive multiple sensory, motor and limbic inputs. In general, these structures project to the hippocampus only via a major convergence area, the parahippocampal region, which has several major subdivisions that are differentiated by input–output organization. The parahippocampal region, at the least, acts as an interface for both incoming and return interactions between the sensory systems and the hippocampal formation. The hippocampal formation is composed of several interacting subdivisions, the dentate

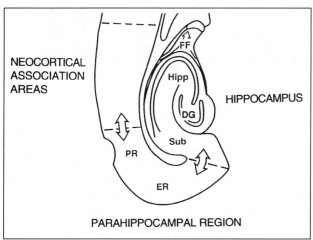

FIG. 4.3.   Schematic diagram of a horizontal section through the rat brain illustrating the locations and crude flow of information from neocortical association areas to the parahippocampal region and then to the hippocampus (Hipp), and then back via the reverse path to the neocortex. DG, dentate gyrus; ER, entorhinal cortex; FF, fimbria fornix; PR, perihinal cortex; Sub, subiculum.

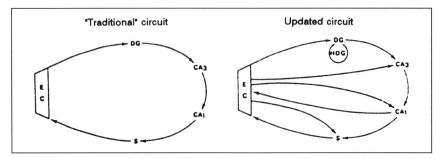

FIG. 4.4.   Diagrammatic representation of connectional "loops" in the flow of information through the hippocampus and entorhinal area. (Left) The simplified and traditional trisynaptic circuit. (Right) The current view of multiple loops between the entorhinal cortex and hippocampal subdivisions. DG, dentate gyrus; EC, entorhinal cortex; HDG, hilus of the dentate gyrus; S, subiculum. From Witter (1989).

gyrus, areas CA3 and CA1 of Ammon's horn, and the subiculum (Figs 4.3, 4.4). As will be seen, cortical representations of events are imposed on these subdivisions of the hippocampus through two major routes.

4.3.1 Cortical inputs to the hippocampal system

The association areas of the neocortex and the olfactory cortex are the cortical afferents for hippocampal processing (Van Hoesen et al. 1972, Krettek & Price 1977, Deacon et al. 1983, Room and Groenewegen 1986). The neocortical structures which project to the hippocampal formation are the temporal, parietal, prefrontal and cingulate areas, each of which is involved with high-level multimodal processing rather than primary sensory processing (Van Hoesen et al. 1972, Insausti et al. 1978a, Goldman-Rakic et al. 1984). The cortical inputs arrive in the broad parahippocampal region that covers the hippocampal formation. This area is composed of several subdivisions: the perirhinal cortex, a transitional area between neocortex and the entorhinal cortex; the entorhinal area composed of multiple subdivisions (primarily the lateral and medial entorhinal areas); and the parasubiculum and presubiculum, transitional areas between the entorhinal cortex and the subiculum, a component of the hippocampal formation.

The multimodal neocortical association areas and the olfactory system project onto lateral parts of the entorhinal and perirhinal areas. These connections are organized systematically, but are unlike the punctate topographies that characterize the primary sensory and motor thalamocortical pathways. The projections onto the parahippocampal gyrus involve large and overlapping zones of projection, an organization of "topographical gradients" (Fig. 4.5). Individual cortical association and olfactory areas project differentially along the parahippocampal cortex such that more rostral cortical inputs, the ones

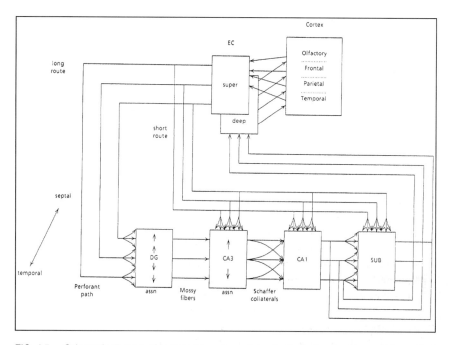

FIG. 4.5.   Schematic diagram of cortical–hippocampal circuits illustrating the topographic gradient in the organization of cortical inputs to the parahippocampal–entorhinal cortex, topographic divergence and association systems in the long route to CA1/subiculum, and relative topographic preservation in the short-route projection onto CA3 and CA1/subiculum. The longitudinal dimension is represented on brain structures on both the vertical axis (top, septal) and the horizontal axis (right, septal). EC, parahippocampal–entorhinal cortex; super, superficial cortical layers; deep, deep, cortical layers; DG, dentate gyrus granule cells; CA3 and CA1, subdivisions of Ammon's horn; SUB, subiculum. From Eichenbaum & Buckingham (1991).

from olfactory and frontal areas, terminate within rostral and ventral parts of the perirhinal and lateral entorhinal cortex; more caudal cortical inputs, the ones from parietal and temporal areas, terminate in more caudal and dorsal parts of the perirhinal and lateral entorhinal cortex (Deacon et al. 1983, Room and Groenewegen 1986).

The perirhinal areas, in turn, project heavily onto entorhinal cortex and contribute to the inputs to the hippocampal formation (see below). The anterior cortical–limbic association areas in the prefrontal, insular and cingulate cortices also project into the entorhinal cortex proper (across species), with overlapping but distinguishable projection areas in the rostral and lateral parts of the entorhinal area. Medial entorhinal cortex receives little sensory input from any of the cortical systems, but does receive a similar pattern of subcortical afferents as more lateral entorhinal areas.

4.3.2 Internal pathways of the hippocampal system

Two main routes project from the parahippocampal areas into the hippocampal formation which we will call the serial and parallel routes, each of which begin and end in the cortical areas of the parahippocampal region.

4.3.2.1 The trisynaptic route

The serial route is the well-known trisynaptic circuit, which begins with the perforant path, which is composed of axons of the entorhinal cortex that penetrate the hippocampal fissure to innervate the dentate gyrus. The perforant path originates in superficial cells of the entorhinal and perirhinal cortices, and the projection into the dentate gyrus involves well-organized, coarse gradients. Granule cells, via the mossy fibres, project to the proximal dendrites of CA3 cells in Ammon's horn. This projection is topographically restricted, with granule cells projecting exclusively to CA3 cells in the same septotemporal level. The CA3 pyramids, in turn, give rise to a large number of collateral outputs. Some of these axons terminate on other CA3 cells throughout the septotemporal axis, others form the earliest extrahippocampal projection, to the lateral septal nucleus, and yet others form the Schaffer collateral system that provides the major long-route input to the pyramids of CA1, terminating along both the apical and basal dendrites of these cells along most of the septotemporal axis. These projections are well organized within a septotemporal level; cells near the dentate gyros give rise to few associational fibres and project to CA1 cells nearest the subiculum, whereas CA3 pyramids further from the dentate gyros give rise to most of the associational system and project to neighbouring CA1 pyramids. CA1 pyramids then project broadly onto the dendritic tree of columns of cells in the subiculum.

4.3.2.2 Parallel routes to Ammon's horn and the subiculum

The alternative, frequently overlooked parallel route involves entorhinal outputs projecting directly to the output cells of CA3, CA1 and the subiculum.

Both the subiculum and all regions of Ammon's horn are the recipients of direct input from the parahippocampal region. The cells in entorhinal cortex just deep to those originating the perforant path project superficially to dendrites in CA1 and the subiculum (Witter et al. 1986, 1988). The organization of these inputs is essentially the same as that of the entorhinal–dentate inputs, although the CA1 termination field may be more widespread. The entorhinal–subicular projections follow the same regional topographical organization as those that characterized the input to dentate gyros and CA3. Recently, Yeckel & Berger

(1990) have shown that the direct entorhinal projections to Ammon's horn are more powerful in controlling hippocampal neuronal activity than activation via the trisynaptic circuit.

4.3.2.3 Hippocampal efferents and the return circuit to cortical systems

The subiculum provides the major subcortical and cortical efferent systems of the hippocampal formation. The subcortical projection is through the fornix and into the ventral striatum and mammilary bodies. The cortical efferents, involving efferents of both CA1 and the subiculum, project primarily to deep layers of the entorhinal cortex, completing the parahippocampal–hippocampal loops. These projections follow the same topographic arrangement as the input connections: a topographic gradient of projections from septotemporal hippocampal areas projecting to lateromedial sites in entorhinal cortex.

The return circuit to the non-hippocampal cortex involves the deep pyramidal cells of entorhinal and perirhinal cortex projecting to the same cortical areas from which inputs originated (Van Hoesen & Pandya 1975a,b, Wyss 1981). Thus the cortical recipients of parahippocampal output include the polymodal association areas of the orbitofrontal, insular and temporal areas, and the unimodal higher cortical areas in the piriform cortex and neocortex (Swanson & Kohler 1986, Witter & Groenewegen 1986, Kosel et al. 1982). The organization of these projections follows that of the input organization: more rostral parts of the parahippocampal gyrus project to rostral cortical areas and more caudal parahippocampal areas to more caudal cortical sites.

4.4 PLASTICITY IN HIPPOCAMPAL CIRCUITS

The neuropsychological consequences of damage to the hippocampal system suggests it is crucial for normal memory. The connectivity of the structure suggests many potential ways in which information could be encoded. In addition, a brain structure crucial for learning and memory would be expected to have some mechanism for information storage and retrieval. One of the first widely known theories to propose a mechanism for storing and retrieving information in neural circuits was Hebb's theory of cell assemblies (1949). According to this view, co-active and potentially interconnected neurons would, after repeated co-activity, become more strongly connected. This change in connection strength implemented learning, its persistence comprised memory, and the reactivation of assemblies of such neurons was memory retrieval or performance. Hebb's theory provided one way in which learning and memory could occur in the brain, through an activity-dependent, associative synaptic plasticity. Long-term potentiation, an electro-physiological phenomenon that resembled Hebb's idea of an activity-dependent, modifiable synapse, was observed in the hippocampus only 26 years later (Bliss & Lomo 1973).

Long-term potentiation

Long-term potentiation (LTP), a rapidly induced form of synaptic plasticity, may reflect an important mechanism of information storage in the hippocampus and other forebrain regions (Lynch 1986, McNaughton & Morris 1987, Bliss & Lynch 1988). LTP is an electro-physiological phenomenon commonly observed by comparing electrically evoked potentials before and after brief, high-frequency electrical pulses are delivered to a pathway in the hippocampus (Fig. 4.6). Several minutes after such stimulation, the magnitude of the evoked potential can increase dramatically, and the change can persist for hours in anaesthetized rodents (Bliss & Lomo 1973), and for weeks in freely moving rats (Staubli & Lynch 1987). LTP is produced easily in each of the cell fields of the hippocampus, although the parameters and mechanisms of LTP vary in the different regions (e.g. Harris & Cotman 1986).

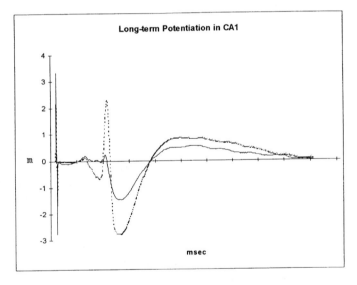

FIG. 4.6.   Long-term potentiation. Schaffer collateral inputs to the dendrites of CA1 cells were stimulated in a rat anaesthetized with urethane. The baseline potential evoked by a 500 µs, 100 µA current produced a negative-going EPSP (excitatory post-synaptic potential) and a very small population spike (solid line). After tetanic stimulation (100 Hz train of 500 µA, 500 µs pulses), the same stimulus produced a dramatic increase in EPSP amplitude, slope and population spike (dotted line). The horizontal tick marks denote 5 ms intervals, the large vertical line at the left of the trace is the stimulation artefact.

In most hippocampal circuits, LTP induction requires glutamate binding to *N*-methyl-D-aspartate (NMDA) receptors (Collingridge et al. 1983). LTP expression, however, does not require NMDA receptors, but instead depends upon the AMPA (alpha-amino-3-hydroxy-5-mettyl-4-isoxazole propionate) receptor, one of several other glutatmate receptors (Muller & Lynch 1988). The induction of LTP in hippocampus and learning that requires the hippocampus may share common mechanisms. (a) Intraventricular administration of aminophosphono-valeric acid (AP5), a selective NMDA receptor antagonist, blocks LTP induction and spatial, but not cued memory acquisition in the water maze (Morris et al. 1986). (b) Spatial learning is impaired when AP5 is concentrated in hippocampus, and LTP blockade in hippocampus is highly correlated with the spatial learning impairment (Butcher et al. 1990). (c) MK801, a non-competitive NMDA receptor antagonist, blocks LTP induction (Abraham & Mason 1988, Gilbert & Mack 1990, Reed & Robinson 1991), and low doses of the drug that attenuate the induction of potentiation in behaving rats (Coté et al. 1995) selectively impairs spatial learning, but not performance (Shapiro & Caramanos 1990, Shapiro & O'Connor 1992).

Spatial working memory, which also depends upon hippocampal function (Olton et al. 1979), may not require NMDA receptor activation if the delay between information presentation and retrieval is brief (Caramanos & Shapiro 1994). Intrahippocampal injection of opiate receptor antagonists may impair this short-term working memory, which may depend upon mossy fibre potentiation (Kesner 1994). However working memory that requires bridging delays longer than some minutes may require NMDA receptors (Tonkiss & Rawlins 1991).

Long-term depression
Long-term depression (LTD) has also been observed in the hippocampus (Dunwiddie & Lynch 1978, Levy & Steward 1979, Bear & Malenka 1994). In the dentate gyrus LTD is produced in synapses that remain inactive during the induction of LTP in other inputs to the same cells (Levy & Steward 1979). In CA1, LTD can be produced when post-synaptic cells are repeatedly and rapidly depolarized while pre-synaptic elements are silent (Pockett et al. 1990). Low frequency stimulation (5 Hz single pulses) can also reverse LTP and produce LTD in previously active CA1 neurons, and this low frequency LTD is blocked by NMDA antagonists. Thus, some forms of LTD can be described by a specific anti-Hebbian learning rule, so that post-synaptic activity not accompanied by pre-synaptic activity will reduce synaptic strength. The relationship between LTD and learning, however, has not been established.

LTP and LTD in hippocampal circuits reflect mechanisms of synaptic plasticity that may enable learning that depends upon these circuits. To the extent that LTP and LTD do reflect crucial mechanisms for hippocampal-dependent learning, the rules that control LTP induction, maintenance and expression will also influence how learning, information storage and retrieval will proceed. However, the relationship between the two well-documented facts of synaptic plasticity in hippocampal circuits and hippocampus-dependent learning and memory is not as clear (Eichenbaum & Otto 1993). The crucial link between the two phenomena requires exploration of the changes in functional neural circuitry that occur during learning. However, this aspect of hippocampal function is just beginning to be explored, and requires analysis of single unit activity in the hippocampus of learning animals.

4.5 INFORMATION CODING BY HIPPOCAMPAL NEURONS

A major constraint for the development of models of hippocampal function and circuitry is the data on functional correlates of the activity of single neurons in the hippocampus. Because the hippocampus is located far from both sensory inputs and motor outputs one might properly expect it to be quite difficult to observe correlations between overt perceptual or behavioural events and neural activity. However, behavioural correlates of hippocampal unit activity are readily observed both in behavioural paradigms for which the hippocampus is crucial and in those for which performance is hippocampal independent. Thus, the challenge lies in the interpretation of the data (see Kubie & Ranck 1983).

The most widely described finding on the functional activity of hippocampal neurons is the discovery of "place cells", hippocampal neurons that fire selectively when the animal is in a particular location in its environment regardless of its orientation or ongoing behaviour (O'Keefe & Dostrovsky 1971). Indeed, together with the observation that animals with hippocampal system damage are severely impaired in a variety of spatial learning tasks, the description of hippocampal place cells has been the basis of a widely held view that the hippocampus supports a cognitive map of the environment (O'Keefe & Nadel 1978). Based solely on the data that support these conclusions, the cognitive mapping hypothesis is a very attractive account of hippocampal processing of perceptual information. However, this hypothesis cannot explain some important aspects of hippocampal function. Neuropsychological data from humans, monkeys and rats indicates that the hippocampal system is critical to many forms of non-spatial learning as well as spatial learning (see above). Furthermore, recording from animals performing a variety of non-spatial learning paradigms reveal behavioural correlates of hippocampal unit activity that are incompatible with the cognitive mapping hypothesis. For example, recordings from rabbits during classical conditioning show that most hippocampal output cells fire in close association with conditioned eyeblinks (Berger et al. 1976). In these experiments the subject was spatially immobilized, thereby holding the "place" of the animal constant; despite this, the variations in neuronal activity associated with specific behaviours were as profound as those of place cells described in freely moving rats.

Odour-guided tasks may help determine whether hippocampal neuronal activity is better related to perceptual or behavioural events. A striking aspect of our findings was that we could identify cells whose activity increased selectively at a particular period associated with each task-relevant event. In each odour-guided task we observed cells that fired prior to or coincident with the behaviour that initiated odour onset, with various phases of stimulus sampling, and with response execution, as if the hippocampus participated in representing each aspect of the experience, with single neurons encoding minute events.

Thus, many hippocampal cells fire tightly locked to behavioural acts that are not directly associated with the task's critical discriminative cues. The firing of many hippocampal cells is strongly influenced by qualities of current and even previous cues as well as with a particular behaviour. Thus, hippocampal cellular activity may be highly dependent both on ongoing behaviour and on task-relevant stimulus properties. Our data from recordings in rats performing a spatial memory task (in the same apparatus in which they performed the above-described olfactory discrimination) also indicate that hippocampal neuronal activity reflects both perceptual and behavioural events. Most hippocampal cells had distinctive place fields as rats performed the spatial memory task, but location did not account for all of the activity of a cell when the rat was in the place field, nor was the location of the rat the only reliable predictor of firing. For many cells, movement speed, direction and turning angle all strongly modulated firing rate within the place field. Indeed, even when the animal was in the place field, the firing rate of some cells was no higher than the out-of-field rate if the animal was moving at a non-optimal speed, or in a non-optimal direction or turning angle (Fig. 4.7). In addition, the activity of these cells was often time-locked to task-relevant approach movements (Eichenbaum 1989b, Wiener et al. 1989).

Some characteristics of hippocampal cellular activity reflect coding properties passed on from hippocampal afferents. Other properties of hippocampal coding appear to reflect a further processing stage, what we call supramodal representations of combinations or conjunctions of perceptually independent events. In our simultaneous odour-discrimination task, some hippocampal cells were differentially activated in relation to the odours presented, to their presentation positions and to the interaction of these two variables (Wiener et al. 1989). Similarly, Wible et al. (1986), observing rats performing a colour-cued delayed non-match to sample task in a Y-maze, found that some hippocampal neurons were differentially active as the rat was in a choice arm associated with a particular colour, a particular position or the interaction of these variables. The perceptual aspects of responses of hippocampal neurons are not solely dependent on spatial configurations of cues, they are also dependent on temporal configurations of task-relevant cues. In our successive odour-discrimination task, some hippocampal cells were activated differentially in relation to the current odour, to the previous odour, and to the sequence of odours presented (Eichenbaum et al. 1986b).

Like neurons in some temporal and parietal association areas projecting to the hippocampal system, hippocampal cells may be consid-

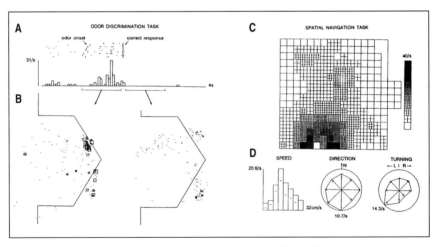

FIG. 4.7.   Analyses of spatial and behavioural correlates of a cell recorded in a rat performing (a,b) the simultaneous odour-discrimination task and (c) performing the place-memory task. (a) Raster display and summary histogram of firing pattern of a cell whose activity is time locked to the discriminative response during presentation of a particular odour configuration. (b) Enlarged schematic view of the odour sampling area showing the location of the rat (dots) and firing rate (squares) at 50ms intervals for 1 s periods indicated in (a). (c) Firing rate map of the same cell when the rat performed a spatial memory task in the same apparatus. The cell had a distinct place field distant from the location of the cul-de-sac where the odour-discrimination task was performed (right). (d) The cell's activity was also significantly tuned to speed, direction and turning angle when the rat was moving through the place field. From Eichenbaum & Wiener (1989b).

ered "polymodal" in that place fields can be supported by stimuli from multiple modalities (Hill & Best 1981). Furthermore, hippocampal place cells demonstrate ultraspecific sensitivities and stimulus invariances similar to those described for neurons in temporal cortex. Maximal response from most hippocampal place cells may require highly specific triggers in the environment (Thompson & Best 1989). Place fields are disrupted only when a large fraction of the cues for spatial orientation are removed (O'Keefe & Conway 1978, Hill & Best 1981); even when a critical cue is removed, the field may be altered only in the dimension associated with that cue (Muller & Kubie 1987). Indeed, several studies have shown that the place field is determined by where the rat "thinks" it is (O'Keefe & Speakman 1987, Eichenbaum & Cohen 1988, Quirk et al. 1990) even when the appropriate stimuli are unavailable, indicating that the sensory stimuli that usually govern the location of the place field are not required at all; this phenomenon may be viewed as an extreme of sensory "constancy", and it might be related to the available sensory input in terms of the capacity of neurons in afferent neocortical areas to persist in firing after a critical stimulus has been removed, or to recurrent activation in the hippocampus.

However, the firing correlates of hippocampal neurons exceed our ability to characterize them simply as the sum of what is transmitted from cortex. First, whereas cortical cells seem to encode the complex configuration of perceptual and behavioural elements that compose a particular percept or action, the hippocampal cells seem to encode relations between independent percepts and/or actions. This difference can be illustrated by considering the "tuning curve" of a cortical neuron (e.g. in striate cortex). Primary visual neurons fire most rapidly when a line of the appropriate orientation moves across the cell's receptive field (Hubel & Wiesel 1977). The firing rate falls off gradually as the line's orientation, location or direction of travel differs quantitatively from the optimal one. By contrast, hippocampal neurons respond to a non-optimal configuration of stimuli in an almost "all or none" fashion. Hippocampal neuronal responses are typically highly selective to a particular location in an environment, but changes in that environment have dichotomous, i.e. non-gradual, effects on spatial firing – they produce either no significant change or a complete alteration in the firing pattern. Although the absence of typical tuning curves may reflect our ignorance of the appropriate stimulus dimension, this property may emerge as a consequence of association rather than convergence of inputs from cortical areas afferent to the hippocampus. The anatomical segregation of functionally distinct cortical inputs may be neither strictly preserved nor completely combined within hippocampal processing. Rather, disparate cortical representations may be associated according to their relevant relationships.

Secondly, even though the sensory–behavioural correlate observed in one behavioural paradigm can be highly specific, the firing correlate of a single hippocampal neuron can change dramatically between behavioural situations. The behavioural correlate of single hippocampal CA1 neurons varied considerably across two quite different situations in rats performing a simultaneous odour-discrimination and spatial-memory task in the same environment (Wiener et al. 1989). Most cells that fired selectively during the sampling of odour cues in the odour-discrimination task also had a place field and other spatial-movement correlates at a locus distant from the odour-sampling area in the spatial-memory task (Fig. 4.7). Each neuron could have a highly specific correlate in both tasks, but there was no obvious relationship between the correlates across tasks.

Three explanations may account for such changes in functional representation. First, apparent alterations in tuning dimensions might be consequent to changes in the activation level of the different inputs each hippocampal neuron receives. As the rat switches its attention across different behavioural situations, the proportion of inputs from various sources might change enormously, resulting in unpredictable changes in the behavioural correlate. Secondly, the hippocampus may be a large-scale massively parallel distributed network in which virtually any item is encoded across a large fraction of the cells (see Eichenbaum & Buckingham 1991). On this view, the pattern of activation in the network (and all of its elements) takes on a different form for each separate representation. Thirdly, the differences in the behavioural correlates may be based on a fundamental feature that is common to both situations. If a higher order property is captured in the firing of hippocampal neurons, one reasonable candidate would seem to be that hippocampal neurons encode abstract relations among cues (see Eichenbaum and Cohen 1988). Thus, one property of hippocampal neuronal activity correlates is preserved across behavioural situations: the representation of relations among critical cues. So far we have not been able to identify a constant relational property that predicts the firing correlates of cells across situations, and therefore we cannot conclude whether a specific relationship is the common "feature" extracted in every situation or whether the relational property changes along with the items represented.

Is the organization of features coded in the hippocampus topographic? Representations of perceptual features in primary sensory neocortical areas are characterized by a spatial topography by which neighbouring neurons have partially overlapping sensory receptive fields and are similar in the specific properties of feature (e.g. edge orientation). A preliminary insight into the topography of hippocampal coding was derived from simultaneous recordings of ensembles of multiple single neurons as rats performed our odour and place-learning tasks (Eichenbaum et al. 1989b). The representation of space in the hippocampus seems to involve a local order but, unlike the representation of visual space in primary sensory neocortex, not a systematic topography of environmental locations mapping onto hippocampal structure. Indeed, place fields of neighbouring neurons tend to overlap and are found in multiple "clusters" of redundant representation of some places and underrepresentation of others. Our recent data collected using more refined methods confirm this observation. Furthermore, cells with closer or more overlapping place fields tend to have similar speed, direction and turning angle correlates. Combined, these data indicate that spatial coding in the hippocampus involves a "patchy" representation of multiple aspects of places (Fig. 4.8).

A similar tendency for "clustering" among the behavioural correlates of hippocampal cells appears in rats performing our odour-guided learning tasks. We compiled data from a single electrode penetration in each rat performing a simultaneous odour-discrimination task, comparing the proportions of cells categorized by one of five functional identifications: goal-approach cells that fired primarily as the rat approached the odour-sampling area, stimulus sampling cells that fired during odour sampling, goal-approach cells that fired as the rat approached the water reward cup, cells that decreased firing during the performance of discrimination trials, and cells with no identified behavioural correlate. Most penetrations demonstrated a striking clustering of behavioural correlates. For example, in one penetration stimulus sampling cells predominated; in another, penetration goal-approach cells predominated (Eichenbaum et al. 1991b). These findings indicate that, as in the place memory task, neighbouring groups of cells tend to overrepresent some of the relevant events and underrepresent others. The observed pattern of place- and odour-task representations in ensembles of neighbouring hippocampal neurons indicated the existence of some form of local order, a "clustering" of functional properties similar to that observed for receptive fields and visual features in the temporal cortex.

Plasticity in hippocampal place cells
The extraordinary fact that hippocampal units encode aspects of task performance in virtually every task that has been tested suggests that the hippocampus may learn to represent salient task features. Such learning within the hippocampal network makes sense given the

remarkable plasticity of connections in the structure, but the evidence supporting this proposal is just beginning to emerge. Hippocampal cell activity changes during spatial learning, and these changes occur rapidly as rats gain experience in an unfamiliar environment (Austin et al. 1990, Austin et al. 1993, Wilson & McNaughton 1993). Place

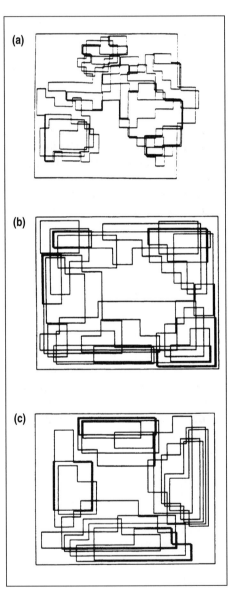

FIG. 4.8.   Clustering. Local groups of hippocampal neurons have place fields that are clustered and overlapped (Eichenbaum et al. 1989b). (a) A square experimental chamber is shown, and the place field boundaries from nine single hippocampal units are outlined. Together, the nine units had 16 subfields that overlapped in three large clusters covering most of the environment. From Eichenbaum et al. (1989b). (b and c) Groups of simulated place fields were also clustered and overlapped. The same criteria to define actual place fields were used to delineate the simulated fields. The figures show the simulated place fields from two different simulations using 15 hidden and 64 output units that differed in the random weights assigned to connections at the start of training. The model in (b) had 12 input cues, the one in (c) four input cues. The simulated place fields from every hidden unit is shown. Note the clustering of subfields in the corners (b) and along the sides (c) in the two simulations. From Shapiro & Hetherington (1993).

fields are relatively large and diffuse when the rat is first introduced to a new environment, and decrease in size and increase in spatial signal as the rat gains familiarity with the environment (Fig. 4.9). This focusing resembles that observed in primary cortices during early development and during learning in adulthood (Hubel & Wiesel 1977, Jenkins et al. 1990) and suggests a mechanism of very rapid learning similar to the competitive learning rules implemented in many network models (Sharp 1991, Hetherington & Shapiro 1993a). The rats explored an enclosed apparatus, and were trained to visit all locations in the apparatus during a recording session. Pre-training took place in a separate apparatus so rats would have familiarity with the task but not the experimental environment. The size of hippocampal place fields, measured by computerized methods, decreased with experience. Most focusing occurred between the first and second recording session, within 1h, but the focusing continued at a lower rate for several days. Focusing most strongly correlated with experience, which accounted for 25% of the variance in place field area. The rapid appearance and persistence of the focusing suggests that a mechanism of synaptic plasticity underlies the phenomenon, rather than a more transient change in the balance of excitation and inhibition. This focusing is also observed in computational models of place fields in neural networks trained to perform spatial discriminations (discussed below).

We have also presented preliminary evidence that NMDA antagonists prevent the normal focusing of place fields that occur with experience (Austin et al. 1990). When rats were given NMDA receptor antagonists, the place fields were unstable, and moved to new locations in the apparatus from one recording session to the next. In rats familiar with the apparatus, having experienced at least four recording sessions before drug treatment, the NMDA antagonist had no obvious effect on the place fields. Thus, the same treatment that attenuates synaptic plasticity and impairs spatial learning may also prevent the establishment of stable place fields representations by hippocampal neurons.

In summary, analyses of hippocampal neuronal encoding suggests that the hippocampus models the salient features of tasks that include both perceptual and behavioural components. Indeed, the hippocampus appears to encode the ongoing episodic structure of the animal acting in its environment, and the structural features representing the episode are learned. The next section describes efforts to account for aspects of the neuropsychological, anatomical and physiological data in computational models of the hippocampal system.

FIG. 4.9.   Place field focusing. The area of hippocampal place fields decreases with experience in an environment. The figure shows an overhead view of an enclosed recording chamber. The large boxes show the place field recorded from a single hippocampal neuron in a 20 min recording session. Each small square shows a location entered by the rat, with firing rate (spikes per second) shown by the line density and scale to the right of each box. Empty squares indicate visited locations containing no cell firing. Empty regions above, below and to the left of the collection of small squares are regions within the camera view, but off limits to the rat. The place field area, measured in camera pixels, includes contiguous pixels containing a firing rate higher than 10% of the maximum rate. (a) The first 20 min session in the environment. (b) The second session in the environment, 30 min after the end of the first. (c) The third session, 4 h after the end of the second. From Austin et al. (1993).

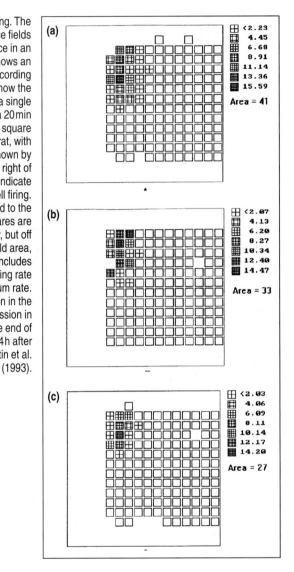

4.6 COMPUTATIONAL DEMANDS FOR A MEMORY SYSTEM

Memory limitations in normal subjects (Bartlett 1932), together with the neuropsychology of amnesia, highlight the computational demands of memory. (a) Memories are associative and content addressable, so that information is stored and retrieved by the attributes of the memory item. Thus, given "a black animal with a white stripe on its back", people can name and give other features of a skunk. This example also illustrates pattern completion, the ability to retrieve entire representations given partial information as a retrieval cue. (b) Memories are encoded, and not stored veridically. Information is lost during encoding, and semantic content is remembered better than perceptual details. Memory retrieval is also a reconstruction process in which "remembered" details are often more influenced by logic or by familiar scripts than the actual experience. (c) Memory is subject to distortion, interference and forgetting, highlighting the need for a systematic organization of memories to avoid catastrophic interference, and a mechanism to prolong information storage. (d) Encoding and retrieval occur flexibly, and use all types of associations to access information. (e) Memories consolidate, or become less susceptible to disruption with time. Of these demands, consolidation, flexible retrieval and interference reduction are especially important for relational memory.

The first three of these memory attributes may be a natural consequence of distributed information storage, in which each memory is encoded and stored using many processing units, with each processing unit participating in many remembered items (Hinton et al. 1986). In distributed memory networks, units become activated as a function of their inputs, representations are defined by the state of activitation within a given population of units, information is stored in weights that interconnect units, and changes in weights constitute learning. The connectivity of the network, and the rules controlling unit activation and weight changes determine how information will be processed in the network and thereby constrain learning and memory. Such networks exemplify content-addressable memory systems, so that units that participate in encoding information also participate in storing that information. Many networks use learning rules that require correlated activity in connected units (e.g. Hebb 1947a) so that units that are co-active become more strongly connected, and the assembly of the co-active units define an active representation. Consequently, the activation of a subset of input units can activate an entire representation by the weighted connections between the input subset and the full set of the receiving units that compose the representation (Marr 1971).

At least two mechanisms of information storage in distributed networks could contribute to information loss, "gist learning" and interference. First, activity dependence and content addressability in the networks will encode similar inputs with similar representations. Secondly, all physical networks have limits that constrain the storage capacity of that network. These limits, including the numbers of units and weights, constrain the number of representations (discriminable states of activation of the network) that could potentially be stored before interference or forgetting occurs. Therefore, interference during storage and retrieval can be viewed as a consequence of distributed network memory systems. One of the challenges in modelling is to explain how such interference is managed.

These constraints on network systems apply to many types of distributed memory systems. However, the directed flexibility of memory ((d) above) may require the recurrent connectivity of processing units. This architecture allows stored representations to activate one another in the absence of other (e.g. perceptual) inputs, and may provide a mechanism for flexible memory retrieval (Hebb 1949). Several models discussed below provide examples of such processing. Finally, the common finding of temporally limited amnesia and the persistence of memories acquired before the onset of amnesia suggests that consolidation ((e) above) requires an understanding of how the memory system handles long-term memory storage. Several models described below propose methods for dividing rapid encoding and long-term storage into separate, interacting modules.

4.6.1 Computational models of the hippocampal system

Many neural architectures could serve as a distributed memory system, but the functional architecture and the neuropsychology of the hippocampal system constrain computational models of memory. Below we describe a selected set of computational models that attempt to explain how the neural properties of the hippocampal system contribute to memory performance. Each of the models implements an hypothesized aspect of hippocampal function that is itself part of a larger memory theory (e.g. consolidation). We compare the network architectures and computational functions with that known about the neuropsychology and neurophysiology of the hippocampal system. From this perspective, two categories of models emerge. The first emphasizes consolidation, an hypothetical process by which the hippocampus contributes to rapid encoding and subsequent storage of long-term memory in the neocortex. The second emphasizes the structure and format of representation and processing that distinguish the hippocampus from other brain areas. Within this second category, one group of models emphasizes unique aspects of stimulus representation and processing that aid memory for all types of learned materials, and a second group emphasizes spatial memory and navigation. Spatial models also come in two types: navigation models, focusing on algorithms for moving through space; and stimulus representation models, focusing on hippocampal place cells.

4.6.2 Rapid encoding and consolidation models

The first computational model of hippocampal function emphasized rapid encoding, pattern completion and interference reduction. Marr (1971) proposed the hippocampus memorized an internal description of the environment. His theory was based on the sequential nature of cortical processing, with the hippocampus receiving convergent inputs from higher cortical areas. Accordingly, the hippocampus encodes and temporarily stores a simple memory, which serves as input for new category formation and enduring storage in the neocortex. Marr's model included three populations of simple linear threshold cells, P1, P2 and P3. P1 represents the cortical input to the hippocampal formation, P2 represents entorhinal cortex and P3 represents the cells within the hippocampus proper. Stored events were patterns of zeros and ones imposed on the P1 units. Information is stored through synaptic plasticity governed by two different learning rules based in part on Hebbian principles (pre- and post-synaptic activation). The topographic organization of the fibres projecting to entorhinal cortex is modelled by dividing P1 and P2 into groups so that cells in one P1 subgroup project only to cells in a corresponding P2 subgroup. The activity in the P2 group impinges on P3, but the group structure is not maintained, so that each P2 block projects sparsely to the entire P3. Finally, P3 units connect with other P3 units and provided the output of the model. Marr intended that each unique input pattern to be stored would evoke a unique output pattern on P3. The P3 to P3 collaterals were intended to support pattern completion, allowing a portion of a previously stored input pattern imposed on P1 to produce the entire pattern in P3. Interference reduction was supported by a variable inhibition that was proportional to the number of active input lines.

Willshaw & Buckingham (1990) analysed Marr's model and implemented it as well as modified versions of the model. They found that a two-layer model without the P2 layer performed as well as the full three-layer model, and that the collateral connections only improved performance slightly. Marr's model provided the conceptual basis for many more recent computational models of hippocampal function. By basing his model on details of neuroanatomy, including a learning mechanism based upon intrahippocampal synaptic plasticity, emphasizing the importance of interference and how it can be reduced by variable threshold activation, and recognizing the importance of understanding the interaction of hippocampus and cortex in consolidation, Marr established several important precedents that remain influential today.

The first theory of hippocampal function and memory emphasized consolidation (Scoville and Milner 1957), and several recent models have addressed this problem by assuming the hippocampus is required for short- or intermediate-term storage, whereas the neocortex is the final repository of memory. Two questions emerge from this perspective. First, how does the hippocampus influence the cortex to enable long-term memory? Secondly, what is special about hippocampal function that allows rapid encoding and temporary memory?

Alvarez & Squire (1994) addressed how hippocampus influences cortical information storage. They emphasized human neuropsychological evidence that new learning is impaired by hippocampal lesions, but that retrieval of memories acquired before the onset of amnesia is intact. The model implemented consolidation through two memory matrices, representing two distinct cortical representations, and a third matrix representing the medial temporal lobe (MTL). The two cortical networks were connected to each other directly and via the (MTL. Rapid encoding was simulated by having (MTL–cortical weights change rapidly, and consolidation was simluated by having cortico-cortical weights change slowly. Random activation of connections between the (MTL and cortical modules also activated the cortical–cortical connections, and their weights were modified through a Hebbian and "winner-take-all" learning rule. Anterograde and temporally limited retrograde amnesia were simulated with the model. This model of consolidation emphasized interactions between the hippocampal system and neocortex, and provides an elegant and simple way in which (MTL output could help cortex encode memories using a biologically reasonable learning rule.

McClelland et al. (1994) also distinguished fast learning in the hippocampus from slow learning in the cortex, and described a model in which the hippocampus reactivates, and thereby "trains" the cortex. McClelland et al. emphasized that a network memory with fast changing weights will not support stable representations required for long-term memory (Grossberg 1987). Rapid changes in synaptic weight produce interference among memory traces, and prevent the accumulation of knowledge in the network. McClelland et al. (1994) propose that the brain solves this problem by having the hippocampus and cortex learn in different ways towards different ends. From this view, the cortex learns slowly, to categorize inputs or "discover structure", whereas the hippocampus learns rapidly, to encode episodes and other information after one exposure to the information. Subsequently, the hippocampus "teaches" the cortex in a manner consistent with integrating the new information with prior knowledge structures by interleaved learning. Normal learning is simulated by presenting new items interleaved with familiar items. Hippocampal lesions are simulated by removing the new patterns from the training corpus after a predetermined number of learning epochs. Thus, the hippocampus was simulated as an input to the cortical network.

O'Reilly & McClelland (1994) extended this approach with a more so-phisticated computational analysis of hippocampal function and a more realistic simulation of hippocampal neuroanatomy and physiology. They assessed the influence of the number, connectivity and mean firing rates of cells in the entorhinal cortex, dentate gyrus and CA3 regions. They also emphasized conflicting constraints on hippocampal function posed by the simultaneous demand for both pattern completion and pat-tern separation. The model proposes ways in which the hippocampal ar-chitecture could minimize the trade-off between these two memory functions. The simulations employ a two-layer network, simulating the dentate gyrus and CA3, both of which receive input from entorhinal cor-tex; CA3 also receives mossy fibre input from the dentate. Both layers are simulated by units organized into sets of "winner-take-all" clusters. Pattern completion is implemented using Marr's method by which feedforward inhibitory neurons were activated in proportion to the number of active input lines. Pattern separation and pattern completion were analysed using conditional probabilities. Input pattern overlap was defined as the probability that active input units are shared, and the output pattern overlap was defined as the probability that output units are shared. Their analyses demonstrated that pattern separation, defined as the reduced overlap of output relative to input patterns, var-ied significantly with the fraction of active neurons participating in a given representation, so that pattern separation increased as the pro-portion of active neurons in the cell layer decreased. The huge number (~106) and sparse activity of dentate granule cells was interpreted as providing a powerful pattern separation device. Two successive lay-ers of "winner-take-all" clusters provided much larger pattern sep-aration than a single layer. The same factors that increased pattern separation also reduced pattern completion, defined as the probability that an output pattern is produced when a partial or noisy input pattern is presented. Analyses of single-layer simulations using an LTP-like learning rule showed that increasing the connection between active and connected input and output units improved pattern completion, but reduced pattern separation.Adding anLTD learning rule that decreased connection strength between inactive input and active output units improved pattern separation and maintained pattern completion, each occurring as a function of input overlap (see also Hetherington & Shapiro 1993a). The balance betweenLTD andLTP defined an input over-lap threshold that determine whether completion or separation occurs. O'Reilly & McClelland (1994) also assessed the memory contribution of dentate to CA3 connections. The results suggested that enhanced pattern separation provided by two consecutive layers outweighed the accompanying reduction in pattern completion produced by the architecture. The most efficient models for maximizing pattern separation and pattern completion were those using the mossy fibre pathway from the dentate to CA3 only for pattern separation, and the direct CA3 input from the entorhinal cortex only for pattern completion. The physiological rationale for these models was that partial inputs could produce lower than threshold activation levels in the dentate, but normal activation in CA3. The O'Reilly & McClelland approach thus provided a powerful analytic method for exploring how connectivity, specific plasticity rules and numeric parameters can influence neural computation that may have evolved to optimize a memory system specialized for rapid encoding of content-addressable, distinct patterns.

Treves & Rolls (1994) also focused on the hippocampus as crucial for temporary storage of episodic or "snapshot" memories that eventually become consolidated and encoded in neocortex. Their theory makes extensive use of the numerical constraints (e.g. cell and synapse number, contact probabilities) and integrates findings from neurophysiology to consider the computational contributions provided by several components of the hippocampal system. In the model, the dentate gyrus stores patterns of entorhinal input through LTP and LTD, which implement Hebbian competitive learning. As in Marr's and McClelland's work, the sparse connections between these areas provides compression and pattern separation of overlapping inputs. The dentate to CA3 projection is a teaching input for CA3 cells, which receives direct entorhinal cortical input too weak to produce enough synaptic change alone to enable learning. Retrieval of information occurs through direct entorhinal input to CA3. Recurrent connections in CA3 implement an autoassociative memory for pattern completion, as in Marr's model. Here, populations of CA3 units encode parts of episodes such as scene fragments, with different populations encoding different fragments, which are linked through the CA3 recurrent pathway. The projection from CA3 to CA1 combines the linked fragments into conjunctions that encode larger parts of the whole scene. The direct projection from perforant path to CA1 elaborates the input from CA3, which had been filtered and reduced through dentate and CA3 processing, so that CA1 encoded an entire episode. Single episodes are stored in the hippocampus for as long as months, and relevant episodes are eventually stored in cortex through polysynaptic pathways from the hippocampus through the subiculum and entorhinal cortex. This long-term storage occurs when cortical neurons are activated by both perceptual information and by stored information returning from the MTL. The coactivation of MTL and cortical neurons allowed LTP of these connections, facilitating storage and later retrieval. Treves & Rolls's model emphasized the physiological and neuroanatomical detail to the perspective advocated by Marr and McClelland. Their simulations demonstrated the potential importance of CA3 collaterals for pattern completion, and establish the importance of this anatomical detail for a fuller understanding of hippocampal function in memory.

Carpenter & Grossberg (1993) take an alternative approach to hippocampal–cortical interactions, proposing that the hippocampus subserves an orientation function assessing the match between sensory input encoded in STM (short-term memory) and recognition codes activated in a cortical attention system. Their attention system was simulated as two layers of units: layer F1 representing conjunctions of sensory features, and layer F2 organized into a competitive layer that received input from F1 and represented recognition codes. Long-term memory is stored via reciprocal connections between F1 and F2. In this model the hippocampal orientation system is activated when too large a mismatch occurs between inputs and memory, which initiates a memory search for a better match between feature conjunctions and recognition codes. A vigilance parameter is used to determine the size of acceptable mismatches. If no acceptable match exists between the F1 input and the set of F2 recognition codes, then unassigned F2 units are recruited to form a new recognition code. This approach of employing the hippocampus as a comparator has been suggested previously (Gray & Rawlins 1986) to account for many aspects of the neuropsychological literature. The model implements this idea in a powerful, content-addressable memory system that can solve interference problems and consolidation.

4.6.3 Models of hippocampal stimulus representation and information processing

An important class of hippocampal system models focuses on the content, format and processing of hippocampal representations, and emphasizes either the encoding of stimulus relationships in general, or that of spatial relationships and navigation in particular.

4.6.3.1 Relational representation models

Gluck & Myers (Gluck & Myers 1993, Myers & Gluck 1994) argue that lesions of the hippocampal system block learning that requires a representation of stimulus–stimulus relationships, but not learning that requires simple stimulus–reinforcement associations. Their model proposes that the hippocampus provides a new representation based upon simultaneously occurring stimuli, and that these representations are conveyed to the cortex to allow long-term memory storage. They propose that the hippocampus encodes co-occurring stimuli either by compressing redundancy or by separating input patterns, and facilitates new learning of representations in the neocortex. (Note that these are the same functions emphasized by Marr, McClelland et al. and Treves & Rolls, described above.) Their model includes a cortical and a hippocampal module, both of which receive sensory input.

The cortical module is trained to activate correctly a single output unit through gradient descent learning. The hippocampal module is an autoencoder, a network trained to produce an output identical to its input through a hidden layer (Hinton et al. 1986). Because the hidden layer contains fewer units than outer layers, the hidden units must encode co-occurrences among the units in the input pattern set. Autoencoder nets have many appealing computational properties, including content-addressable memory, and powerful abilities to separate similar patterns and to complete patterns to partial inputs (Hinton et al. 1986). The autoencoder was trained by back-propagation of error, a powerful supervised learning algorithm (Rumelhart et al. 1986). The hidden units in the autoencoder project to the cortical module, and enable cortical storage of autoencoded representations. The simulations showed the hippocampal module was required for many of the tasks impaired in animals with hippocampal lesions, including negative pattern learning and contextual conditioning, but was not necessary for simple conditioning and stimulus discriminations. The dual use of the hidden layer for both generating an autoencoded representation and for providing a training signal for the cortex module is intriguing, and suggests how hippocampal representations may be usefully recoded in downstream brain regions. From a computational perspective, this model advances the consolidation view by adding representational structure to the information processed by the hippocampus. The model also provides a supervised learning version of proposals that the hippocampus works as an autoassociative net (e.g. Marr 1971, McNaughton & Morris 1987, Treves & Rolls 1994).

Schmajuk and colleagues (Schmajuk 1990, Schmajuk & DiCarlo 1992, Schmajuk et al. 1993) also attempted to simulate selective learning impairments produced by hippocampal lesions. Like Gluck & Myers (1993), they emphasized that the hippocampus is crucial for some forms of classical conditioning, as well as spatial learning. In addition to encoding stimulus representations, Schmajuk's models propose that the hippocampus computes predictions, thus adding the crucial dimension of time. Schmajuk's models compute "aggregate predictions" of environmental events generated from spatial and temporal maps encoded in the hippocampal representation. These aggregate predictions, or expectancies, generate an error signal when mismatches occur between expected and actual stimuli (Schmajuk & DiCarlo 1992). The error signal is used in a biologically plausible implementation of back-propagation of error using feedback. In the model, detector units learn to encode values of either spatial or temporal conditioned stimuli through the presentation of unconditioned stimuli. The detector units connect to association units that form the link between the conditioned stimuli detectors and the network output. The association units are connected to both an output unit and a hippocampal unit, which feeds back to the association units via non-modifiable connections. Only the connections between the detector and association units are modifiable. A more extensive model included hidden units that receive inputs from several detector units and allowed the formation of configural representations (Schmajuk & DiCarlo 1992). Schmajuk et al. (1993) proposed a three-component model of navigation that included a goal-seeking mechanism, a cognitive map and a route-finding mechanism. The cognitive map encoded adjacent places in a heteroassociative network, which allowed each place to predict views of available adjacent places, and thus navigation. The cognitive map of places and views was proposed to be encoded in neocortex.

The models provide an important advance, because they demonstrate that one tractable network architecture can account for a wide range of spared and impaired learning tasks, including classical conditioning and spatial learning. The models do so by including representations of spatial and temporal information. The models also simulate some aspects of hippocampal single unit activity, albeit indirectly. Schmajuk's models make several other important contributions, including simulation of real-time neural activation, biologically reasonable supervised learning rules, analysis of the network activity in comparison with neural activity, and physiological as well as behavioural predictions.

Many of the computational properties described above were anticipated by Lynch and collegues (Lynch 1986, Lynch & Baudry 1988), who focused on the importance of the hippocampal system in representational memory. The theory focused on olfactory memory, but emphasized that the hippocampus encodes contextual information from all modalities, and generates expectancies about the stimuli likely to be encountered in an environment. Context is similar to stimulus relations (Gluck & Myers 1993) and to spatial and temporal maps (Schmajuk et al. 1993), and Lynch and colleagues advanced the art by describing how the processing of context may occur in anatomical and physiological detail. They propose that dentate neurons are massively activated by actual or anticipated movements, and that this activity was maintained by an excitatory feedback loop through cycling. Entorhinal synapses onto dentate granule cells are activated selectively by odours, and the combination of odour stimuli and movements produced potentiation.

The selective set of highly active granule cells activate a subset of CA3 neurons through mossy fibres, while non-selective activity of the dentate activates feedforward inhibition, reducing activity of the remaining CA3 neurons and increasing the signal to noise ratio of encoded odours. The active mossy fibres undergo short-term potentiation, setting the stage for associative encoding (e.g. odours with objects) in the CA3 association network. The alternating encoding of an object and an odour (e.g. in a place in a maze) produces alternating activity in populations of CA3 cells, which have interconnections via the CA3 association pathway. This alternating activation maintains two separate representations, but each produces expectancy of the other. CA1 cells combine active CA3 populations through an "AND" mechanism, and encoded the link between the sequentially separated individual representations. Thus, the CA3 association pathway encodes a linked list of objects, and the sequences of these objects as such, or episodes, are encoded in CA1. Furthermore, the spatial and temporal distance between items is encoded by the synaptic strength in the CA3 association network.

Lynch and colleagues implemented different aspects of this theory in executable simulations of the hippocampus and pyriform cortex (e.g. Ambros-Ingerson et al. 1990). Most striking were their discoveries that specific circuits and biophysical properties of neurons in superficial layers of cortex together provide powerful computational mechanisms for encoding and storing hierarchically structured memories. The biological properties included sparse and uniform connectivity of principal inputs, asymmetric collateral connections, distinct firing modes during performance and learning, the prolonged hyperpolarization of neurons that occurs after strong depolarization, the elevated threshold for activating NMDA receptors relative to that for producing action potentials, and local regions of inhibition produced by interneurons. Sensory inputs were presented in bursts analogous to sniffing, so that a stimulus is sampled several times in rapid succession during each presentation. The presentation format and network details provided a temporal winnowing function, so that cells encoding a stimulus early in sampling were refractory and unavailable later in sampling, so that fewer neurons were activated in each successive sample. The computational consequence of this architecture comprised a top-down hierarchical search, with more inclusive categories activated first, and individual exemplars activated last (e.g. bird, waterfowl, duck, mallard). This mechanism helped to overcome the trade-off between storing exemplars and storing prototypes, because both exemplars and prototypes were encoded in the hierarchical representation. The models provide the important advance of showing how cortical networks can implement the power of representational hierarchies. In addition, the model provided many strong physiological predictions at the level of single units, synaptic plasticity and learning.

The computational power of biological detail has been further advanced by Hasselmo and colleagues, who have demonstrated the importance of neuromodulation in memory function (Hasselmo et al. 1994, Hasselmo 1995; see also Hirsh 1980). Hasselmo and colleagues, like Marr, McClelland and Treves & Rolls (above), emphasized the importance of the CA3 association pathway as an autoassociative memory. In the model, learning predominates when principal inputs activate CA3 cells and cholinergic activity inhibits recurrent activity. Conversely, recall predominates when intrinsic feedback is strong and cholinergic activity is reduced. Unfamiliar inputs produce no match in the feedback network, no feedforward increase in CA3 activity, increased cholinergic activity, and enhanced plasticity in the principal inputs to CA3. Familiar inputs increase recurrent feedback, inhibits cholinergic input and thus generates recall. Cholinergic activity therefore determines whether the network learns, chunks or recalls, and is similar to the vigilance parameter in Carpenter & Grossberg's (1993) model. Low acetylcholine (ACh) input allows only novel inputs (orthogonal to all stored patterns) to be learned. Input patterns with partial overlap with previously stored patterns leads to retrieval of those old patterns, but no new storage. Moderate ACh levels partly suppress recall of old patterns, and both new and familiar patterns are activated simultaneously, and fused or chunked. High ACh levels suppress recall, and new items are learned as independent events even if they overlap with previously stored patterns.

Hasselmo (1995) expanded the CA3 model into a model of hippocampal function that emphasized rapid encoding of episodic, configural and relational memory. The model excluded the subiculum, but included the medial septal area, entorhinal cortex, dentate gyrus, CA3 and CA1, with rough approximation of the connectivity of these areas. Each region included feedback inhibition, and all regions were modulated by cholinergic input, except the entorhinal cortex. The model formed distinct episodic memories for overlapping input patterns, learned both a negative pattern and a relational learning task, but failed to learn a relational learning task. In episodic learning, the network separated, stored and completed overlapping inputs. The model produced sparser representation as more patterns were stored, suggesting it was approaching saturation. The model learned the negative patterning task, but not if the entorhinal cortex to dentate gyrus and CA1 connections were removed. The models demonstrate how consideration of neuromodulators can contribute to a computational analysis of hippocampal and memory function.

4.6.4 Models of spatial navigation and spatial information processing

Although general theories argue that spatial information provides only an excellent example of the relational information encoded by the hippocampus, all successful models of hippocampal function will ultimately have to account for its role in spatial learning. Furthermore, spatial information processing provides an important window into hippocampal function, and the processing of spatial representations will illustrate at least a major subset of operations performed on all hippocampal representations.

Worden (1992) emphasized the importance of spatial navigation abilities for survival, the profound spatial navigation impairment produced by hippocampal lesions, and the importance of geometric constraints for solving navigation problems. Worden makes explicit claims about the stimulus representation and processing required for spatial navigation, and claims the central role of the hippocampus is to retrieve, manipulate and organize geometrically related memoranda (fragments), by a process called "fragment fitting". The fragments are pieces of organized information, such as local views, which contain representations of a relatively small number of objects, their spatial interrelationships and other properties. The model fits fragments together by rotation and translation, and produces a combined and organized set of fragments relevant to reaching a goal from a familiar place; a map. The model navigates to goals hidden from view by computing a spatial version of transitive inference. The geometric assumptions of the model also provided flexible memory retrieval. Worden's model navigated, included non-spatial information as part of a geometrically organized representation scheme, and was based on important and powerful assumptions about specialized computational devices.

McNaughton and colleagues (McNaughton & Morris 1987, McNaughton & Nadel 1989) showed that aspects of hippocampal anatomy and physiology may be well suited to spatial navigation. Like Worden, this perspective emphasizes the importance of local views as input to the hippocampus. McNaughton & Morris (1987) show how hippocampal anatomy and physiology could implement an associative matrix memory. McNaughton & Nadel (1989) describe how representations of successive local views of the environment can be linked to representations of movements to compute spatial trajectories. The hippocampal pathways are modelled as a series of associative matrix memory networks connected with rough anatomical accuracy. Input from the inferotemporal cortex signals the nature of objects in the visual field (local view) of the animal. The hippocampus encodes local views, identified with places, and parietal cortex encodes the animal's movements. The model assumes that place cells are local view cells. The local view information is combined with movement information through a feedback loop from the hippocampus to parietal cortex, which also provides input to the hippocampus. During exploration, a local view is associated with a representation of the previous local view and movement. After learning, a place–movement configuration evokes the local view expected to follow a given movement in a given place. Thus, adjacent local views represented in the hippocampus are linked to one another via feedback connections from the parietal cortex, and this feedback circuit provides a mechanism for computing trajectories. This model provides an explanation for the finding that place cells continue to fire in their usual place field in the absence of external cues (O'Keefe and Speakman 1987).

Touretzky & Redish (1995) advanced McNaughton's ideas in a computational theory of navigation that is implemented in an executable model and in a navigating robot. Implementing McNaughton's ideas, Touretzky & Redish's theory is that place units in the hippocampus combine information about perceived local views with information about movements to compute locations and allow navigation to goals. Visual, vestibular and motor efference copies are assumed to provide sufficient input for computing head direction and allow path integration. A path integrator provides a prediction about current location, and provides input for updating and correcting place units. The place units are initially computed from local views, which include information about the distance, bearing and types of landmark. In familiar environments, the place units are also informed by the path integrator. The model accounts successfully for the behavioural results of several navigation experiments with rodents, as well as for some important behavioural correlates of hippocampal place cells.

4.6.4.1 Place field models

To the extent that computational models of hippocampal spatial function and navigation are biologically correct, the properties of hippocampal place fields should exist in the models. One strategy for devising a biologically correct model of navigation and hippocampal function is a bottom-up modelling of place fields, toward the goal of discovering the computational properties conferred by such a representation.

Zipser's (1985) model emphasized the results of environmental dilation, which produces scaling of place fields (Muller & Kubie 1987). Thus, a CA1 cell recorded in a rat chasing food pellets in a cylinder 1 m in diameter having a place field 10 cm across typically had a place field 16 cm across when the recording was done in a cylinder 2 m in diameter (Muller & Kubie 1987). Zipser argued that place field scaling disproved models of place fields based upon absolute distances to visual stimuli.

Zipser's model used the visual angle subtended by identified cues as input to hidden units, which after training using back-propagation, had activation patterns that resembled place fields and scaled with environmental dilation.

Shapiro & Hetherington (1993) used the same basic architecture as Zipser's, and also used back-propagation to train three layer networks to produce location information from visual angle inputs. Like hippocampal place cells, the activation of simulated place units varied smoothly with spatial position in patterns that resembled place fields. Some units had multiple subfields, the fields showed graceful degradation, so that simulations removing single visual cues often had no effect on the fields, and some of the units were active equivalently in all locations, resembling silent or noisy cells. When groups of units were considered together, the simulated place fields overlapped in multiple clusters, as do actual neural ensembles in hippocampus (Eichenbaum et al. 1989b, O'Keefe & Recce 1993). Parameters in the model were varied to generate predictions for place fields in different environments and lesion conditions. Two predictions from the visual angle models are that place fields should preferentially occur near cues, and that large cues should alter place fields more than smaller cues. In tests of these predictions, the first appears to be true, the second false (Hetherington & Shapiro 1997).

Sharp's place field model used a biologically plausible, competitive learning rule. The model was a three-layer network in which two layers were competitive-learning, pattern-classification devices. The simulated environment was a cylinder with eight point stimuli on its periphery. Two types of input unit responded to distance to one of the stimuli: one type responded to a pre-specified range of distances to a stimulus, the other type responded to distance and direction to a stimulus (Sharp 1991). The input units projected to a middle layer, which provided the first layer of competitive learning interactions, and this layer in turn projected to a final competitive learning layer, which simulated the hippocampus. In this model, place fields developed that were resistant to cue removal, that scaled to environment dilation and that often produced silent cells (Sharp 1991). The place fields were learned representations that focused with training, and thus resembled the development of actual place field (Austin et al. 1990, 1993).

Burgess et al. (1994) further advanced place field modelling by embedding simulated place field in a larger network model of rat navigation. The model includes a feedforward, competitive learning network that simulates place cells. In the model, animals learn about spatial environments through exploration, during which sensory configurations corresponding to locations are learned. The location information is pooled and combined with head direction information through a reinforcement signal generated by reaching a goal. Goal cells form a population vector (Georgopoulis et al. 1986) that points toward the goal throughout the environment, with the magnitude of the vector coding the distance to the goal. The model uses a feed-forward series of projections (sensory, entorhinal, place, subicular, goal cells), which finally project to cells in the motor system. Entorhinal cells encode conjoint input from two sensory cells, and fire in the centroid defined by the distance to the two encoded cues. The relative location of the rat with respect to the centroid (ahead or behind) is encoded by the phase of the theta rhythm (a 4–12Hz dendritic oscillation paced by the medial septum). O'Keefe and colleagues have observed that as rats cross a place field, place cells fire progressively earlier in theta phase. Downstream brain areas could thus decode relative positions based on the theta phase of the place cell firing. Entorhinal cells project to place cells, which are organized into competitive learning pools, as are the downstream subicular cells. The subiculum combines the inputs of many place fields, including non-overlapping ones, into a population code for relative location across the environment. The subicular cells, together with head direction cells, project to goal cells that encode the eight compass points; sets of eight goal cells encode each goal. Learning occurs in the connection from the subicular to the goal cells when a reinforcer is encountered. The goal cells are divided into populations that respond to different head directions by connections with head direction cells (e.g. in post-subiculum (Taube et al. 1990)), and the reinforcer is gated by these heading signals. The model learned rapidly to encode environments, showed latent learning, and navigated to goals even when the direct route is blocked by a barrier. Although the model could encode multiple goals, no description was given of how different goals were retrieved or input to the model. The model produced realistic-looking place fields that appear similar to those recorded from the entorhinal cortex, subiculum and CA fields in the hippocampus. The model included many components of the hippocampal system and predicts the existence of goal cells one synapse downstream of the subiculum.

4.6.4.2 Linked place fields and cognitive mapping

Biological detail confers powerful computational advantages to network models. One detail that has been considered in models of place fields and navigation is the CA3 recurrent network. Several models suggest that plasticity in the recurrent connections in CA3 could serve a cognitive mapping function that supports memory, sequence learning and trajectory computation (Lynch & Baudry 1988, Muller et al. 1991,

Hetherington & Shapiro 1991, 1993b; Schmajuk & Thieme 1993, Levy 1994). This suggestion differs from Marr's notion of a recurrent auto-association matrix for pattern completion, and follows from Hebb's (1949) idea of phase sequences. CA3 may implement a specific case of a Hebb cell assembly in which, for example, place cells with overlapping or neighbouring place fields become functionally linked, and sequences of linked fields may activate one another.

Hetherington & Shapiro (1991, 1993b) trained a recurrent network using back-propagation to compute trajectories to goals. The network navigated to the goals even if simulated visual cues were present only at a starting point and then removed, corresponding to the performance of rats trained to navigate to a goal in a radial maze under similar constraints (O'Keefe & Speakman 1987). The hidden units' activity in the network resembled place fields, showed robust pattern completion and had simulated place fields that persisted after the visual cues were removed (as in O'Keefe & Speakman 1987). The model computed trajectories by forming positive connections between units with overlapping or neighbouring fields, and inhibitory connections between units with distant fields. When one location was represented, the set of units active in that location activated another set of units representing a neighbouring location, and inhibited the units representing distant locations. The model demonstrated that trajectories can be computed by selective enhancement of connections between place units, and provided physiologically testable predictions based upon the recurrent computation posited to occur in CA3, and perhaps the dentate gyrus (Hetherington et al. 1994).

Muller et al. (1991) proposed a similar mechanism, implemented in CA3 that computes a directed graph. The graph model proposes that the LTP of CA3 association fibres should strengthen connections among CA3 cells with overlapping or neighbouring place fields. Thus, distance is represented as synaptic strength among the CA3 neurons. With a simple Hebb-like rule of synaptic modification in a simulation, the connectivity of CA3 place cells could come to represent environmental connectivity, with nothing more than synaptic plasticity and experience in an environment. Thus a graph-like arrangement of place cells could arise in CA3 through simple experience, an LTP rule of synaptic plasticity and a random association pathway. Note that the graph model does not posit that anatomically neighbouring cells excite one another, but rather that cells that fire in neighbouring or overlapping places in an environment should excite one another (Muller et al. 1991). Simulations demonstrated that the graph model can perform important computations, including sequence formation, "bee-line" trajectories and barrier circumvention (Muller et al. 1996).

Levy and colleagues (Minai & Levy 1993, Levy 1994, Minai et al. 1994, Prepscius & Levy 1994) have shown that input sequences can be learned rapidly using biologically plausible learning rules embedded in a simulation of the recurrent CA3 pathway. Furthermore, the architecture can encode and disambiguate several sequences, as well as compress sequences to allow, for example, the hippocampus to represent a goal shortly after being presented with stimuli associated with a starting point. Granger et al. (1994) simulated the detailed temporal properties governing LTP induction in a network model, and discovered that such a network encoded, parsed and retrieved random sequences in a highly efficient manner.

Together, the different implementations of sequence processing based on the recurrent architecture of the CA3 layer continue to address important questions about this representational and processing style, including its computational and biological plausibility, the impact of different learning rules on the speed of sequence encoding and retrieval, capacity limits for storing multiple sequences, and how overlapping sequences can be kept separate or joined when useful (e.g. use in novel or concatenated trajectories). Most importantly, this style of computation suggests a mechanism for implementing a cognitive map that may be sufficient for spatial computations (given appropriate geometric information as input) as well as episodic and other forms of relational representation, as described in the next section.

4.6.5 An integration: the hippocampus as a memory map

Perhaps the two most crucial features of hippocampal system-dependent memory are the flexible use of information obtained in many contexts that is used to solve tasks in novel ways, and the ability to distinguish between stimuli that share many features but differ in organization. These features, flexibility and resistance to interference, are central to the utility of relational representations. We describe below how hippocampal circuits may compute these properties.

This proposal assumes that memory storage and retrieval are not veridical, but involve compression and reconstruction of information. We assume that cortical regions distinguish, separate and categorize sensory information into identifiable stimuli (e.g. Marr 1971, Carpenter & Grossberg 1993). The hippocampal system rapidly encodes relationships among these stimuli as relational representations, which increases the differences among these representations, and links relational representations to one another in abstract, multidimensional maps (Hirsh 1974, O'Keefe & Nadel 1978, Eichenbaum & Cohen 1988, Gluck & Myers 1993, Schmajuk et al. 1993). The encoding of relational representations also serves to compress the huge amount of perceptual data represented in sensory cortical assemblies into a compact code in the hippocampus (Gluck & Myers 1993). Activation of hippocampal assemblies in turn activates cortical regions from medial temporal to other multimodal association cortices that reconstruct perceptual attributes of memories (Alvarez & Squire 1994). Hippocampal function is crucial in any situation in which new relational representations must be created, or in which new sequences of such representations must be constructed. The output from the hippocampus allows these relational representations to be consolidated in many cortical regions, and to influence behaviour (O'Reilly & McClelland 1994, Alvarez & Squire 1994).

The proposal has three central ideas: First, the relationships among identified stimuli are stored as sets of synaptic weights on groups of single cells in hippocampus. The convergence of many axons from the entorhinal cortex onto single hippocampal neurons and the synaptic plasticity that allows individual synapses to potentiate or depress lets hippocampal cells respond to specific combinations of inputs. Thus, hippocampal neurons are relational cells. Secondly, an hierarchical organization of relational representations is encoded by recurrent connections among relational cells. By encoding relationships among relational cells, the recurrent architecture of the hippocampus can represent hierarchical information as locations within a multidimensional space (O'Keefe & Nadel 1978). Just as relationships among stimuli (e.g. the sizes of several stimuli in an environment) can encode a location, relationships among locations (e.g. distances among locations) can encode a map of an environment. Thirdly, the hippocampal network operates to increase directly differences between similar input patterns (i.e. it performs pattern separation) (Marr 1971, McClelland et al. 1994, Treves & Rolls 1994). Because physical space is easy to visualize, we will first describe these processes and representations primarily using examples from spatial processing, and then extend the proposal to other domains.

4.6.6 Conjunctive encoding forms relational units

From this view, relational representations encode specific relationships between sets of identified cues. For example, the set of retinal angles formed by each member of a set of visual cues can define a unique location and provide sufficient input for the defining properties of place cells (O'Keefe & Nadel 1978, Zipser 1985, Sharp 1991, Shapiro & Hetherington 1993). The convergence of entorhinal cortex axons onto single hippocampal cells, which allows the cells to respond to and encode conjunctions of these values (Barnes et al. 1990), specifies a multidimensional location (e.g. the conjoint retinal angle of several cues define a two-dimensional location). Because relational items coded with similar inputs in one dimension can be separated by differences in another dimension, storing conjunctions of inputs increases the dimensionality of the representation, which can help separate similar items. The process of conjunctive encoding accounts for other patterns of single-unit activity that have been recorded in the hippocampus in many experiments in rats, primates and humans, e.g. place, face and word cells (O'Keefe & Dostrovsky 1971, Heit et al. 1988, Ono et al. 1991; see also below).

The conjunctions that define a unique relational unit are presumably stored by the same mechanisms that support LTP and LTD. Because only 1% of a hippocampal neuron's inputs are required to fire a hippocampal (CA1) cell (Andersen 1990), each cell can, in principle, participate in many relational representations, each encoded by a small subset of its inputs. This functional architecture is reflected in chronic recording studies showing that individual CA1 units have several different behavioural correlates in different tasks, even within the same environment (e.g. Kubie & Ranck 1983, Wiener et al. 1989).

4.6.7 Recurrent connections form hierarchies of relational units
Cells within the dentate gyrus or CA3 lamina of the hippocampus interconnect to form "maps", which compose a second order of relational representations. Thus, interconnected place units form a spatial map of neighbouring locations (O'Keefe & Nadel 1978) and the connections within these lamina (e.g. among dentate gyrus or CA3 neurons) will be enhanced among functional neighbours, defined as synaptically connected cells that have similar response properties (e.g. overlapping or neighbouring place fields) located anatomically across the hippocampus (Hetherington & Shapiro 1991, Muller et al. 1991). Appropriately timed pre- and post-synaptic activation of these cells will produce either LTP or LTD of connections from one cell to the other. The strength of connections between two cells encodes the functional proximity or distance of the two cells along a given dimension in the map (e.g. spatial proximity). The hypothesis predicts that if functional proximity is encoded by the synaptic strength among CA3 neurons, then pairs of interconnected CA3 cells with overlapping place fields should share stronger synapses than pairs of cells with non-overlapping place fields. Furthermore, the timing requirements for induction of LTP suggest that animals using consistent spatial paths should develop directional place fields. Because the animal would reliably occupy one position before another, the CA3 cells upstream of, and earlier in the trajectory relative to, the recorded cell would reliably fire before the recorded cell, and not vice versa. This architecture also provides a mechanism for generating expectancies. The modulation of the recurrent pathway by ACh, as

described by Hasselmo, provides an important control of sequence storage and retrieval. If direction is coded by recurrent connections, then learning to perform regular trajectories should produce directional place fields (Hetherington & Shapiro 1993b). Finally, just as one unit can help represent many types of relationships, each unit can serve in many types of map (Wiener et al. 1989).

Third-order relational representations may be formed by more prolonged recurrent activation within maps. The physiological properties of recurrent circuits confer several important properties to maps: the ability to complete patterns (Treves & Rolls 1994), the ability to form active, self-sustaining cell assemblies that can act as working memory (e.g. Taketani et al. 1992), and the ability to activate sequences of assemblies within a map that can represent, for example, spatial trajectories. Higher order relational representations can be formed by recurrent architectures (e.g. the recurrent activation of sequences might encode episodes). Because recurrent networks can, in principle, compute anything (i.e. are Turing equivalent), and the functional capacity of hippocampal circuits is presumably limited, not all of these functions should be expected to be implemented in the structure. Nonetheless, this recurrent architecture provides a mechanism for encoding potentially unlimited hierarchies of relational representations.

4.6.8 Recurrent activation provides flexibility

Several of the models described above view the recurrent network properties of CA3, or the re-entrant connections between cortex and hippocampus, as a mechanism for generating linked, sequential representations (McNaughton & Nadel 1989). Levy (1994) has shown that input sequences can be learned rapidly using biologically plausible learning rules embedded in a simulation of the recurrent CA3 pathway. The model encodes, compresses and disambiguates between sequences, to compute a goal rapidly after being presented with stimuli associated with a starting point. Furthermore, different sequences with identical sections, thus containing choice points where the sequences diverge, are computed correctly, based on goals. Recent simulations of the "cognitive graph" model proposed by Muller and colleagues, based on a recurrent architecture of linked CA3 place cells, demonstrates the flexibility required by the relational memory system. The active vector of hippocampal neurons representing, for example, a place, will most strongly activate (or tend to activate) neurons encoding adjacent places, and less strongly activate more distance locations. Under appropriate conditions, an entire sequence of representations, from a location to a goal, will tend to be activated. The simulations, which focus on spatial processing, show that the network can navigate around obstacles and generate novel routes to goals. Generalizing from this type of network provides the computational framework for understanding relational memory.

4.6.9 Non-spatial relational encoding

Maps of relational units are not limited to encoding spatial representations but include other relational representations, such as those for faces, words, odours and other stimuli. One crucial assumption is that hippocampal units encode unique combinations of inputs to define relational units. The shape and hairiness of a head are principal components that activate face units in the anterior inferotemporal cortex (Young & Yamane 1992). If our proposal is correct and if these units influence activity in the medial entorhinal cortex, then single-unit activity in the entorhinal cortex should vary quantitatively along these facial dimensions and, in turn, should activate hippocampal units to encode and store unique faces. Analogously, the syntactic frame of word strings could define unique verbal items, and interconnected verbal units may form a semantic map (see O'Keefe and Nadel 1978). Single hippocampal units in humans do respond to words (Heit et al. 1988). However, the absence of probe tests, such as comparing synonyms to homonyms, prevented the structure of the representation from being analysed. Interconnected olfactory sampling units (Wiener et al. 1989) may form a map of odours with similar perceptual or contingent properties. Other experiments using single-unit data recorded from behaving animals can determine whether neuron activity is directly related to the functions proposed here. The sensory and behavioural correlates of hippocampal single-unit activity are consistent with the concept of relational cells. A crucial test of the role of recurrent connections in forming hierarchical representations would be selectively to lesion the recurrent pathways in the dentate gyrus or CA3 and test spatial learning. Although the method for performing this type of lesion has yet to be developed, pharmacological techniques may enhance or depress either principal inputs or recurrent connections (Hasselmo 1995).

4.6.10 Distances between representations encode differences between stimuli

An important challenge for the relational representation view is to specify the kinds of relationship that need the hippocampal system for normal learning, and how these are encoded by hippocampal circuits. Recurrent distributed networks can be described as abstract maps, with weights among processing units defining distances between representations. We propose that the primary relationship encoded by the hippocampus is that of distance, defined in the analytic geometric sense as the multidimensional distance (e.g. the dot product between two vectors) between stimuli encoded by the cortex. Just as single hippocampal neurons encode all types of relational stimulus, the distances among hippocampal vectors encode all types of differences among those stimuli. When sequences of stimuli are discriminated (as in working memory and spatial tasks), the hippocampus will encode those sequences based upon perceptual input as well as goal information, which may be encoded by pre-frontal cortical areas. During memory retrieval, the recurrent network will activate the same sequences, generating predictions of expected events. Note that each vector in a sequence can potentially activate any vector previously associated with the first. If Levy is correct, and sequences can be compressed, this architecture provides a mechanism for transitive inference. Thus, conjunctive encoding of inputs onto groups of single cells define configural stimuli, and recurrent activation of such stimuli provides the flexibility for relational representations. From this view, the hippocampal system is not only responsible for snapshot memory, encoded by parahippocampal regions, but for linking snapshots into dynamic movies, carried out by recurrent networks, perhaps in CA3, dentate gyrus or cortico-hippocampal connections.

4.7 IMPLICATIONS FOR HUMAN MEMORY AND THE NEUROPSYCHOLOGY OF AMNESIA

In our view, the basic architecture of the hippocampal system thus provides a memory map, and as in the phase sequences described by Hebb, one that uses synaptic plasticity to encode organized sequences of representations. This view predicts that representations required for many types of task will be represented and encoded by the hippocampal system as maps, with salient stimulus conjunctions defining nodes in that map, and differences between those stimuli defining interstimulus distances. The distances, perhaps encoded by synaptic weights among CA3 neurons, provide a way in which sequential activation of similar stimuli (i.e. adjacent places) occur, and provides a mechanistic basis for the flexible use of relational representations. These representations form the input to neocortical regions, which ultimately store the continuing history of the organism.

Thus, the incoming stream of perceptual information that is processed by neocortex is encoded as a sequence of unique episodes by the hippocampus, each episode containing elements that both separate and identify it from other episodes, and serve as relational links to other episodes. Healthy people can thereby remember episodes from the past, the elements comprising the episodes and can describe the sequence of events as they unfolded. Furthermore, each remembered episode, as well as the sequence in which it occurred, can provide associations for new and distinct pathways for retrieval. The cognitive, emotional and behavioural goal guiding behaviour at any one time also guides the retrieval pathway. People with damage to the hippocampal system can neither encode the unfolding, episodic stream nor link the incoming episode with the myriad potential relationships with past episodes. Because a crucial site of synaptic plasticity is damaged, the encoding of relational representations is prevented. Because the circuitry that enables sequential links among relational representations are also damaged, the ability to encode this "narrative stream" is also impaired. Finally, the ability to form new retrieval routes is impaired, a consequence of losing the substrate for sequential memory encoding.

REFERENCES

Abraham, W. C. & S. E. Mason 1988. Effects of the NMDA receptor/channel antagonists CPP and MK801 on hippocampal field potentials and long-term potentiation in anesthetized rats. *Brain Research* **462**, 40–6.

Alvarez, P. & L. R. Squire 1994. Memory consolidation and the medial temporal lobe: a simple network model. *Proceedings of the National Academy of Sciences USA* **91**, 7041–5.

Amaral, D. G. & M. P. Witter 1989. The three-dimensional organization of the hippocampal formation: a review of anatomical data. *Neuroscience* **31**, 571–91.

Ambros-Ingerson, J., R. Granger, G. Lynch 1990. Simulation of paleocortex performs hierarchical clustering. *Science* **247**, 1344–8.

Andersen, P. 1990. Synaptic integration in hippocampal CA1 pyramids. *Progress in Brain Research* **83**, 215–22.

Austin, K. B., W. F. Fortin, M. L. Shapiro 1990. Place fields are altered by NMDA antagonist MK–801 during spatial learning. *Society for Neuroscience Abstracts, 20th Annual Meeting*, **16**, 263, abstract 113.11.

Austin, K. B., L. H. White, M. L. Shapiro 1993. Short- and long-term effects of experience on hippocampal place fields. *Society for Neuroscience Abstracts, 23rd Annual Meeting* **19**, 797.

Barnes, C.A., B. L. McNaughton, S. J. Mizumori, B. W. Leonard, L. H. Lin 1990. Comparison of spatial and temporal characteristics of neuronal activity in sequential stages of hippocampal processing. *Progress in Brain Research* **83**, 287–300.

Bartlett, F. C. 1932. *Remembering*. London: Cambridge University Press.

Bear, M. F. & R. C. Malenka 1994. Synaptic plasticity: LTP and LTD. *Current Opinion in Neurobiology* **4**, 389–99.

Berger, T., B.Alger, R. F. Thompson 1976. Neuronal substrate of classical conditioning in the hippocampus. *Science* **192**, 483–5.

Bliss, T. V. P. & T. Lomo 1973. Long-lasting potentiation of synaptic transmission in the dentate area of the anaesthetized rabbit following stimulation of the perforant path. *Journal of Physiology* **232**, 331–56.

Bliss, T. V. P. & M. A. Lynch 1988. Long-term potentiation of synaptic transmission in the hippocampus: properties and mechanisms. In *Long-term potentiation: from biophysics to behavior*, P. W. Landfield & S. A. Deadwyler (eds), 3–72. New York: A. R. Liss.

Burgess, N., M. Recce, J. O'Keefe 1994. A model of hippocampal function. *Neural Networks* **7**, 1065–1081.

Butcher, S. P., S. Davis, R. G. M. M. Morris 1990. A dose-related impairment of spatial learning by the NMDA receptor antagonist, 2-amino–5-phosphovalerate (AP5).*European Neuropsychopharmacology* **1**, 15–20.

Caramanos, Z. & M. L. Shapiro 1994. Spatial memory and *N*-methyl-D-aspartate receptor antagonists APV and MK–801: memory impairments depend on familiarity with the environment, drug dose, and training duration. *Behavioural Neuroscience* **108**, 30–43.

Carpenter, G. A. & S. Grossberg 1993. Normal and amnesic learning, recognition and memory by a neural model of cortico-hippocampal interactions. *TINS* **16**(4), 131–7.

Cohen, N. J. 1984. Preserved learning capacity in amnesia: Evidence for multiple memory systems. In *The neuropsychology of memory*, N. Butters & L. R. Squire (eds). New York: Guilford Press.

Cohen, N. J. & L. R. Squire 1980. Preserved learning and retention of a pattern-analysing skill in amnesia: dissociation of knowing how and knowing that. *Science* **210**, 207–10.

Collingridge, G. L., G. L. Kehl, H. McLennan 1983. Excitatory amino acids in synaptic transmission in the Schaffer collateral-commisural pathway of the rat hippocampus. *Journal of Physiology (London)* **334**, 33–46.

Corkin, S. 1968. Acquisition of a motor skill after bilateral medial temporal lobe excision. *Neuropsychologia* **6**, 225–65.

Corkin, S. 1984. Lasting consequences of bilateral medial temporal lobectomy: clinical course and experimental findings. *H. M. Seminars in Neurology* **4**, 249–59.

Coté, D., E. L. Hargreaves, M. L. Shapiro 1995. Low doses of MK–801 impair primed burst potentiation in the dentate gyrus of freely moving rats. *Society for Neuroscience Abstracts, 24th Annual Meeting*, **21**, 442.

Deacon, T. W., H. Eichenbaum, P. Rosenberg, K. W. Eckman 1983. Afferent connections of the perirhinal cortex in the rat. *Journal of Comparative Neurology* **220**, 168–90.

Dunwiddie, T. & G. Lynch 1978. Long-term potentiation and depression of synaptic responses in the rat hippocampus: localization and frequency dependency. *Journal of Physiology* **276**, 353–67.

Eichenbaum, H. & N. J. Cohen 1988. Representation in the hippocampus: what do the neurons code? *Trends in Neurosciences* **11**, 244–8.

Eichenbaum, H. & T. Otto 1993. LTP and memory: can we enhance the connection. *Trends in Neuroscience* **16**, 163–4.

Eichenbaum, H., A. Fagan, N. J. Cohen 1986a. Normal olfactory discrimination learning set and facilitation of reversal learning after combined and separate lesions of the fornix and amygdala in rats: implications for preserved learning in amnesia. *Journal of Neuroscience* **6**, 1876–84.

Eichenbaum, H., M. Kuperstein, A. Fagan, J. Nagode 1986b. Cue-sampling and goal-approach correlates of hippocampal unit activity in rats performing an odor discrimination task. *Journal of Neuroscience* **7**, 716–32.

Eichenbaum, H., A. Fagan, P. Mathews, N. Cohen 1988a. Hippocampal system dysfunction and odour discrimination: impairment or facilitation depending on cognitive strategies. *Behavioural Neuroscience* **102**, 331–9.

Eichenbaum, H., A. Fagan, P. Mathews, N. J. Cohen 1988b. Hippocampal system dysfunction and odour discrimination learning in rats: impairment or facilitation depending on representational demands. *Behavioural Neuroscience* **102**, 3531–42.

Eichenbaum, H., P. Mathews, N. J. Cohen 1989a. Further studies of hippocampal representation during odour discrimination learning. *Behavioural Neuroscience* **103**, 1207–16.

Eichenbaum, H., S. I. Wiener, M. Shapiro, N. J. Cohen 1989b. The organization of spatial coding in the hippocampus: a study of neural ensemble activity. *Journal of Neuroscience* **9**, 2764–75.

Eichenbaum, H., T. Otto, C. G. Wible, J. Piper 1991. Building a model of the hippocampus in olfaction and memory. In *Olfaction as a model for computational neuroscience*, H. Eichenbaum & J. Davis (eds). Cambridge, MA: MIT Press.

Eichenbaum, H. & J. Buckingham 1992. Studies on hippocampal processing: experiment, theory, and model. In *Neurocomputation and learning: foundations of adaptive networks*, M. Gabriel & J. Moore (eds). Cambridge, MA: MIT Press.

Eichenbaum, H., T. Otto, N. J. Cohen 1992. The hippocampus – what does it do? *Behavioural and Neural Biology* **57**, 2–36.

Georgopoulis, A. P., A. B. Schwartz, R. E. Kettner 1986. Neuronal population coding of movement direction. *Science* **233**, 1416–19.

Gilbert, M. E. & C. M. Mack 1990. The NMDA antagonist, MK–801, suppresses long-term potentiation, kindling, and kindling-induced potentiation in the perforant path of the unanesthetized rat. *Brain Research* **519**, 89–96.

Gluck, M.A. & C.A. Myers 1993. Hippocampal mediation of stimulus representation: a computational theory. *Hippocampus* **3**, 491–516.

Goldman-Rakic, P. S. 1995. Cellular basis of working memory. *Neuron* **14**, 477–85.

Goldman-Rakic, P. S., L. D. Selemon, M. L. Schwart 1984. Dual pathways connecting the dorsolateral prefrontal vortex with the hippocampal formation and parahippocampal cortex in the rhesus monkey. *Neuroscience* **12**, 719–43.

Graf, P. & D. L. Schacter 1985. Implicit and explicit memory for new associations in normal and amnesic subjects. *Journal of Experimental Psychology: Learning, Memory, and Cognition* **11**, 501–18.

Graf, P., L. R. Squire, G. Mandler 1984. Amnesic patients perform normally on one kind of memory test for previously presented words. *Journal of Experimental Psychology: Learning, Memory, and Cognition* **10**, 164–78.

Granger, R., J. Whitson, J. Larson, G. Lynch 1994. Non-Hebbian properties of long-term potentiation enable high-capacity encoding of temporal sequences. *Proceedings of National Academy of Sciences, USA* **91**(21), 10104–8.

Gray, J.A. & J. N. P. Rawlins 1986. Comparator and buffer memory: an attempt to integrate two models of hippocampal function. In *The hippocampus*, vol. 4, R. L. Isaacson & K. H. Pribram (eds), 159–202. New York: Plenum Press.

Grossberg, S. 1987. Competitive learning: from interactive activation to adaptive resonance. *Science* **11**, 23–63.

Harris, E. W. & C. W. Cotman 1986. Long-term potentiation of guinea pig mossy fibre responses is not blocked by *N*-methyl-D-aspartate antagonists. *Neuroscience Letters* **70**, 132–7.

Hasselmo, M. 1995. A network model of the hippocampus combining self-organization and associative memory function. *Journal of Neuroscience*, in press.

Hasselmo, M. E. & E. Barkai 1995. Cholinergic modulation of activity-dependent synaptic plasticity in the piriform cortex and associative memory function in a network biophysical simulation. *Journal of Neuroscience* **15**, 6592–604.

Hasselmo, M., E. Schnell, E. Barkai 1995. Dynamics of learning and recall at excitatory recurrent synapses and cholinergic modulation in rat hippocampal region CA3. *Journal of Neuroscience* **15**, 5249–62.

Hebb, D. O. 1949. *The organization of behaviour*. New York: Wiley.

Heit, G., M. E. Smith, E. Halgren 1988. Neural encoding of individual words and faces by the human hippocampus and amygdala. *Nature* **333**, 773–5.

Hetherington, P. A. & M. L. Shapiro 1991. A recurrent PDP model simulates hippocampal place cell activity in goal-directed, sequential behaviour. *Third IBRO World Congress of Neuroscience: Abstracts*, 168.

Hetherington, P. A. & M. L. Shapiro 1993a. Simulated Hebb cell assemblies require potentiation, depression, and functionally segregated dendrites for stable and persistent representations. *Network* **4**, 135–53.

Hetherington, P. A. & M. L. Shapiro 1993b. A simple network model simulates hippocampal place fields II: goal directed behaviour and "memory fields". *Behavioural Neuroscience*, **107**(3), 434–43.

Hetherington, P. A. & M. L. Shapiro 1997. Hippocampal place fields are altered by the removal of single visual cues. *Behavioural Neuroscience* **111**, 20–34.

Hetherington, P. A., K. A. Austin, M. L. Shapiro 1994. The ipsilateral associational pathway in the dentate gyrus: an excitatory feedback system that supports NMDA-dependent long-term potentiation. *Hippocampus* **4**(4), 422–38.

Hill, A. J. & P. J. Best 1981. Effects of deafness and blindness on the spatial correlates of hippocampal unit activity in the rat. *Experimental Neurology* **74**, 204–17.

Hinton, G. E., J. L. McClelland, D. E. Rumelhart 1986. Distributed representations. In *Parallel distributed processing: explorations in the microstructure of cognition,* vol. 1, *Foundations*, J. L. McClelland & D. E. Rumelhart (eds), 77–109. Cambridge, MA: MIT Press.

Hirsh, R. 1974. The hippocampus and contextual retrieval of information from memory: a theory. *Behaviour and Biology* **12**, 421–44.

Hirsh, R. 1980. The hippocampus, conditional operations and cognition. *Physiology and Psychology* **8**, 175–82.

Hubel D. H. & T. N. Wiesel 1977. Ferrier Lecture. Functional architecture of macaque monkey visual cortex. *Proceedings Royal Society of London, Series B* **198**, 1–59.

Insausti, R., D. G. Amaral, W. M. Cowan 1978. The entorhinal cortex of the monkey: II. Cortical afferents. *Journal of Comparative Neurology* **264**, 356–95.

Jenkins, W. M., M. M. Merzenich, G. Recanzone 1990. Neocortical representational dynamics in adult primates: implications for neuropsychology. *Neuropsychology* **28**, 573–84.

Jones, E. G. & T. P. S. Powell 1970. An anatomical study of converging sensory pathways within the cerebral cortex of the monkey. *Brain* **93**, 793–820.

Kesner, R. P. 1994. *Working memory is impaired by intrahippocampal injections of opiate antagonists*. Winter Conference on Neurobiology of Learning and Memory, Park City, UT, January.

Kesner, R. P., B. L. Bolland, M. Dakis 1993. Memory for spatial locations, motor responses, and objects: triple dissociation among the hippocampus, caudate nucleus, and extrastriate visual cortex. *Experimental Brain Research* **93**, 462–70.

Kosel, K. C., G. W. Van Hoesen, D. L. Rosene 1982. Non-hippocampal cortical projections from the entorhinal cortex in the rat and rhesus monkey. *Brain Research* **214**, 201–13.

Krettek, J. E. & J. L. Price 1977. Projections from the amygdaloid complex and adjacent olfactory structures to the entorhinal cortes and to the subiculum in the rat and cat. *Journal of Comparative Neurology* **172**, 723–52.

Kubie, J. L. & J. B. Ranck 1983. Sensory–behavioural correlates in individual hippocampus neurons in three situations: space and context. In *The hippocampus*, W. Seifert (ed.), 433–47. New York: Academic Press.

Levy, W. B. 1994. Unification of hippocampal function via computational considerations. World Congress on Neural Networks – San Diego, Lawrence Erlbaum, Inc., Hillsdale, NJ, IV-661–IV 666.

Levy, W. B. & O. Steward 1979. Synapses as associative elements in the hippocampal formation. *Brain Research* **175**, 233–45.

Lynch, G. 1986. *Synapses, circuits, and the beginnings of memory*. Cambridge MA: MIT Press.

Lynch, G. & M. Baudry 1988. Structure–function relationships in the organization of memory. In *Perspectives in memory research*, M. S. Gazzaniga (ed.), 23–92. Cambridge, MA: MIT Press.

Marr, D. 1971. Simple memory: a theory for archicortex. *Philosophical Transactions of the Royal Society, Series B* **262**, 23–81.

McClelland, J. L., B. L. McNaughton, R. C. O'Reilly 1994. Why there are complementary learning systems in the hippocampus and neocortex: insights from the successes and failures of connectionist models of learning and memory. *Parallel Distributed Processing and Cognitive Neuroscience Technical Report PDP CNS.94.1*.

McDonald, R. J. & N. M. White 1993. A triple dissociation of memory systems: hippocampus, amygdala, and dorsal striatum. *Behavioural Neuroscience* **107**, 3–22.

McNaughton, B. L. & R. G. M. Morris 1987. Hippocampal synaptic enhancement and information storage within a distributed memory system. *Trends in Neurosciences* **10**, 408–15.

McNaughton, B. L. & L. Nadel 1989. Hebb-Marr networks and the neurobiological representation of action in space. In *Neuroscience and connectionist theory*, M. A. Gluck & D. E. Rumelhart (eds), 1–64. Hillsdale, NJ: Lawrence Erlbaum Associates Inc.

Minai, A. A. & W. B. Levy 1993. Sequence learning in a single trial. World Congress on Neural Networks, Lawrence Erlbaum Associates, Inc., Hillsdale, NJ, II-505–II-508.

Minai, A. A., G. L. Barrows, W. B. Levy 1994. Disambiguation of pattern sequences with recurrent networks. World Congress on Neural Networks – San Diego, Lawrence Erlbaum, Inc. Hillsdale, NJ, IV-176–IV-81.

Morris, R. G. M., E. Anderson, G. S. Lynch, M. Baudry 1986. Selective impairment of learning and blockade of long-term potentiation by an N-methyl-D-aspartate receptor antagonist, AP5. *Nature* **319**, 774–6.

Morris, R. G. M., P. Garrud, J. N. P. Rawlins, J. O'Keefe 1982. Place navigation impaired in rats with hippocampal lesions. *Nature* **297**, 681–3.

Muller, R. U. & J. L. Kubie 1987. The effects of changes in the environment on the spatial firing of hippocampal complex-spike cells. *Journal of Neuroscience* **7**, 1951–68.

Muller, D. & G. Lynch 1988. Long-term potentiation differentially affects two components of synaptic responses in hippocampus. *Proceedings of the National Academy of Sciences USA* **85**, 9346–50.

Muller, R. U., J. L. Kubie, R. Saypoff 1991. The hippocampus as a cognitive graph (abridged version). *Hippocampus* **1**, 243–6.

Muller, R. M., M. Stead, J. Pach 1996. The hippocampus as a cognitive graph. *Journal of General Physiology* **106**, 663–94.

Myers, C. & M. Gluck 1994. Context, conditioning, and hippocampal re-representation. *Behavioural Neuroscience* **108**, 835–47.

O'Keefe, J. & D. H. Conway 1978. On the trail of the hippocampal engram. *Physiology and Psychololgy* **2**, 229–38.

O'Keefe, J. & J. Dostrovsky 1971. The hippocampus as a cognitive map. Preliminary evidence from unit activity in freely moving rats. *Brain Research* **34**, 171–5.

O'Keefe, J. & L. Nadel 1978. *The hippocampus as a cognitive map*. Oxford: Oxford University Press.

O'Keefe, J. & M. L. Recce 1993. Place relationship between hippocampal place units and the EEG theta rhythm. *Hippocampus* **3**, 317–30.

O'Keefe, J. & A. Speakman 1987. Single unit activity in the rat hippocampus during a spatial memory task. *Experimental Brain Research* **68**, 1–27.

Olton, D. S., J. T. Becker, G. E. Handlemann 1979. Hippocampus, space, and memory. *Brain Behaviour and Science* **2**, 313–65.

Ono, T., K. Nakamura, M. Fukada, R. Tamura 1991. Place recognition responses of neurons in monkey hippocampus. *Neuroscience Letters* **121**, 194–8.

O'Reilly, R. C. & J. L. McClelland 1994. Hippocampal conjunctive encoding, storage, and recall: avoiding a trade-off. *Parallel Distributed Processing and Cognitive Neuroscience Technical Report PDP CNS.94.4.*

Otto, T., F. Schottler, U. Staubli, H. Eichenbaum, G. Lynch 1991. Hippocampus and olfactory discrimination learning: effects of entorhinal cortex lesions on olfactory learning and memory in a successive-cue, go/no-go task. *Behavioural Neuroscience* **105**, 111–19.

Packard, M. G., R. Hirsh, N. M. White 1989. Differential effects of fornix and caudate nucleus lesions on two radial maze tasks: evidence for multiple memory systems. *Journal of Neuroscience* **9**, 1465–72.

Phillips, R. G. & J. E. LeDoux 1992. Differential contribution of amygdala and hippocampus to cued and contextual fear conditioning. *Behavioural Neuroscience* **106**, 274–85.

Pockett S., N. H. Brookes, L. J. Bindman 1990. Long-term depression at synapses in slices of rat hippocampus can be induced by bursts of postsynaptic activity. *Experimental Brain Research* **80**(1), 196–200.

Quirk, G. J., R. U. Muller, J. L. Kubie 1990. The firing of hippocampal place cells in the dark depends on the rat's recent experience. *Journal of Neuroscience* **10**, 2008–17.

Reed, G. D. & G. B. Robinson 1991. Effect of MK801 on long-term potentiation in the hippocampal dentate gyrus of the unanesthetized rabbit. *Annals of the New York Academy of Sciences USA* **627**, 381–4.

Room, P. & H. J. Groenewegen 1986. Connections of the parahippocampal cortex in the cat. I. Cortical afferents. *Journal of Comparative Neurology* **251**, 415–50.

Rumelhart, D. E., G. E. Hinton, R. J. Williams 1986. Learning representations by back-propagating errors. *Nature* **323**, 533–6.

Schacter, D. L. 1985. Multiple forms of memory in humans and animals. In *Memory systems of the brain*, N. M. Weinberger, J. L. McGaugh, G. Lynch (eds), 351–80. New York: Guilford Press.

Schacter, D. L. 1987. Implicit memory: history and current status. *Journal of Experimental Psychology: Learning, Memory and Cognition* **13**, 510–18.

Schacter, D. L. & E. Tulving (eds) 1994. *Memory systems 1994*. Cambridge, MA: MIT Press.

Schmajuk, N. A. 1990. Role of the hippocampus in temporal and spatial navigation: an adaptive neural network. *Behaviour and Brain Research* **39**, 205–29.

Schmajuk, N. A. & J. J. Dicarlo 1992. Stimulus configuration, classical conditioning, and hippocampal function. *Psychology Review* **99**, 268–305.

Schmajuk, N. A., A. D. Thieme, H. T. Blair 1993. Maps, routes, and the hippocampus: a neural network approach. *Hippocampus* **3**, 387–400.

Scoville, W. B. & B. Milner 1957. Loss of recent memory after bilateral hippocampal lesions. *Journal of Neurology, Neurosurgery and Psychiatry* **20**, 11–12.

Shapiro, M. L. & Z. Caramanos 1990. NMDA antagonist MK–801 impairs acquisition but not performance of spatial working and reference memory. *Psychobiology* **18**, 231–43.

Shapiro, M. L. & P. A. Hetherington 1993. A simple network model stimulates hippocampal place fields: parametric analyses and psychological predictions. *Behavioural Neuroscience* **107**, 34–50.

Shapiro, M. L. & C. O'Connor 1992. *N*-Methyl-D-aspartate receptor antagonist MK–801 and spatial memory representation: working memory is impaired in an unfamiliar environment but not in a familiar environment. *Behavioural Neuroscience* **106**, 604–12.

Shapiro, M. L. & D. S. Olton 1994. Hippocampal function and interference. In *Memory systems*, D. L. Schacter & E. Tulving (eds), 87–117. Cambridge, MA: MIT Press.

Sharp, P. E. 1991. Computer simulation of hippocampal place cells. *Psychobiology* **19**(2), 103–15.

Sherry, D. F. & D. L. Schacter 1987. The evolution of multiple memory systems. *Psychological Review* **94**(4), 439–54.

Shimamura, A. P. 1986. Priming effects in amnesia: evidence for a dissociable memory function. *Quarterly Journal of Experimental Psychology* **38A**, 619–44.

Squire, L. R. 1987. *Memory and brain*. New York: Oxford University Press.

Squire, L. R. 1992. Declarative and nondeclarative memory: multiple brain systems supporting learning and memory. *Journal of Cognitive Neuroscience* **4**(3), 232–43.

Squire, L. R., A. P. Shimamura, D. G. Amaral 1989. Memory and the hippocampus. In *Neural models of plasticity*, J. Byrne & W. Barry (eds). New York: Academic Press.

Staubli, U. & G. Lynch 1987. Stable hippocampal long-term potentiation elicited by "theta" pattern stimulation. *Brain Research* **435**, 227–34.

Staubli, U., G. Ivy, G. Lynch 1984. Hippocampal denervation causes rapid forgetting of olfactory information in rats. *Proceedings of the National Academy of Sciences USA* **81**, 5885–7.

Swanson, L. W. & C. Kohler 1986. Anatomical evidence for direct projections from the entorhinal area to the entire cortical mantle in the rat. *Journal of Neuroscience* **6**, 3010–23.

Taketani, M., J. Ambros-Ingerson, R. Myers, R. Granger, G. Lynch 1992. Is field CA3 a reverberatory short term memory system? *Society for Neuroscience Abstracts* **18**, 1211.

Taube, J. S., R. U. Muller, J. B. Ranck Jr 1990. Head-direction cells recorded from the postsubiculum in freely moving rats. I. Description and quantitative analysis. *Journal of Neuroscience* **10**, 420–35.

Thompson, L. T. & P. J. Best 1989. Place cells and silent cells in the hippocampus of freely-behaving rats. *Journal of Neuroscience* **9**, 2382–90.

Tonkiss, J. & J. N. P. Rawlins 1991. The competitive NMDA antagonist AP5, but not the non-competitive antagonist MK801, induces a delay-related impairment in spatial working memory in rats. *Experimental Brain Research* **85**, 349–58.

Touretzky, D. S. & A. D. Redish 1995. A multiple representation theory of rodent navigation. Unpublished manuscript.

Treves A. & E. T. Rolls 1994. Computational analysis of the role of the hippocampus in memory. *Hippocampus* **4**(3), 374–91.

Tulving, T. E. & D. L. Schacter 1990. Priming and human memory systems. *Science* **247**, 301–6.

Van Hoesen, G. W. & D. N. Pandya 1975a. Some connections of the entorhinal (area 28) and perirhinal (area 35) cortices of the rhesus monkey. I. Temporal lobe afferents. *Brain Research* **95**, 1–24.

Van Hoesen, G. W. & D. N. Pandya 1975b. Some connections of the entorhinal (area 28) and perirhinal (area 35) cortices of the rhesus monkey. III. Efferent connections. *Brain Research* **95**, 39–59.

Van Hoesen, G. W., D. N. Pandya, N. Butters 1972. Cortical afferents to the entorhinal cortex of the rhesus monkey. *Science* **175**, 1471–3.

Warrington, E. K. & L. Weiskrantz 1970. The amnesic syndrome: consolidation or retrieval? *Nature* **228**, 628–30.

Wible, C. G., R. L. Findling, M. Shapiro, E. J. Lang, S. Crane, D. S. Olton 1986. Mnemonic correlates of unit activity in the hippocampus. *Brain Research* **399**, 97–110.

Wiener, S. I., C. A. Paul, H. Eichenbaum 1989. Spatial and behavioural correlates of hippocampal neuronal activity. *Journal of Neuroscience* **9**, 2737–63.

Willshaw, D. J. & J. T. Buckingham 1990. An assessment of Marr's theory of the hippocampus as a temporary memory store. *Philosophical Transactions of the Royal Society, London, Series B* **329**, 205–15.

Wilson, M. A. & B. L. McNaughton 1993. Dynamics of the hippocampal ensemble code for space. *Science* **261**, 1055–8.

Witter, M. P. 1989. Connectivity of the rat hippocampus. In *The hippocampus – new vistas* V. Chan-Palay & C. Koeler (eds), 53–79. New York: A. R. Liss.

Witter, M. P. & H. J. Groenewegen 1986. Connections of the perihippocampal cortex in the cat. III. Cortical and thalamic efferents. *Journal of Neurology* **252**, 1–31.

Witter, M. P., A. W. Griffioen, B. Jorritsma-Byham, J. L. M. Krijnen 1988. Entorhinal projections to the hippocampal CA1 region in the rat: an underestimated pathway. *Neuroscience Letters* **85**, 193–8.

Worden, R. 1992. Navigation by fragment fitting: a theory of hippocampal function. *Hippocampus* **2**(2), 165–88.

Wyss, J. M. 1981. An autoradiographic study of the efferent connections of the entorhinal cortex in the rat. *Journal of Comparative Neurology* **199**, 495–512.

Yeckel, M. F. & T. W. Berger 1990. Feedforward excitation of the hippocampus by afferents from the entorhinal cortex: redefinition of the role of the trisynaptic pathway. *Proceedings of the National Academy of Sciences, USA* **87**, 5832–6.

Young, M. P. & S. Yamane 1992. Sparse population coding of faces in the inferotemporal cortex. *Science* **256**, 1327–31.

Zipser, D. 1985. A computational model of hippocampal place fields. *Behavioural Neuroscience* **99**, 1006–18.

CHAPTER 5

Voluntary movement: computational principles and neural mechanisms

Apostolos P. Georgopoulos

5.1 VOLUNTARY MOVEMENT DEFINED

Movements of body parts comprise a large variety of motions (e.g. from small finger movements to locomotion) produced for various behavioural purposes (e.g. reach towards an object, manipulate an object, run away from a predator). Which of these movements are voluntary? Clearly, reaching to an object of interest is a voluntary motor act, but is arm swinging during walking, or running for life from a predator voluntary as well? In a way they are not because, for example, the arms swing while we walk without our intentionally willing them to do so, and we run away from a predator because our life is in imminent danger and, therefore, we have no choice. However, in both these cases, we can do otherwise *if we choose to do so*: we can walk without swinging our arms, and we can stay immobile when the predator approaches. However, we *cannot stop* other movements that are usually the result of brain damage, especially in a group of nuclei within the so-called basal ganglia. For example, people with lesions of a small nucleus in the basal ganglia, the subthalamic nucleus, frequently move their arms unwillingly in wild, throwing motions, a condition called hemiballismus; and the various dyskinesias consist of movements of body parts that happen without the patients willing them to, but also without the patients *being able to stop them* either. Therefore, these movements are called *involuntary*. Strangely, the best definition of *voluntary movement* seems to be the opposite of involuntary movement, that is a movement that *can be suppressed* (or not initiated at all) *at will*. This comes from the fact that involuntary movements are well defined and possess the cardinal feature that they come and go by themselves, and that they cannot be suppressed or not initiated. This then serves as a good background against which to define voluntary movements.

5.2 COMPUTATIONAL ASPECTS OF VOLUNTARY MOVEMENTS

Practically all voluntary movements are quite complex across several dimensions. Consider, for example, reaching towards and manipulating an object of interest: the reaching movement looks graceful and feels effortless, and the hand manipulates the object by continuous, expert movements. This apparently simple, natural act involves the co-ordinated activation and relaxation of many muscles acting about several joints of the arm and the hand each of which possesses a number of degrees of freedom in motion and which, together, provide an enormously complex system from the computational point of view. Then consider playing the piano, dancing or an acrobatic performance: the complexity now extends to the time as well as the space dimension; not only is a precise coordination of muscles and joints needed to achieve a particular movement, but the movements of different body parts also have to be co-ordinated continuously in time and space for these motor skills to be performed. Lastly, consider standing on a tightrope. In this case you need just the opposite, that is to suppress irrelevant movements and assume a posture that will balance yourself very precisely so that the centre of gravity of your body does not fall outside the safe margin dictated by your stance and you do not fall on the ground. All these cases are quite different and can be performed well after a period of practice. The computations involved, if one were to solve these problems in a straightforward, brute-force manner, are prohibitively large. This is due mainly to the combinatorial aspect of the problem, in the sense that the same goal can be achieved in an almost infinite number of combinations of muscle activations and joint motions; for example, you can reach an object through a very large number of movement trajectories which correspond to a large number of different combinations of muscles and joints. Although these are serious issues for modellers, fortunately, they do not seem to pose problems for the organism because movements are typically performed in a stereotypical manner and with several constraints, so that the degrees of freedom are reduced appreciably. For example, quadruped locomotion involves regular alternation of stance and swing phases associated with cyclical changes in many joint angles and concomitant activation and relaxation of flexor and extensor muscles acting about those joints; this reduces the practically infinite ways of combining the motion of all the joints in four limbs, and the activation of muscles in these limbs, to specific constrained, co-ordinated motions and muscle activations. Similarly, the reaching movement involves well co-ordinated and tightly linked motions about the shoulder and elbow joints (Soechting & Lacquaniti 1981) that position the hand in desired locations in space. This reduction in the degrees of freedom is a common property in the motor system (Bernstein 1967). It seems that the brain controls movements of the limbs as a constrained, linked system rather than as an aggregate of independent units. In this chapter we discuss the properties of reaching movements and the neural mechanisms involved in their control.

5.3 REACHING MOVEMENTS

Reaching movements involve motions at the shoulder and elbow joints. These motions result from the application of torques generated about each joint by the contraction of muscles. The muscles activated and the temporal course of the intensity of their contraction will depend on the movement trajectory in space, the velocity of the movement and the magnitude and direction of fixed or changing external loads. The relations between the temporal pattern of these torques and the trajectory of the hand are complicated even for two-dimensional hand trajectories (Hollerbach & Flash 1982). This is true both for deriving the trajectory given the torques (integral kinematics) and for deriving the torques at each joint given the trajectory (inverse kinematics).

In general, the patterns of activation of muscles during reaching movements are very complicated. This is due to several factors. First, these movements are implemented by the concomitant contraction of several muscles. Therefore, a population of muscles has to be considered rather than an agonist–antagonist pair, as is usually the case for movements around joints possessing a single degree of freedom (e.g. elbow). Secondly, the exact contribution of each muscle to the torques generated at each joint in the course of the movement is often difficult to measure because the direction along which a muscle will exert its mechanical action may change during the movement. Thirdly, a complete analysis of the muscular patterns of activity subserving these movements has to take into account the relative timing differences between the evolving contractions of the muscles involved, because such differences may affect the movement trajectory. This problem is further complicated by methodological considerations. For example, muscle activation is usually assessed using electromyographic (EMG) methods, yet there is no general agreement concerning the relations between the EMG activity and the force exerted by the muscle. This is an especially difficult problem in the case of pinnate muscles, the fibres of which do not run along the axis between the insertion points of the muscle; in this case, for an approximate assessment of the relation between the EMG activity and the force developed along that axis and within different compartments of these muscles, the geometrical arrangement of the fibres must be considered.

In spite of these complexities, some principles of muscle activation during reaching are evident. For example, in an EMG analysis of movements made by monkeys in eight different directions on a plane, it was found that at least ten muscles acting on the shoulder joint and girdle were involved (Georgopoulos et al. 1984). The magnitude of EMG activation was correlated significantly among several muscles, which suggests that the movements were subserved by muscle synergies. Moreover, these synergies differed in an orderly fashion from the direction of movement. Although similar considerations may apply to unconstrained reaching movements in three-dimensional space, at the present time we lack an adequate description of the simultaneous muscle patterns in this general case.

5.4 PATHS AND TRAJECTORIES

A path is the sequence of positions that the hand follows in space; a trajectory is the time sequence of these successive positions (Hollerbach & Flash 1982). Handpaths of unconstrained reaching movements made on the sagittal (Soechting & Lacquaniti 1981, Atkeson & Hollerbach 1985) or horizontal (Morasso 1981, Gordon et al. 1994) plane are usually straight or slightly curved. Their velocity profile is dome shaped and, if no emphasis is placed on accuracy, it is single peaked. The curve may become slightly asymmetric with practice, with the ascending, accelerating slope steeper than the descending, decelerating slope (Beggs & Howarth 1972). The shape of the velocity profile is essentially unaffected by the location of the movement vector in space, in contrast to joint motion (Morasso 1981).

The shape of the velocity profile is probably determined by the strategy for making the movement (Nelson 1983). First of all, a basic strategy that subjects follow in reaching is to arrive near the target with a single movement that covers most of the distance to be travelled. Moreover, the acceleration of the movement changes continuously, so that there is no portion of the movement in which the velocity is constant. We do not know why or how this strategy is adopted. It is acquired gradually during infancy, and breaks down in Parkinson's disease. The initial reaching response of infants is composed of a series of smaller movements, and it is only later that the large amplitude, initial component develops (von Hofsten 1979). In Parkinson's disease the first movement component is too small, and a series of smaller movements is employed by the patient to get to the target (Flowers 1975).

5.5 ACCURACY OF REACHING

The accuracy of reaching is defined with respect to its target. The trajectory itself is not commonly constrained, although accuracy boundaries could be placed on it as well. P. M. Fitts investigated the accuracy of open-loop reaching at targets in different locations in extrapersonal space (discussed in Georgopoulos 1986). In the first series of experiments pilots memorized the letter-coded locations of 20 targets and reached with a pencil at a requested target while fixating a red light in front of them. The subjects did not see the target areas which were constructed like a bull's eye, so that the accuracy of reaching could be determined directly. Movements directed straight ahead were most accurate, whereas those directed low, on either side and slightly behind were least accurate.

In two-dimensional reaching movements, the errors in pointing comprise errors relating to the direction and amplitude of movement (Gordon et al. 1994). The variability of movement end-points along the axis of movement reflects errors in movement amplitude and increase markedly and non-linearly with distance from the origin of the movement. On the other hand, the variability of movement end-points perpendicular to the axis of the movement reflects errors in the direction of the movement, and is generally smaller than the variability due to amplitude. Moreover, directional errors increase proportionally with distance, which indicates that the directional variability, in *angular* terms, is constant and independent of distance. These findings suggest that the direction and amplitude of movement are planned separately.

5.6 MOVEMENT TIME AND THE SPEED–ACCURACY TRADE-OFF

The duration of the reaching movement is a behaviourally important variable because it specifies how quickly the target will be reached.

With respect to dynamics, changing the time of moving between two points involves a substantial recomputation of the joint motion dynamics. Hollerbach & Flash (1982) found that these computations could be simplified by scaling the joint torques according to the speed desired. Indeed, it seems that human subjects adopt a strategy compatible with this scaling procedure (Hollerbach & Flash 1982). These results suggest that the overall movement speed could be specified at a behavioural level and implemented with no increase in computational load. This would be a behavioural advantage for the subject, especially during motor learning. For example, "one might conceive of a practice strategy beginning with slow movements to learn the basic torque profiles, then simply scaling these profiles to increase the speed of movement" (Hollerbach 1982: 192).

In the absence of accuracy constraints, the movement time tends to remain constant as the amplitude of the movement increases, due to an increase of movement speed with movement amplitude. However, in the presence of accuracy constraints, there is a trade-off between the speed and the accuracy of the reaching movement such that more accurate movements are performed more slowly, and, conversely, faster movements are less accurate. This phenomenon has been studied extensively (see Keele 1981, for a review). It seems that the increase in movement time under conditions of increased accuracy requirements results from an increase in the number of corrective movements that bring the hand on the target following the large amplitude, first component of the movement.

5.6.1 Information transmission

Fitts (1954) applied an information–theoretical approach to the relations linking movement time, accuracy and distance. He calculated the rate of information transmission during an aimed movement as follows:

$$I_p = -\frac{1}{t}\log_2\left(\frac{W}{2A}\right)$$

where I_p, the index of performance, is the information transmitted in bit/s, t is the movement time, W is the target width, and A is the movement amplitude. The term $-\log_2(W/2A)$ is the index of task difficulty. It is a composite measure of informational load, relating to both accuracy and distance. The upper limits of information transmitted by human subjects vary with the task (Fitts 1954) and decrease with age (Welford et al. 1969).

5.7 DEVELOPMENT OF REACHING IN INFANCY

The capacity to reach to objects of interest develops gradually over a period of several months after birth. However, a rudimentary form of eye–hand co-ordination is present in the newborn (von Hofsten 1982), and it is on this background that visual reaching is established. The characteristics of forward extensions of the arm towards a moving target were investigated in infants from the 15–18th to the 36th week of age (von Hofsten 1979). Remarkable changes in reaching skill were observed, so that at the end of the observation period it closely resembled the adult pattern. At the age of 12–16 weeks, reaching consisted of a series of movements, as judged by the zero crossings in the acceleration record. About 80% of reachings consisted of three or more serial movements. This resulted in long, fragmented movement paths, in which the first movement covered no more than 40% of the total distance. In contrast, at 36 weeks of age, the first movement covered more than 70% of the total distance. In addition, there was a decrease in the fragmentation of reaching. In fact, the essence of the development lay in the gradual build-up of a dominance of the first movement towards the target, so that at the end of the observation period the reaching response consisted predominantly of one forceful movement that brought the hand near the target, a pattern which resembles that observed in adults. It is interesting that reaching was better to a fast-moving target (15 and 30 cm/s), as compared with a stationary or slowly moving (3.4 cm/s) target. In fact, there were clear indications that some of the reaching movements were predictive in nature (von Hofsten 1980).

5.8 VISUAL GUIDANCE OF REACHING

The behavioural repertoire of reaching to a target does not consist of the arm movement alone but includes concomitant movements of the eyes and the head towards the target. All these responses are generated in parallel, for the latency of *muscle* (EMG) activation of the head and arm muscles, and of changes in the electro-oculogram are almost identical when subjects are instructed to track a visual target, when it appears, by eye, head and hand as quickly as possible, without specifying a sequence in those movements (Biguer et al. 1982). In contrast, the latency of the onset of the *movement* of the eyes, head and arm differ, that of the saccade being the shortest and that of the arm being the longest (Biguer et al. 1982). This is due to the different inertial loads that have to be overcome before movement begins. These observations concerning the practically simultaneous muscle activation and the rank ordering of the onset times of the eye, head and arm movements in reaching seem to reflect a central pattern, because they were unaffected when vision of the arm was eliminated (Biguer et al. 1982). The sequencing of movement onsets can be of particular significance, because the eye movement may be completed before the arm movement has even started, due to the high velocity of the saccade (Biguer et al. 1982). In fact, if eye or head movements are not allowed, reaching to eccentric targets is very inaccurate (Prablanc et al. 1979a). The contribution of the eye and head movements to the accuracy of reaching is probably due to both the foveation of the target *and* the visual monitoring of the hand movement, because allowing the saccade to occur in the absence of vision of the hand did not improve reaching accuracy at eccentric targets (Prablanc et al. 1979a).

This brings us to the question of visual guidance of reaching. There are at least three aspects of this problem: first, visual localization of the target in extrapersonal space and suitable coding of that information for use by the arm motor system; secondly, visual monitoring of the hand before and during its movement through space; and, thirdly, visual adjustment of the final position of the hand to touch, grasp or retrieve successfully the object of interest.

The coding of absolute target position in space is a large subject that is usually treated in the context of perception rather than movement. It will suffice to mention that the perceived location of the target need not coincide with the location used by the motor system to direct the arm. This was shown, for example, in experiments in which subjects were asked to hit with a hammer targets illuminated at different positions in space during the onset of a saccade (Skavenski & Hansen 1978). Remarkably, the subjects hit the targets accurately, despite the fact that they were uncertain about the location of the target and their high success rate.

The monitoring of the arm and hand motion throughout reaching is apparently important for accurate performance. Reaching is more accurate in the presence than in the absence of vision of the arm just before (Prablanc et al. 1979b) and during the movement (Conti & Beaubaton 1976, Prablanc et al. 1979a,b). Since this improvement was observed even for movements that were completed within 200 ms, it was proposed (Paillard 1982) that visual cues from arm motion are being processed at higher speeds than the times (190–260 ms) assumed necessary to utilize external visual feedback (Keele & Posner 1968).

Two visual systems that process information related to the movement of the arm and hand during reaching have been identified (Paillard 1982, Jeannerod & Biguer 1982). Their contribution to the visual guidance of movement and the cues they use have been studied in experiments that allowed separate control of target and hand vision through a coloured filter in normal and split-brain monkeys (Beaubaton et al. 1978). In other experiments, continuous or stroboscopic illumination was used to dissociate position from motion cues during the course of prismatic adaptation in human subjects (Paillard et al. 1981). It was found that one system utilizes central vision (8°), is facilitated by the presence of a foveated target, and analyses positional (displacement) cues, because it is unaffected under conditions of stroboscopic illumination (Paillard et al. 1981). Presumably this system subserves the accurate placement of the hand on the target near the end of the reaching movement. The other system employs peripheral vision and analyses motion cues, as evidenced by its impairment under conditions of stroboscopic illumination. More importantly, the motion cues that seem to be meaningful to this system are those arising from the motion of the arm when *actively* moved by the subject but not when passively moved by the experimenter (Paillard et al. 1981). These findings are consistent with earlier results which suggested that the development of visually guided reaching depends on "self-produced movement with its concurrent visual feedback" (Held & Hein 1963). In general, the two visual systems mentioned above resemble the distinction made previously by Trevarthen (1968).

Paillard (1982) has summarized the implications of these findings as follows. There are three aspects of visual information that are utilized in reaching. The first concerns the visual localization of the target in space.Although this information can be restricted to one hemisphere, it can effectively be used to trigger reaching by either arm. The second piece of visual information concerns the relative position of hand and target; and the third comes from the motion of the limb across the visual fields. The last two cues are processed most efficiently by the hemisphere contralateral to the moving arm (Beaubaton et al. 1978).

5.9 SPATIAL PLANNING OF REACHING

Reaching as a behavioural act is the result of a complex sensorimotor coordination. Reaching itself is a complicated multijoint movement directed to a defined point in space and performed under behavioural and biomechanical constraints. In self-paced, cyclical tasks in which alternate reaching movements are performed between two targets, the planning, initiation and execution of successive movements will overlap partially in time. In contrast, in reaction time (RT) tasks in which, for example, a fast aiming movement has to be made in response to a stimulus, it can be assumed that a good part of the planning process happens during the RT. Several aspects of this process have been studied successfully using RT paradigms, such as the specification of the direction and extent of movement (Gordon et al. 1994), as discussed above.

In general, it has been assumed that the duration of the RT reflects the difficulty in generating a response, given a certain stimulus. The least complicated case is that of a *simple* RT task, in which a response (e.g. movement of the hand) is required as soon as a stimulus is presented. In contrast, in *choice* RT tasks the response is contingent on making a decision concerning specific attributes of the stimulus. For example, given a set of two responses (e.g. movement of the left or right hand) and two stimuli (e.g. a blue and a red light), a choice RT task could be as follows: "move the right hand in response to the blue light, and the left hand in response to the red light". Choice RT increases with the number of alternatives N involved in decision-making; in fact it is a linear function of stimulus uncertainty ($\log_2 N$) (Hick 1952).

Is the RT of a movement aimed at a target a simple or a choice RT? It is not a simple RT because the response is constrained by the location of the stimulus, but if it is a choice RT, what are the choices? Assuming that the movement starts from the same point in space and is of constant amplitude and accuracy, it is reasonable to suppose that the choices will be determined by the number of targets presented in a task, because each target specifies a different movement. Yet, it is remarkable that the RT under these conditions may increase only slightly, or not at all, with stimulus uncertainty (Sanders 1967, Georgopoulos et al. 1981), probably because reactions toward the source of stimulation are fast (Simon 1969) and because aimed movements are usually highly practised and possess a high degree of spatial compatibility with the target. Both of these factors have been shown to reduce the effect of stimulus uncertainty on choice RT (Mowbray & Rhoades 1959, Brainard et al. 1962). Therefore, reaching movements seem to be generated very efficiently, as if there were a short link between the target and the movement directed to it. This link is probably based on the strong similarity between the ways in which the target and the aimed movement are coded spatially, according to theories of stimulus–response compatibility in the spatial domain (Fitts & Seeger 1953, Wallace 1971, Duncan 1977).

Another interesting feature in the planning of reaching movements is that they can be elicited in quick succession as responses to changing targets during the RT, without the delays usually observed in other tasks under similar conditions; that is, without a psychological refractory period (PRP). The PRP is a delay beyond the normal RT that is observed in the response to the second of two stimuli presented in quick succession. The occurrence of a PRP has been well documented (for a review see Bertelson 1966). The most widely accepted explanation is the single-channel theory, which postulates that there exists a gated channel of limited capacity that cannot handle the stimulus–response requirements of both stimuli simultaneously; therefore, the generation of responses to the two stimuli are treated sequentially and without overlap. When the second stimulus is presented during the RT to the first stimulus, the successive processing of information results in a delayed response to the second stimulus (i.e. in addition to its own RT); this additional delay equals approximately $RT_1 - ISI$ (where RT_1 is the RT to the first stimulus, and ISI is the interstimulus interval). Indeed, a PRP of the predicted magnitude has been observed in several studies (for a review see Bertelson 1966). It is remarkable, therefore, that a PRP is practically not observed when the required responses are reaching movements. This has been documented in behavioural experiments in monkeys (Georgopoulos et al. 1981) and human subjects (Soechting & Lacquaniti 1983, Massey et al. 1986), and in neurophysiological studies in the motor cortex of monkeys (Georgopoulos et al. 1983b).

These results probably reflect the highly efficient information processing of aimed movements due most probably to the high spatial stimulus–response compatibility and extensive practice, as discussed above. In fact, the information transmitted during the second of two reaching movements made in quick succession was much more than that of a single reaching movement (Massey et al. 1986), as evidenced by its shorter duration in spite of its larger amplitude and constant accuracy.

5.10 EFFECTS OF BRAIN LESIONS

Reaching to targets is affected by general motor disorders that affect the initiation, performance or braking of the movement. These disorders include, for example, paralysis or paresis, akinesia, hypotonia and ataxia. In some cases it is difficult to distinguish between such a fundamental disorder and a particular defect in reaching. In contrast, the accuracy of reaching can be affected in the presence of normal motor function. This is mostly observed with lesions of the posterior parietal areas of the cerebral cortex. Defects in reaching have been observed in both human subjects and subhuman primates. For example, lesions of the posterior parietal cortex of monkeys result in defective reaching to visual targets in space (Ettlinger & Kalsbeck 1962, LaMotte & Acuna 1975).

The most interesting cases are furnished by patients suffering from "optic ataxia" (Hécaen & de Ajuriaguerra 1954, Rondot et al. 1977,

Perenin & Vighetto 1993). These patients usually do not have impaired vision or impaired hand or arm movements, but show a severe impairment in visually guided reaching in the absence of perceptual disturbance in estimating distance. In several cases an oculomotor disorder may be present, but in others eye movements are normal. Misreaching cannot be accounted for by motor disability of the limb or a visual defect. Thus, other movements are performed well, and visual functions in the field where misreaching occurs are carried out normally, despite the occasional presence of amblyopia.

The syndrome of optic ataxia is complex, and several variants of it exist. The brain damage in cases of optical ataxia has been localized in the parietal cortex (angular and/or supramarginal gyrus), its underlying white matter and/or the posterior part of the corpus callosum. Although some of the defects in eye–hand co-ordination in that syndrome can be attributed to the destruction of the parietal cortex itself, others are best understood as disconnection syndromes produced by the interruption of pathways linking the posterior parietal and prestriate cortex to the precentral premotor and motor areas on the same (ipsilateral) and the contralateral side (Ferro et al. 1983). For example, suppose that the pathway connecting the right parietal cortex with the right frontal cortex is interrupted, then: (a) the visual control of the left hand (i.e. contralateral to the side of the lesion) will be affected, since the corticospinal pathway from the precentral motor areas is crossed; and (b) the eye–hand co-ordination will be affected in the left hemifield, because the parietal cortex controls spatial operations in the contralateral hemifield; a patient with such defects has been described (Castaigne et al. 1975). Suppose now that, in addition to a lesion of the right parietal cortex, the crossed pathway connecting the right parietal with the left frontal cortex has also been interrupted; then, the visual control of both hands will be impaired when operating in the left homonymous half-fields; such a case has indeed been described (Castaigne et al. 1971). Cases with various combinations of lesions corresponding to a rich variety of defects in eye–hand co-ordination have also been described (Ferro et al. 1983).

5.11 NEURAL STUDIES OF REACHING

Several brain areas are involved in the initiation and control of reaching. The study of the role of the various areas in this function was made possible by the advent of a technique that allowed the recording of the activity of single cells in the brain of behaving animals during reaching. This technique (Lemon 1984) is indispensable for the study of neural mechanisms underlying motor aspects of behaviour. Typically, monkeys are trained to perform various motor tasks and then microelectrodes are inserted through the dura into the brain area of interest to record extracellularly the electrically isolated action potentials of single cells. This combined behavioural–neurophysiological experiment provides a direct and sensitive tool with which the brain mechanisms underlying performance can be studied. An important finding from such studies has been that several brain areas are involved in reaching, including areas of the cerebral cortex and various subcortical structures. The first cortical area investigated was the posterior parietal cortex (Hyvärinen & Poramen 1974, Mountcastle et al. 1975). It was found that cells in Brodmann's areas 5 and 7 changed activity with reaching in the absence of driving from the somatic periphery. Although the changes in cell activity associated with reaching could be observed in the absence of visual guidance (Hyvärinen & Poramen 1974, Mountcastle et al. 1980), cell activity was usually modulated more strongly when the animal reached with the eyes open. Indeed, a particular class of cells could qualify for an "eye–hand co-ordination" function because the changes in their activity was most intense when the monkey tracked a moving visual target with both the eyes and the hand (Mountcastle et al. 1975).

Porter and Lewis (1975) studied the changes in activity of motor cortical cells while monkeys reached out and manipulated a handle in front of them. It was found that single cells changed their activity during the task and that the latency of activation of different cells shifted to later times as more distal parts of the limb became involved in the motor act. This question of the sequential activation of motor cortical populations in reaching and grasping was investigated in more detail by Murphy et al. (1985). The activity of single cells in the forelimb area of the motor cortex was recorded in a task in which monkeys pointed to targets in front of them. The functional relation between the recording locus and the joint of the arm was determined by intracortical microstimulation. Thus a cell could be classified as relating mainly to movements at the shoulder, elbow, hand or fingers. It was found that in the pointing task cells were generally activated sequentially, from proximal to distal, reflecting the sequential engagement of successively more distal parts of the arm.

Murphy et al. (1982) also investigated the possible relations between motor cortical cell activity and joint motion and EMG activity in muscles of the forelimb during reaching. There were three main findings of this study. First, no simple relation was observed between single cell activity and the EMG, even when the muscle from which the EMG was recorded was activated by intracortical microstimulation. Secondly, single cells related to motion about the shoulder or elbow joints behaved similarly in the task, although the motions produced about these joints could be quite different. Thirdly, the discharge of shoulder-related cells seemed to vary systematically with the movement trajectory. These results indicate that the relations between single-cell activity in the motor cortex and components (joint rotation, EMG activity) of reaching are complex.

5.11.1 Directional tuning of motor cortical cells

Reaching movements possess two spatial components, namely direction and amplitude. The activity of single cells is directionally tuned, in that cell activity is highest for a given direction ("preferred direction") of movement (for reviews see Georgopoulos 1990, Georgopoulos et al. 1993) or isometric force (Georgopoulos et al. 1992) and decreases gradually with directions farther and farther away from the preferred one (Fig. 5.1). Typically, the frequency of discharge is a linear function of the direction cosines of the movement vector (relative to its origin), or, equivalently, of the cosine of the angle formed between the direction of a particular movement and the cell's preferred direction (Fig. 5.1). These relations have been documented for planar pointing movements (Georgopoulos et al. 1982, Kalaska et al. 1989, Fu et al. 1993), for free pointing movements in three-dimensional space (Schwartz et al. 1988, Caminiti et al. 1990), for continuous planar movements (Schwartz 1993), and for isometric force pulses (Georgopoulos et al. 1992). Changes in cell activity relate the direction, and not to the end-point of the movement (Georgopoulos et al. 1985). Directional tuning is observed for cells with different types of resting firing pattern, including cells with low-rate, regular spike trains, cells with bursting patterns, and cells with high frequency of discharge (Taira & Georgopoulos 1993). Preferred directions differ for different cells and are uniformly distributed in three-dimensional space (Fig. 5.2, reproduced on p. 151) (Schwartz et al. 1988, Caminiti et al. 1990). They are multiply represented on the cortical surface and tend to cluster in columns (Georgopoulos et al. 1984). The preferred direction is very similar for movements of different amplitudes (Fu et al. 1993), although it can change when the origin of the movement changes (Caminiti et al. 1990). Finally, cell activity during the reaction time relates predominantly to the direction of the upcoming movement. In contrast, relations to movement amplitude are more prominent during the movement time (Fu et al. 1995).

5.11.2 Direction of reaching and neuronal populations: the neuronal population vector

The broad directional tuning indicates that a given cell participates in movements of various directions, and that a movement in a particular

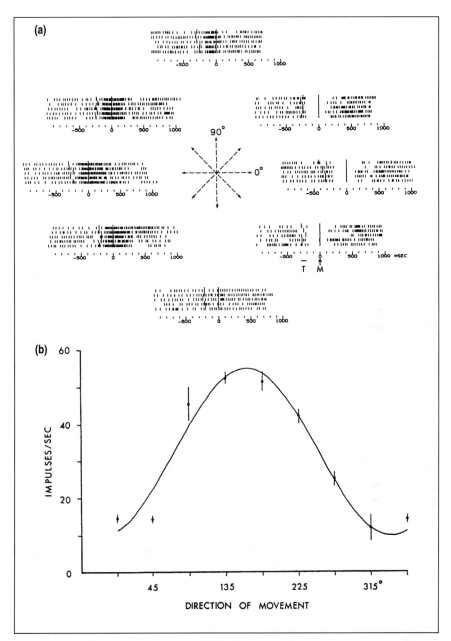

FIG. 5.1. Directional tuning. (a) impulse activity during five trials in which equal-amplitude movements were made in eight directions from the centre of the working surface towards peripheral targets, as indicated by the diagram in the centre. The rasters are aligned to the onset of movement M. Longer vertical bars preceding movement onset denote the time of stimulus onset (target) onset T. (b) Plot of the average frequency of discharge during the time interval from the onset of the target to the end of the movement against the direction of the movement. Points are means of five trials ±SEM; the curve is a fitted sinusoidal function. From Georgopoulos et al. (1982). Reproduced with permission of the publisher. Copyright by the Society for Neuroscience.

direction will involve the activation of a whole population of cells. Given that single cells are directionally tuned, we proposed a vectorial neural code for the direction of reaching by the neuronal ensemble (Georgopoulos et al. 1983a, 1986, 1988): (a) a particular vector represents the contribution of a directionally tuned cell and points in the cell's preferred direction; (b) cell vectors are weighted by the change in cell activity during a particular movement; and (c) the sum of these vectors (i.e. the population vector) provides the unique outcome of the ensemble coding operation. The population vector points in the direction of the movement (Fig. 5.3, reproduced on p. 151) (Georgopoulos et al. 1983a, 1986, 1988). The population vector approach has proved useful not only in studies of the motor cortex but also in studies of other motor areas (for a review see Georgopoulos et al. 1993). Moreover, it can be generalized to other, non-motor problems, such as the coding of faces in the inferotemporal cortex (Young & Yamane 1992). The following are some general properties of the neuronal population vector.

5.11.2.1 The neuronal population vector predicts the direction of reaching for movements of different origin

In these experiments monkeys made movements that started from different points, were in the same direction but described parallel trajectories in three-dimensional space. Under these conditions, the population vector in the motor cortex predicted well the direction of the reaching movement (Kettner et al. 1988, Caminiti et al. 1991).

5.11.2.2 The direction of reaching is predicted well by neuronal population vectors in different cortical layers

The average absolute angle between the population vector calculated from cells in the upper layers (II and III) and the direction of movement was $4.31° \pm 2.98°$ (mean $\pm$ SD, $N = 8$ movement directions), compared with $2.32° \pm 2.06°$ for the lower layers (V and VI) (Georgopoulos 1990). This finding suggests that the ensemble operation of the population vector can be realized separately in the upper and lower layers. This is important because that information can then be distributed to different structures according to the differential projections from the upper and lower layers (Jones & Wise 1977).

5.11.2.3 The neuronal population coding of the direction of reaching is resistant to loss of cells

The population coding described above is a distributed code and, as such, does not depend exclusively on any particular cell. This robustness was evaluated by calculating the population vector from progressively smaller samples of cells randomly selected from the original population (Georgopoulos et al. 1988); it was found that the direction of the population vector can be reliably estimated from as few as 100–150 cells. In fact, recent work has shown that the population vector can be optimally calculated from a much smaller number of cells (Salinas & Abbott 1994).

5.11.2.4 The neuronal population vector predicts the direction of isometric force

This finding (Georgopoulos et al. 1992) established the fact that the coding of directional information applies to the motor output in general, even in the absence of joint motion. Moreover, it showed that the direction specified by the motor cortex is not that of the total force exerted by the subject but that of the dynamic component of the force, that is the component of the force remaining after a constant, static force is subtracted.

5.11.2.5 The neuronal population vector transmits directional information comparable with that transmitted by the direction of movement

In the usual studies in two-dimensional space, monkeys (Georgopoulos et al. 1982) and human subjects (Georgopoulos & Massey 1988) moved a manipulandum from the centre of a planar working surface to a target on a circle. In this case, the direction of the target is the ideal direction: if the subject's movements were straight lines from the centre to the target, the subject's performance would be perfect, and we could say that the movement transmitted the maximum possible information. However, movements rarely end dead on target, and therefore, the infor-mation transmitted is rarely maximal: the more the dispersion of the movement endpoint around the target, the less the information transmitted. Now, this dispersion can be split into errors in the amplitude of movement and errors in the direction of movement; accordingly, the information transmitted by the amplitude and the direction of movement can be studied separately. As we were interested in the control of the direction of movement, we asked subjects to "move in the direction of the target" without imposing restrictions on the amplitude or the end-point of the movement: this provided a purely directional task (Georgopoulos & Massey 1988). The calculation of the information transmitted by the direction of movement involves the construction of a "performance matrix" in which the ideal and actual directions are tabulated, and from which the information transmitted can be computed (Georgopoulos & Massey 1988). Essentially the same technique can be used to calculate the information transmitted by the direction of the population vector. Since the population vector is the vectorial sum of weighted contributions of individual cells, and since these weights can vary from trial to trial due to intertrial variability in neuronal discharge, then the direction of the population vector can vary somewhat from trial to trial. This variation in the direction of the population vector can be treated in exactly the same way as the direction of movement, and the information transmitted calculated. Indeed, we calculated the information transmitted by the direction of movement and the direction of the population vector (Georgopoulos & Massey 1988) and found the following. First, the information transmitted by both these measures increases with input information but more slowly than the maximum possible, and it tends to saturate at high levels of input information. This loss of information is probably due to noise generated during the initial (perceptual) and successive (perceptual–motor) processing stages. Secondly, the information transmitted by the population vector was consistently higher than that transmitted by the movement by approximately 0.5 bit. This means that an additional loss of information is incurred between the motor cortex and the movement. However, this loss differs from the previous one, as it does not increase with increasing stimulus information but remains constant at about 0.5 bits at all levels of input information. This loss could occur during processing in other motor structures or at the stage of biomechanical implementation of the movement.

5.11.3 Time-varying properties of the neuronal population vector

5.11.3.1 The neuronal population vector predicts the movement trajectory in continuous, tracing movements

In this experiment (Schwartz 1993, 1994) monkeys were trained to trace smoothly with their index finger sinusoids displayed on a screen, from one end to the other. The direction of the population vectors, calculated successively in time along the trajectory, changed throughout the sinusoidal movement, closely matching the smoothly changing direction of the finger path. Moreover, a neural "image" of the sinusoidal trajectory of the movement was obtained by connecting successive population vectors tip-to-tail. This finding suggests that the length of the population vector carries information concerning the instantaneous velocity of the movement.

5.11.3.2 The neuronal population vector predicts the direction of reaching during the reaction time

This is the simplest case of predicting the direction of an upcoming movement. Given that the changes in cell activity in the motor cortex precede the onset of movement by approximately 160–180 ms, on average (Georgopoulos et al. 1982), it is an important finding that the population vector predicts the direction of the upcoming movement during

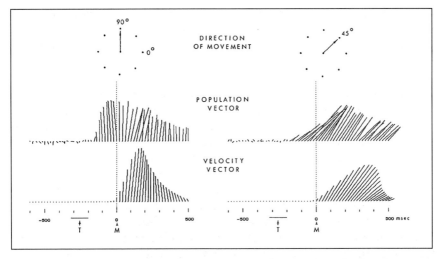

FIG. 5.4.   Time-varying population vector. The population vector points in the direction of movement well before the movement begins. The results for two movement directions in two-dimensional space are illustrated (top); the population vector was calculated every 20 ms (middle); the average instantaneous (20 ms bin) velocity of the movement is also shown (bottom). Before the target onset T, the population vector is very small in length and its direction varies from moment to moment. Well before the onset of movement M, it increases in length and its direction points in the direction of the upcoming movement. This finding suggests that even the earliest inputs to the motor cortex are relevant in the direction of the upcoming movement. From Georgopoulos et al. (1984). Reproduced with permission of the publisher.

that period during which the movement is being planned (Georgopoulos et al. 1984, 1988) (Fig. 5.4).

5.11.3.3 The neuronal population vector predicts the direction of reaching during an instructed delay period

In these experiments the monkeys were trained to withhold the movement for a period of time after the onset of a visual cue signal and to move later in response to a *go* signal. During this instructed delay period the population vector in the motor cortex computed every 20 ms gave a reliable signal concerning the direction of the movement that was triggered later for execution (Georgopoulos et al. 1989a).

5.12 NEURAL MECHANISMS OF COGNITIVE PROCESSING: NEURONAL POPULATIONS AS KEYS FOR UNDERSTANDING

The results summarized above underscore the operational usefulness of the neuronal population vector for monitoring in time the directional tendency of the neuronal ensemble. We took advantage of this property and used the population vector as a probe to decipher the neural processing of directional information during two cognitive operations, one involving memory holding and the other mental rotation.

5.12.1 Memory holding

In these experiments (Smyrnis et al. 1992), two rhesus monkeys were trained to move a handle on a two-dimensional work surface in directions specified by a light on the plane. They first captured with the handle a light on the centre of the plane and then moved the handle in the direction indicated by a peripheral light (*cue* signal). The signal to move (*go* signal) was given by turning off the centre light. The following tasks were used. In the *non-delay task* the peripheral light was turned on at the same time as the centre light went off. In the *memorized delay task* the peripheral light stayed on for 300 ms (cue period) and the centre light was turned off 450–750 ms later (delay period). Finally, in the *non-memorized delay task* the peripheral light stayed on continuously, whereas the centre light went off 750–1050 ms after the peripheral light came on. Recordings in the arm area of the motor cortex showed changes in single-cell activity in all tasks. The population vector was calculated every 20 ms, following the onset of the peripheral light. There are two aspects of the information carried by the population vector. One concerns its direction, which can be interpreted as the directional information carried by the directional signal; the other aspect concerns the length of the population vector, which can be regarded as the strength of the directional signal carried. The direction of the population vector during the memorized delay period was close to the direction of the target (Fig. 5.5). The length of the population vector reflects the strength of the directional signal. It is interesting that the population vector length was similar in the cue period but was longer during the memorized versus the non-memorized part of the delay. This is shown in Figure 5.6, which illustrates the time-course of the length of the population vector in the two delay tasks. Three phases can be distinguished in this time-course. First, there is an initial increase of the vector length during the 300 ms of the delay period; this increase is similar for both tasks. Secondly, this increase subsides during the rest of the non-memorized delay period but continues at a somewhat higher level during the memorized delay period; the latter difference is indicated in Figure 5.6 by stippling. Finally, there is a steep increase in the population vector length following the *go* signal, at the end of the delay period. Thus the memorized task is distinguished from the non-memorized one by the higher population signal during that part of the delay period during which the instructed direction had to be kept in memory.

FIG. 5.2.   Preferred directions (unit vectors) of 475 motor cortical cells in three-dimensional space. From Schwartz et al. (1988). Reproduced with permission of the publisher. Copyright by the Society for Neuroscience.

FIG. 5.3.   Population coding of movement direction. The *blue lines* represent the vectorial contributions of individual cells in the population (N = 475). The movement direction is in *yellow* and the direction of the population vector in *red*. From Georgopoulos et al. (1988). Reproduced with permission of the publisher. Copyright by the Society for Neuroscience.

From Chapter 6, Studying brain function with neuroimaging (Frith & Friston), pp. 169–96

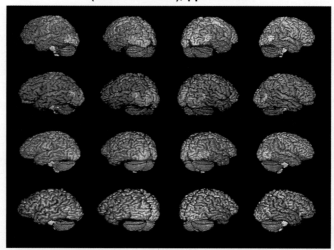

FIG. 6.2. The location of the brain activity associated with the passive viewing of visual motion: human V5. Reproduced from Watson et al. (1993).

From Chapter 8, The architecture of working memory (Jonides & Smith), pp. 243–76

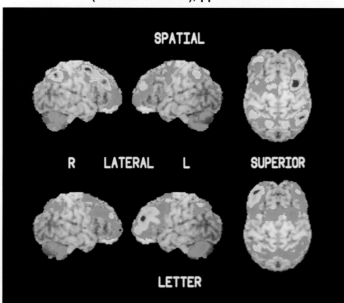

FIG. 8.4. Six PET images from the three-back experiment described in the text. Each row contains right and left lateral views as well as a superior view of a reconstructed brain (from a structural magnetic resonance image) on which have been superimposed PET activations that are shown in colour code. Red and bright yellow areas indicate the highest levels of brain activation. The top row presents images that resulted from subtracting the spatial control from the spatial memory condition; the bottom row presents the images for the verbal memory minus the verbal control conditions.

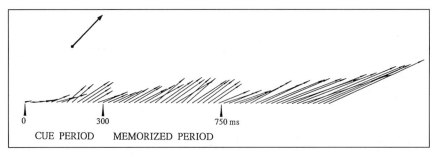

FIG. 5.5. Memorized population vector: direction. Population vectors in the memorized delay task for the direction indicated are plotted every 20 ms. The arrow on top indicates the direction of the *cue* signal present during the first 300 ms of the delay period. From Smyrnis et al. (1992).

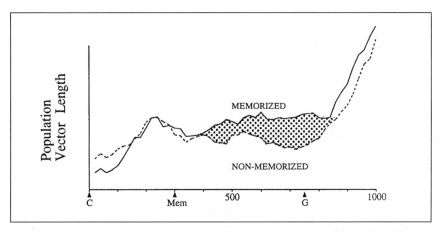

FIG. 5.6. Memorized population vector: length. The length of the mean resultant of the population vector is plotted against time for the two delay tasks. G, Minimum time of onset of the *go* signal. From Smyrnis et al. (1992).

The directional information carried by the population vector in the memorized task identifies the memorized information in a direct fashion. Moreover, this analysis provided an insight concerning the time-course of encoding and holding directional information. For that purpose we used the length of the population vector, which can be regarded as reflecting the strength of the directional signal in the neuronal ensemble. The population vector length showed an initial increase which started approximately 100 ms following the cue onset and peaked at 250 ms. This increase was very similar in both the memorized and the non-memorized delay tasks (Fig. 5.6). This initial peak can be interpreted as reflecting an encoding process. A second phase followed which differed in the memorized and the non-memorized tasks in that a higher, sustained signal was present during the memorized delay period but not during the non-memorized delay (stippled area in Fig. 5.6). This could reflect a holding-in-memory process. Following the onset of the *go* signal, the population vector length increased similarly in all tasks used. These findings are interesting because the increase in the signal during the memorized delay period was observed in the absence of the target; however, one would have expected that the signal would be stronger in the presence rather than in the absence of the visual stimulus. This finding strengthens our interpretation of this increase as a memory signal, in contrast to a sensory one and raises the more general possibility that the motor cortex may be particularly involved when only part of the visual information about an upcoming movement is provided.

5.12.2 Memorized trajectories of complex movements

The studies summarized above dealt with motor cortical activity during tasks requiring memorization of simple pointing movements. A different question concerns the neural mechanisms subserving memorized, complex movement trajectories. This problem was investigated in a recent study (Ashe et al. 1993) in which two monkeys were trained to perform from memory an arm movement with an orthogonal bend, first up and then to the left, following a waiting period. They held a two-dimensional manipulandum over a spot of light at the centre of a planar work surface. When the light went off, the animals were required to hold the manipulandum there for 600–700 ms and then move the handle up and to the left to receive a liquid reward. There were no external signals concerning the go time or the trajectory of the movement. Following 20 trials of the memorized movement trajectory, 40 trials of visually triggered movements in radially arranged directions were performed. The activity of 137 single cells in the motor cortex was recorded extracellularly during performance of the task. A good percentage (62.8%) of cells changed activity during the waiting period. Other cells did not change activity until after the 600 ms minimum waiting time was over, and, occasionally, cell activity changed almost exactly at 600 ms after the centre light was turned off. However, the most interesting observation was that a few cells changed activity exclusively during the execution of the memorized movement (see Ashe et al. 1993: Fig. 5); these cells were completely inactive during performance of similar movements in the visually guided control task. These findings suggest that performance of a movement trajectory from memory may involve a specific set of cells, in addition to the cells activated during both visually guided and memorized movements. This idea is in accord with the results of modelling studies summarized below.

5.12.3 Mental rotation

The second cognitive process we chose for study involved a transformation of an intended movement direction. In these studies we first carried out psychological experiments in human subjects. Then we trained monkeys to perform the same task and recorded the activity of single cells in the brain of these animals during performance of the task. Finally, we tried to connect the neural results with those of the human studies and interpret the latter on the basis of the former: the objective is to get as close as possible in relating neurophysiology and cognitive psychology. I describe below these steps as they were applied to a particular problem of a mental transformation of movement direction.

The task required subjects to move a handle at an angle from a reference direction defined by a visual stimulus on a plane. Since the reference direction changed from trial to trial, the task required that in a given trial the direction of movement be specified according to this reference direction. In the psychological studies (Georgopoulos & Massey 1987) human subjects performed blocks of 20 trials in which the angle by which the subjects had to move away from the stimulus direction and its departure (counterclockwise or clockwise) were fixed, although the reference direction varied. Seven angles (5–140°) were used. The basic finding was that the time to initiate a movement (reaction time) increased in a linear fashion with the angle. The most parsimonious hypothesis to explain these results is that subjects arrive at the correct direction of movement by shifting their motor intention from the reference direction to the movement direction, travelling through the intermediate angular space. This idea is very similar to the mental rotation hypothesis of Shepard & Cooper (1982) to explain the monotonic increase of the reaction time with orientation angle when a judgement has to be made whether a visual image is a normal or mirror image: in both cases a mental rotation is postulated. In fact, the mean rates of rotation and their range among subjects were very similar in the perceptual (Shepard & Cooper 1982) and motor (Georgopoulos & Massey 1987) studies. Moreover, when the same subjects performed both perceptual and motor rotation tasks, their processing rates were positively correlated (Pellizzer & Georgopoulos 1993), which indicates similar processing constraints for both tasks.

In the *neurophysiological studies* (Georgopoulos et al. 1989b, Lurito et al. 1991), two rhesus monkeys were trained to move the handle 90° and counterclockwise from the reference direction; these trials were intermixed with others in which the animals moved in the direction of

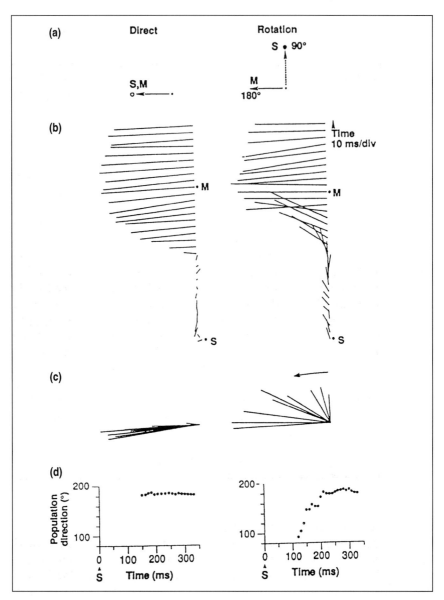

FIG. 5.7.   Mental rotation of the population vector. Time evolution of the neuronal population vector when the movement was in the direction of a stimulus or 90° counterclockwise from it. (a) Task: (o) dim and (●) bright light; (....) stimulus S and (—) movement M direction. (b) Neuronal population vectors calculated every 10 ms from the onset of the stimulus S at positions shown in (a) until after the onset of the movement M. When the population vector lengthens, for the direct case (left) it points in the direction of the movement, whereas for the rotation case it points initially in the direction of the stimulus and then rotates counterclockwise (from 12 o'clock to 9 o'clock) and points in the direction of the movement. (c) Ten successive population vectors from (b) are shown in a spatial plot, starting from the first population vector that increased significantly in length. Note the counterclockwise rotation of the population vector (right). (d) Scatter plots of the direction of the population vector as a function of time, starting from the first population vector that increased significantly in length after stimulus onset S. For the direct case (left), the direction of the population vector is in the direction of the movement (≈180°); for the rotation case (right) the direction of the population vector rotates counterclockwise from the direction of the stimulus (≈90°) to the direction of the movement (≈180°). From Georgopoulos et al. (1989b). Reproduced with permission by the publisher. Copyright AAAS.

the target. When the time-varying neuronal population vector was calculated during the reaction time, it was found that it rotated from the stimulus (reference) to the movement direction through the counterclockwise angle, when the animal had to move away from the stimulus, or in the direction of the stimulus, when the animal had to move towards it. This is illustrated in Figure 5.7. It is remarkable that the population vector rotated at all, and also that it rotated through the smaller, 90° counterclockwise angle. These results showed clearly that the cognitive process in this task truly involves a rotation of an analogue signal. The occurrence of a true rotation was further documented by showing that there was a transient increase during the middle of the reaction time in the recruitment of cells with preferred directions in between the stimulus and movement directions: this indicated that the rotation of the population vector was not the result of varying activation of just two cell groups, one with preferred directions centred on the stimulus and another in the movement direction. Therefore, this rotation process, "sweeping" through the directionally tuned ensemble, provided for the first time a direct visualization of a dynamic cognitive process. In this respect, it is noteworthy that the population vector is, in essence, a measure that can take continuous values in direction.

In summary, the results of these studies provide the neural correlates of a dynamic cognitive representation (Freyd 1987). The essential contribution of this work is in the neural identification and visualization of the time-varying, dynamic representation of direction in the motor cortex when a transformation of this direction is required and achieved. Interestingly, the mean rotation rate and the range of rates observed for different reference directions were very similar to those obtained in the human studies.

5.12.4 Context-recall memory scanning

The neural correlates of visuomotor memory scanning were investigated recently (Pellizzer et al. 1995). A monkey was trained to exert a force pulse on a two-dimensional semi-isometric manipulandum in eight different directions. The force exerted was displayed as a feedback cursor. The memory task can be divided into three parts: (a) a sequential presentation of three or four yellow stimuli, which stayed on the screen; (b) one of the stimuli, except the last one, changed from yellow to blue which identified it as the test stimulus, and gave the *go* signal; (c) the correct response was to the stimulus that succeeded the test stimulus during the initial presentation. This task required the memorization of the order of presentation of the stimuli, but not of their position in space which was still available. In a control task, one stimulus was presented and the response was made after the go signal. The activity of 544 cells in the motor cortex was recorded during perform-ance of the two tasks. The salient finding of the study was that cell activity usually reflected first the direction of the test stimulus, then switched to reflect the direction of the response, when the test stimulus was the second in the sequence. This was true both for the case of single cells, which showed abrupt changes in activity reflecting the two differ-ent directions, as well as for the population vector, which also showed an abrupt shift from the direction of the test stimulus to that of the motor response. Another finding was that the time for which neural activity reflected the direction of the test stimulus, and, correspond-ingly, for which the population vector stayed in that direction, was ap-proximately 100–150 ms. These results indicate that the neural process that underlies memory scanning is quite different from that which un-derlies mental rotation: whereas the latter involves an apparently con-tinuous change of direction of the population vector, the memory scan-ning seems to involve abrupt shifts of the population vector from one direction to another. Accordingly, the neural events in the mental rota-tion task reflect a *transformation* of movement direction, whereas those in the context-recall task reflect a *selection* of a direction from a list.

5.13 NEURAL NETWORK MODELLING OF MOTOR CORTICAL DIRECTIONAL OPERATIONS

The time-varying directional operations summarized above have been modelled using a massively interconnected artificial neural network that consists of directionally tuned neurons and produces as an out-come the neuronal population vector (Georgopoulos et al. 1993, Lukashin & Georgopoulos 1993, 1994a,b). This network has repro-duced well many of the experimental findings and has led recently to a novel hypothesis on how memorized movement trajectories could be stored in the synaptic connections of overlapping neural networks (Lukashin et al. 1994). The idea is that there is a general-purpose net-work that is involved in all kinds of movements, memorized or not, but which carries no information about memorized trajectories of specific shapes (e.g. circles, ellipses, scribbles) and which, if activated alone, would produce straight-line trajectories. It is now hypothesized that there are also networks highly specific for a particular trajectory (e.g. clockwise circle) which are interconnected with the general-purpose network: when a specific trajectory needs to be performed, the appro-priate specific network fuses with the general-purpose network and, as one network now, produces the desired trajectory. It is remarkable that the size of the specific network need only be less than 5% of the size of

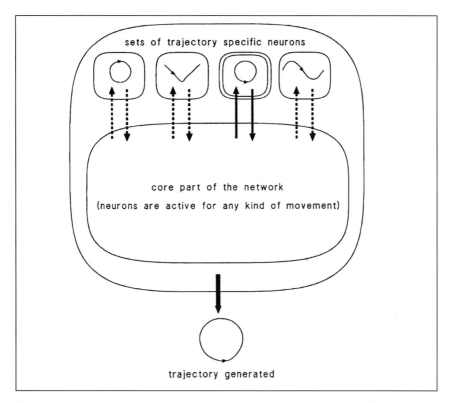

FIG. 5.8.   Overlapping neural networks. The neural network for generating four different types of neural-vector trajectories. All units in the core part are interconnected with each other and with all units in the trajectory-specific sets. All units in each trajectory-specific set are interconnected with one another and with all units in the core part. There are no connections between different trajectory-specific sets. Heavy arrows (solid and dashed) indicate that this is a feedback network, and that the connections between the core part and the trajectory-specific parts are adjusted during the training of the network to generate different types of trajectory. The double ovoid indicates that this particular set is currently activated, and connections between the core part and this set (solid arrows) determine the shape of generated neural-vector trajectory. Single ovoids indicate that the other three trajectory-specific parts of the network are inhibited, and that the connections between the core part and these sets (dashed lines) do not interfere with the dynamics. From Lukashin et al. (1994).

the general-purpose network for the desired trajectory to be effectively stored and reproduced (Lukashin et al. 1994). This idea is illustrated in Figure 5.8. It is noteworthy that such very specific cells have been observed at low proportions in neurophysiological recordings during performance of memorized trajectories (Ashe et al. 1993).

   The idea of the existence of very specialized networks raises the question of the degree of specialization and of how such networks are created in the first place. We can only speculate on these issues. With respect to the general-purpose network, it is reasonable to assume that it is present at birth, since it is assumed to subserve all movements. There are several possibilities concerning the specialized networks. One possibility is that a number of small networks, specific for basic shapes (e.g. straight lines, curves, and some combinations thereof—"motor shape primitives"), are present at birth. Then, motor learning for other, complex motor acts would consist of adjusting the strength of the connections between the general-purpose and specific networks. This idea implies that all the specialized primitives are used routinely, although not as frequently as the general-purpose network. Another idea is that innate specific networks code for more complicated shapes and are large in number. The mechanism of motor learning would then be similar to that described above, but in this case only a small number of the specialized networks would be used. This means that a number of the complex, specialized networks may never be used. This situation would be similar to that encountered in the immune system in which there is a large potential for making a large number of antibodies, of which, however, only some may actually be made, depending on the exposure of the organism to specific antigens. In both cases there is a selection (selection of a specialized trajectory or selection of an antibody) from the large ensemble available. Finally, an intermediate hypothesis would be that we start with motor shape primitives but that the more complex trajectories resulting from the combination of these primitives to the general network become themselves very specialized and behave as such in the formation of other trajectories in novel associations.

5.14 SPINAL CORD AND REACHING

Reaching involves motion at the shoulder and elbow joints. Behaviourally, there is little doubt that these two joints are controlled as one functional unit (Soechting & Lacquaniti 1981). Descending motor commands from the motor cortex and other brain areas influence the proximal arm motoneurons, i.e. those innervating muscles acting on the elbow and/or shoulder, through a set of interneurons located at the C3–C4 spinal segments, that is above the segments of the proximal motor nuclei. These interneurons ("C3–C4 propriospinal neurons", Lundberg 1979) have been studied extensively in the cat. They receive monosynaptic inputs from several supraspinal sources, including the pyramidal (i.e. corticospinal), rubrospinal, reticulospinal and tectospinal tracts, and they distribute their axons to several proximal motoneuronal pools. Selective section of the output from these propriospinal neurons to their target motoneurons results in abnormal reaching with normal grasping, and similar effects are observed when the corticospinal input to the propriospinal neurons is removed (Alstermark et al. 1981). These results indicate that the C3–C4 propriospinal system is concerned with the neural integration of the reaching movement at the spinal level and that the motor cortex and other areas control reaching, most probably through that system. This motor cortical control is also exerted at other levels within the propriospinal system; for example, there is direct corticospinal input on a key inhibitory interneuron which mediates inhibition from afferent fibres to propriospinal neurons (Alstermark et al. 1984). This peripherally initiated inhibition of the propriospinal neurons is important in limiting the reaching movement, because lack of peripheral input results in consistent hypermetria in reaching (Alstermark et al. 1986).

The results summarized above indicate that a large part of neural integration of the reaching movement is accomplished in the spinal cord. In a way, this is qualitatively similar to the sophisticated integration observed in spinal circuits underlying locomotion (Grillner 1981): both cases involve the production of complicated motor outputs, complicated in the sense of involving the time-varying control of several muscles and of more than one joint. It is possible, and even probable, that the detailed organization and the neural integration of the reaching movement need not be the concern, or the burden, of the motor cortex or other motor areas. These various areas could be concerned, instead, with the initiation and ongoing control of reaching according to internally generated goals, as, for example, in drawing, or according to information from exteroceptors, as, for example, in reaching towards a visual or an auditory object. These functions would then be accomplished by the activation of neuronal populations in different brain areas, including the motor cortex, which, in turn, would engage the spinal "reaching" circuits (Georgopoulos 1988).

5.15 CONCLUDING COMMENTS

Voluntary movement is still an evolving "hot" topic in behavioural, neural and modelling research. The problems involved are very challenging and not easily amenable to simple solutions. Although simplistic solutions are abundant, true advancements are hard to come by. A major question is, how do such diverse brain structures as the cerebral cortex, basal ganglia and cerebellum co-operate to produce grafecul, accurate and seemingly effortless reaching movements? The neuronal population vector analysis is a first step in "breaking" the code by which individual brain areas process directional information. The fact that this code applies to several areas involved in motor control suggests that the interactions among areas could be expressed within a common, population–vectorial framework. In addition, the fact that the time-varying population vector can provide crucial information on how directional information is being processed in different tasks, opens up the possibility that the dynamic interplay of the areas involved could also be expressed and elucidated within this population–vectorial framework. For this purpose, simultaneous recordings from various areas will be needed, a technically difficult but not insurmountable task. Modern functional brain-imaging techniques (e.g. functional magnetic resonance imaging) could provide useful guidance as to which areas are involved in a task, and, therefore, which areas to record from simultaneously. This combination of approaches should lead to an efficient and effective approach to understanding the real-time, dynamic co-operation of diverse brain areas in planning, initiating and controlling voluntary movements.

ACKNOWLEDGEMENTS

This work was supported by United States Public Health Service grant NS17413, the United States Department of Veterans Affairs and the American Legion and University of Minnesota Brain Sciences Chair.

REFERENCES

Alstermark, B., A. Lundberg, U. Norrsell, E. Sybirska 1981. Integration in descending motor pathways controlling the forelimb in the cat. 9. Differential behavioural defects after spinal cord lesions interrupting defined pathways from higher centres to motoneurons. *Experimental Brain Research* **42**, 290–318.

Alstermark, B., A. Lundberg, S. Sasaki 1984. Integration in descending motor pathways controlling the forelimb in the cat.10. Inhibitory pathways to motoneurons via C3–C4 propriospinal neurons. *Experimental Brain Research* **56**, 279–92.

Alstermark, B., T. Gorska, T. Johannisson, A. Lundberg 1986. Hypermetria in forelimb target-reaching after interruption of the inhibitory pathway from forelimb afferents to C3–C4 propriospinal neurons. *Neuroscience Research* **3**, 457–61.

Ashe, J., M. Taira, N. Smyrnis, G. Pellizzer, T. Georgakopoulos, J. T. Lurito, A. P. Georgopoulos 1993. Motor cortical activity preceding a memorized movement trajectory with an orthogonal bend. *Experimental Brain Research* **95**, 118–30.

Atkeson, C. G. & J. M. Hollerbach 1985. Kinematic features of unrestrained vertical arm movements. *Journal of Neuroscience* **5**, 2318–30.

Beaubaton, D., A. Grangetto, J. Paillard 1978. Contribution of positional and movement cues to visuo-motor reaching in split-brain monkey. In *Structure and function of cerebral commissures*, vol. I, I. Russell, M. W. van Hoff, G. Berlucci (eds), 371–84. Baltimore, MD: University Park.

Beggs, W. D. A. & C. I. Howarth 1972. The movement of the hand towards a target. *Journal of Experimental Psychology* **24**, 448–53

Bernstein, N. A. 1967. *The coordination and regulation of movements*. New York: Pergamon.

Bertelson, P. 1966. Central intermittency twenty years later. *Quarterly Journal of Experimental Psychology* **18**, 153–63.

Biguer, B., M. Jeannerod, C. Prablanc 1982. The coordination of eye, head, and arm movements during reaching at a single visual target. *Experimental Brain Research* **46**, 301–4.

Brainard, R. W., T. S. Irby, P. M. Fitts, E. A. Alluisi 1962. Some variables influencing the rate of gain of information. *Journal of Experimental Psychology* **63**, 105–10.

Caminiti, R., P. B. Johnson, Y. Burnod, C. Galli, S. Ferraina 1990. Shift of preferred directions of premotor cortical cells with arm movements performed across the workspace. *Experimental Brain Research* **83**, 228–32.

Caminiti, R., P. B. Johnson, C. Galli, S. Ferraina, Y. Burnod, A. Urbano 1991. Making arm movements within different parts of space: the premotor and motor cortical representation of a coordinate system for reaching at visual targets. *Journal of Neuroscience* **11**, 1182–97.

Castaigne, P., B. Pertuiset, P. Rondot, J. De Recondo 1971. Ataxie optique dans les deux hemichamps visuels homonymes gauches apres exerese chirurgicale d'un aneurysme arteriel de la paroi du ventricule lateral. *Revue Neurologique (Paris)* **124**, 261–8.

Castaigne. P., P. Rondot, J. L. R. Dumas, P. Tempier 1975. Ataxie optique localisee au cote gauche dans les deux hemichamps visuels homonymes gauches. *Revue Neurologique (Paris)* **131**, 23–8.

Conti, P. & D. Beaubaton 1976. Utilization des informations visuelles dans le controle du mouvement: etude de la precision des pointages chez l'homme. *Travail Humaine* **39**, 19–32.

Duncan, J. 1977. Response selection rules in spatial choice reaction tasks. In *Attention and performance*, vol. VI, S. Dornic (ed.), 49–61. Hillsdale, NJ: Lawrence Erlbaum Associates Inc.

Ettlinger, G. & J. E. Kalsbeck 1962. Changes in tactile discrimination and in visual reaching after successive and simultaneous bilateral posterior parietal ablations in the monkey. *Journal of Neurology, Neurosurgery and Psychiatry* **25**, 256–68.

Ferro, J. M., J. M. Bravo-Marques, A. Castro-Caldas, L. Antunes 1983. Crossed optic ataxia: possible role of the dorsal splenium. *Journal of Neurology, Neurosurgery and Psychiatry* **46**, 533–9.

Fitts, P. M. 1954. The information capacity of the human motor system in controlling the amplitude of movement. *Journal of Experimental Psychology* **47**, 381–91.

Fitts, P. M. & C. M. Seeger 1953. S–R compatibility: spatial characteristics of stimulus and response codes. *Journal of Experimental Psychology* **46**, 199–210.

Flowers, K. 1975. Ballistic and corrective movements on an aiming task. *Neurology* **25**, 413–21.

Freyd, J. J. 1987. Dynamic mental representation. *Psychological Review* **94**, 427–38.

Fu, Q.-G., J. L. Suarez, T. J. Ebner 1993. Neuronal specification of direction and distance during reaching movements in the superior precentral premotor area and primary motor cortex of monkeys. *Journal of Neurophysiology* **70**, 2097–116.

Fu, Q.-G., D. Flament, J. D. Coltz, T. J. Ebner 1995. Temporal coding of movement kinematics in the discharge of primary motor and premotor neurons. *Journal of Neurophysiology* **73**, 836–54.

Georgopoulos, A. P. 1986. On reaching. *Annual Review of Neuroscience* **9**, 147–70.

Georgopoulos, A. P. 1988. Neural integration of movement: role of motor cortex in reaching. *FASEB Journal* **2**, 2849–57.

Georgopoulos, A. P. 1990. Neurophysiology of reaching. In *Attention and performance* Vol. XIII, M. Jeannerod (ed.), 227–63. Hillsdale, NJ: Lawrence Erlbaum Associates Inc.

Georgopoulos, A. P. & J. T. Massey 1987. Cognitive spatial–motor processes. 1. The making of movements at various angles from a stimulus direction. *Experimental Brain Research* **65**, 361–70.

Georgopoulos, A. P. & J. T. Massey 1988. Cognitive spatial–motor processes. 2. Information transmitted by the direction of two-dimensional arm movements and by neuronal populations in primate motor cortex and area 5. *Experimental Brain Research* **69**, 315–26.

Georgopoulos, A. P., J. F. Kalaska, R. Caminiti, J. T. Massey 1982. On the relations between the direction of two-dimensional arm movements and cell discharge in primate motor cortex. *Journal of Neuroscience* **2**, 1527–37.

Georgopoulos, A. P., R. Caminiti, J. F. Kalaska, J. T. Massey 1983a. Spatial coding of movement: a hypothesis concerning the coding of movement direction by motor cortical populations. *Experimental Brain Research Supplement* **7**, 327–36.

Georgopoulos, A. P., J. F. Kalaska, R. Caminiti, J. T. Massey 1983b. Interruption of motor cortical discharge subserving aimed arm movements. *Experimental Brain Research* **49**, 327–40.

Georgopoulos, A. P., J. F. Kalaska, J. T. Massey 1981. Spatial trajectories and reaction times of aimed movements: effects of practice, uncertainty, and change in target location. *Journal of Neurophysiology* **46**, 725–43.

Georgopoulos, A. P., J. F. Kalaska, M. D. Crutcher, R. Caminiti, J. T. Massey 1984. The representation of movement direction in the motor cortex: Single cell and population studies. In *Dynamic aspects of neocortical function*, G. M. Edelman, W. M. Cowan, W. E. Gall (eds), 501–24. New York: Wiley.

Georgopoulos, A. P., J. F. Kalaska, R. Caminiti 1985. Relations between two-dimensional arm movements and single cell discharge in motor cortex and area. 5: Movement direction versus movement endpoint. *Experimental Brain Research Supplement* **10**, 176–83.

Georgopoulos, A. P., A. B. Schwartz, R. E. Kettner 1986. Neuronal population coding of movement direction. *Science* **233**, 1416–19.

Georgopoulos, A. P., R. E. Kettner, A. B. Schwartz 1988. Primate motor cortex and free arm movements to visual targets in three-dimensional space. II. Coding of the direction of movement by a neuronal population. *Journal of Neuroscience* **8**, 2928–37.

Georgopoulos, A. P., M. D. Crutcher, A. B. Schwartz 1989a. Cognitive spatial-motor processes. 3. motor cortical prediction of movement direction during an instructed delay period. *Experimental Brain Research* **75**, 183–94.

Georgopoulos,A. P., J. T. Lurito, M. Petrides,A. B. Schwartz, J. T. Massey 1989b. Mental rotation of the neuronal population vector. *Science* **243**, 234–6.

Georgopoulos, A. P., J. Ashe, N. Smyrnis, M. Taira 1992. Motor cortex and the coding of force. *Science* **256**, 1692–5.

Georgopoulos, A. P., M. Taira, A. V. Lukashin 1993. Cognitive neurophysiology of the motor cortex. *Science* **260**, 47–52.

Gordon, J, M. F. Ghiraldi, C. Ghez 1994. Accuracy of planar reaching movements. I. Independence of direction and extent variability. *Experimental Brain Research* **99**, 97–111.

Grillner, S. 1981. Control of locomotion in bipeds, tetrapods, and fish. In *Handbook of physiology – the nervous system,* vol. II, *Motor control*, V. B. Brooks (ed.), 1179–236. Bethesda, MD: American Physiological Society.

Hécaen, H. & J. De Ajuriaguerra 1954. Balint's syndrome (psychic paralysis of visual fixation) and its minor forms. *Brain* **77**, 373–400.

Held, R. & A. Hein 1963. Movement-produced stimulation in the development of visually guided behaviour. *Journal of Comparative Physiology Psychology* **56**, 872–6.

Hick, W. E. 1952. On the rate of gain of information. *Quarterly Journal of Experimental Psychology* **4**, 11–26.

Hollerbach, J. M. 1982. Computers, brains and the control of movement. *Trends in Neurosciences* **5**, 189–92.

Hollerbach, J. M. & T. Flash 1982. Dynamic interactions between limb segments during planar arm movement. *Biological Cybernetics* **44**, 67–77.

Hyvärinen, J. & A. Poramen 1974. Function of the parietal associative area 7 as revealed from cellular discharges in alert monkeys. *Brain* **97**, 673–92.

Jeannerod, M. & B. Biguer 1982. Visuomotor mechanisms in reaching within extrapersonal space. In *Analysis of visual behaviour*, D. J. Ingle, M. A. Goodale, R. J. W. Mansfield (eds), 387–409. Cambridge MA: MIT.

Jones, E. G., & S. P. Wise 1977. Size, laminar and columnar distribution of efferent cells in the sensory-motor cortex of monkeys. *Journal of Comparative Neurolology* **175**, 391–438.

Kalaska, J. F., D. A. D. Cohen, M. L. Hyde, M. Prud'homme 1989. A comparison of movement direction-related versus load direction-related activity in primate motor cortex, using a two-dimensional reaching task. *Journal of Neuroscience* **9**, 2080–102.

Keele, S. W. 1981. Behavioural analysis of movement. In *Handbook of physiology – the nervous system,* vol. II. *Motor control*, V. B. Brooks (ed.), 1391–414. Bethesda, MD: American Physiological Society.

Keele, S. W. & M. I. Posner 1968. Processing of visual feedback in rapid movements. *Journal of Experimental Psychology* **77**, 155–8.

Kettner, R. E., A. B. Schwartz, A. P. Georgopoulos 1988. Primate motor cortex and free arm movements to visual targets in three-dimensional space. III. Positional gradients and population coding of movement direction from various movement origins. *Journal of Neuroscience* **8**, 2938–47.

LaMotte, R. H. & C. Acuna 1975. Defects in accuracy of reaching after removal of posterior parietal cortex in monkeys. *Brain Research* **139**, 309–26.

Lemon, R. N. 1984. *Methods for neuronal recording in conscious animals.* Chichester, UK: Wiley.

Lukashin, A. V. & A. P. Georgopoulos 1993. A dynamical neural network model for motor cortical activity during movement: Population coding of movement trajectories. *Biological Cybernetics* **69**, 517–24.

Lukashin, A. V. & A. P. Georgopoulos 1994a. A neural network for coding of trajectories by time series of neuronal population vectors. *Neural Computation* **6**, 19–28.

Lukashin, A. V. & A. P. Georgopoulos 1994b. Directional operations in the motor cortex modelled by a neural network of spiking neurons. *Biological Cybernetics* **71**, 79–85.

Lukashin, A. V., G. L. Wilcox, A. P. Georgopoulos 1994. Overlapping neural networks for multiple motor engrams. *Proceedings of the National Academy of Sciences USA* **91**, 8651–4.

Lundberg, A. 1979. Integration in a propriospinal motor centre controlling the forelimb in the cat. In *Integration in the nervous system*, H. Asanuma & V. J. Wilson (eds), 47–64. Tokyo: Igaku-Shoin.

Lurito, J. L., T. Georgakopoulos, A. P. Georgopoulos 1991. Cognitive spatial–motor processes. 7. The making of movements at an angle from a stimulus direction: studies of motor cortical activity at the single cell and population levels. *Experimental Brain Research* **87**, 562–80.

Massey, J. T., A. B. Schwartz, A. P. Georgopoulos 1986. On information processing and performing a movement sequence. *Experimental Brain Research Supplement* **15**, 242–51.

Morasso, P. 1981. Spatial control of arm movements. *Experimental Brain Research* **42**, 223–7.

Mountcastle, V. B., J. C. Lynch, A. P. Georgopoulos, H. Sakata, C. Acuna 1975. Posterior parietal association cortex of the monkey: command functions for operations within extrapersonal space. *Journal of Neurophysiology* **38**, 871–908.

Mountcastle, V. B., B. C. Motter, R. A. Andersen 1980. Some further observations on the functional properties of neurons in the parietal lobe of the waking monkey. *Behavioural Brain Sciences* **3**, 520–2.

Mowbray, G. H. & M. V. Rhoades 1959. On the reduction of choice reaction times with practice. *Quarterly Journal of Experimental Psychology* **11**, 16–23.

Murphy, J. T., H. C. Kwan, W. A. MacKay, Y. C. Wong 1982a. Activity of primate precentral neurons during voluntary movements triggered by visual signals. *Brain Research* **236**, 429–49.

Murphy, J. T., H. C. Kwan, W. A. MacKay, Y. C. Wong 1982b. Precentral unit activity correlated with angular components of a compound arm movement. *Brain Research* **246**, 141–5.

Murphy, J. T., Y. C. Wong, H. C. Kwan 1985. Sequential activation of neurons in primate motor cortex during unrestrained forelimb movement. *Journal of Neurophysiology* **53**, 435–45.

Nelson, W. L. 1983. Physical principles for economies of skilled movements. *Biological Cybernetics* **46**, 135–47.

Paillard, J. 1982. The contribution of peripheral and central vision to visually guided reaching. In *Analysis of visual behaviour*, D. J. Ingle, M. A. Goodale, R. J. W. Mansfield (eds), 367–85. Cambridge, MA: MIT.

Paillard, J., P. Jordan, M. Brouchon 1981. Visual motion cues in prismatic adaptation: evidence of two separate and additive processes. *Acta Psychologica* **48**, 253–70.

Pellizzer, G. & A. P. Georgopoulos 1993. Common processing constraints for visuomotor and visual mental rotation. *Experimental Brain Research* **93**, 165–72.

Pellizzer, G., P. Sargent, A. P. Georgopoulos 1995. Motor cortical activity in a context-recall task. *Science* **269**, 702–5.

Perenin, T. & A. Vighetto 1983. Optic ataxia: a specific disorder in visuomotor coordination. In *Spatially oriented behaviour*, A. Hein & M. Jeannerod (eds), 305–26. New York: Springer.

Porter, R. & M. M. Lewis 1975. Relationship of neuronal discharges in the precentral gyrus of monkeys to the performance of arm movements. *Brain Research* **98**, 21–36.

Prablanc, C., J. F. Echallier, E. Komilis, M. Jeannerod 1979a. Optimal response of eye and hand motor systems in pointing at a visual target. I. Spatiotemporal characteristics of eye and hand movements and their relationships when varying the amount of visual information. *Biological Cybernetics* **35**, 113–24.

Prablanc, C., J. F. Echallier, M. Jeannerod, E. Komilis 1979b. Optimal response of eye and hand motor systems in pointing at a visual target. II. Static and dynamic visual cues in the control of hand movement. *Biological Cybernetics* **35**, 183–7.

Rondot, P., J. de Recondo, J. L. R. Dumas 1977. Visuomotor ataxia. *Brain* **100**, 355–76.

Salinas, E. & L. F. Abbott 1994. Vector reconstruction from firing rates. *Journal of Computational Neuroscience* **1**, 89–107.

Sanders, A. F. 1967. Some aspects of reaction processes. *Acta Psychologica* **27**, 115–30.

Schwartz, A. B. 1993. Motor cortical activity during drawing movements: population representation during sinusoid tracing. *Journal of Neurophysiology* **70**, 28–36.

Schwartz, A. B. 1994. Direct cortical representation of drawing. *Science* **265**, 540–2.

Schwartz, A. B., R. E. Kettner, A. P. Georgopoulos 1988. Primate motor cortex and free arm movements to visual targets in three-dimensional space. I. Relations between single cell discharge and direction of movement. *Journal of Neuroscience* **8**, 2913–27.

Shepard, R. N. & L. A. Cooper 1982. *Mental images and their transformations*. Cambridge, MA: MIT.

Simon, J. R. 1969. Reactions toward the source of simulation. *Journal of Experimental Psychology* **81**, 174–6.

Skavenski, A. A. & R. M. Hansen 1978. Role of eye position information in visual space perception. In *Eye movements and the higher psychological functions*, J. W. Senders, D. F. Fisher, R. A. Monty (eds), 15–34. Hillsdale, NJ: Lawrence Erlbaum Associates Inc.

Smyrnis, N., M. Taira, J. Ashe, A. P. Georgopoulos 1992. Motor cortical activity in a memorized delay task. *Experimental Brain Research* **92**, 139–51.

Soechting, J. F. & F. Lacquaniti 1981. Invariant characteristics of a pointing movement in man. *Journal of Neuroscience* **1**, 710–20.

Soechting, J. F. & F. Lacquaniti 1983. Modification of trajectory of a pointing movement in response to a change in target location. *Journal of Neurophysiology* **49**, 548–64.

Taira, M. & A. P. Georgopoulos 1993. Cortical cell types from spike trains. *Neuroscience Research* **17**, 39–45.

Trevarthen, C. B. 1968. Two mechanisms of vision in primates. *Psychologische Forschung* **31**, 299–337.

von Hofsten, C. 1979. Development of visually directed reaching: the approach phase. *Journal of Human Movement Studies* **5**, 160–78.

von Hofsten, C. 1980. Predictive reaching for moving objects by human infants. *Journal of Experimental Child Psychology* **30**, 369–82.

von Hofsten, C. 1982. Eye–hand coordination in the newborn. *Developmental Psychology* **18**, 450–61.

Wallace, R. J. 1971. S–R compatibility and the idea of a response code. *Journal of Experimental Psychology* **88**, 354–60.

Welford, A. T., A. H. Norris, N. W. Shock 1969. Speed and accuracy of movement and their changes with age. *Acta Psychologica* **30**, 3–15.

Young, M. P. & S. Yamane 1992. Sparse population coding of faces in the inferotemporal cortex. *Science* **256**, 1327–31.

CHAPTER 6

Studying brain function with neuroimaging

Christopher D. Frith & Karl J. Friston

6.1 INTRODUCTION

On 4 August 1881, a landmark meeting took place to consider the problem of attributing function to a particular cortical area (see Phillips et al. 1984). This meeting highlighted the fundamental dialectic of brain organization. On the one hand there is functional segregation, such that neurons with the same function tend to be grouped together in a circumscribed brain area (Zeki 1978). Given such a principle it should be possible to produce a map of the cortex in which every area has its own specific function On the other hand, given the dependence of cerebral activity on underlying connections (Phillips et al. 1984), there is functional integration, such that function must depend upon interactions between widely distributed neurons. Given this principle, a circumscribed area can have no function of its own. Specific functions will only emerge from interactions between many brain areas. In 1875, Ferrier had demonstrated that electrical stimulation of a particular area of motor cortex in the dog or monkey would elicit movements in a specific limb. He concluded that control of movement could be mapped onto motor cortex. However, Goltz (1881), while accepting these results, considered the stimulation method did not conclusively demonstrate functional segregation, since the movements elicited might have originated in related pathways, or current could have spread to distant centres. This argument is still unresolved. However, the principle of correlating a behaviour with cerebral excitation is still the principal method employed today to study brain function. There have been major advances in technique and theory over the past century and, with modern methods of functional imaging, such studies can now be applied to man (Posner & Raichle 1994). However, the question still remains of whether the physiological changes elicited by sensorimotor or cognitive processes are better explained by functional localization, or in terms of distributed changes mediated by neural interactions. The question itself has important implications for data analysis and interpretation, and applies to all techniques of functional brain imaging. To underscore this point we will introduce various types of experimental design and statistical analysis under the headings of (i) localizing cerebral functions and (ii) characterizing distributed changes. since different kinds of analysis are appropriate to these different views of brain function. To show that these analyses are largely independent of the measurement techniques used we will present analyses of data sets from functional magnetic resonance imaging (fMRI) and positron emission tomography (PET) in parallel. First, however, we will give a brief account of how these recently developed methods for imaging brain function work.

6.2 BLOOD FLOW AS AN INDEX OF NEURAL ACTIVITY

Shortly after the first investigations of brain function, Roy & Sherrington (1890) proposed that brain activity might cause local changes in blood flow: "Bearing in mind that strong evidence exists of localization of function in the brain, we are of the opinion that an automatic mechanism ... is well fitted to provide for a local variation of the blood supply in accordance with local variations of the functional activity". There is now ample evidence in favour of this proposal from studies of animals and man (for a review see Raichle 1987). Hill (1926) was the first to demonstrate that nerve impulse activity increases oxygen consumption. A number of detailed studies since (e.g. Mata et al. 1980) have shown that this increase in metabolism occurs not in the cell bodies but in the neuropil, the cell-free region containing the synaptic connections between axons and dendrites. This change in metabolism does not distinguish between inhibitory and excitatory activity.

Since the brain stores no oxygen and little glucose, the energy requirements for continuous neural activity depend on local blood supply. A high degree of coupling between energy metabolism and blood flow has been demonstrated (Sokoloff 1981), but the relationship is not perfect. A number of studies have demonstrated that the local increase in blood flow exceeds the local tissue requirements for oxygen.

For example, Fox & Raichle (1986) observed that vibrotactile stimulation of the fingers of one hand produced a 31% increase in blood flow localized in the contralateral hemisphere, while the increase in oxygen consumption was only 6%. This is a very important observation, since, first, it shows that blood flow is a more sensitive index of neural activity than are more direct measures of metabolism and, secondly, it provides the basis for new methods of measuring blood flow using MRI (see below). First, however, we describe one of a number of well-established techniques for measuring regional cerebral blood flow (rCBF) using radioactive tracers.

6.2.1 Positron emission tomography

Radioactive tracers were first used to measure regional blood flow in animals (Landau et al. 1955) and later in humans (Lassen et al. 1963). Currently the most widely used tracer is $^{15}O_2$, i.e. oxygen in which one electron has been removed from the normal atom to give an unstable form that will eventually emit one positron. $^{15}O_2$ is injected into a vein as water ($H_2^{15}O$). The advantage of this tracer is that it has a very short half-life (~2 min). This means that several scans (currently up to 12) can be performed on the same volunteer, allowing direct comparison of conditions within subjects. The associated disadvantage of a short half-life is that a cyclotron, the particle accelerator used to generate the tracer, must be close to the camera. Thus every PET facility must house a cyclotron as well as a camera. In consequence, PET scanning is very expensive and there are relatively few centres where such equipment is available.

At the beginning of a typical PET scan a small amount of radiolabelled water is injected into a vein. After about 30 s the tracer starts to enter the brain, and the following 30 s, in which radiation in the brain rises to a maximum, is the critical window during which a picture of rCBF is obtained. The ^{15}O reverts to ^{16}O by emission of a positron. This travels a few millimetres before interacting with an electron to produce two annihilation photons which travel away at 180° from each other. These two photons are detected by the imaging device, using radiation detectors connected by electronic coincidence circuits that record an event only when two photons arrive simultaneously. By the use of these coincidence detectors the line along which the photons have travelled can be measured very accurately (Fig. 6.1). The major factor determining the ultimate spatial resolution of PET is the distance travelled by a positron before its annihilation, which is ~2–3 mm. The sensitivity of the imaging device is equal throughout the brain, rather than being higher on the surface than in deeper structures. The scanner therefore produces an image of the density of radiation throughout the brain during the 30 s window. This recorded tissue radioactivity is a

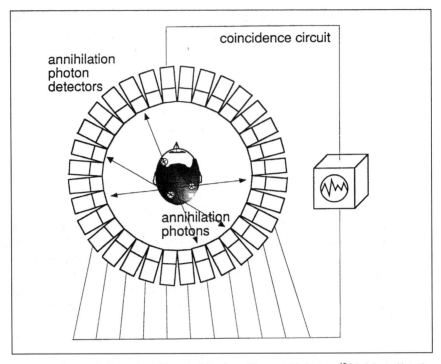

FIG. 6.1.   Schematic illustration of the principle of PET. The unstable isotope ^{15}O is injected into the bloodstream, with water as the vehicle and enters the brain. When a positron is emitted it meets an electron, resulting in an annihilation event which sends out two photons at 180°. The rings of detectors around the head detect these events as coincidences, and a very accurate map of the density of radiation throughout the brian can be constructed.

nearly linear function of local blood flow in the tissue. The end result is a series of scans from a single volunteer showing the pattern of neural activity averaged across the ~30s of each scan which reflects whatever mental processes were engaged during that scan.

6.2.2 Functional magnetic resonance imaging

MRI is well established as the best technique for obtaining *in vivo* images of brain structure. If the brain is placed in a strong, uniform magnetic field and an appropriate radiofrequency pulse is transmitted through it, the effects of the resulting resonance in atomic nuclei can be detected in a receiver coil placed around the head. This technique can be used to detect hydrogen nuclei attached to oxygen in the form of water. From such measurements an image of the brain can be formed in which tissue of different density such as grey and white matter can clearly be distinguished. These images have good spatial resolution of approximately

2 mm and temporal resolution of the order of seconds. At the beginning of the 1990s, various techniques were developed which permit MRI to be used to measure brain function in terms of blood flow. One of these methods, blood oxygen level dependent contrast (BOLD), depends on the uncoupling between blood flow and oxygen consumption discussed above. As already mentioned, during neural activity there is a large increase in blood flow, but a much smaller increase in oxygen consumption. In consequence, there is an increase in the proportion of oxygenated haemoglobin in local tissue. Since oxygenated haemoglobin has different magnetic properties from the deoxygenated form, increases in blood flow produce changes in the intensity of the signals measured by MRI. The best techniques for using MRI to measure brain function have yet to be established, but there are already many published studies demonstrating the viability of the technique (see e.g. Turner & Jezzard 1994). A major difference between MRI and PET is that, in the former, the information from which the images are derived is collected sequentially. This means that the image of the top of the brain could be reflecting activity occurring at a slightly different time from the image of the bottom of the brain. This problem can be resolved by using fast data acquisition techniques such as echo planar imaging (EPI).

One important result to emerge concerns the temporal resolution of techniques that depend upon blood-flow measurement. It seems that there is a lag of 5–8s between changes in neural activity and the associated change in blood flow (Friston et al. 1994). Thus neither PET nor fMRI are ever going to approach the millisecond temporal resolution of techniques such as EEG and MEG (see Ch. 7). The major advantage of fMRI over PET, once this new methodology has become fully established, lies in the fact that no radiation is involved. A single volunteer can therefore be scanned repeatedly without any associated risk.

In the remainder of this chapter we discuss the experimental designs and data analyses required to link cognitive processes and brain function using PET and fMRI. We illustrate the different techniques that can be applied with two of our own data sets from PET and fMRI respectively. We also discuss other experiments in which the same experimental designs have been applied.

6.3 LOCALIZING CEREBRAL FUNCTION

Functional imaging, used in conjunction with cognitive (Posner et al. 1989) or sensorimotor subtraction (Zeki et al. 1991), has been extremely successful in establishing functional specialization as a principle of brain organization in man. In such studies images of blood flow are collected in at least two different conditions (e.g. while moving the fingers and while at rest). The images are then compared in order to find areas where the experimental task is associated with more blood flow than the control task. These areas of increased blood flow are typically referred to as "activations". There are two basic approaches to identifying the location of these changes: (a) difference or change score mapping and (b) statistical parametric mapping (SPM). The fundamental difference between these approaches is in the question asked, namely: (a) Is the activation big (change score), or (b) is the activation reliable (SPM)? A reliable activation is large relative to the underlying variability in blood flow at that location. SPMs therefore use both change scores and the error variance estimated at each point (or voxel) in the image. These estimates are combined to produce a test quotient (e.g. a t statistic or a correlation coefficient). A major advantage of the SPM approach is that it can take advantage of a wide range of well-established statistical techniques such as ANOVA (Analysis of Variance), ANCOVA (Analysis of Covariance) and regression.

Statistical parametric maps are images in which voxels are, under a null hypothesis, distributed according to a (statistical) probability density function. The maps are essentially images of significance. The simplest forms are t maps, based on repeated measurements, in two brain states, of rCBF (or equivalent) data at each voxel. More sensitive and general approaches have been developed for experiments using many conditions in many subjects. In its original form, SPM uses ANCOVA (analysis of covariance) to compute the t statistic and remove the confounding effects of global CBF differences (Friston et al. 1990, 1991a, Ramsay et al. 1993). Because relatively few scans can be performed on each volunteer using PET, it is necessary to combine data from several subjects in order to detect activations. The precise number of subjects required will depend on the size of the activation to be detected and on the number of conditions to be compared. In our laboratory each subject undergoes 12 scans, which is the maximum allowed under current radiation safety regulations. If each condition is replicated three or four times (i.e. there are four or three different conditions in the experiment, respectively) a group of six subjects will be sufficient to detect 2–5% changes in blood flow. The need to combine data from different scans and from different subjects gives rise to many problems. In a typical experimental session the subject must lie in the scanner for 2.5h with scans being done roughly every 10 min. In spite of the use of some kind of head holder, it is inevitable that there will be some head movement during the course of the session. Fortunately, there are standard methods for "realigning" the sequence of brain images which are extremely accurate. A more difficult problem results from the need to combine data from brains of different people which vary widely in size and shape. A number of techniques have been developed that allow brains to be "normalized" to a standard space (e.g. Friston et al. 1991a). Such techniques are now fairly standard. However, it is not possible to compensate fully for the differences between subjects without reducing the resolution of the image. In consequence, although the theoretical resolution available from PET is of the order of 2–3mm, the resolution in a typical multisubject activation study will be of the order of 10–15mm. In addition to permitting the averaging of data from groups of subjects, normalization of the brain images allows the location of activations to be reported in terms of standard spatial co-ordinates (usually based on the brain atlas of Talairach & Tournoux 1988). This is a great help when comparing studies done at different centres.

For fMRI data the situation is slightly different. Large numbers of scans can be obtained from a single subject. Thus weak activation signals can be detected without the need for intersubject averaging. On the other hand, there are special problems associated with fMRI because of its higher spatial and temporal resolution. The high spatial resolution of the order of 2–3mm means that even small movements can have a dramatic effect on the image. It is therefore important for the images to be realigned accurately before attempting to detect the locations of activations. The high temporal resolution means that scans can be obtained more rapidly (e.g. once every second) than the change in blood flow being measured. As already documented, when neural activity increases in a location there is a delay of several seconds before local blood flow increases. The precise form of this increase in flow over time is know as the "haemodynamic response function". The delay in the increase in blood flow means that, in a sequence of fMRI images, the image showing activation occurs much later than the image that coincided with the event which caused the neural activity leading to the change in blood flow. Because a single PET scan takes 30s or more, the haemodynamic response function has little impact on the data.

The fundamental hypothesis underlying brain imaging studies is that regional physiology is significantly correlated with some stimulus or task parameter (or mental state). For fMRI data the correlation coefficient can be used directly (after accounting for the effects of the haemodynamic response function). In PET the end result is equivalent, but is derived in terms of the t statistic: the ANCOVA generates rCBF means and an associated error variance at each voxel, for all experimental conditions. These estimates are used to compute a t statistic. The t statistic is defined by a contrast, based on a time-dependent stimulus or task parameter. The resulting t statistic reflects the correlation between rCBF and the contrast (parameter). Correlation coefficients (fMRI) or contrasts (PET) allow arbitrary non-pair-wise and graded comparisons, as well as the assessment of interaction terms (see below). This flexibility takes data analysis, and consequently experimental design, beyond the simple subtraction framework and into the realm of parametric studies and factorial designs. These different types of analysis can be classified as categorical, parametric and factorial.

6.3.1 Categorical analysis

This is simply the comparison of one set of conditions with another and is predicated on cognitive subtraction (Petersen et al. 1988, Posner et al. 1989). The assumption underlying this approach is that the difference between two tasks can be characterized by a separable cognitive or sensorimotor component, and that the locations of rCBF differences identify the corresponding functionally specialized area. Early applications of the subtraction technique range from the cortical anatomy of word processing (Petersen et al. 1988) to functional specialization in extrastriate cortex (Lueck et al. 1989, Zeki et al. 1991). The latter studies involved presenting visual stimuli with and without some specific attribute (e.g. colour, motion). The areas identified by subtraction are believed to be homologous to areas in monkeys which show selective electrophysiological responses to equivalent visual stimuli (Fig. 6.2, which appears on p. 152).

We illustrate the various data analysis techniques discussed in this chapter by applying them to data from two of our own experiments, one involving fMRI and the other PET. The fMRI experiment examined the brain activity associated with simple visual stimulation. This stimulation (at 16 Hz) was provided by goggles fitted with light-emitting diodes. The light stimulation was off for the first ten scans (30 s), on for the second ten scans, off for the third ten scans, and so on. The resulting data were a series over time of 64 single coronal brain slices (5 mm thick, 64 × 64 voxels) through the calcarine sulcus and extrastriate areas. EPI was used to obtain images every 3 seconds from a single subject using a 4.0 T whole-body system. The images were reconstructed, and scaled so that the mean image was the same for all scans.

Figure 6.3a shows the SPM{ρ} based on our fMRI data and highlights regions where blood flow was positively correlated with photic stimulation. The SPM{ρ} is simply an image of the correlation coefficient between the fMRI data and the variable labelled "contrast", which codes for the presence or absence of light. The regions highlighted include the primary visual cortex (V1; BA 17) and a set of extrastriate regions (the cuneus, BA 18,19; unilateral lingual gyrus, BA 18; and a bilateral dorsal signal in the region of the middle occipital gyrus). In other words,

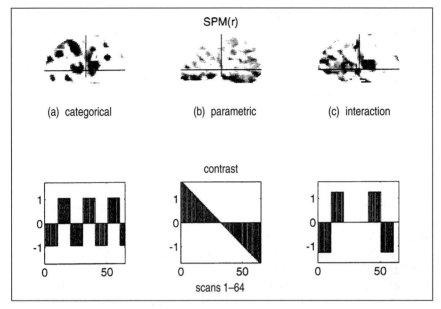

FIG. 6.3.   (a) A voxel-wise correlation of the fMRI signal and stimulus parameters. The upper image is a statistical parametric map of the correlation coefficient (SPM{ρ}) contrasting no stimulation with photic stimulation superimposed in a coronal brain slice through the occipital cortex. The correlation coefficient has been transformed to the *t* statistic to facilitate visual interpretation. The darker portions of the image (black: $t = 12.0$) show the more significant areas of correlation, which are located in primary visual cortex. The lower image shows the contrast used to calculate the correlation. This corresponds to the sequence of 64 scans assigned a value of −1 for no stimulation and +1 for photic stimulation. Stimulation can be seen to occur in alternating blocks of ten scans. (b) A parametric or graded contrast tests for linear time effects in the fMRI data set. The darker areas, where activity decreased over time, are in the lingual and fusiform gyri. (c) The SPM{ρ} from a test for an interaction between the haemodynamic activation due to photic stimulation and time. The contrasts, shown in the lower figure, compare increases in activity associated with photic stimulation in the first two blocks of scans, with decreases in the last two blocks. The corresponding SPM{ρ} highlights those regions in which physiological activation has adapted by the second stimulation. These were in the primary visual cortex (V1).

the light stimulation has activated most of the primary and secondary visual cortex.

Our PET data were obtained from six subjects scanned 12 times (every 10 min) whilst performing one of two verbal tasks. The subjects performed the two tasks in alternation. The first task (control) was repeating a letter presented aurally at a rate of one letter every 3 s (word shadowing). The second task (experimental) was a paced verbal fluency task, where the subjects responded with a word that began with the letter presented (e.g. A – apple; word generation). In both tasks the subject heard a series of sounds and spoke a series of words. Only in the experimental task did the subjects themselves have to generate the words to be spoken. Comparison of these two tasks should identify brain areas concerned with word generation. Scans were obtained using a CTI PET camera (model 953B CTI Knoxville, TN, USA). Reconstructed images had a resolution of 5.2mm (Townsend et al. 1992, Spinks et al. 1992). ^{15}O was administered intravenously as a radio-labelled water infused over 2min. Total counts per voxel during the build-up phase of radioactivity served as an estimate of rCBF (Fox & Mintun 1989). To facilitate intersubject pooling, data were stereo-tactically normalized (Friston et al. 1989, 1991b) to the space defined by the brain atlas of Talairach & Tournoux (1988).

Figure 6.4a shows the SPM{t} based on the PET data and compares the verbal fluency conditions with word shadowing. The regions identified include the anterior cingulate, the left dorsolateral prefrontal cortex

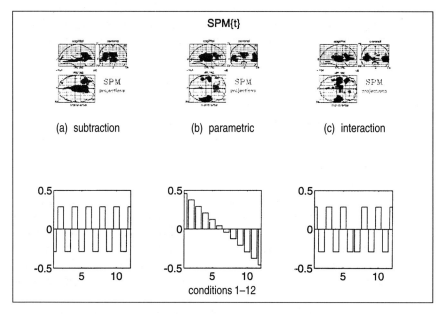

FIG. 6.4.   (a) As Figure 6.3a, but using a contrast (weighted sum of mean rCBFs) following a voxel-wise analysis of rCBF variance of the PET data. This generates statistical parametric maps of the t statistic (SPM{t}) for a subtraction of word shadowing (odd-numbered) conditions from verbal fluency (even-numbered) conditions. The areas activated are shown as three projections through the brain and include left DLPFC and anterior cingulate. (b) A contrast used to identify regions whose rCBF declines linearly with time in the PET data set. The regions identified are in the right and left auditory cortex. (c) A contrast testing for an interaction between the rCBF activation due to verbal fluency (compared with word shadowing) and time. The corresponding SPM{t} highlights those regions where the physiological activation shows adaptation with sustained performance. The areas identified include auditory cortex, thalamus and Broca's area.

(DLPFC) (including BA 44 – Broca's area) and subcortical structures. In this example the cognitive component, which distinguishes between verbal fluency and word shadowing, is complex. It will include intrinsic word generation and working memory. The results can be interpreted as showing a predilection of left DLPFC and anterior cingulate for the intentional and mnemonic aspects of word finding.

Cognitive subtraction is conceptually simple and is a very effective method in functional mapping. It does, however, depend on the assumption that the activating tasks differ in components that can be purely inserted or removed without any alteration in the function of the remaining components. However, there are many situations for which this assumption does not apply. For example, consider a simple GO/NO-GO paradigm. In this task there are two kinds of trial. On the GO trials the subject presses a button when the light comes on. On the NO-GO trials the subject does nothing when the green light comes on. Each of these types of trial is associated with a particular cognitive process. By subtracting a task in which there are only GO trials we should be able to identify the activity associated with the NO-GO trials. This assumption is invalid. If we remove the NO-GO trials from the task then the responses to the GO trials become much faster. Thus, removing one component of the task has changed the nature of the remaining components. It has therefore been necessary to develop alternatives to cognitive subtraction. One such alternative is to explore correlations between regional activity and graded cognitive or sensorimotor parameters.

6.3.2 Parametric analysis

The premise here is that regional physiology will vary monotonically and systematically with some parameter of cognitive or sensorimotor processing. For example, time-dependent changes are clearly central to studies of learning and memory. Many animal models of procedural learning depend on habituation and adaptation, at either a behavioural or an electrophysiological level. In the context of functional imaging, physiological adaptation to a challenge is simply the change in rCBF activation over time.

The example given (Figs 6.3b, 6.4b) uses time as a stimulus parameter (see contrasts). The resulting SPM{ρ} (fMRI) and SPM{t} (PET) pick out regions where the rCBF declines linearly with time. These include the lingual and fusiform gyri (fMRI – photic stimulation) and the temporal regions bilaterally and the anterior cingulate (PET – word generation). Interestingly, in the PET data, the left temporal areas segregate into a periauditory region and the posterior superior temporal gyrus (BA 22, Wernicke's area) reflecting the different functions of these areas.

Recent examples of this approach include the experiments done by Grafton et al. (1992), who demonstrated significant correlations over time between rCBF and the performance of a visually guided motor tracking task (using a pursuit rotor device) in the primary motor area, supplementary motor area and pulvinar thalamus. The authors associated this distributed network with early procedural learning. On the sensory side, Price et al. (1992) have demonstrated a remarkable linear relationship between rCBF in periauditory regions (BA 41,42) and frequency of aural word presentation (Fig. 6.5). Significantly, this correlation was not observed in Wernicke's area, where rCBF appeared to correlate, not with the rate of presentation of the stimuli, but with the presence or absence of semantic content.

Of special interest are recent studies by Grasby et al. (1993, 1994) on verbal memory. In the first study a categorical comparison was made between two conditions in which subjects heard and recalled a short list of five words or a long list of 15 words. It was assumed that the areas of extra activity associated with the long list were concerned with long-term memory, since a list of 15 words is well above short-term memory span while five words are below it. In the second experiment a parametric design was used in which 12 different list lengths were used, varying from two to 13 words. The brain areas in which

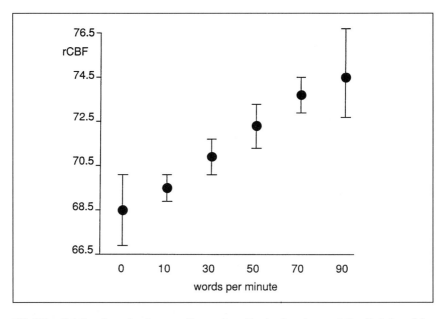

FIG. 6.5.   Relation of rCBF in primary auditory cortex with rate of word presentation. Data from Price et al. (1992).

rCBF correlated with list length were essentially the same as those observed in the first study (DLPFC bilaterally, anterior cingulate cortex, thalamus, posterior cingulate cortex and pre-cuneus). However, the precise form of the relationship (Fig. 6.6) showed that rCBF increased rapidly across the short list lengths, but then levelled out at a list length of about eight words. This pattern closely resembles the performance of the subjects who never recalled more than about eight words, even from the longer lists. Indeed, the correlation between words recalled in each condition and rCBF in the relevant brain areas was approximately 0.9. These results suggest that the major brain areas highlighted in both experiments were associated with a limited capacity, working-memory system which became saturated with lists of seven or more items. The information needed to make this interpretation was not available in the first, categorical experiment.

In these studies the parameter of interest was varied across several scans in a single subject. However, the same type of analysis can be applied when a parameter has been measured in a series of subjects. For example, current symptomatology was assessed in a group of schizophrenic patients in whom resting rCBF was assessed (Liddle et al. 1992). A significant correlation was found between measures of the

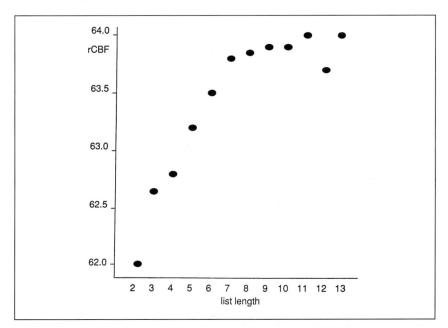

FIG. 6.6.   Average rCBF from a system of "memory" areas (prefrontal cortex, thalamus, etc.) related to the lengths of word lists being memorized. Little increase in activity can be observed after reaching "span" (seven words). Data from Grasby et al. (1994).

severity of psychomotor poverty of speech, etc., and rCBF in the left DLPFC. Patients with marked psychomotor poverty showed low rCBF in left DLPFC.

6.3.3 Interactions and factorial designs

An interaction is basically a change in a change. It is associated with factorial designs where two (or more) treatments are combined in the same experiment. The effect of one treatment, on the effect of the other, is assessed by the interaction term. Figure 6.4c shows a contrast testing for an interaction between rCBF changes due to verbal fluency (compared with word shadowing) and time. The SPM{t} shows those regions which show a physiological adaptation, or regions where activations are attenuated when performing the verbal fluency task, but not when performing the word shadowing task. These regions include the periauditory areas on both sides and, on the left, Broca's area (BA 44) and the mediodorsal thalamus. One might suggest that these regions are implicated in learnable sensorimotor or cognitive components specific to verbal fluency performance. Note that Broca's area adapts in terms of its differential response to verbal fluency, but is not subject to non-specific time effects. The main areas of adaptation during photic stimulation in the fMRI experiment are centred on V1 (Fig. 6.3c).

Factorial designs of this sort have a wide range of applications. The first PET experiment to use this approach was perhaps the simplest imaginable and examined the interaction between motor activation (sequential finger opposition paced by a metronome contrasted with rest) and time. The subjects were scanned six times, alternating motor performance with rest (Friston et al. 1992a). Significant adaptation was seen in the cerebellar cortex (ipsilateral to the hand moved) and cerebellar nuclei. These results are consistent with the electrophysiological studies done by Gilbert & Thach (1977), who demonstrated a reduction in simple and complex spike activity of Purkinje cells in the cerebellum during motor learning in monkeys. Psychopharmacological activation studies provide another example of a factorial design (Friston et al. 1992b). In these studies subjects perform a series of rest–activation pairs before and after the administration of a centrally acting drug. The interaction term reflects the modulatory drug effect on the task-dependent physiological response. The effects of buspirone (a 5-HT$_{1A}$ receptor partial agonist) and apomorphine (a non-selective dopamine agonist) on changes in rCBF associated with word-list learning have been examined extensively. Although these drugs act on different neurotransmitter systems they both impair the learning of word lists. However, the PET studies suggest that these drug effects occur in different brain regions. Thus, apomorphine produced an attenuation of memory induced activity in prefrontal cortex. This is the cortical area with the highest concentration of dopamine receptors. In contrast, buspirone attenuated memory-induced activations in retrosplenial cortex, a location consistent with the particular mode of action of this drug. In principle, it should be possible to use this technique to identify the location at which a particular neurotransmitter has its effect in the extended neural system that underlies any particular cognitive process (Grasby et al. 1992).

6.3.4 The functional anatomy of memory

Another important application of the factorial design is in dual task interference paradigms. Dual task interference has been widely used in cognitive psychology to identify discrete cognitive modules. The best known example of the use of this technique is probably in studies of working memory. Baddeley and his colleagues (e.g. Baddeley 1986) have proposed that working memory consists of two components: a central executive and a slave system specific to the material being remembered (e.g. the articulatory loop for verbal material and the visuospatial scratch pad for visuospatial material). The demonstration of the independence of these modules depends, in part, upon the effect of interference in dual task paradigms. Thus, function of the articulatory loop is impaired by concurrent articulation (saying "blah blah blah"), but not by a non-verbal spatial task (e.g. tapping out a pattern of key presses). The opposite pattern of interference is found for the visuospatial scratch pad. In contrast, the central executive is interfered with by any task which requires focused attention and response selection. The same approach can be used in functional brain imaging to isolate independent neural systems.

A recent example of this sort of experiment used the interaction between the difficulty of a distractor task and focal activations due to a memory task to separate out cognitive and associated neural components underlying long-term memory (Shallice et al. 1994). The subjects had to learn paired associates consisting of a category and an exemplar (e.g. poet – Browning). A single presentation of 15 such pairs is sufficient for subjects to achieve recall of approximately 80%. There are two major processes leading to successful recall. The first of these, priming, is largely automatic and does not require deliberate attention during acquisition. In such a case the subject will not recollect having been presented with the word "poet", but reports that "Browning" was the first example that came to mind. The second process underlies episodic memory and does require deliberate attention during acquisition. In such a case the subject recollects the experimenter reading out the

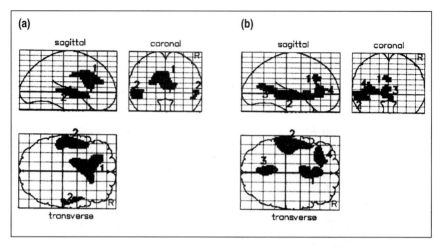

FIG. 6.7.   Memory acquisition in the presence of a difficult distractor task (a) and an easy distractor task (b). The figure shows SPM projections through the brain with areas of significantly increased rCBF. Activity in the anterior cingulate (1) and temporal cortex (2) is present in both conditions. With difficult distraction, memory is impaired and activity in the retrosplenial cortex (3) and in left DLPFC (4) is eliminated. Data from Shallice et al. (1994).

pair, poet – Browning. If the subject is given a difficult distractor task (e.g. choice reaction time) during the acquisition phase, then episodic memory is impaired while priming remains intact. Subjects were scanned during acquisition in four different conditions. The design was a 2 × 2 factorial experiment. One treatment had either a high or a low memory load, while the other involved a difficult or easy distractor task. Figure 6.7a shows the activations associated with a memory load in the presence of a difficult distractor, while Figure 7b shows the activations in the presence of an easy distractor. In Figure 7b we expect to see activations associated with priming and with episodic memory processes, while in Figure 7a we expect to see only activations associated with priming, because the difficult distractor task has largely eliminated episodic processes. The difference between these two difference images (i.e. the interaction) will pick out the activations associated with episodic memory processes. Formal analysis confirms the visual impression gained from the two figures. Episodic memory processes during acquisition are associated with activity in left prefrontal cortex and retrosplenial cortex (Shallice et al. 1994).

6.3.5 The use of interactions to test a lesion–deficit model

The lesion–deficit model assumes that a localized brain lesion will cause impairment in a specific cognitive function. This assumption is predicated upon the existence of functional segregation in the brain. In the context of human neuroimaging, the lesion–deficit approach usually tries to establish a three-way link between sensorimotor or cognitive deficit, focal disturbances in neurophysiology and the functional anatomy of normal subjects. Such an approach requires a mixed factorial design in which one factor contrasts different conditions in the same subject, while the other contrasts different groups of subjects. Our example comes from the study of motor control in patients with Parkinson's disease (Playford et al. 1992). These patients have particular difficulties when they have to initiate or select responses with no external cues to guide selection. A series of PET studies has revealed a distributed system of brain areas that is activated when normal subjects have to select a sequence of responses at random (Deiber et al. 1991, Frith et al. 1991), a paradigm example of a situation in which there are no external cues to help the subject make his choice. The areas activated include the DLPFC, supplementary motor area (SMA) and anterior cingulate cortex. In the study of Parkinson's disease there were two conditions (producing a sequence of four possible joystick movements at random versus producing the same response every time) and two groups (Parkinson's disease patients and normal controls). The rate of response was constrained to be the same in both groups by using a pacing tone. The interaction between groups and conditions reveals those areas where the activation associated with internally guided response selection is significantly reduced in the Parkinson's disease patients. These areas were SMA, anterior cingulate and contralateral putamen (Fig. 6.8). Further experiments (essentially three-way

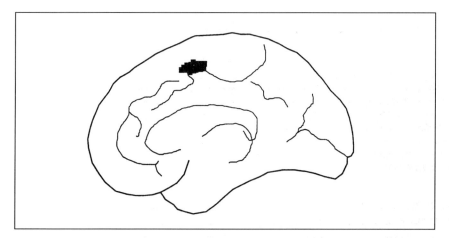

FIG. 6.8.   An area of increased rCBF in medial premotor cortex (supplementary motor area) associated with self-generated movements of a joystick. In patients with Parkinson's disease there is significantly less increase of activity in this area. From Playford et al. (1992).

factorial designs) have shown that this effect can be modulated by treatment with dopamine agonists such as apomorphine. In patients with Parkinson's disease treated with apomorphine the symptoms are improved and the activation in the SMA associated with internally guided response selection is normalized (Jenkins et al. 1992).

6.3.6 Functional segregation is not enough

In the studies of verbal fluency and internally guided response selection, a complex cognitive process was associated with activity in several brain regions (DLPFC, anterior cingulate cortex, SMA, etc.). One approach to this finding is to propose that each area is associated with a different cognitive component. For example, DLPFC might be concerned with working memory for the sequence produced so far, while ACC is concerned with selection of the next response. New and more subtle tasks could then be developed to examine such hypotheses using subtractive logic. But, however good the evidence is for such functional segregation, it is still necessary to address the problem of how these segregated areas interact with one another. Inevitably there will be some (higher order?) cognitive functions which depend upon interactions between areas rather than activity in a single circumscribed area. How can we characterize activations distributed across many areas?

6.4 CHARACTERIZING DISTRIBUTED CHANGES

A single cortical region is implicated in a distributed system by virtue of its functional interactions with the other regions. The identification of distributed systems therefore relies on the characterization of neuronal interactions and correlations. In current analyses of imaging data there are two distinct themes: (a) the extraction or identification of distributed systems using the observed correlations in rCBF (functional connectivity); and (b) the assessment of effective connections which mediate the interactions within these systems. Here we focus on functional connectivity as a method of characterizing distributed systems.

In the past two decades the concepts of functional and effective connectivity have been most thoroughly elaborated in the analysis of multi-unit recordings of separable neuronal spike trains, recorded simultaneously from different brain areas (Gerstein & Perkel 1969, Gerstein et al. 1989). Temporal coherence among the activity of different neurons is commonly measured by cross-correlating their spike trains. The resulting correlograms are then interpreted as a signature of functional connectivity (Aertsen & Preissl 1991, Gochin et al. 1991). More generally, functional connectivity refers to the observed temporal correlation between two electro/neurophysiological measurements from different parts of the brain (Friston et al. 1992c). Functional connectivity can be defined as the temporal correlation between spatially remote neurophysiological events.

This concept is best illustrated by an example of a study of the responses of single nerve cells to visual stimulation. Many nerve cells can be found in visual cortex which respond only when an object is moved in a certain direction across a circumscribed area (the receptive field) on the retina. It is possible to record simultaneously from two such cells which respond to the same direction of movement, but are associated with different, and non-overlapping areas on the retina which we might call areas A and B. If two objects move across the retina, one through area A and one through area B, then both cells will become active at the same time. However, the two patterns of activity will not show any temporal relationships, i.e. they will uncorrelated. If, however, a single object (say a long bar) is moved across the retina and extends into areas A and B simultaneously, then both cells will become active in a correlated manner (Engel et al. 1990). This implies that when the two fields are stimulated by a single object the associated cells become effectively connected. As yet the mechanism by which the connection is achieved remains unknown. The index of connectivity in this case is the extent to which the activity in the two cells is correlated over time. Precisely the same index can be derived for large brain areas containing many cells. With PET and fMRI we do not simply record activity in two such areas, but from the whole brain. The problem with such data is to develop methods for revealing patterns of connectivity.

6.4.1 Distributed systems, spatial modes and functional connectivity

One of the best approaches to characterizing the spatiotemporal organization of these correlations, for both multiple spike trains and the electroencephalogram EEG, is to segregate the data into a small number of independent components or patterns of correlated activity (Dvorak & Holden 1991). This sort of analysis can now be applied to functional imaging data (Friston et al. 1992c) and extracts truly distributed brain systems with dense functional interconnections. These patterns, called "spatial modes" (principal components or eigenimages) are derived using singular value decomposition or principal component analysis of PET or fMRI time series (Friston et al. 1992c). Each mode represents a highly interconnected and independent system, which is active, to a greater or lesser extent, during the conditions under which subjects are scanned. The relative activity of a given mode across the different conditions is used to attribute a functional role to that mode (see Fig. 6.9).

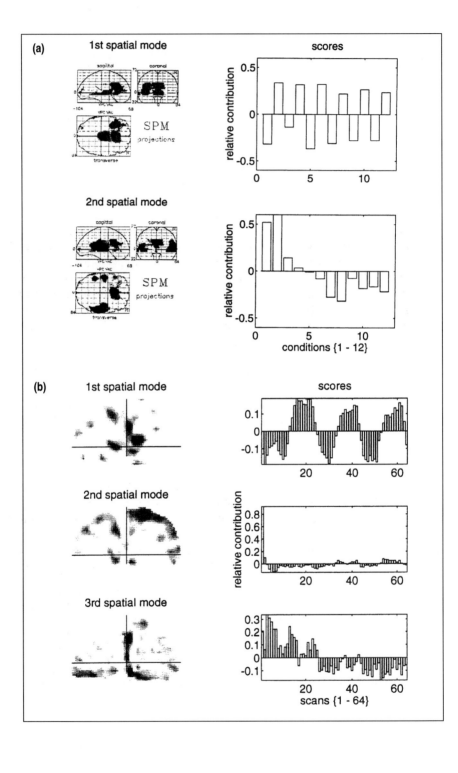

6.4.2 PET data

The first two spatial modes of the verbal fluency data accounted for most (84%) of the variance observed. The first mode accounted for 68% and the second for 16% of variance. The first spatial mode is shown in Figure 6.10a and has positive loadings in the anterior cingulate (BA 24,32), the left DLPFC (BA 46), Broca's area (BA 44), the thalamic nuclei and in the cerebellum. Negative loadings were seen bitemporally and in the posterior cingulate. This profile is the verbal fluency profile shown in Figure 6.4a (left) (see also Frith et al. 1991). The component scores, reflecting the contribution of this spatial mode to each condition (Fig. 6.9a, right) testify to this interpretation. The first mode is prevalent in the verbal fluency tasks with correspondingly negative scores in word shadowing. The second principal component had its highest positive loading in the anterior cingulate and appears to correspond to a highly non-linear, monotonic time effect with greatest prominence in the first three conditions (Fig. 6.9a, bottom right). These two spatial modes may represent an intentional system critical for the intrinsic generation of words and a second attentional system the physiology of which changes monotonically with time. In the analyses described in the first section of this chapter the correlations and contrasts were used to test hypotheses about the effects of the experimental conditions on brain activity. Such analyses are hypothesis led. In contrast, the analyses described in this section of the chapter are data led. The component scores emerge from the most prominent pattern of physiological correlations and are unconstrained by any *a priori* ideas about the effects of the different conditions.

6.4.3 fMRI data

The fMRI data segregated into three spatial modes. These are shown in Figure 6.9b. The similarity with the PET findings is striking: The largest mode (accounting for 48%) was introduced by experimental design

---

FIG. 6.9.   (a) A principal component (PC) analysis of the PET verbal fluency data. Left: SPM{PC} of the first two principle components or spatial modes. The first (top) has the largest eigenvalue, or in other words accounts for the most rCBF variance. Note the similarity between this spatial mode and the SPM{t} in Figure 6.4a. The first two principal components account for a substantial amount of variance (84%). This means that nearly all the rCBF changes can reproduced by some combination of these two modes. (Right) The principal component scores for the corresponding spatial modes. These scores represent the degree to which each mode is expressed in each condition. Clearly the first mode is strongly associated with the different word tasks and the second with time effects. The gray scale is arbitrary. (b) The same as (a) but for the fMRI data. (Left) The first three modes. The first SPM{PC} (top) accounts for 48% of the variance. Note the similarity between this spatial mode and the SPM{} in Figure 6.3a. (Right) The principal component scores for the corresponding spatial mode. The first mode is strongly associated with photic stimulation, the second represents a transient due to magnetic saturation and the third corresponds to time effects.

FIG. 6.10.   The standard SPM projections through the brain show the pattern of functional connectivity shown by normal volunteers in a PET experiment on word generation. Areas within each figure are positively related. The relationship between the figures is reciprocal, i.e. increases in left frontal activity (a) are associated with decreases in temporal lobe activity (b). Part (c) shows a measure of the extent to which this pattern of activity was present in four groups of volunteers. The three groups of chronic schizophrenic patients show significantly less connectivity of the normal kind. These three groups differed in terms of their speech behaviour (poverty of speech, odd speech and normal speech, respectively) but all showed a lack of the normal pattern of connectivity. From Friston & Frith (1995).

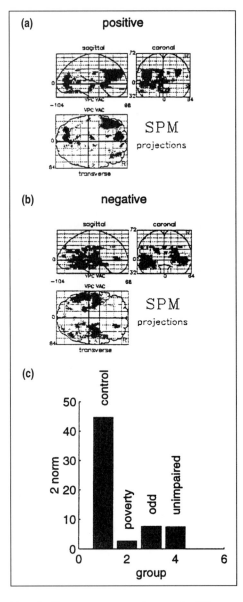

and corresponds to the photic stimulation response shown in Figure 6.3a (top). The third mode reflects time effects (which may be due to subject movement) of a complex nature, which were most evident in the medial cortex, extending from the cuneus to lingual gyrus. The second mode accounts for 21% of the variance, but does not have a counterpart in the PET data. This modality-specific mode is evident only in the first few scans. It can be attributed to the effects of progressive magnetic saturation, which is most pronounced in voxels containing cerebrospinal fluid, which takes a long time to return to equilibrium in high magnetic fields. This result illustrates another benefit that can be achieved with unconstrained analysis in terms of spatial modes. The second and third modes have identified what are essentially nuisance variables irrelevant to the experimental design, i.e. subject movement and magnetic saturation. The first mode is, by definition, independent of the other modes and reflects true physiological variance uncontaminated by these nuisance factors.

As yet few studies have been done that have applied this method of analysis to data from PET or fMRI. The mapping of cognitive processes in both the normal and the abnormal case has been dominated by the lesion–deficit model. A discrete brain area is assumed to have a discrete cognitive function such that damage to that area will result in a circumscribed cognitive deficit. However, there is a class of disorders for which this approach may well not be appropriate. About 100 years ago the distinction was made between the organic and the functional psychoses (or perhaps, neurological and psychiatric patients). The functional psychoses, of which the most common is schizophrenia, were (and are) believed to be biological in origin, but were not associated with any detectable brain lesion or neuropathological marker. Wernicke (1906) made the suggestion that these disorders resulted from damage to the organ of association, by which he meant the long fibres connecting high-level association areas. In other words, disorders such as schizophrenia do not result from abnormalities in discrete brain areas, but from disconnections within distributed brain systems. We have taken the first steps in testing this hypothesis by applying measures of functional connectivity to PET data from chronic schizophrenic patients and controls (Friston & Frith 1995). All subjects performed the verbal fluency task described above. The control subjects showed the strongly interconnected network of areas we have already described, including the reciprocal relationship between DLPFC and superior temporal cortex. Such connectivity was strikingly absent in the schizophrenic patients, particularly that between DLPFC and left temporal lobe (see Fig. 6.10). Recently, a number of authors (e.g. Murray & Lewis 1987, Breslin & Weinberger 1990) have suggested that schizophrenia is a neurodevelopmental disorder (and have even provided a small amount of evidence in favour of this hypothesis). Developmental disorders in general are likely to be characterized by failures and abnormalities of connections between brain areas, whether the associated cognitive abnormalities are manifested early (as in developmental dyslexia) or late (as in schizophrenia). Analysis of brain imaging data in terms of functional (and effective connectivity) may be particularly suitable for the study of such groups.

6.5 CONCLUSION

The analysis of localized and distributed cerebral function has been examined by reviewing a series of complementary data analysis techniques. To date the functional imaging literature has focused almost exclusively on subtraction techniques and (explicitly or implicitly) on functional segregation, as a principle of brain organization. An alternative framework has been introduced, in terms of analysing spatial modes defined by their functional interconnectivity. This approach appears to be very good at identifying separable distributed systems and processes. We have focused on PET and fMRI data, but the same techniques can be applied to any method for imaging brain function. A major strength of the techniques we have described is that they are all derived from the classical statistical methods first proposed by Fisher (1942) and developed intensively since then. There are, of course, novel problems associated with brain imaging because the data consist of a very large number of non-independent voxels extended in space and time. We have not addressed these problems directly in this chapter; discussion of the relevant theory and techniques can be found in Friston (1995). All the methods we have described are parametric and assume that the data are continuous and (roughly) normally distributed. Re-cently, techniques have been developed which permit non-parametric approaches to be applied to brain imaging data. These techniques are independent of the underlying distribution, but (for the moment) are very demanding on computing time. However, the driving force behind the analysis of functional brain images should be theories of brain function rather than statistical techniques. For this reason we have organized our chapter in terms of functional segregation and functional integration. Over the next few years, largely because of the new vistas opened up by functional brain imaging experiments, new theories of brain function are going to emerge and new analytical techniques will be continually developed to accommodate them.

REFERENCES

Aertsen, A. & H. Preissl 1991. Dynamics of activity and connectivity in physiological neuronal networks. In *Nonlinear dynamics and neuronal networks*, H. G. Schuster (ed.), 281–302. New York: VCH.

Baddeley, A. 1986. *Working Memory*. Oxford: Oxford University Press.

Breslin, N. A. & D. R. Weinberger 1990. Schizophrenia and the normal functional development of the prefrontal cortex. *Development and Psychopathology* **2**, 409–24.

Deiber, M.-P., J. G. Colebatch, K. J. Friston, P. D. Nixon, R. S. J. Frackowiak, R. E. Passingham 1991. Cortical areas and the selection of movements. *Experimental Brain Research* **84**, 393–402.

Dvorak, I. & A. V. Holden 1991. *Mathematical approaches to brain functioning diagnostics*. Manchester: Manchester University Press.

Engel, A. K., P. König, C. M. Gray, W. Singer 1990. Stimulus-dependent neuronal oscillations in cat visual cortex: inter-columnar interaction as determined by cross-correlation analysis. *European Journal of Neuroscience* **2**, 588–606.

Ferrier, D. 1875. Experiments on the brain of monkeys. *Proceedings of the Royal Society of London* **23**, 409–30.

Fisher, R. A. 1942. *Statistical methods for research workers*. Edinburgh: Oliver & Boyd.

Fox, P. T. & M. A. Mintun 1989. Non-invasive functional brain mapping by change distribution analysis of averaged PET images of $H^{15}O_2$ tissue activity. *Journal of Nuclear Medicine* **30**, 141–9.

Fox, P. T. & M. E. Raichle 1986. Focal physiological uncoupling of cerebral blood flow and oxidative metabolism during somatosensory stimulation in human subjects. *Proceedings of the National Academy of Sciences, USA* **83**, 1140–4.

Friston, K. J. 1995. Statistical parametric mapping: ontology and current issues. *Journal of Cerebral Blood Flow & Metabolism* **15**, 361–70.

Friston, K. J. & C. D. Frith 1995. Schizophrenia: a disconnection syndrome? *Clinical Neuroscience* **3**, 89–97.

Friston, K. J., R. E. Passingham, J. G. Nutt, J. D. Heather, G. V. Sawle, R. S. J. Frackowiak 1989. Localisation in PET images: direct fitting of the intercommissural (AC–PC) line. *Journal of Cerebral Blood Flow and Metabolism* **9**, 690–5.

Friston, K. J., C. D. Frith, P. F. Liddle, R. J. Dolan, A. A. Lammertsma, R. S. J. Frackowiak 1990. The relationship between global and local changes in PET scans. *Journal of Cerebral Blood Flow and Metabolism* **10**, 458–66.

Friston, K. J., C. D. Frith, P. F. Liddle, R. S. J. Frackowiak 1991a. Plastic transformation of PET images. *Journal of Computer Assisted Tomography* **15**, 634–9.

Friston, K. J., C. D. Frith, P. F. Liddle, R. S. J. Frackowiak 1991b. Comparing functional (PET) images: The assessment of significant change. *Journal of Cerebral Blood Flow Metabolism* **11**, 690–9.

Friston, K. J., C. D. Frith, R. E. Passingham, P. F. Liddle, R. S. J. Frackowiak 1992a. Motor practice and neurophysiological adaptation in the cerebellum: a positron tomographic study. *Proceedings of the Royal Society of London, Part B* **248**, 223–8.

Friston, K. J., P. M. Grasby, C. J. Bench, C. D. Frith, P. J. Cowen, P. F. Liddle, R. S. J. Frackowiak, R. Dolan 1992b. Measuring the neuromodulatory effects of drugs with positron emission tomography. *Neuroscience Letters* **141**, 106–10.

Friston, K. J., C. D. Frith, P. F. Liddle, R. S. J. Frackowiak 1992c. Functional connectivity: the principal-component analysis of large (PET) data sets. *Journal of Cerebral Blood Flow and Metabolism* **13**, 5–14.

Friston, K. J., P. Jezzard, R. Turner 1994. Analysis of functional MRI time-series. *Human Brain Mapping* **2**, 69–78.

Frith, C. D., K. J. Friston, P. F. Liddle, R. S. J. Frackowiak 1991. Willed action and the prefrontal cortex in man: a study with PET. *Proceedings of the Royal Society of London, Part B* **244**, 241–6.

Gerstein, G. L. & D. H. Perkel 1969. Simultaneously recorded trains of action potentials: analysis and functional interpretation. *Science* **164**, 828–30.

Gerstein, G. L., P. Bedenbaugh, A. M. H. J. Aertsen 1989. Neuronal assemblies. *IEEE Transactions on Biomedical Engineering* **36**, 4–14.

Gilbert, P. F. & C. W. T. Thach 1977. Purkinje cell activity during motor learning. *Brain Research* **128**, 309–28.

Gochin, P. M., E. K. Miller, C. G. Gross, G. L. Gerstein 1991. Functional interactions among neurons in inferior temporal cortex of the awake macaque. *Experimental Brain Research* **84**, 505–16.

Goltz, F. 1881. In *Transactions of the 7th International Medical Congress* vol. 1, W. MacCormac (ed.), 218–28. London: J. W. Kolkmann.

Grafton, S., J. Mazziotta, S. Presty, K. J. Friston, R. S. J. Frackowiak, M. Phelps 1992. Functional anatomy of human procedural learning determined with regional cerebral blood flow and PET. *Journal of Neuroscience* **12**, 2542–8.

Grasby, P. M., K. J. Friston, C. Bench, P. J. Cowen, C. D. Frith, P. F. Liddle, R. S. J. Frackowiak, R. J. Dolan 1992. Effect of the 5-HT$_{1a}$ partial agonist buspirone on regional cerebral blood flow in man. *Psychopharmacology* **108**, 380–6.

Grasby, P. M., C. D. Frith, K. J. Friston, C. Bench, R. S. J. Frackowiak, R. J. Dolan 1993. Functional mapping of brain areas implicated in auditory–verbal memory function. *Brain* **116**, 1–20.

Grasby, P. M., C. D. Frith, K. J. Friston, J. Simpson, P. C. Fletcher, R. S. J. Frackowiak, R. J. Dolan 1994. A graded task approach to the functional mapping of brain areas implicated in auditory-verbal memory. *Brain* **117**, 1271–82.

Hill, A. V. 1926. The heat production of nerve. *Journal of Pharmacology and Experimental Therapeutics* **29**, 161–5.

Jenkins, I. H., W. Fernandez, E. D. Playford, A. J. Lees, R. S. J. Frackowiak, R. E. Passingham, D. J. Brooks 1992. Impaired activity of the supplementary motor area in Parkinson's disease is reversed when akinesia is treated with apomorphine. *Annals of Neurology* **32**, 749–57.

Landau, W. M., W. H. J. Freygang, L. P. Roland, L. Sokoloff, S. S. Kety 1955. The local circulation of the living brain: values in the unanesthetized and anesthetized cat. *Transactions of the American Neurological Association* **80**, 125–9.

Lassen, N. A., K. Hoedt-Rasmussen, S. C. Sorensen, E. Skihoj, S. Cronquist, B. Bodforss, E. Eng, D. H. Ingvar 1963. Regional cerebral blood flow in man determined by krypton–85. *Neurology* **13**, 719–27.

Liddle, P. F., K. J. Friston, C. D. Frith, S. R. Hirsch, T. Jones, R. S. J. Frackowiak 1992. Patterns of cerebral blood flow in schizophrenia. *British Journal of Psychiatry* **160**, 179–86.

Lueck, C. J., S. Zeki, K. J. Friston, M. P. Deiber, P. Cope, V. J. Cunningham, A. A. Lammertsma, C. Kenard, R. S. J. Frackowiak 1989. *Nature* **340**, 386–9.

Mata, M. D., D. J. Fink, H. Gainer, C. B. Smith, L. Davidsen, H. Savaki, W. J. Schwartz, L. Sokoloff 1980. Activity-dependent energy metabolism in rat posterior pituitary primarily reflects sodium pump activity. *Journal of Neurochemistry* **34**, 213–15.

Murray, R. M. & S. W. Lewis 1987. Is schizophrenia a developmental disorder? *British Medical Journal* **295**, 681–2.

Petersen, S. E., P. T. Fox, M. I. Posner, M. Mintun, M. E. Raichle 1988. Position emission tomographic studies of the cortical anatomy of singleward processing. *Nature* **331**, 585–9.

Phillips, C. G., S. Zeki, H. B. Barlow 1984. Localization of function in the cerebral cortex. *Brain* **107**, 327–61.

Playford, E. D., H. I. Jenkins, R. E. Passingham, J. Nutt, R. S. J. Frackowiak, D. J. Brooks 1992. Impaired mesial frontal and putamen activation in Parkinson's disease. *Annals of Neurology* **32**, 151–61.

Posner, M. I. & M. E. Raichle 1994. *Images of mind*. New York: W. H. Freeman.

Posner, M. I., J. Sandson, M. Dhawan, G. L. Shulman 1989. Is word recognition automatic: a cognitive anatomical approach. *Journal of Cognitive Neuroscience* **1**, 50–60

Price, C., R. J. S. Wise, S. Ramsay, K. J. Friston, D. Howard, K. Patterson, R. S. J. Frackowiak 1992. Regional response differences within the human auditory cortex when listening to words. *Neuroscience Letters* **146**, 179–82.

Raichle, M. E. 1987. Circulatory and metabolic correlates of brain function in normal humans. In *Handbook of physiology: the nervous system*, vol. 5, F. Plum & V. Mountcastle (eds), 643–74. Baltimore/Bethesa:American Psychological Society/Williams & Wilkins.

Ramsay, S. C., K. Murphy, S. A. Shea, K. J. Friston, A. A. Lammertsma, J. C. Clark, L. Adams et al. 1993. Changes in global cerebral blood flow in humans: effects on regional cerebral blood flow during a neural activation task. *Journal of Physiology* **471**, 521–34.

Roy, C. S. & C. S. Sherrington 1890. On the regulation of the blood supply of the brain. *Journal of Physiology* **11**, 85–108.

Shallice, T., P. Fletcher, C. D. Frith, P. Grasby, R. S. J. Frackowiak, R. J. Dolan 1994. Brain regions associated with acquisition and retrieval of verbal episodic memory. *Nature* **368**, 633–5.

Sokoloff, L. 1981. Relationships among local functional activity, energy metabolism and blood flow in the central nervous system. *Federation Proceedings* **40**, 2311–16.

Spinks, T. J., T. Jones, D. L. Bailey, D. W. Townsend, S. Grootoonk, P. M. Bloomfield, M. C. Gilardi et al. 1992. Physical performance of a positron tomograph for brain imaging with retractable septa. *Physics in Medicine and Biology* **37**, 1637–55.

Talairach. J. & P. Tournoux 1988. *A co-planar stereotaxic atlas of a human brain*. Stuttgart: Thieme.

Townsend, D. W., A. Geissbuhler, M. Defrise, E. J. Hoffman, T. J. Spinks, D. L. Bailey, M. C. Gilardi et al. 1992. Fully three dimensional reconstruction for a PET camera with retractable septa. *IEEE Transactions of Medical Imaging* **M1–10**, 505–12.

Turner, R. & P. Jezzard 1994. Magnetic resonance functional imaging of the brain at 4T. *MAGMA* **2**, 147–56.

Watson, J. D. G., R. Myers, R. S. J. Frackowiak, J. V. Hajnal, R. P. Woods, J. C. Mazziotta, S. Shipp, S. Zeki 1993. Area V5 of the human brain. *Cerebral Cortex* **3**, 79–94.

Wernicke, C. 1906. *Grundrisse der Psychiatrie*. Leipzig: Thieme.

Zeki, S. 1978. Functional specialisation in the visual cortex of the monkey. *Nature* **274**, 423–8.

Zeki, S., J. D. G. Watson, C. J. Lueck, K. J. Friston, C. Kennard, R. S. J. Frackowiak 1991. A direct demonstration of functional specialisation in human visual cortex. *Journal of Neuroscience* **11**(3), 641–9.

CHAPTER 7

Electrical and magnetic readings of mental functions

Marta Kutas & Anders Dale

Ever since Berger's (1929) discovery that brain electrical activity (electroencephalogram (EEG)) can be measured at the human scalp, it has been assumed that in these voltage fluctuations are hidden the mysteries of the workings of the human mind. While classical neurophysiologists questioned the likelihood that such "simple" fluctuations could be the key to the complexities of understanding, talking, reasoning, imagining and supposing, the past 70 years have proven otherwise. A large body of evidence has shown that electrical and magnetic activity (human or otherwise) encode information about brain states and brain processes and, by inference, about mental states and mental processes. The exact mapping from neural structures to sensory, perceptual and cognitive processes and states is not at all transparent, but all neuroimaging techniques are based on the assumption that such mappings exist and are decipherable.

In this chapter we examine the nature of the mapping between perception, movement and cognition on the one hand and electrical and magnetic activity at various scalp locations on the other. In this regard, it is important to remember that the brain's currency at a neurophysiological level is electrochemical activity. It is the pattern of electrical activity at the scalp that doctors and scientists alike take to be a sign of how and how well the brain is functioning. As we will document, electrical and magnetic activity can be used within the context of psychological experiments to assess the brain's sensitivity to various experimental manipulations, and thereby to constrain psychological theories of various cognitive and behavioural phenomena. The chapter starts with a few references to some basics of electrical (event-related potentials (ERPs)) and magnetic (event-related fields (ERF)) recording. This is followed by a short tutorial on the physiology and physics of electrical and magnetic activity, a discussion of the types of inference that can and cannot be drawn from such measurements, and a cursory overview of the most widely used terms in cognitive electrophysiology. We conclude with a few specific examples of cognitive ERP and ERF research.

7.1 EVENT-RELATED ACTIVITY: ELECTRICAL (ERPS) AND MAGNETIC (ERFS)

An ERP/ERF experiment requires a willing participant, electrodes for recording the brain wave activity or a magnetometer, some means of presenting stimuli, amplifiers and a digitizer that turns the analogue data into a digital form for storage, further representation and analyses. Technical details about electrodes, electrode placement, amplifiers, magnetic recordings, digitization and analyses can be found in a number of articles and books (Cooper et al. 1974, Regan 1989, Hamalainen et al. 1993, Rugg & Coles 1995).

There are many ways to look at electrical and magnetic activity in both the temporal and spatial domains. The emphasis of this chapter is on scalp activity, specifically that which is time-locked or synchronized to some external stimulus or event. Typically, the earliest or so-called "exogenous" components of the ERP are used in a clinical setting to assess the integrity of the peripheral or central nervous system, although they are clearly essential for understanding cognitive effects as well (for more in-depth discussion see Desmedt 1988, Starr & Don 1988, Regan 1989). Since the evoked response to a single stimulus at the scalp is quite small (5–10µV), it must be extracted from the background activity via averaging. Averaging enhances the signal (or whatever is invariant from trial to trial) and reduces what is random (noise) to nearly zero, improving the signal-to-noise ratio by a factor proportional to the square root of the number of trials. Since the assumptions of averaging are often violated, single-trial ERP data have also been examined using pattern recognition techniques, cross-correlation, Woody filter and step-wise discriminant analysis (e.g. Glaser & Ruchkin 1976, Gevins & Remond 1987), although averaging remains the most common technique.

7.1.1 How ERPs are generated by the brain

The net flow of current across the neural membrane generates an electric potential in the conductive media both inside and outside the cells. It is this electric potential that forms the basis for the electrophysiological recordings made both invasively, by lowering electrodes into the brain, and non-invasively, by placing electrodes on the scalp for EEG/ERP (Nicholson & Freeman 1975, Nunez 1981). The same transmembrane current flows are also responsible for the magnetic fields recorded outside the head for MEG (the magnetoencephalogram). Viewed from outside the neurons, each patch of membrane acts as a tiny current source or sink, depending on whether the net local current flow is outward or inward, respectively. The electric potential Φ and magnetic field $\bar{\mathbf{B}}$ are given by the following linear differential equations (Hamalainen, et al. 1993)

$$\nabla \cdot (\sigma \nabla \Phi) = \nabla \cdot \bar{\mathbf{J}}^i \tag{1}$$

$$\nabla \cdot \bar{\mathbf{B}} = 0 \tag{2}$$

$$\nabla \times \bar{\mathbf{B}} = \mu_0 \left(\bar{\mathbf{J}}^i - \sigma \nabla \Phi \right) \tag{3}$$

where $\bar{\mathbf{J}}^i$ are the impressed currents, corresponding to microscopic non-Ohmic transmembrane currents due to ionic concentration gradients, and σ represents the electrical conductivity.[1] Φ, $\bar{\mathbf{B}}$ and $\bar{\mathbf{J}}^i$ all vary as functions of both space and time, while σ is assumed to vary as a function of space but not as a function of time. These equations can, in principle, be used to calculate the potential and magnetic field anywhere inside or outside the head for any arbitrary distribution of neural membrane currents. It is not essential to understand the details of these equations for the purposes of this chapter. However, it is important to understand certain simple properties of these equations for the subsequent discussion:

(a) Both the electric potential and the magnetic field at time t depend on the membrane currents only at time t; in other words, the propagation of the potential and magnetic fields is essentially instantaneous.

(b) All three equations are linear, i.e. if $\bar{\mathbf{B}}_1, \bar{\mathbf{J}}^i_1, \Phi_1$ and $\bar{\mathbf{B}}_2, \bar{\mathbf{J}}^i_2, \Phi_2$ both satisfy the equations, then so must $c_1 \bar{\mathbf{B}}_1 + c_2 \bar{\mathbf{B}}_2$, $c_1 \bar{\mathbf{J}}^i_1 + c_2 \bar{\mathbf{J}}^i_2$, and $c_1 \Phi_1 + c_2 \Phi_2$ where c_1 and c_2 are scalar constants. Hence, the potential and magnetic field produced by a weighted sum of two current source distributions are equal to a weighted sum of the fields produced by each current source distribution alone.

Consequently, the electric potential and magnetic field generated by a particular spatial distribution of current sources and sinks can be computed either by adding up the individual contributions of each current source and sink in the entire source space or, alternatively, by partitioning the source space into a number of regions, calculating the contributions of all the sources and sinks within each region, and then adding together the contribution of each region. In either case, the resultant field is the same. For simplicity we will assume that the sources and sinks are inside an infinite homogeneous conductor; that is, that the conductivity σ is constant. Although an infinite homogeneous conductor is not a very good model of a human head, as the conductivity of brain, skull and air are quite different, on the whole the principles we discuss below generalize to more realistic conductors.

The potential produced by a single current source within such a homogeneous conductor is given by

$$\Phi_1 = \frac{s}{4\pi\sigma r} \tag{4}$$

where s is the strength of the current source (or sink, if s is negative), and r is the distance from the source to the measuring point. First, let us consider the case of a current source and a current sink of equal strength s, located at distances r_1 and r_2, respectively, from the measuring point. The potential produced by this dipole can be calculated by adding the separate contribution from each source and sink,

$$\Phi_2 = \frac{s}{4\pi\sigma r_1} - \frac{s}{4\pi\sigma r_2} = \frac{s}{4\pi\sigma}\left(\frac{1}{r_1} - \frac{1}{r_2}\right) \tag{5}$$

However, if the distance between the dipole and the measuring point is several times greater than that between the dipole sink and source, the equation can be simplified as follows:[2]

$$\Phi_2 \approx \left(\frac{1}{4\pi\sigma}\right)\frac{s\vec{d}\cdot\vec{r}}{r^3}, \quad r \gg d \tag{6}$$

where $\vec{d}$ is the vector from the dipole source to the sink, and $\vec{r}$ is the vector from the centre of the dipole to the measuring point. Note that, while the potential produced by a source or sink (monopole) falls off as r^{-1} with distance, the potential produced by a dipole falls off more rapidly, specifically as r^{-2}. The potential produced by any arbitrary collection of sources and sinks can be expressed in terms of a multipole expansion:

$$\Phi \approx \Phi_1 + \Phi_2 + O\left(r^{-3}\right) \tag{7}$$

where Φ_1 is a monopolar term, as in Equation 4, Φ_2 is a dipole term, as in Equation 6, and $O(r^{-3})$ represents so-called quadropolar, octopolar and higher order terms which fall off as r^{-3}, or faster, with distance. Hence, we see that the electric potential produced by a collection of current sources and sinks within a region can be approximated closely by considering only the monopolar and dipolar terms, as long as the size of the region is small relative to the distance at which the measurements are made.

Now, recall that the current sources and sinks in the brain correspond to currents flowing through neural membranes. Since the total amount of current leaving a cell must equal the total amount of current entering the cell, the monopolar term in the multipole expansion of the source–sink distribution of a cell must equal zero. Thus, under these circumstances, where activity of neurons in a patch of tissue is observed at a distance much greater than the linear extent of the patch, only the dipolar term of the multipole expansion need be considered. In short, the distribution of sources and sinks within such a patch can be represented by a single so-called "equivalent dipole" located in the middle of the patch.

If the sources and sinks are distributed in an approximately radially symmetric fashion within the patch of tissue, the dipole term vanishes. This is known as a "closed field" source configuration. For example, if we assume that all the dendrites of the neurons illustrated in the top row of Figure 7.1 are activated to a similar extent, on average, then the current sources and sinks in a given cell will be distributed in an approximately radially symmetric fashion, and the resulting dipole moment vanishes. In other words, no potential would be recorded at a distance. Figure 7.1 also shows two other examples of closed fields, where the net dipole moment of the collection of cells is zero, either because the cells are oriented in a random fashion (middle row), or because the activity of the cells is not synchronized (bottom row).

In summary, we see that a patch of brain tissue produces an externally observable electric potential or magnetic field if, and only if, (a) the average distribution of sources and sinks within the neuron in the patch is distributed in a non-radially symmetric fashion, (b) the neurons are aligned in some systematic fashion, and (c) the neurons are activated in a synchronized fashion, as illustrated in Figure 7.2. The neocortex is one of the main structures of the brain which satisfies all these constraints. It is organized as a large folded sheet a few millimetres thick.About 70% of the cells in the neocortex are pyramidal cells which have apical

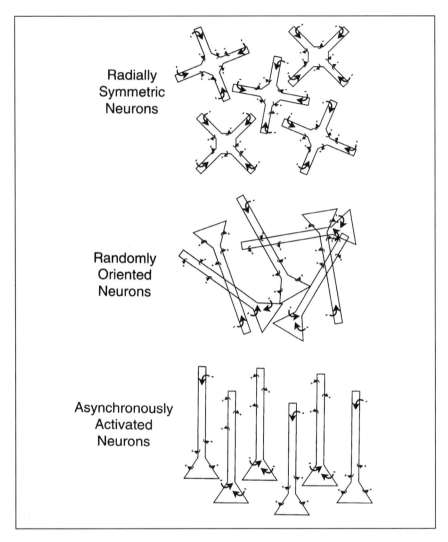

FIG. 7.1.   Examples of self-cancelling or closed field source configurations. Neurons which are radially symmetric, randomly oriented or asynchronously activated do not produce externally observable electric or magnetic fields.

dendrites extending from the soma towards the surface of the sheet, which gives the cortex a columnar appearance. When the proximal parts of the apical dendrites of a cell are activated, currents flow into the cell around the soma, and currents flow out of the cell at more distal sites, thus creating an approximately dipolar source–sink configuration oriented perpendicularly to the cortical sheet (Nunez 1981). Similarly, if

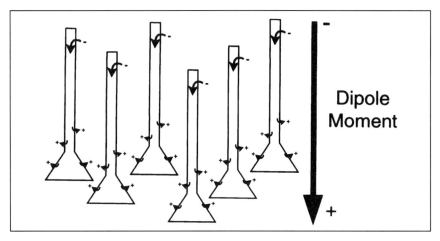

FIG. 7.2.   Open field source configuration. Neurons which are non-radially symmetric, spatially aligned and synchronously activated add up to produce externally observable electric and/or magnetic fields.

the distal parts of the dendrites are activated, a dipole field of the opposite orientation is generated. Of course, the potential and magnetic field produced by a single cortical pyramidal neuron are quite weak, but those produced by a patch of cortex containing hundreds of thousands of such cells may be strong enough to be detected even at a considerable distance from the patch. These are believed to be the primary source of scalp-recorded ERPs and associated ERFs.

Since non-invasive measurements of electric potential and magnetic field are made at a distance of at least 1 cm from the nearest cortex and the thickness of the cortex is, at most, a few millimetres, we can approximate the source–sink distribution within a patch of cortex by a single equivalent dipole located in the middle of the patch and oriented perpendicularly to it. For that given dipole the electric potential $\Phi_i(t)$ measured at the ith electrode at time t can be expressed as

$$\Phi_i(t) = e_i s(t) \tag{8}$$

where $s(t)$ is the strength of the dipole, and e_i is a scalar constant which depends on the location and orientation of the dipole as well as on the conductive properties of the head. Similarly, the magnetic field $\bar{\mathbf{b}}_i(t)$ measured at the ith sensor location can be expressed as

$$\bar{\mathbf{b}}_i(t) = \bar{\mathbf{m}}_i s(t) \tag{9}$$

where $\bar{\mathbf{m}}_i$ is a three-vector constant which depends on the location and

orientation of the dipole and the conductive properties of the head
(Grynszpan & Geselowitz 1973, Cuffin & Cohen 1977, Oostendorp &
van Oosterom 1989). Since a magnetic sensor (superconducting quan-
tum interference device (SQUID)) does not measure the magnetic field
vector at a point, but rather the scalar magnetic field component in
some particular direction, we can rewrite Equation (9) as

$$b_i(t) = m_i s(t) , \qquad (10)$$

where b_i is the scalar magnetic measurement, and m_i is a scalar coefficient relating the dipole strength s to the measurement. Because of the
linear nature of the forward equations we can express the electric potential and magnetic field generated by the entire cortex as

$$\Phi_i(t) = \sum_j^p e_{i,j} s_j(t) \qquad (11)$$

and

$$b_i(t) = \sum_j^p m_{i,j} s_j(t) \qquad (12)$$

where p is the number of patches, s_j is the strength of the equivalent
dipole in patch j, and $e_{i,j}$ and $m_{i,j}$ are scalar constants relating the jth
patch to the ith electric and magnetic recording sites, respectively. Note
that Equations (11) and (12) are of exactly the same form, i.e. the
instantaneous electric and magnetic measurements are both linearly
related to the instantaneous dipole strengths. This makes it possible to
combine these equations into a single equation for the combined electric and magnetic measurements

$$\bar{\mathbf{x}}(t) = \sum_j^p \bar{\mathbf{g}}_j s_j(t) , \qquad (13)$$

where $\bar{\mathbf{x}}$ is an n-dimensional vector of combined electric and magnetic
measurements (where n is the total number of sensors, electric plus
magnetic), and $\bar{\mathbf{g}}_j$ is a so-called gain vector specifying the electric and
magnetic measurement at each sensor generated by a unit of dipole
strength at the jth patch.

Equation (13) can be written even more compactly, in matrix form, as

$$\bar{\mathbf{x}}(t) = \mathbf{G}\bar{\mathbf{s}}(t) \qquad (14)$$

where $\mathbf{G}$ is an n by p matrix whose jth column is the gain vector
$\bar{\mathbf{g}}_j$ for the jth dipole, and $\bar{\mathbf{s}}$ is a vector of dipole strengths.

Although, as we have seen, electric and magnetic signals are generated by the brain in a very similar way, the two types of measure do provide somewhat different views of the underlying brain activity. This is because the electric and magnetic recordings are affected differently by factors such as head shape, and dipole location and orientation.[3] For instance, the magnetic field strength falls off much more rapidly with the depth of a dipole than does the electric potential. Furthermore, while the electric potential is affected by dipoles of any orientation, the magnetic field is mainly sensitive to the tangential component of the dipole moment, i.e. the portion of the dipole oriented tangentially to the scalp. A purely radially oriented dipole, regardless of depth, produces almost no magnetic field outside the head.

In practical terms, this means that MEG is mostly sensitive to superficial, largely tangentially oriented dipoles. Given that the primary source of the MEG and EEG are the cortical pyramidal cells, oriented perpendicularly to the cortical sheet, it follows that the MEG is mostly sensitive to activity in the superficial parts of the sulci, and much less sensitive to activity on the crowns of gyri or in the depths of sulci. While the MEG provides only a limited view of brain activity compared with the EEG, it has the advantage of being largely unaffected by skull and conductive inhomogeneities in the intervening tissue. This makes the magnetic field easier to model quantitatively than the electric potential, for which the exact shape and conductive properties of the head have to be taken into account.

In summary, the MEG mostly provides information about the synchronous activation of parallel-oriented populations of pyramidal cells located superficially within cortical sulci. The EEG provides a broader picture of underlying neuronal activity, which includes both superficial and deep sources at various orientations relative to the scalp. However, since the EEG and MEG provide somewhat complementary information about the same underlying brain activity, the broadest picture of this activity can be obtained by combining the two kinds of measure (Wood et al. 1985, Dale & Sereno 1993).

7.1.2 What can be inferred from ERPs?

In this section we discuss how ERPs can be used to make inferences about cognitive processes and their associated neural activity. The classical approach has been to identify certain so-called "components" of the ERP, usually positive or negative peaks with characteristic scalp distributions and latencies, which can be shown to be reliably correlated with particular experimental manipulations. It is often assumed that, since such a peak is correlated with a particular cognitive process, it can in fact be used as a physiological index of that process. Based on this reasoning, it follows that the timing of the process can be inferred from the latency of the corresponding peak, and the degree of activation or "strength" of the process can be inferred from the amplitude of or area under the peak. Moreover, according to this view, the question of whether two experimental conditions involve the same cognitive process reduces to the question of whether both conditions evoke the same component. It may be worthwhile to examine more closely the assumptions implicit in this reasoning.

Before doing so, however, it is important to note that there is no single, universally accepted definition of an ERP component. In some cases, "component" merely refers to a peak or a trough in the waveform. According to one of its more common usages, which we will call "functional", "component" refers to a delineated waveform feature whose approximate polarity, latency and scalp distribution are predictable from experimental (psychological) manipulations (Donchin 1979); in this view, the fact that an ERP is generated by the brain is taken to be irrelevant. At the other extreme, in a more "physiological" view, an ERP component is presumed to be the reflection of the activity of a particular generator or set of generators in the brain (Nunez 1981). Although few researchers start by explicitly defining their usage of the word "component", the majority seem to have adopted a position which is intermediate between or a combination of the "functional" and "physiological" usages. Let us examine the assumptions of this generic combined usage of the term.

From the discussions in the previous section, recall that neural activity in a particular location in the brain produces a characteristic spatial pattern of electric and magnetic measurements (cf. the gain vector in Eq. (13)). The definition of a "component" in terms of a characteristic scalp distribution thus implies that the neural activity associated with a particular component has a characteristic spatial distribution within the brain. The strength of such a component is often defined in terms of the peak measurement at a particular electrode within a particular latency range. This component strength is then used to infer something about the brain's sensitivity to some experimental variable. However, the idea that a peak measured at a given electrode reflects only the activity of a particular process implicitly assumes that the potential recorded at that electrode is affected by that process, and by that process alone. This assumption is potentially troubling, since we know that even highly localized foci of activity within the brain may produce widespread potential distributions on the scalp, and it is highly unlikely that there would only be a single process active at any given moment.

We will show the consequences of this assumption via a number of simple simulations. Let's imagine, for instance, that three processes (L,

R and M) involve neural activity at different locations, and that the current distributions in the tissue activated by each can be approximated by radially oriented dipoles on the left (L), right (R) and middle (M) of the brain, respectively. The scalp distributions of the potential generated by each of these dipoles in a homogeneous spherical head are shown on the left in Figure 7.3; the simulated ERP waveforms from 16

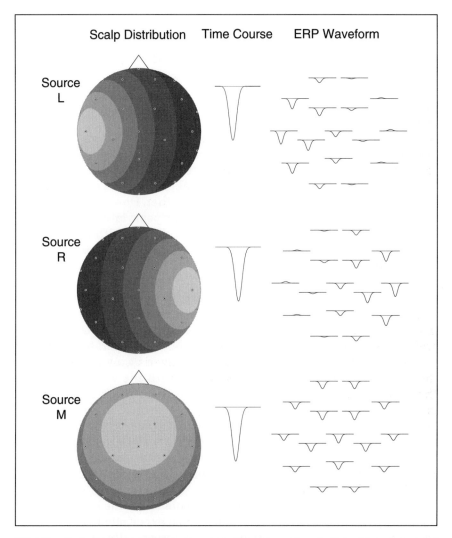

FIG. 7.3.   Scalp distribution, time-course and resulting ERP waveform for three different simulated neural generators. Sources L, R and M are represented by radially oriented dipoles located on the left, right and middle of the head, respectively.

different locations on the scalp generated by each of these dipoles are shown on the right. Clearly, the scalp distributions of the potentials generated by these three dipoles overlap greatly. In fact, dipole M would affect peak amplitude at all the electrodes. Thus, there is no simple measure at any electrode that can be used as a pure index for the activity of any of the three processes.

It may be argued that different components can be distinguished based on their scalp distributions, since the potentials generated by each of the dipoles L, R and M are quite distinguishable. However, consider the example shown in Figure 7.4 wherein the processes L and R are both activated but with slightly different latencies. The scalp distributions produced by the combination of these two dipoles, as shown on the bottom at three different latencies, is quite different from either one alone. In fact, the combined scalp distribution of L and R looks somewhat similar to that produced by dipole M (see Fig. 7.3). This example also illustrates another common misconception in ERP analysis based on peak amplitude or area measurements. It is often assumed that a peak reflects the same process at all electrodes, such that differences in peak latency at various locations can be taken to reflect propagation of the process from one side of the head to the other. However, the current example shows that continuous changes in peak latency across the scalp may instead be due to multiple fixed dipoles with different but overlapping time-courses. In fact, as we shall see later, changes in scalp distribution over time necessarily imply that several generators with different time-courses must be involved.

The fact that different brain generators produce widespread, overlapping potential distributions makes it essential to have a method for extracting the signal produced by each generator. As we see in the next section, if the scalp distribution of each generator is known, then the contribution of each generator is given by a weighted sum of the potentials recorded at each electrode, with the weights given by the least-squares solution. This makes it possible to determine the time-course of activation of each generator, and in turn to determine whether or not the same generator is involved in different experimental conditions. By this account, the contribution to the ERP of a particular source can be thought of as a component, and we can investigate how this component is affected by various experimental manipulations.

Unfortunately, however, we usually do not know the scalp distributions of all the generators involved in a given experiment. The problem of finding these scalp distributions is essentially equivalent to localizing all the generators, which, as we see in the next section, is a decidedly non-trivial problem. Nonetheless, as we show next, it is still

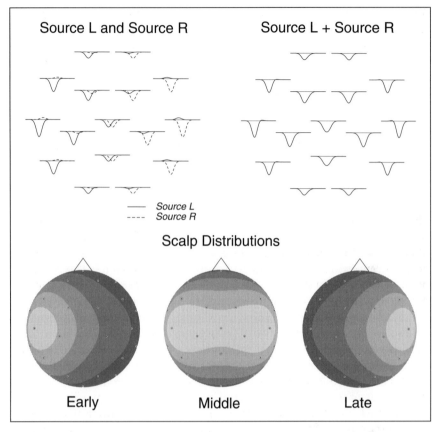

FIG. 7.4.   Spatial superpositioning of ERP waveforms produced by the two generators L and R. The difference in latency between sources L and R results in a gradual change in scalp distribution over time.

possible to draw certain important inferences about the underlying brain activity from ERP recordings without localizing the sources.

First, let us compare the ERPs from two experimental conditions (A and B). If A-ERP and B-ERP are (statistically) indistinguishable (across all electrode sites), then we can safely conclude that the pattern of data appears consistent with the hypothesis that the two conditions are identical. But can we safely offer this as evidence or proof that the brain activity evoked by the two conditions is identical? No! There are several reasons, other than the actual identity of the underlying neural activity, as to why the ERPs from two conditions could appear to be identical. For example, the EEG and MEG simply may not be the correct techniques for detecting the difference because the configuration of active generators generate no dipole moment (so-called closed fields). Another possible way we could easily be led astray would be if the measurements were not sensitive enough due to inappropriate temporal and/or spatial sampling, a poor recording technique or a similar factor.

Conversely, if the A-ERP and B-ERP do differ reliably, then it is safe to conclude (or as safe as science ever allows us to be) that the brain activity and the mental activities it subserves are different in the two conditions. For the moment we need not concern ourselves with either the nature or the cause of the difference. The fact is that the ERP difference indicates that some difference exists and, sometimes, being able to conclude that two conditions are different is a critical finding in and of itself. Any such ERP difference, obtained when by all psychological accounts the conditions were expected to be identical, should lead to a reformulation of the current working hypothesis that supports or at least allows the difference.

Of course, identifying a difference is merely the first step in a much longer process of ERP analysis. At a minimum, we can use the timing of the onset of an ERP difference to make additional inferences about the timing of the associated mental activity. If time t is the earliest time at which ERPs from the two conditions differ significantly, then we can conclude that the brain activity differs between the two conditions at time t. However, we may not conclude that there was no difference in brain activity before time t, because such differences simply may not be detectable with ERPs, as discussed above. In other words, the onset of the latency of the ERP difference must be taken as an upper limit on the time by which the brain must have processed the stimuli sufficiently to distinguish them.

It is also possible to make some inferences based on the spatial distribution of the ERPs. If a given condition involves only a single generator, then the ERP waveform for that condition must have the same scalp distribution across its entire extent. That is,

$$\bar{\mathbf{x}}(t) = \bar{\mathbf{g}} \cdot \mathbf{s}(t)$$

for all time points t, where $\bar{\mathbf{x}}(t)$ is the electric or magnetic recording vector, $s(t)$ is the strength of the generator and $\bar{\mathbf{g}}$ is the gain vector for the generator. Practically speaking, this means that if the scalp distribution changes over time we can conclude that there must be more than a single generator involved. In fact, we can go further than that by applying principal component analysis (PCA) to determine the minimum number of spatial basis vectors needed to account for the waveforms (Donchin 1979, Press et al. 1990). If a given set of ERP waveforms requires k basis vectors, i.e. PCA finds k significant "components",[4]

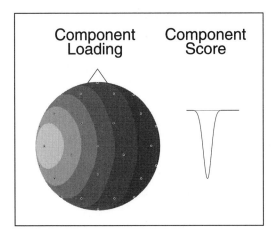

FIG. 7.5.   Result of applying spatial PCA to the ERP waveform produced by the single generator L. Note that the component loading and score accurately reflect the scalp distribution and time-course, respectively, of source L as shown in Figure 7.3.

then there must be at least k generators involved. Applying this PCA to the ERP produced by a single generator L in Figure 7.3 yields a single significant principal component, with the scalp distribution (known as the "loading") and time-course (known as the "score") shown in Figure 7.5. Note that the spatial distribution and time-course of this principal component are the same as that of generator L. Applying this analysis to an ERP waveform produced by two generators, such as the sum of dipoles L and R shown in Figure 7.4, yields two significant components, with the scalp distributions and scores shown in Figure 7.6. Note that, while the number of principal components in this case accurately reflects the number of generators,[5] the scalp distributions of the principal components and their scores do not reflect the actual scalp distributions and time-courses of the generators. This illustrates the point that PCA may be useful for providing a (lower) estimate of the number of generators, even though the principal component vectors do not necessarily correspond to the scalp distributions of actual sources, and their scores do not necessarily correspond to the time-courses of the actual sources.

In order to determine the actual scalp distributions and time-courses of activation of the generators of our observed ERPs and ERFs, we first have to determine the locations of these generators. In the next section we examine this so-called "source localization problem" more closely.

7.1.3 Source localization
Recall that if the locations and orientations of a set of k dipoles are known, then the combined electric and/or magnetic measurements can be expressed as a weighted sum of k gain vectors $\bar{\mathbf{g}}_j$, (see equations (13) and (14)),

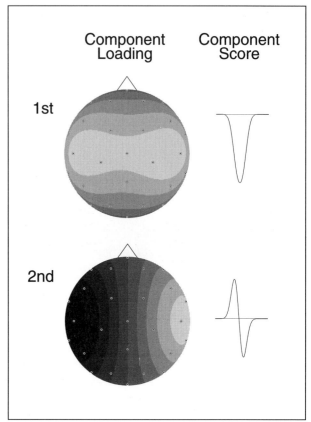

Component
Loading

Component
Score

1st

2nd

FIG. 7.6.   Result of applying spatial PCA to the ERP waveform produced by the two generators L and R. Note that, while the number of principal components (two) accurately reflects the number of sources, the component loadings and scores do not reflect the scalp distribution or time-course of either generator.

$$\bar{\mathbf{x}}(t) = \sum_{j}^{k} \bar{\mathbf{g}}_j \cdot \bar{\mathbf{s}}_j(t) = \mathbf{G}\bar{\mathbf{s}}(t) \qquad (15)$$

where the gain vectors $\bar{\mathbf{g}}_j$ depend on the locations and orientations of the dipoles, the locations of the sensors, and the shape and conductive properties of the head (Grynszpan & Geselowitz 1973, Cuffin & Cohen 1977, Nunez 1981, Oostendorp & van Oosterom 1989, Hamalainen 1993). Thus, the so-called "forward problem" of determining the electric potential and magnetic field produced by a given set of dipoles has a well-defined and unique solution. On the other hand, the so-called "inverse problem" of determining the locations, orientations and time-courses of the set of dipoles producing the electric and magnetic recordings is ill posed, i.e. it has no unique solution. In other words, there are, in general, infinitely many distributions of dipoles inside the brain which are consistent with any set of electric and/or magnetic recordings (Nunez

1981, Sarvas 1987). In order to overcome this fundamental ambiguity, it is necessary to impose some additional constraints on the solution.

The most common approach to this problem is to model the generators as some fixed number of so-called "equivalent dipoles", each representing the activity within some volume of tissue. The electric and magnetic recordings can be expressed as

$$\bar{\mathbf{x}}(t) = \sum_{j}^{k} \bar{\mathbf{g}}_j\left(\bar{\mathbf{r}}_j, \bar{\mathbf{d}}_j\right)\bar{s}_j(t) \tag{16}$$

where k is the number of equivalent dipoles, $s_j(t)$ is the strength of the jth dipole, and the gain vector $\bar{\mathbf{g}}_j\left(\bar{\mathbf{r}}_j, \bar{\mathbf{d}}_j\right)$ for the jth dipole is an explicit function of the dipole location $\bar{\mathbf{r}}_j$ and orientation $\bar{\mathbf{d}}_j$. The dipole locations, orientations, and strengths can be estimated by the method of least-squares (Oostendorp & van Oosterom 1989, Scherg 1989), i.e. by minimizing the error measure

$$E = \int_{t_0}^{t_1} dt \left\| \bar{\mathbf{x}}(t) - \bar{\mathbf{x}}_{obs}(t) \right\|^2$$

where $\bar{\mathbf{x}}_{obs}(t)$ is the observed electric and magnetic recording, and $\bar{\mathbf{x}}(t)$, the predicted recording, is given by Equation (16). Note that, while the relationship between dipole strength and electric or magnetic recordings is a simple, linear one, the recordings depend on the dipole location and orientation in a non-linear way. No efficient method for minimizing such non-linear cost functions is known, making it impractical to localize more than a few dipoles using this approach. Moreover, in general, it is impossible to know *a priori* how many equivalent dipoles to use.

Another approach to the inverse problem is to model the brain electric or magnetic generators as an essentially continuous dipole distribution, rather than as some pre-specified number of discrete equivalent dipoles. As discussed in a previous section, most of the observed electric and magnetic recordings are thought to be generated by post-synaptic currents in the apical dendrites of cortical pyramidal cells. Hence, we may assume that the dipole moment is zero everywhere except in the cortical gray matter, and that the local dipole moment is oriented perpendicularly to the cortical sheet. Given these assumptions, the inverse problem reduces to one of estimating dipole strength everywhere over the folded cortical surface.

Since dipole strength and electric or magnetic recordings are linearly related, the problem is a linear one. However, the number of dipole patches needed adequately to represent the cortical surface is much greater than the number of electric and/or magnetic sensors that can practically be applied, and hence the problem remains underdetermined. A common way to deal with this problem is to choose the so-called "minimum-norm solution", that is, the "shortest" dipole strength vector $\bar{\mathbf{s}}(t)$ satisfying

$$\bar{\mathbf{x}}_{obs}(t) = \mathbf{G}\bar{\mathbf{s}}(t)$$

(Hamalainen & Ilmoniemi 1984, Smith et al. 1990, Wang et al. 1992, Dale & Sereno 1993). The minimum-norm solution $\hat{\mathbf{s}}(t)$ is given by

$$\hat{\mathbf{s}}(t) = G^{\dagger}\mathbf{x}(t) \tag{18}$$

where
$$\mathbf{G}^{\dagger} = \mathbf{G}^{T}\left(\mathbf{G}\mathbf{G}^{T}\right)^{-1}$$

is the Moore–Penrose pseudo-inverse of the gain matrix $\mathbf{G}$. Although the minimum-norm constraint does provide a unique solution to the inverse problem, there is no guarantee that the solution is the correct one. In order further to disambiguate the inverse problem in a principled way, it is essential to impose additional constraints that are based on biological insights (Dale & Sereno 1993).

A particularly promising source of such additional constraints is functional imaging techniques, such as functional magnetic resonance imaging (fMRI) and, to a lesser extent, positron emission tomography (PET) (see Ch. 6). Although these techniques provide little information about the fine-grained temporal sequence of brain activity, they do provide information about average brain activity with relatively high and uniform spatial resolution (Belliveau et al. 1991, Ogawa et al. 1992). It seems reasonable to assume that the bioelectrical activity which is responsible for the observed electric and magnetic recordings is also likely to cause changes in metabolic and haemodynamic processes, which can be seen using fMRI or PET. The so-called linear estimation approach (Smith et al. 1990), of which minimum-norm estimation is a special case, makes it possible to use such functional imaging data as "soft" constraints on the inverse solution (Dale & Sereno 1993), thus potentially combining the spatial resolution of fMRI and the temporal resolution of EEG and MEG.

7.2 THE TERMS USED IN COGNITIVE ELECTROPHYSIOLOGY

By contrast to every other brain imaging technique, cognitive ERP research has a respectable history – 30 years of research unearthing the sensitivity of scalp activity to sensory, perceptual, motor and cognitive processes. It is important to note that much of this work was carried out during a period when there were no electrode caps (i.e. each electrode was placed by hand) and amplifiers and computing power were prohibitively expensive. Moreover, by today's standards, the computers were excruciatingly slow and, perhaps for related reasons, few sophisticated analytical or graphical techniques existed. As a consequence, an undue emphasis was placed on looking at the ERP waveform, specifically at the largest effects on peaks and troughs that could readily be discerned with the eye. In the previous section we detailed why this approach may be problematic. However, whatever might have been missed, the effects that have been reported tended to be the largest, the most reliable and undeniably real; thus, each must be explained by any viable theory of the function under study. Moreover, despite the technical differences between the various brain imaging techniques, it is our belief that much time can be saved by using this history to guide contemporary research in brain imaging for cognitive purposes. No single chapter could do justice to all the published observations on ERPs and their implications. Thus, this section is intended not to encourage continued peak labelling, but rather to provide the reader with an idea of the vast data base on cognitive ERP effects via quick reference to most of the terms in the various cognitive domains that can serve as keywords in library searches.

7.2.1 Event-preceding negativities including the CNV, O-wave, E-wave, PINV and SPN

The behaviourist tradition led to the discovery of the first of many "endogenous" ERP components linked to some cognitive process. While the primary aim of this research was to use exogenous evoked potential (EP) components to examine effects of conditioning on sensory processing, one of the more startling findings was a scalp negativity during the interval between a warning stimulus and the warned event (Fig. 7.7). Grey Walter et al. (1964) called this shift the *contingent negative variation* (CNV) or *expectancy wave* to underscore that it was the contingency between the stimuli and not the processing of either *per se* that was critical for its elicitation.

The early research revealed that the CNV varies systematically in its distribution across the scalp as a function of stimulus modality, task parameters and response requirements. Nonetheless, the negativity is referred to as *the* CNV, presumably to highlight the functional equivalence of the underlying processes, although there is no consensus as to exactly what these are. The proposals include cortical excitability, wherein the specific region of the cortex about to receive information was prepared to do so, arousal, attention, uncertainty, preparedness,

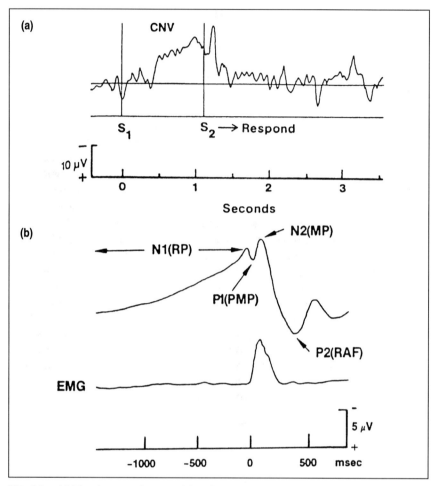

FIG. 7.7. (a) The slow negative potential, called the contingent negative variation (CNV), which builds during the interval between two stimuli. (b) The basic components of a movement-related potential elicited by a voluntary hand or arm movement. The waveform is labelled according to two of the more common nomenclatures. RP, readiness potential; MP, motor potential; PMP, pre-motion positivity; RAF, reafference potential. Movement onset is at zero. Between the movement-related potential and the time-line is the muscle activity (electromyogram) recorded from the responding arm. This figure was originally published as Figure 3 in Kutas and Hillyard (1985). Reprinted by permission of Lippincott/Harper & Row.

receptiveness, resource mobilization, level of effortful involvement and motivation (for a review see McCallum & Curry 1993).

In the 1970s, studies with long foreperiods led to the suggestion that the CNV did not index a single cognitive process but rather the sum of an *orienting* or *O-wave* that reflected processing of the warning stimulus and an *expectancy* or *E-wave* that developed in anticipation of the impending stimulus and/or response. To this day, it remains an open question whether there exists a subcomponent to the CNV that is not strictly tied to either the stimuli or the upcoming response but only to the contingency between the two. A recent proposal equates the "true" CNV with the *stimulus preceding negativity* (SPN) (e.g. Damen & Brunia 1994).

Typically, the CNV resolves (i.e. returns to baseline) or falls into a late positive component. However, under certain circumstances or in some patient populations (e.g. schizophrenic, neurotic), it is maintained for some time following the imperative stimulus, and is thus referred to as the *post-imperative negative variation* (PINV).

More recent classifications of slow potentials (longer than 1 s in duration) distinguish between those related to preparation, anticipation and expectation (largest at parietal sites) and those related to holding information in working memory (largest at frontal sites). Such investigations are based on the working hypothesis that the topography of the slow waves reflects the relative activity of cortical areas involved in solving the problem at hand, while their durations and amplitudes index the duration and degree of effort invested in particular processing steps, respectively (e.g. Roesler & Heil 1991).

7.2.2 Movement-related activity including the RP or BSP, LRP or CMA, MPN and ERN

At about the same time as the discovery of the CNV, a slow negative shift with a somatotopic distribution along the central sulcus was observed preceding self-paced voluntary movements; this was called the *Bereitschaftspotential* (BSP) or *readiness potential* (RP) (see Fig. 7.7b). Subsequently, movement-related potentials (MPs) were analysed into a series of subcomponents preceding and following movement onset (e.g. Shibasaki et al. 1980).

The movement potential component of greatest cognitive interest has been the RP, as it represents brain activity the generation of which is endogenous rather than stimulus driven. The RP starts approximately 1 s prior to a voluntary movement at the scalp, subdurally (Neshige et al. 1988) and in magnetic recordings (e.g. Cheyne et al. 1991, Kristeva et al. 1991). Given that the RP precedes movement onset, varies with responding member, specific features (force, speed and complexity) of the impending movement, and performance, it has been taken as an index of motor preparation. Some researchers prefer that the RP be replaced by a more neutral term such as *movement-preceding negativity* MPN (Bocker et al. 1994) so as to mirror its counterpart, the stimulus-preceding negativity.

The RP prior to hand movements is larger over contralateral than ipsilateral central sites. This fact has been used to derive a measure called the *lateralized readiness potential (LRP)* or *corrected motor asymmetry (CMA)* from activity time-locked to the stimulus. Specifically, the LRP derivation is based on the notion that the late half of the CNV in a warned reaction-time task must include the RP. One common method (among several) of calculating the LRP involves: (1) recording from left and right central sites for movements with each hand; (2) subtracting the potential ipsilateral to the responding hand from the potential contralateral to it; and (3) averaging the values for the two hands. The resulting average measure is the LRP. In this way asymmetrical activity that is the same for both left- and right-hand movements is eliminated while the activity associated with side of movement remains (reviewed in Coles et al. 1995).

Studies of the LRP led to the discovery of the the *error-related negativity* (ERN) on those trials in a choice reaction-time task in which the wrong response was executed (e.g. Gehring et al. 1993, Falkenstein et al. 1995); presumably the ERN reflects a system involved in the detection of and compensation for response errors.

7.2.3 Information processing effects including P300, P3a, P3b, novel P3, LPC, N200, SW, MMN, P165, Na and Dm.

The other ERP component routinely used to analyse the structure of the human information processing system was discovered as the heyday of the behaviourist tradition was drawing to a close and the information processing approach to cognition was taking hold. From the information processing point of view, cognition is an ordered sequence of processing stages, each of which performs a specific mental operation and takes a measurable amount of time to complete. Psychologists have been challenged to discover the stages (representations and processes), their durations and their order of occurrence. The great hope of the information processing approach is that psychological functions can be mapped onto brain functions via the language of information, defined in terms of reduction in uncertainty.

In the late 1960s, a positive ERP component with a peak latency around 300ms (P300) was offered as a correlate of stimulus uncertainty because its amplitude varied inversely with stimulus uncertain-ty and its latency indicated when the uncertainty was reduced (for reviews see Pritchard 1981, Donchin & Coles 1988, Johnson 1988). The important finding was that exactly the same physical stimulus sometimes did and sometimes did not elicit a P300 depending upon the task demands and decisions rendered, i.e. upon its informational value. For instance, a large P300 is elicited by the presence of a stimulus that is unexpected as well as by the absence of one that is expected.

The relationship between the P300 and expectancy has been studied most extensively in the *oddball task*. In this paradigm individuals are asked to detect improbable (5–25%) targets or "oddballs" that occur unpredictably in a random sequence of non-target, non-oddball, so-called "standard" or background stimuli. Although the oddball task is considered the prototypical P3-eliciting paradigm, even in this task the ERPs to targets often contain both an early, frontally distributed positivity (P3a) and a later, larger and posteriorly distributed positivity (P3b) (e.g. Squires et al. 1975). These two subcomponents of the P3 often overlap and are difficult to disentangle. Other components characteristic of ERPs to oddballs include a modality-dependent negativity (N200) preceding the P300 (e.g. Simson et al. 1977), and a subsequent *slow wave* (SW) that is positive posteriorly but negative frontally (e.g. Ruchkin et al. 1982) (Fig. 7.8).

As long as people pay some attention to the stimulus sequence, the amplitude of P3 to the oddballs is inversely related to its probability of occurrence, with contributions from its probability within a given period of time (*temporal probability*), globally across an entire block

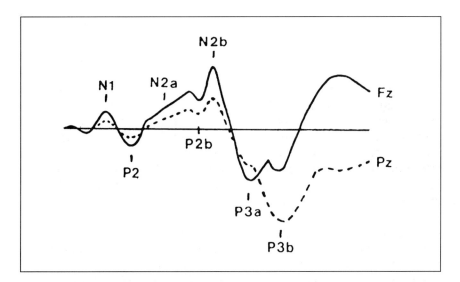

FIG. 7.8.   Schematic representation of the component structure for the ERP to a deviant stimulus under detection conditions including the N2a (MMN), N2b, P3a, P3b and SW components. The solid line represents recordings from a midline frontal site and the dashed line the recording from a midline parietal site. Reprinted from Naatanen et al. (1982) with kind permission of Elsevier Science NL, Sara Burgerhartstraat 25, 1055 KV Amsterdam, The Netherlands.

of trials (*global probability*), and more locally in terms of both the immediate stimuli (*local probability*) and the fine structure of the stimulus sequence (*sequential probability*). It is important to note, however, that it is subjective not objective probability that is the more critical determinant of P3 amplitude (reviewed in Picton & Hillyard 1988). For example, in an oddball task when more than two different stimuli are used, P300 amplitude is determined by the probability of the relevant stimulus category rather than the probability of each individual stimulus. In short, the P300 seems to index the operation of adaptive brain systems that anticipate the occurrence of significant environmental events and react to unexpected discrepancies therein. Specific proposals have suggested that the P300 reflects updating of working memory (Donchin & Coles 1988), cognitive closure (Verleger 1988) and transfer of information to consciousness (Picton 1992).

Remarkably similar P300s are recorded in the visual, auditory and tactile modalities in a variety of paradigms. Again, it is the presumed functional significance of the positivity and the experimental conditions that lead to its elicitation, rather than the identity of its underlying neural generators that serve as the criteria for defining a P300. As yet there is no general consensus on the generator(s) of the P300, although a number of sites, including the hippocampus, parietal regions, locus coeruleus and temporoparietal junction, have been proposed, examined and implicated (see e.g. Swick et al. 1994).

The peak latency of the P300 to task-relevant stimuli varies from around 300 to 1000ms as a function of the difficulty of the categorization. By contrast to RT (reaction time) measures, the peak latency of the P3b is disproportionately sensitive to stimulus evaluation (encoding, recognition, classification) relative to response selection and execution processes (e.g. Magliero et al. 1984). Accordingly, P3b latency has been taken as an upper limit on the time it takes to reach the perceptual decision that an informative event has occurred. The latency of the preceding N200 likewise varies positively with the difficulty of the discrimination for stimulus categorization (Ritter et al. 1979).

Identifying a positivity as *the* P3 is problematic. Most researchers have skirted the problem by referring to any positivity after 300ms as a *late positive component* (*LPC*) or simply a member of the P3 family. Others have placed greater emphasis on a topographical criterion, although often implicitly in combination with sensitivity to experimental manipulations: thus, the "true" P3b or parietal P3 is sensitive to probability and task relevance, while the P3a or frontal P3 is smaller, earlier, and presumably does not require attention. It is unclear by these criteria whether the P3a differs from the *novel P3* which also is early, has a frontal maximum and is elicited by infrequently occurring "novel" events such as dog barks interspersed in a sequence of tones in an oddball task (Courchesne et al. 1975). Similarly controversial is whether the so-called *difference related to memory* (Dm) is merely a modulation in P3 amplitude or an endogenous event that just happens to overlap with the P3, although one can use the measure regardless of the answer. The Dm refers to the greater late positivity during encoding (study) of items that will later be remembered, relative to those that will not; it is hypothesized to reflect some aspect of elaborative processing (Paller et al. 1987). The Dm and P3b have different scalp distributions, as do P3s in different situations (Johnson 1993).

The N200 component, often preceding the P3b, since its discovery, has experienced a similar fractionation (N2a, N2b, N2c) based on its different distributions and functional roles (sensory processing, orienting). By some accounts, the *N2a* in an oddball task is also known as the *mismatch negativity* (MMN), since its amplitude is a function of the degree of mismatch between different standard stimuli (Naatanen 1992), even if the stimuli are being ignored (see Fig. 7.8). Other components such as the *P165* and *Na* also have been identified following various subtractions of ERPs to targets and non-targets in variants of the oddball task with and without attention (Goodin et al. 1978, Ritter et al. 1982).

7.2.4 Attention-related effects including N1, Nd, processing negativity, P1 and selection negativity

A major issue that arose from the view of the mind as a limited-capacity information processor was the exact location of the "attentional" bottleneck. Electrophysiological studies designed to address this issue have implicated both early (N1 and P2) and later components of the ERP. Initially, the larger negativity observed in response to exactly the same stimuli when they were attended than inattended was called the *N1 attention effect* and presumed to be a physiological index of an early selection process. Experiments in the late 1970s, however, showed that neither the onset nor the duration of this enhanced negativity always mirrored that of the exogenous N1 component; the effect was early for easy selections but later for more difficult ones. As this effect of auditory attention was best visualized by subtracting the ERPs to stimuli when unattended from those to the same stimuli when attended, it was called the *Nd* or *negative difference*; the same effect is sometimes also referred to as the *processing negativity* (for a review see Naatanen 1992). Nd amplitude is presumably some function of the amount of processing resources allocated for focused or divided attention, although the nature of the processing resources remains unknown. It is now argued that the Nd comprises an early frontocentral phase and a later more frontal phase (Naatanen 1992).

ERP studies of selective attention have also been conducted in vision. Relative to unattended stimuli, those in the focus of attention produce enhanced sensory-evoked P1 (80–100 ms) and N1 (140–190 ms) components in tasks involving sustained attention, spatial cueing and visual search. The P1 effect has a focus over the ventrolateral extrastriate cortex, while the N1 effect has a somewhat more dorsal focus over occipito-parietal cortex. Selection among stimuli based on features such as colour, spatial frequency, contour, size and shape is accompanied by a larger, longer latency negativity between 150–350 ms over posterior sites and is called the *selection negativity* (SN) (for a review see Hillyard 1993).

7.2.5 Language-related effects including N400, N280 or LPN, P600 or SPS, and LAN

When people read sentences such as "He shaved off his moustache and city" versus "He shaved off his moustache and beard", the most striking feature of the ERP to the anomalous (as opposed to the expected congruent) word is a negativity starting around 200 ms and peaking around 400 ms (*N400*); (Fig. 7.9). An N400 is reliably elicited by semantic anomalies in written text and speech at different points in a sentence as well as in a variety of languages, including the handshapes of American Sign Language (for a review see Kutas & Van Petten 1994). Despite this family resemblance, N400s do differ in latency and scalp distribution, even within presumably similar experimental tasks. The problem of uniquely identifying a negativity as an N400 is further exacerbated by comparisons across paradigms employing single words in unstructured lists, word pairs related along various dimensions, and sentences in tasks requiring different decisions (such as lexical decisions, grammatical judgement).

All word-like stimuli elicit some N400 activity, its amplitude being sensitive to a variety of factors including frequency of usage, repetition and predictability. ERPs to words also contain a negativity at around 280 ms (*N280*) which, unlike the right posterior predominance of the N400, has a maximum over left frontal sites (Neville et al. 1992). The functional significance of this negativity (also known as the *lexical processing negativity* (LPN)), is unknown, although its latency does vary systematically with the frequency of the eliciting word (King & Kutas 1995a) (see Fig. 7.9).

At least three different classes of ERP events have been described in association with more syntactic aspects of sentence processing: (a)

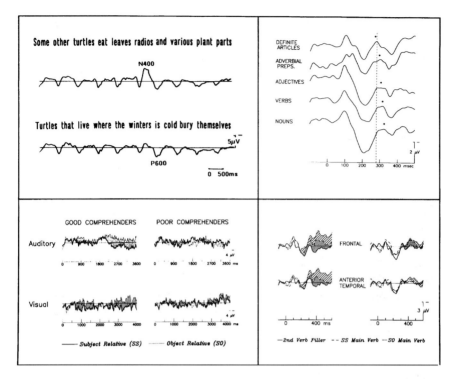

FIG. 7.9.   Various ERP effects elicited during language processing. (Top left) Over sentence average ERP data showing an N400 elicited by semantic violations and a P600 elicited by grammatical violations occurring in written text read one word at a time for comprehension. (Top right) The lexical processing negativity (LPN) to various word classes, showing how LPN (previously known as N280) varies in latency with frequency and length. From King & Kutas (1995a). (Bottom left) Over sentence averages for written and spoken sentences with embedded relative clauses for good and poor comprehenders. Auditory and visual data are from two different subject groups. Data from Mueller et al. (1977). (Bottom right) Left anterior negativity (LAN) for main clause verbs in three different sentence types, two with embedded relative clauses (subject and object relatives, SS and SO, respectively) and one with no clauses (filler). Data from King and Kutas (1995b).

the *P600* or *syntactic positive shift* (SPS), which may be a member of the P3 family, but is elicited by some types of grammatical error (see Fig. 7.9); (b) a frontocentral negativity with a left hemisphere tendency, which is also seen in word pair studies; and (c) a *left anterior negativity* (LAN) from 300 to 700 ms or so, elicited by words that signal the need for reference back to an item earlier in the sentence (see Fig. 7.9), which at a non-linguistic level may be related to working-memory usage (for a general review and further references see Kutas & Kluender 1994, Kutas & Van Petten 1994, Osterhout & Holcomb 1995).

7.3 EXAMPLES OF ERP STUDIES IN COGNITIVE NEUROSCIENCE

7.3.1 Mental chronometry

People generally take (a) longer to reject "brane" than "hime" as words in the English language, (b) longer to pronounce "dough" than "cough", (c) longer to name the colour of the ink in which a word is printed if the word refers to a different colour than if it refers to the same colour, (d) longer to respond to a particular letter (H) when it is surrounded by a different letter (SSHSS) than when it is surrounded by the same letter (HHHHH), and (e) longer to respond to a stimulus to the right of fixation with the left hand and a stimulus to the left of fixation with the right hand than vice versa. Understanding these patterns of behaviour continues to be a significant component of experimental psychology and cognitive neuroscience.

According to the information processing framework, the answer to each of these questions is a matter of pinpointing the stage(s) at which there is interference that contributes to the slowed RT. Both RT and ERP measures are useful in this regard; in particular, ERPs provide dependent variables that are sensitive to the activity of relatively circumscribed parts of the processing system. For example, variables such as stimulus–response compatibility that alter the timing of response processes typically have very little, if any, effect on P3 latency, whereas manipulations that increase the difficulty of perceptual discriminations and categorizations do.

This said, how can such observations be used to determine why RTs in some of the conditions outlined above are slowed relative to others? In brief, several laboratories have done so by comparing the effects of manipulations like these on RT, P3b latency, electromyographic (EMG) or muscle activity, and LRP measures (for a review see Coles et al. 1988). Whenever P3 latency (defined by functional and distributional criteria) is unchanged while RT is prolonged, then the prolongation is attributed to some aspect of response selection or execution rather than before it. On the other hand, when P3 latency and RT are both prolonged, then the onus is placed on some aspect of stimulus evaluation (with or without the involvement of response-related processes). Moreover, whenever response-related processes are implicated, then the nature and time-course of their contributions can be delineated by examining the temporal relations among the EMG, the actual response and the LRP. Such data have been used to pinpoint the locus of interference in a number of paradigms wherein some "incongruence" or "conflict" has resulted in a delayed overt response. The LRP is taken to reflect response preparation and its timing an indication of when; moreover, its polarity can be taken as a sign of what response has been prepared.

On the whole, the patterns of brain, muscle and behavioural activity in conflict situations have revealed that on many incongruent trials, the incorrect response had in fact been activated before the correct one. The results of these experiments indicate that information flow is not always discrete (all-or-none) in the strictest sense, as partial analysis of the stimulus does indeed affect the response system (for reviews see e.g. Coles et al. 1988, 1995). The ERP data have thus been instrumental in diverting the research focus from choosing between all-or-none versus continuous models to the delineation of the factors that determine when each is the more appropriate characterization. Data from these types of experiment have also demonstrated that different stimulus features are not only processed independently of each other but also at different rates. It is likely that it is from this temporal patterning of feature selection that an apparent information processing structure emerges.

It is important to note that these ERP components are most useful in answering questions of this type when used in combination with, rather than instead of, the more traditional chronometric measures. That said, the P3 and LRP are especially valuable indices of informational transactions because they can be measured even on trials where no response need be made, as in the NO-GO trials of a GO/NO-GO paradigm

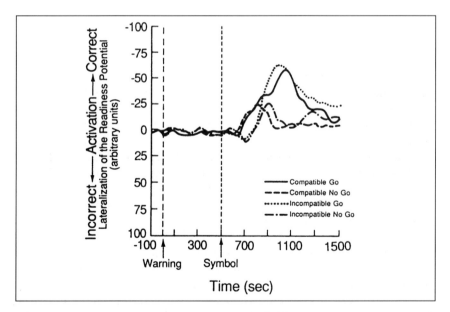

FIG. 7.10.   Lateralized readiness potential (LRP) on GO/NO-GO trials. Note the presence of significant LRP on NO-GO trials. From Osman et al. (1992) with permission of the authors and publisher.

(e.g. Osman et al. 1992) (Fig. 7.10). We can determine the time-course of feature extraction and information use by placing contingencies on how people respond to certain stimulus configurations. In a typical example, response contingencies are set so that one hand is equated with stimuli in one location and the other hand with stimuli in a different location, but whether or not a response is actually required depends on stimulus colour. The latency and polarity of the LRP under such circumstances can be used to determine whether colour is processed before or after location in space. This general logic can be used to test other hypotheses about the relative timing of distinct processes in a variety of complex acts such as speech production. Moreover, even when a person responds, LRP parameters can be used to reveal if and when they changed their mind, so to speak.

7.3.2 Attention

ERPs have been particularly useful in investigating the timing, level of analysis and anatomical loci of attentional selection in the brain. The beauty of the ERP technique in this endeavour is that it allows an examination of stimuli that are unattended with the same resolution as those at the centre of attention. ERP data have thus provided an unparalleled look at the suppressed processing of feature and semantic information when unattended in vision, audition and somatosensation, as well as information about just how effective attentional selection is (i.e. the width of the attentional beam or spotlight); the natures of the processing of both attended and unattended information have been found to vary depending on the input modality, stimulus features and task (for references see e.g. Hillyard 1993).

ERP and MEG data have provided some of the strongest evidence for early selection of sensory inputs based on spatial location; that is, an effect of focused auditory attention as early as 20ms post-stimulus under conditions of high sensory load (Woldorff et al. 1993). These data are in line with those observed for attention-sensitive single units from primary auditory cortex in monkeys. The magnetic data implicated the auditory cortex of the supratemporal plane (in or near Heschl's gyrus). Subsequent attention-related effects also appear to emanate from different regions of the auditory cortex depending on the nature of the selection required.

A variety of neuroimaging and neuropsychological studies have led to the view that there are many parts to the neural circuitry responsible for co-ordinating attentional resources during visual analyses, including the dorsolateral prefrontal cortex, the anterior cingulate, the posterior parietal lobe and the pulvinar nucleus of the thalamus (Posner & Dehaene 1994). It remains to be seen which of these structures contribute to the scalp-recorded activity. Much of the current-day ERP/ERF research is aimed at defining the nature and time-course of attentional control by the anterior and posterior attentional systems over sensory projection areas.

An elegant example of how ERPs have been used to delineate attention-related processes can be seen in the work of Woods et al. (1991). These researchers recorded ERPs to all events and reaction times to some in a multidimensional dichotic listening variant of a prototypic ERP selective attention paradigm. Specifically, people were asked to attend to tone bursts of a designated pitch in a particular ear and to respond to occasional (20%) stimuli that were 20 ms shorter in duration than the more frequent (80%) standard stimuli; thus, target stimuli were defined by three features – ear of delivery (right or left), pitch (250, 1000 or 4000hz) and duration (short or long). The relevant comparisons involved the ERPs to the standard stimuli when attended versus when inattended. This clever design allowed the authors to use the different ERP patterns to determine whether the brain was sensitive to differences in tone frequency (as would be expected from previous data), and also whether the brain processes pitch and location information differently and, if so, what the time-courses of the processing of each of these features and their conjunction might be.

The ERPs to tones of different pitches differed at 100 ms (N100 component) regardless of attention in a way that reflected tonotopic organization in the eliciting area. By contrast, the attention effects for pitch, ear of delivery, and the pitch–ear conjunction, although statistically different from each other, did not show tonotopy, thereby implicating the involvement of non-tonotopic regions of the auditory cortex. The attention-related differences (Nd) for both pitch and location started fairly early (80–120 ms) and showed slightly different topographies; thus, we can infer that these two features were analysed independently and in parallel starting by 80 ms at the latest. After 120 ms, in addition to the pitch and location Nds, conjunction-specific Nds appeared, indicating that conjunction processing lagged individual feature analysis somewhat. By 400 ms, the Nds to individual features disappeared, leaving Nd activity strictly in response to stimuli that had both the relevant pitch and location (Fig. 7.11). The different Nd distributions indicated that, whereas either individual feature Nd could be accounted for by the activation of auditory cortical fields, the conjunction Nd (400–900 ms) implicated the frontal lobes.

7.3.3 Language

One domain of cognition that has been revolutionized by the advent of various neuroimaging techniques is language. Whatever else language

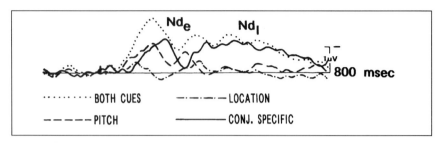

FIG. 7.11.   Timing of feature processing including time-courses of Nd frequency, Nd location, Nd to both frequency and location and Nd that is conjunction specific. Nd refers to negative difference: e, early, l, late. Modified from Woods et al. (1994) with permission of the authors and publisher.

may be it is a compelling process that takes place in real time and in a large part outside of awareness until the input makes sense or not. Neuropsychological and neuroimaging data have implicated many areas of the brain (other than the classical Broca's and Wernicke's areas) in language processing. While these different areas may not all be active simultaneously, the relevant processes must overlap considerably in time. It is for this reason in particular that ERP/ERF activity which tracks language as it is being decoded and interpreted has been especially informative (for further discussion see Kutas & King 1996).

An elegant example of how ERPs can be used to investigate psycholinguistic questions can be found in the work of Garnsey et al. (1989). These researchers exploited the fact that semantic anomalies elicit N400s in order to evaluate two alternative hypotheses about the strategies that guide sentence parsing when there is a momentary ambiguity about syntactic structure. "Parsing" refers to the process of figuring out the syntactic relations between words in a sentence (i.e. who did what to whom). In English, determining the grammatical function (e.g. subject, object) of each word in a sentence is usually relatively easy, as this information is correlated with word order. However, there are exceptions; for instance, in *wh*-questions, where the questioned element occurs at the beginning of a sentence (e.g. *Which customer did the secretary call?*), there is no way of knowing what the grammatical function (subject, object, object of preposition) of the questioned element (*Which customer*) is until later in the sentence.

Sentence processing theorists have opposing hypotheses about what the parser does in cases where the function of an element is ambiguous. For instance, in the example above, the noun phrase *which customer* might automatically be assigned as the direct object of the clause, if the parser follows a "first resort" strategy. In this case, the disambiguating information in the verb "call" which occurs later in the sentence would tell the parser that its initial assignment was correct, because *which customer* is the direct object of call. However, if the parser were following a "last resort" strategy, then no grammatical role would be assigned to "which customer" until more information was available. Both strategies have costs and benefits. The first resort strategy is effective if *which customer* is the direct object; however, if it is not, as in "Which customer did the secretary call *about*?", then the parser incurs a great computational penalty in reanalysing "which customer" as the object of a preposition instead. The last resort strategy is necessarily less efficient in the early, ambiguous region of the sentence, but ensures no delays whenever the function of "which customer" is not the expected one.

Garnsey et al. constructed sentences with embedded *wh*-questions wherein the questioned element was either plausible or implausible as a direct object of the subsequent verb.

(a) The businessman knew which customer the secretary *called* _____ at home.

(b) The businessman knew which article the secretary *called* _____ at home.

These were randomly interspersed with simple declarative control sentences which either did or did not contain a semantically anomalous word. The beauty of this design is that the noun phrase "which article" in (b) isn't plausible as a direct object and will therefore elicit an enhanced N400 wherever in the sentence the parser assigns it as such. If the first resort strategy is in effect, the N400 will be observed early, namely at the verb "call", which is the first place the parser might assign a direct object role. On the other hand, according to the last resort strategy, the N400 should not appear until later in the sentence at the word "at", when it becomes unambiguous that "which article" serves the direct object role.

An N400 was observed at "called" and this was taken as evidence for the first resort strategy. Note that, in this example, the N400 is not to be taken as a direct reflection of role assignment, but rather of the incongruity that is either a consequence of making an implausible role assignment or of evaluating the possibility of that assignment. While other viable interpretations for this outcome have since been proposed,[6] these are independent of the choice of the N400 as a measure, and the Garnsey et al. study remains a good example of how ERPs can be used to limit the number of viable explanations for certain linguistic phenomena.

Examples of this type are increasing daily. Equally powerful is the use of ERPs to investigate speech comprehension and aspects of parsing and integration beyond the level of individual words (Kutas & King 1996) in reading and listening to sentences with simple and complex syntax. What is remarkable is how similar sentence-level ERP effects are for written text presented one word at a time and for natural speech (e.g. Osterhout & Holcomb 1993, Mueller et al. 1997). Such data have also shown the necessity of taking individual differences in comprehension skills into account from the earliest stages of sensory analysis through comprehension (King & Kutas 1995b) (see Fig. 7.9, bottom right).

7.3.4 Memory: electrophysiological data on encoding and retrieval processes

ERPs are sensitive indicators of physical, perceptual and conceptual changes in the environment, both intentional and/or conscious and involuntary and/or unconscious. Clearly, an appreciation of change requires some trace or memory of past events. ERPs have been used to investigate aspects of the formation, maintenance (repetition) and retrieval of such memory traces (for reviews see Kutas 1988, Johnson 1995, Rugg 1995).

The earliest ERP studies of memory dealt with the timing of retrieval from short-term memory. Later ERP studies of memory focused on the amplitude of the P3 during encoding as a predictor of subsequent memory performance. These investigations were motivated by the hypothesis that P3 amplitude reflected the updating of one's mental model of the "environment" and evidence from intracranial recordings that potentials in the amygdala-hippocampal regions of humans co-occurred with the scalp-recorded P3 component. The story was some-what complicated by the fact that humans and monkeys with damage to the medial temporal lobe did not necessarily show reduced P3 ampli-tudes at the scalp. While this issue remains unsettled, studies con-ducted to test the updating of working memory hypothesis of the P3 have nonetheless contributed to our understanding of memory and the brain. Proponents of the levels of processing framework had predicted that under most circumstances items that were processed more "deeply" (meaningfully) would be better remembered than items that were processed at only a shallow level (orthographically or phonologi-cally in the case of words). Such predictions were confirmed by many studies wherein the nature of encoding was manipulated; the behav-ioural data allowed the inference that the way in which a stimulus is encoded is a critical determinant of the probability of its recognition or recall. However, the ERP data recorded in such tasks demonstrated more directly that the brain processes during encoding were in fact different within 200–300 ms of stimulus presentation. Moreover, ERPs recorded during the study phase sorted as a function of subsequent memory performance have revealed different classes of people including those who choose to use "maintenance" versus "elaborative" rehearsal strategies to remember (e.g. Fabiani et al. 1990). Again, while this should come as no great surprise, ERPs provide more precise online evidence of the timing of these strategic choices.

Much current ERP research is aimed at testing various hypotheses about the proposed implicit/explicit distinction in long-term memory. By definition, amnesics do not perform as well as non-brain-damaged individuals on traditional tests of recognition and recall, and yet there are situations wherein the accuracy or speed of their performance can only be interpreted as indicating that they do have some memory for an event which they say they do not remember (Squire et al. 1993). Similar dissociations between memory measured "directly" and "indirectly" have been observed for non-brain-damaged individuals as well. ERPs have been used to examine the issue of whether, and if so how, performance in implicit and explicit memory tests are subserved by different neural systems operating on the same or different representations, and the time-courses of these processes.

A good example is a study by Paller (1990) on "directed forgetting". In this experiment individuals were exposed to words printed in red or green ink and asked to remember the "red" ones and forget the "green" ones. After the study phase, half the participants were asked to use three-letter stems as cues to recall words they had just studied while the other half were asked to write down the first word that came to mind in response to each stem. Thus both groups were exposed to the same stimuli, but differed in what they had to do. Both groups also were asked to recall as many of the words (green or red) as they could in any order (free recall).

As expected, everyone recalled more of the words that they had been directed to remember than those they had been directed to forget. But directed forgetting had no differential effect on stem completion; the stems were completed with equivalent numbers of "red" and "green" words. Thus, Paller obtained the expected pattern of dissociation of the effect of directed forgetting on recall versus priming. Moreover, Paller found that the ERPs recorded during encoding (study phase) were sensitive to subsequent recall but not to priming; that is, items that would be recalled had larger late positivities than those that would not be recalled, but there were no signs in the ERP of subsequent performance in the stem completion priming task. This pattern supports a difference between the encoding factors that are important for explicit versus implicit memory performance.

In a subsequent series of studies, Paller et al. (1995) combined behavioural and electrophysiological measures to examine the processes underlying implicit (priming) and explicit (recollection) memory performance. Across a series of studies, ERPs were recorded during an implicit test of memory (either threshold identification or lexical decision) following study manipulations that either influenced behavioural priming measures but not recognition performance, or vice versa. For example, people were asked to image a word and compare its size with that of the cathode ray tube in front of them in order to process the item deeply, or instead to count the number of syllables in the word in order to process it to a shallow level; this study manipulation had the effect of varying recognition but not priming performance. In other experiments, priming but not recognition performance was manipulated by varying the physical features of the studied items from the study to the test phase. The results thus far indicate that: (a) ERPs and behavioural measures reflect different aspects of memory-related processes; (b) at least partly different brain mechanisms support priming and recollection, with the electrophysiological signs of priming occurring earlier than those of recollection (after 300 ms); and (c) recollection processes may come into play even under nominally implicit tests of memory that have no immediate consequence on behavioural measures of priming.

Another contemporary line of research uses very slow potentials to examine retrieval processes from long-term memory. In one typical approach exemplified by the work of Roesler and his colleagues (e.g. Roesler et al. 1995), young adults were asked to learn various lists of facts by heart on one day and to make decisions about them on another. The materials were constructed so as to take advantage of the so-called "fan effect". This refers to the observation that the time taken to verify a proposition about a concept depends on the number of links which that concept has with other concepts in memory; more links translate into slower decision times. Thus, it is possible to vary the difficulty of retrieving an item by increasing the number of links between it and other items. In practice, this means teaching a person many facts about some items, a moderate number of facts about other items, and only a single fact about yet other items.

The relevant electrophysiological data are the slow potentials recorded for several hundreds of milliseconds during the act of retrieval. The results of these studies suggest a close relationship between different neocortical structures and different retrieval processes. For example, there appears to be a pronounced DC-like negative potential over left frontal sites during retrieval of almost any semantically encoded item (Fig. 7.12) where amplitude varies with the size of the fan. This effect was seen together with other more task-specific slow potentials the amplitude, timing and distribution of which varied with the nature of the information retrieved (general versus specific concepts, verbal

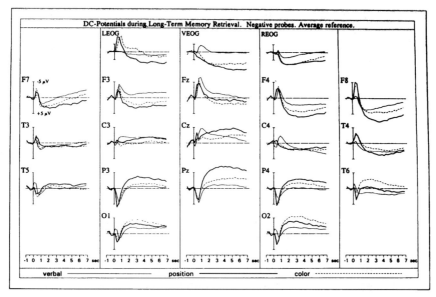

FIG. 7.12.   Very slow potentials related to memory retrieval in three experimental conditions. Recordings are relative to an average reference and across subjects and different levels of fan. From Roesler et al. (1995) with permission of the authors and publisher.

versus spatial materials, etc.) and the decision (yes or no) required (for a review see Heil et al. 1994). Most importantly, all these studies revealed a pronounced negative slow wave that was temporally related to retrieval, the spatial topography of which reflected the type of material that was being retrieved and the amplitude of which varied with the difficulty of the retrieval. These results fit with the notion that the brain areas involved in explicit memory are the same ones that are needed for encoding and perception; there is no single memory store for all memories. In addition, the ERP data offer a real-time view of the time-course and relative location of retrieval processes.

7.3.5 Electrophysiological studies of neural plasticity

Nature or nurture? It's almost outdated to pose the question, for when it comes to brain development (and the associated perceptual, cognitive and motor functions), the answer is most certainly "Both to some degree". So, the better questions are what is the impact of each and with what time-course? For example, how do the brain and behaviours of someone who has hearing differ from those of someone who is born deaf? Exactly what is the auditory cortex of a deaf individual doing? These are the sorts of question that are being asked and answered using ERP/ERF recordings. Insofar as a deaf individual's brain responses to visual and somatosensory stimuli differ, we can infer that different brain systems are involved in their processing.

Neville and her colleagues (for a review see Neville 1995) addressed these questions by comparing the scalp-recorded visual EPs of hearing adults, congenitally deaf adults (individuals who have been deprived of auditory input since birth), and hearing adults whose first language was American Sign Language by virtue of having been born to deaf parents. In a number of studies, they found that the visual EPs of deaf individuals were in fact different from those of hearing individuals, especially for stimuli occurring in the periphery. Specifically, early sensory compoments (N150 and P230) were larger in amplitude for the deaf. The larger N150 over frontal and temporal regions was taken as consistent with the hypothesis that auditory areas deprived of their normal input were processing visual information instead, while the larger amplitude P230s over occipital sites were hypothesized to reflect structural changes in the intact visual areas.

Neville & Lawson (1987a–c) also pursued this question within a selective attention task that required detection of motion in different regions of visual space. While there were some similarities in the overall pattern of attention-related effects in the deaf and hearing subjects, there were also some notable distribution differences, especially for stimuli in the periphery. For example, deaf individuals had larger attention effects on both the N1 component and a subsequent latency positivity (PD) and showed these effects at the occipital sites – locations where the hearing group had no such effects. Deaf individuals also had larger N1 effects over the left hemisphere than hearing individuals, regardless of the visual field of presentation. These ERP results indicate that the neural systems which mediate attention to visual space and perception of motion are different in part in hearing and congenitally deaf individuals.

The interpretation of these differences is clarified in part by comparing them with the ERPs of hearing individuals born to deaf parents and whose first language is American Sign Language. With this comparison we can determine the extent to which each of these group differences in attention is attributable to sensory deprivation versus the acquisition of a visuospatial language. Relative to the hearing and congenitally deaf individuals, these hearing-of-deaf adults show very similar ERP waveform morphologies; differences occur primarily in the size and distribution of the attention effects (Fig. 7.13). On the one hand, the hearing-of-deaf look more like the hearing in that they do not show the large N1 or PD effects at the occipital sites. On the other hand, the hearing-of-deaf are more similar to the deaf in the lateral distribution of their attention effects; that is, they show large effects over the left hemisphere in response to left visual field stimuli. As the larger ERP (N1 and PD) effects over the occipital region are specific to individuals who are deaf, they are probably a consequence of auditory deprivation since birth. In contrast, the apparently greater involvement of the left hemisphere in attentional selection based on motion for both the deaf and the hearing-of-deaf (relative to normal hearing) individuals is most consistent with an explanation based on the early acquisition of sign language.

Mapping via magnetic recording techniques has also been used to investigate the reorganization of the somatosensory system in humans. For instance Mogilner, et al. (1993) used magnetic recordings to

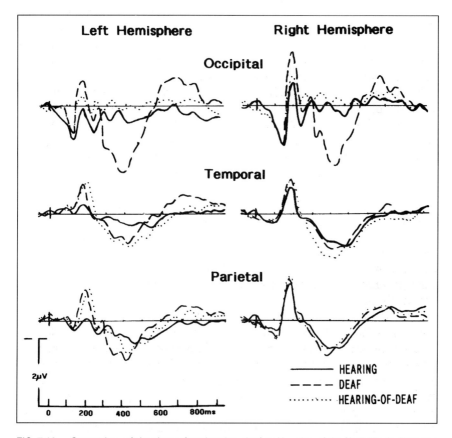

FIG. 7.13. Comparison of visual ERPs from hearing, deaf and hearing-of-deaf individuals. Note that only deaf individuals show large occipital N1 and later positivity. Both deaf and hearing-of-deaf show large N1 over left hemisphere temporal and parietal sites. Thus, the occipital effects are related to altered sensory experience, whereas as the temporal and parietal effects are more likely due to altered language experience (a visuospatial manual language). Adapted from Neville & Lawson (1987c) with permission of the authors and publisher.

compare the somatosensory map of the hand areas of a group of control people with those obtained from two adult men both before and after surgical separation of congenitally webbed fingers. The pre-surgical recordings revealed that hand areas of the abnormal hand in these two patients were quite small and unusual in their lack of a consistent topography; however, a few weeks after surgery, a normal somatotopic organization was evident. Somatosensory reorganization in humans has also been observed in MEG recordings of a patient with an amputated limb; via behavioural testing this patient felt touch as well as heat and cold in the phantom limb when a certain area on his cheek or a few inches above the amputation line were stimulated (Yang et al. 1994). The MEG patterns revealed no real "hand" area in the hemisphere contralateral to the amputated limb, but a normal topographically organized area in the other hemisphere; moreover, the presumed hand area was activated by touching either the lower face or the upper arm 10cm above the line of amputation. This is one of the strongest pieces of evidence of cortical remapping in humans following abnormal experience. All in all, these data support the emerging view that receptive fields and cortical maps are dynamic in the face of experience, rather than static and inborn.

7.4 CONCLUSIONS

The reader should now have a good idea of the many types of question that have proven amenable to the ERP methodology. Different aspects of the ERP/ERF are sensitive to stimulus parameters, response parameters, preparation, modulation and direction of attention, establishing expectancies and noticing violations thereof, discrimination, categorization, decision-making, conscious recollection and implicit processing among other factors. ERPs can be used not only to help determine which factors influence brain activity, mental state and/or an individual's behaviour but also to provide some important information about the time-course of their influences. This time-course of sensitivity to experimental and internal variables can be combined with other neural-imaging techniques of greater spatial but coarser temporal resolution to unfold the active brain areas across time.

ACKNOWLEDGEMENTS

The preparation of this chapter was supported in part by HD22614, AG08313 and MH52893 to M. Kutas. A. Dale was supported by a post-doctoral fellowship from the Norweigan Research Council and a grant from ONR N00014–94–1–

0856 to M. I. Sereno. The helpful comments of J. Weckerly, M. Rugg and L. Anllo-Vento on an earlier draft were much appreciated, as is the constant input from J. King on many fronts.

NOTES

1. More generally, σ denotes a tensor, to allow for anisotropic conductivity.
2. The corresponding equation for the magnetic field produced by a current dipole is

$$\bar{\mathbf{B}}_2 \approx \left(\frac{\mu_0}{4\pi}\right)\frac{s\bar{\mathbf{d}}\times\bar{\mathbf{r}}}{r^3}, r \gg d \,,$$

where μ_0 is the permeability of free space.
3. These differences are reflected in the $e_{i,j}$ and $m_{i,j}$ in Equations (11) and (12).
4. Note that the "components" derived from PCA do not necessarily correspond to the ERP components as defined above.
5. Note that, if two or more generators are strongly correlated in time, the number of principal components may be lower than the actual number of generators.
6. See e.g. Fodor (1989) for a thorough review of the issues involved in processing empty categories. More recent work has favoured models where the parser maintains parallel syntactic analyses in certain situations (e.g. Gibson 1990). Moreover, MacDonald et al. (1992) provide evidence that there are working memory-related individual differences in the computation of such multiple analyses, thereby muddying the interpretation of Garnsey et al.'s data somewhat. If subjects were maintaining multiple syntactic analyses, the N400 observed may simply have reflected the fact that the "first resort" is one of several analyses that is being pursued.

REFERENCES

Belliveau, J. W., D. N. Kennedy Jr, R. C. McKinstry, B. R. Buchbinder, R. M. Weisskoff, M. S. Cohen, J. M. Vevea et al. 1991. Functional mapping of the human visual cortex by magnetic resonance imaging. *Science* **254**, 716–19.

Berger, H. 1929. Uber das Elektrekephalogramm des Menschen. *Archiv für Psychiatrie und Nervenkrankheiten* **87**, 527–70.

Bocker, K. B., C. H. Brunia, P. J. Cluitmans 1994. A spatio-temporal dipole model of the readiness potential in humans. I. Finger movement. *Electroencephalography and Clinical Neurophysiology* **91**, 275–85.

Cheyne, D., R. Kristeva, L. Deecke 1991. Homuncular organization of human motor cortex as indicated by neuromagnetic recordings. *Neuroscience Letters* **122**, 17–20.

Coles, M. G. H., G. Gratton, E. Donchin 1988. Detecting early communication: using measures of movement-related potentials to illuminate human information processing. *Biological Psychology* **26**, 69–89.

Coles, M. G. H., H. G. O. M. Smid, M. K. Scheffers, L. J. Otten 1995. Mental chronometry and the study of human information processing. In *Electrophysiology of mind: event-related potentials and cognition*, M. D. Rugg & M. G. H. Coles (eds), 86–131. Oxford: Oxford University Press.

Cooper, R., J. W. Osselton, J. C. Shaw 1974. *EEG technology*. London: Butterworths.

Courchesne, E., S. A. Hillyard, R. Galambos 1975. Stimulus novelty, task relevance and the visual evoked potential in man. *Electroencephalography and Clinical Neurophysiology* **39**, 131–42.

Cuffin, B. N. & D. Cohen 1977. Magnetic fields of a dipole in special volume conductor shapes. *IEEE Transactions on Biomedical Engineering* **24**, 372–81.

Dale, A. M. & M. I. Sereno 1993. Improved localization of cortical activity by combining EEG and MEG with MRI cortical surface reconstruction: a linear approach. *Journal of Cognitive Neuroscience* **5**(2), 162–76.

Damen, E. J. & C. H. Brunia 1994. Is a stimulus conveying task-relevant information a sufficient condition to elicit a stimulus-preceding negativity? *Psychophysiology* **31**, 129–39.

Desmedt, J. 1988. Somatosensory evoked potentials. In *Human event-related potentials*, T. W. Picton (ed.), 159–244. New York: Elsevier.

Donchin, E. 1979. Event-related brain potentials: a tool in the study of human information processing. In *Evoked brain potentials and behaviour*, H. Begleiter (ed.), 13–88. New York: Plenum.

Donchin, E. & M. G. H. Coles 1988. Is the P300 component a manifestation of context updating? *Behavioural Brain Sciences* **11**, 357–74.

Fabiani, M., D. Karis, E. Donchin 1990. Effects of mnemonic strategy manipulation in a Von Restorff paradigm. *Electroencephalography and Clinical Neurophysiology* **75**, 22–35.

Falkenstein, M., J. Hohnsbein, J. Hoormann 1995. Event-related potential correlates of errors in reaction tasks. *Electroencephalography and Clinical Neurophysiology* **44**, 287–96.

Fodor, J. D. 1989. Empty categories in sentence processing. *Language and Cognitive Processes* **4**, 155–209.

Garnsey, S. M., M. K. Tanenhaus, R. M. Chapman 1989. Evoked potentials and the study of sentence comprehension. *Journal of Psycholinguistic Research* **18**, 51–60.

Gehring, W. J., B. Goss, M. G. Coles, D. E. Meyer, E. Donchin 1993. A neural system for error detection and compensation. *Psychological Science* **4**, 385–90.

Gevins, A. S. & A. Remond (eds) 1987. Methods of analysis of brain electrical and magnetic signals. *EEG handbook* I Revised series. Amsterdam: Elsevier.

Gibson, E. 1990. Recency preference and garden-path effects. In *Program of the Twelfth Annual Conference of the Cognitive Science Society*, 372–9. Hillsdale, NJ: Lawrence Erlbaum.

Glaser, E. M. & D. S. Ruchkin (eds) 1976. In *Principles of neurobiological signal analysis*. New York: Academic Press.

Goodin, D. S., K. C. Squires, B. H. Henderson, A. Starr 1978. An early event-related cortical potential. *Psychophysiology* **4**, 360–5.

Grynszpan, F. & D. B. Geselowitz 1973. Model studies of the magnetocardiogram. *Biophysical Journal* **13**, 911–25.

Hamalainen, M. S. & R. J. Ilmoniemi 1984. *Interpreting measured magnetic fields of the brain: estimates of current distribution*. Report TKK-F-A559, Department of Technical Physics, Helsinki University of Technology.

Hamalainen, M. S., R. Hari, R. J. Ilmoniemi, J. Knuutila, O. V. Lounasmaa 1993. Magnetoencephalography – theory, instrumentation, and applications to noninvasive studies of the working human brain. *Reviews of Modern Physics* **65**, 413–97.

Heil, M., F. Roesler, E. Hennighausen 1994. Slow potentials during long-term memory retrieval. In *Cognitive electrophysiology*, H. Heinze, T. Muente, G. R. Mangun (eds), 149–68. Boston: Birkhauser.

Hillyard, S. A. 1993. Electrical and magnetic brain recordings: contributions to cognitive neuroscience. *Current Opinions in Neurobiology* **3**, 217–24.

Johnson Jr, R. 1988. The amplitude of the P300 component of the event-related potential: Review and synthesis. In *Advances in psychophysiology*, P. K. Ackles, J. R. Jennings, M. G. H. Coles (eds), 69–138. Greenwich, CT: JAI.

Johnson Jr, R. 1993. On the neural generators of the P300 component of the event-related potential. *Psychophysiology* **30**(1), 90–7.

Johnson Jr., R. 1995. Event-related potential insights into the neurobiology of memory systems. In *Handbook of neuropsychology*, vol. 10, R. Johnson Jr (ed.), 135–64. Amsterdam: Elsevier.

King, J. W. & M. Kutas 1995a. A brain potential whose latency indexes the length and frequency of words. *Newsletter of the Centre for Research in Language* **10**(2), 3–9.

King, J. W. & M. Kutas 1995b. Who did what and when? Using word- and clause-related ERPs to monitor working memory usage in reading. *Journal of Cognitive Neuroscience* **7**, 378–97.

Kristeva, R., D. Cheyne, L. Deecke 1991. Neuromagnetic fields accompanying unilateral and bilateral voluntary movements: topography and analysis of cortical sources. *Electroencephalography and Clinical Neurophysiology* **81**, 284–98.

Kutas, M. 1988. Review of event-related potential studies of memory. In *Perspectives in memory research*, M. S. Gazzaniga (ed.), 181–218. Cambridge, MA: MIT Press.

Kutas, M. & S. A. Hillyard 1985. Event-related potentials and psychopathology. In *Psychobiology and foundations of clinical psychiatry*, section 4, *Psychiatry*, J. O. Cavenar Jr (ed.), Ch. 62, 1–17. Philadelphia, PA: Lippincott/Harper & Row.

Kutas, M & J. W. King 1996. The potentials for basic sentence processing: differentiating integrative processes. In *Attention and performance*, vol. 16, T. Inui & J. L. McClelland (eds), 501–46. Cambridge, MA: MIT Press.

Kutas, M. & R. Kluender 1994. What is who violating: a reconsideration of linguistic violations in light of event-related brain potentials. In *Cognitive electrophysiology*, H. Heinze, T. Muente, G. R. Mangun (eds). La Jolla, CA: Birkhauser Boston.

Kutas, M. & C. Van Petten 1994. Psycholinguistics electrified. In *Handbook of psycholinguistics*, M. A. Gernsbacher (ed.), 83–143. San Diego, CA:Academic Press.

MacDonald, M. C., M. A. Just, P. A. Carpenter 1992. Working memory constraints on the processing of syntactic ambiguity. *Cognitive Psychology* **24**, 56–98.

Magliero, A., T. R. Bashore, M. G. H. Coles, E. Donchin 1984. On the dependence of P300 latency on stimulus evaluation processes. *Psychophysiology* **21**, 171–86.

McCallum, W. C. & S. H. Curry (eds) 1993. *Slow potential changes in the human brain*, NATO ASI series A: Life Sciences 254. New York: Plenum.

Mogilner, A., J. A. Grossman, U. Ribary, M. Joliot, J. Volkmann, D. Rapaport, R. W. Beasley et al. 1993. Somatosensory cortical plasticity in adult humans revealed by magnetoencephalography. *Proceedings of the National Academy of Sciences, USA* **90**(8), 3593–7.

Mueller, H. M., J. W. King, M. Kutas 1997. Event-related potentials elicited by spoken relative clauses. *Cognitive Brain Research* **5**(3), 193–203.

Naatanen, R. 1992. *Attention and brain function*. Hillsdale, NJ: Lawrence Erlbaum.

Naatanen, Simpson, Lake 1982. Stimulus deviance and evoked potentials. *Biological Psychology* **14**, 53–98.

Neshige, R., H. Luders, H. Shibasaki 1988. Recording of movement-related potentials from scalp and cortex in man. *Brain* **111**, 719–36.

Neville, H. J. 1995. Developmental specificity in neurocognitive development in humans. In *The cognitive neurosciences*, M. S. Gazzaniga (ed.), 219–31. Cambridge, MA: MIT Press.

Neville, H. J. & D. Lawson 1987a. Attention to central and peripheral visual space in a movement detection task: an event-related potential and behavioural study. I: Normal hearing adults. *Brain Research* **405**, 253–67.

Neville, H. J. & D. Lawson 1987b. Attention to central and peripheral visual space in a movement detection task: an event-related potential and behavioural study. II: Congenitally deaf adults. *Brain Research* **405**, 268–83.

Neville, H. J. & D. Lawson 1987c. Attention to central and peripheral visual space in a movement detection task. III: Separate effects of auditory deprivation and acquisition of a visual language. *Brain Research* **405**, 284–94.

Neville, H. J., D. L. Mills, D. S. Lawson 1992. Fractionating language: different neural subsystems with different sensitive periods. *Cerebral Cortex* **2**(3), 244–58.

Nicholson, C. & J. A. Freeman 1975. Theory of current source-density analysis and determination of conductivity tensor for Anuran cerebellum. *Journal of Neurophysiology* **38**, 356–68.

Nunez, P. L. 1981. *Electric fields of the brain*. New York: Oxford University Press.

Ogawa, S., D. W. Tank, R. Menon, J. M. Ellermann, S. G. Kim, H. Merkle, K. Ugurbil 1992. Intrinsic signal changes accompanying sensory stimulation: functional brain mapping with magnetic resonance imaging. *Proceedings of the National Academy of Sciences, USA* **89**, 5951–5.

Oostendorp, T. F. & A. van Oosterom 1989. Source parameter estimation in inhomogeneous volume conductors of arbitrary shape. *IEEE Transactions on Biomedical Engineering* **36**, 382–91.

Osman, A., J. R. Bashore, M. G. H. Coles, E. Donchin, D. E. Meyer 1992. On the transmission of partial information: inferences from movement-related brain potential. *Journal of Experimental Psychology: Human Perception and Performance* **18**, 217–32.

Osterhout, L. & P. J. Holcomb 1993. Event-related potentials and syntactic anomaly: Evidence of anomaly detection during the perception of continuous speech. *Language & Cognitive Processes* **8**, 413–37.

Osterhout, L. & P. J. Holcomb 1995. Event-related potentials and language comprehension. In *Electrophysiology of mind: event-related potentials and cognition*, M. D. Rugg & M. G. H. Coles (eds), 171–215. Oxford: Oxford University Press.

Paller, K. A. 1990. Recall and stem-completion priming have different electrophysiological correlates and are modified differentially by directed forgetting. *Journal of Experimetnal Psychology: Learning, Memory, and Cognition* **16**, 1021–32.

Paller, K. A., M. Kutas, A. R. Mayes 1987. Neural correlates of encoding in an incidental learning paradigm. *Electroencephalography and Clinical Neurophysiology* **67**, 360–71.

Paller, K. A., M. Kutas, H. K. McIsaac 1995. Monitoring conscious recollection via the electrical activity of the brain. *Psychological Science* **6**, 107–11.

Picton, T. W. 1992. The P300 wave of the human event-related potential. *Journal of Clinical Neurophysiology* **9**(4), 456–79.

Picton, T. W. & S. A. Hillyard 1988. Endogenous event-related potentials. In *Human event-related potentials*, T. W. Picton (ed.), 361–426. New York: Elsevier.

Posner, M. I. & S. Dehaene 1994. Attentional networks. *Trends in Neuroscience* **17**, 75–9.

Press, W. H., B. P. Flannery, S. A. Teukolsky, W. T. Vetterling 1990. *Numerical recipes in C: the art of scientific computing*, 59–70 New York: Cambridge University Press.

Pritchard, W. S. 1981. Psychophysiology of P300: a review. *Psychological Bulletin* **89**, 506–40.

Regan, D. 1989. *Human brain electrophysiology: evoked potentials and evoked magnetic fields in science and medicine*. New York: Elsevier.

Ritter, W., R. Simson, H. G. Vaughan, D. Friedman 1979. A brain event related to the making of a sensory discrimination. *Science* **203**, 1358–61.

Ritter, W., R. Simson, H. G. Vaughan, M. Macht 1982. Manipulation of event-related potential manifestations of information processing stages. *Science* **218**, 909–11.

Roesler, F. & M. Heil 1991. Toward a functional categorization of slow waves: taking into account past and future events [comment; see comments]. *Psychophysiology* **28**, 344–58.

Roesler, F., M. Heil, E. Hennighausen 1995. Distinct cortical activation patterns during long-term memory retrieval of verbal, spatial, and color information. *Journal of Cognitive Neuroscience* **7**, 51–65.

Ruchkin, D. S., R. Munson, S. Sutton 1982. P300 and slow wave is a message consisting of two events. *Psychophysiology* **19**, 629–42.

Rugg, M. D. 1995. ERP studies of memory. In *Electrophysiology of mind: event-related brain potentials and cognition*, M. D. Rugg & M. G. H. Coles (eds), 132–170. Oxford: Oxford University Press.

Rugg, M. D. & M. G. H. Coles 1995. *Electrophysiology of mind: event-related brain potentials and cognition*. Oxford: Oxford University Press.

Sarvas, J. 1987. Basic mathematical and electromagnetic concepts of the biomagnetic inverse problem. *Physics in Medicine and Biology* **32**, 11–22.

Scherg, M 1992. Functional imaging and localization of electromagnetic brain activity. *Brain Topography* **5**, 103–11.

Shibasaki, H., G. Barrett, E. Halliday, A. M. Halliday 1980. Components of the movement-related cortical potential and their scalp topography. *Electroencephalography and Clinical Neurophysiology* **49**, 213–26.

Simson, R., H. G. Vaughan, W. Ritter 1977. The scalp topography of potentials in auditory and visual discrimination tasks. *Electroencephalography and Clinical Neurophysiology* **42**, 528–35.

Smith, W. E., W. J. Dallas, W. H. Kullmann, H. A. Schlitt 1990. Linear estimation theory applied to the reconstruction of a 3-D vector current distribution. *Applied Optics* **29**, 658–67.

Squire, L. R., B. Knowlton, G. Musen 1993. The structure and organization of memory. *Annual Review of Psychology* **44**, 453–95.

Squires, K. C., N. K. Squires, S. A. Hillyard 1975. Vertex evoked potentials in a rating-scale detection task: relation to signal probability. *Behavioural Biology* **13**, 21–34.

Starr, A. & M. Don 1988. Brain potentials evoked by acoustic stimuli. In *Human event-related potentials*, T. W. Picton (ed.), 97–158. New York: Elsevier.

Swick, D., M. Kutas, H. J. Neville 1994. Localizing the neural generators of event-related brain potentials. In *Localization and neuroimaging in neuropsychology*, A. Kertesz (ed.), 73–122. San Diego, CA: Academic Press.

Verleger, R. 1988. Event-related potentials and cognition: a critique of the context updating hypothesis and an alternative interpretation of P3. *Behavioural Brain Sciences* **11**(3), 343–56.

Walter, W. G., R. Cooper, V. J. Aldridge, W. C. McCallum, A. L. Winter 1964. Contingent negative variation: an electric sign of sensorimotor association and expectancy in the human brain. *Nature* **203**, 380–4.

Wang, J. Z., S. J. Williamson, L. Kaufman 1992. Magnetic source images determined by a lead-field analysis: the unique minimum-norm least-squares estimation. *IEEE Transactions on Biomedical Engineering* **39**, 665–75.

Woldorff, M. G., C. C. Gallen, S. A. Hampson, S. A. Hillyard, C. Pantev, D. Sobel, R. E. Bloom 1993. Modulation of early sensory processing in human auditory cortex during auditory selective attention. *Proceedings of the National Academy of Sciences, USA* **90**, 8722–6.

Wood, C. C., D. Cohen, B. N. Cuffin, M. Yarita, T. Allison 1985. Electrical sources in human somatosensory cortex: identification by combined magnetic and potential recordings. *Science* **227**, 1051–53.

Woods, D. L., K. Alho, A. Algazi 1991. Brain potential signs of feature processing during auditory selective attention. *Neuroreport* **2**, 189–92.

Woods, D. L., K. Alho, A. Algazi 1994. Stages of auditory feature conjuction: an event-related potential study. *Journal of Experimental Psychology: Human Perception and Performance* **20**(1), 81–94.

Yang, T. T., C. C. Gallen, V. S. Ramachandran, S. Cobb, B. J. Schwartz, F. E. Bloom 1994. Noninvasive detection of cerebral plasticity in adult human somatosensory cortex. *Neuroreport* **5**, 701–4.

CHAPTER 8

The architecture of working memory

John Jonides & Edward E. Smith

8.1 INTRODUCTION

We begin with a simple observation: cognition requires memory. Every intelligent being has some form of memory play a critical role in its higher cognitive function. This is true of any complex computing device, it is true of any animal that is respected for its cognitive skill, and it is true of humans. In fact, the role played by memory in cognition is sufficiently complex that just a single memory will not do. Rather, computers, humans and other animals have all developed (some by evolution, some by design) multiple memory systems that aid in higher level cognition. Our goal in this chapter is to examine one of these systems, working memory, so as to reveal its architecture and illustrate its role in cognitive functioning. Perhaps the best way to begin is with an example which captures the role of memory systems in cognition and highlights some of the features that working memory must have to support higher cognitive function.

Think about mental arithmetic. One of the products of the extensive training we receive in school is the ability to execute arithmetic operations without the use of external aids. Of course, our ability to do this is limited to the solution of relatively simple problems, but in the solution of even these problems we can see the elements of a complex cognitive skill that requires extensive use of memory. To illustrate, think about the operations required to solve the following addition problem "in your head":

$$
\begin{array}{r}
8\ 3\ 6 \\
+\ \underline{4\ 2\ 9} \\
\end{array}
$$

Most people begin by computing the sum of 6 and 9, storing the units digit of this sum (5) and carrying the tens digit (1) over to the next column. Then they add this carried digit to the 3 and 2, to give them the desired tens digit, 6. To this point, they would have to hold in memory the original problem and the partial solution of 65. Next, they would move to the third column of the original problem, add the digits there to arrive at 12, which they would append to the 65 that is already computed to arrive at the final sum, 1265. Intuition suggests that this is a common strategy, and careful research confirms it. Hitch (1978) conducted a series of experiments demonstrating that this sort of right-to-left strategy is common to mental-addition problems like this one. He showed, for example, that restricting people so they had to write their answers in a left-to-right order resulted in more errors than allowing them to write their answers in a right-to-left order, agreeing with the hypothesis that the mental addition steps are carried out from right to left.

One particularly interesting feature of Hitch's (1978) analysis of mental addition is the model he proposed. An adaptation of this model to the current example is illustrated in Figure 8.1. The model has two main components, one for long-term memory and one for working memory. The long-term memory component stores various pieces of information relevant to doing mental arithmetic, including the strategy of going from right to left and the library of number facts that we have learned in the past. These are part of our more or less permanent repository of information, allowing us to solve arithmetic problems as well as many other types of problem that we face. The solution process itself, however, is accomplished by working memory. This structure consists of two components. One is a storage buffer that temporarily holds information about the problem at hand. It also is responsible for storing information that is accrued as the problem is solved, such as the fact that the rightmost digit of the solution will be a "5". A storage component is a necessary part of working memory for two reasons. First, in order to solve problems, we must have a temporary representation of the problem at hand. Secondly, mental arithmetic (and most other complex cognitive skills) involves a number of operations that produce intermediate information. These intermediate products must be stored as well as the original problem.

The other component of working memory has been called a "central executive" (Baddeley & Hitch 1974), but is perhaps better labelled a "set

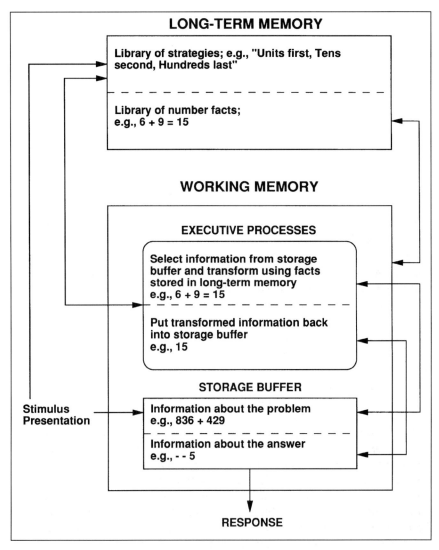

FIG. 8.1.   A flow chart after Hitch (1978) showing the processing components necessary to conduct mental arithmetic. Note that long-term and working memory are both required, and that working memory itself is composed of a storage buffer and a set of executive processes.

of executive processes". These processes are presumably responsible for controlling the computations that are performed on the contents of working memory. In performing mental arithmetic, for example, the executive processes would include: shifting attention from the ones column of the problem to the tens column, and then to the hundreds column as the solution progresses; scheduling the actual numerical operations performed (such as looking up arithmetic rules in long-term memory, applying these rules to the current contents of working memory, adding any carryover from the previous column, and so on); and inhibiting or suppressing the numbers in the problem that have already been taken into consideration. Note that, as the name implies, executive processes control lower-level computational processes. That is, they are not the simple computations such as adding 6 to 9; rather, they are processes such as scheduling the order in which 6 and 9 should be added as compared with 3 and 2. Note further that this characterization of executive processes implies that they are several in number. In our illustration, one is attentional, being able to focus attention on one part of a problem to the temporary exclusion of others. Another process is inhibition, being able to inhibit previous information that was the focus of attention so that new information can be put into the spotlight for current processing. Yet another process is a scheduling operation that allows us, for example, properly to order our work on the units digits before working on the tens digits. Still another process might be setting priorities for different tasks if we are doing something else at the same time that we are trying to solve this arithmetic problem. (For example, although you might make more errors, you could probably work on the mental arithmetic problem in our example at the same time as trying to follow a conversation.) Viewed in this way, the term "central executive" may be just a convenient umbrella for a constellation of processes, all of which are variously involved in higher mental function, and all of which make use of the storage buffers of working memory.

Note that several characteristics of working memory are implied by this analysis. First, its capacity to store information is limited (see e.g. Miller 1956). The reason that we cannot solve mental arithmetic problems of any arbitrary size is not because we cannot do the calculations; rather, it is because we cannot store the problem and its solution as we work through it. A second characteristic of working memory is that its contents can be encoded and updated quickly and frequently (see e.g. Sternberg 1966). You can work on one problem, and then replace it with a new one or some other piece of information quite quickly. Thirdly, the information that is stored in working memory can be accessed quickly (Sternberg 1966, 1975), e.g. it takes only a very short time to retrieve, say, the tens digits of the problem when they are needed. Fourthly, the contents of working memory are fragile; they do not stay in memory long unless there is constant attention to them (Brown 1958, Peterson & Peterson 1959). For example, if you were distracted while solving the mental addition problem that we have illustrated, it would soon be lost so that you could not return to it and pick up where you left off. Finally, as the model proposed by Hitch (1978) illustrates, working memory is not an end in itself; it is a system that is designed to serve higher mental processes (Baddeley 1986).

At this point, we have a reasonably clear idea of the psychological functions of working memory and of its major behavioural characteristics. We can turn now to considering the architecture of working memory in more detail, which will lead us to an examination of its neural implementation. Let us begin with working memory for verbal information (such as arithmetic problems), since this is probably the most frequently used part of the working memory system for humans.

8.2 VERBAL WORKING MEMORY

8.2.1 Behavioural evidence

You can get a reasonably clear idea of the major components of verbal working memory by thinking about a common example, storing a telephone number. Once you have found the number you want in a directory, what is involved in storing it? First, of course, the number must be placed in a storage buffer of the sort we described in connection with our analysis of mental arithmetic. Consistent with our description of that buffer, however, we know that the number will be quickly forgotten if attention is not paid to it constantly. For verbal material such as telephone numbers, our introspections tell us that paying attention is accomplished by covertly speaking the number repeatedly, what psychologists have called "maintenance rehearsal" or "rehearsal". This example suggests, then, that there are two components to verbal working memory, a storage site and a rehearsal process that recirculates the contents of storage for as long as needed.

Going beyond introspection, we can document the functional separability of verbal storage and verbal rehearsal by examining some behavioural experiments. The logic of these studies is this: if there are two components of working memory that are separable, then one ought to be able to identify two experimental variables, where one variable influences the operation of the first component of working memory but not the second, and the other variable influences the operation of the second component of working memory but not the first. This pattern of results is called a "double dissociation". If one could not find a double dissociation for two putative components of working memory, then it would not be clear what is meant by the claim that they are "functionally separable". Of course, it may not be easy to identify two variables that have the predicted effects. Happily, however, there have been some successful behavioural studies of storage and rehearsal in verbal working memory that provide compelling evidence for the notion that there are two components, i.e. that provide a double dissociation.

The experiments are based on a view of rehearsal that characterizes it as a kind of internal tape-recorder loop that recycles the contents of a verbal storage buffer. Baddeley et al. (1975) reasoned that if rehearsal is like a tape loop of limited length, then the number of items one should be able to rehearse and keep refreshed should be limited by the length of the items themselves. They confirmed this prediction in a series of experiments showing that longer words are more poorly remembered than shorter words, even when the words have the same number of syllables. For example, compare the words "bishop" and "voodoo"; it takes longer to articulate the second of these than the first, even though they are both two-syllable words. Baddeley et al. (1975) demonstrated that the immediate recall of lists composed of words that take longer to articulate was poorer than the immediate recall of lists of shorter words. This result has been interpreted as evidence that word length affects the success of rehearsal without affecting the storage of words per se.

Another variable that affects verbal working memory is phonemic similarity (e.g. Conrad 1964, 1970). Words that all sound alike are more difficult to remember than are words that sound different from one another. The effect of phonemic similarity has been attributed to the storage component of working memory, specifically to confusion that occurs among items stored in a verbal buffer. Presumably, the features of the items become interposed with one another, resulting in a loss of item information, which, in turn, results in poorer recall (Baddeley et al. 1984, Baddeley 1986).

Now we have evidence of two variables that affect verbal working memory: word length and phonemic similarity. If these two variables have their effects by influencing the operation of rehearsal and storage respectively, then one ought to find independent effects of them if they are simultaneously applied in a single experiment (see Garner et al. 1956). That is, the decrement in recall due to the words taking longer to articulate should be completely unaffected by whether or not the words sound alike; similarly, the decrement in recall due to the words sounding alike should be completely unaffected by whether or not the words take a relatively long time to articulate. Longoni et al. (1993) tested this prediction and confirmed it. This provides evidence of the functional separability of these two stages in working memory.

8.2.2 Neuropsychological evidence

Establishing functional independence raises the possibility that storage and rehearsal are anatomically separable as well. That is, if one could define the neuroanatomical circuitry of verbal working memory, it might be possible to isolate a component of the circuitry that represents storage and a component that represents rehearsal. Of course, this need not be so. It could be that the representations of storage and rehearsal are so distributed in the brain, with substantial overlap, that it would not be practically possible to isolate one from the other anatomically.

It turns out, however, that it is possible to separate storage and rehearsal components. Several studies using positron emission tomography (PET) (see Ch. 6) have now led to a reasonably clear view of which parts of the verbal working memory circuitry are devoted to storage, and which parts are devoted to rehearsal. Consider one experiment from our laboratory (Smith et al. 1996; see also Paulesu et al. 1993, Awh et al. 1996). The task required subjects to maintain verbal information in working memory continuously, thereby forcing them to use storage and rehearsal strenuously. Subjects saw a stream of single letters appear on a screen, each for 0.5 s, with 2.5 s intervening between letters. As each letter appeared, subjects had to decide whether or not it matched the letter that had appeared two items back in the sequence (hence this is called a "two-back" task). Note that, in order to be successful in this condition, subjects must always maintain in memory representations of the two most recent letters to compare with the current one, and constantly update their representations as new letters appear.

Two control conditions were also tested. One control required subjects to search for a single target letter in a sequence similar to that presented in the two-back condition. The visual and response events in this "search" task were quite similar to those in the two-back task, but the working memory requirements were minimal. When brain activations in this search task were subtracted from those in the two-back task, two major sites of activation were revealed. One was in posterior parietal cortex in the left hemisphere. What is its function? An answer comes from noting that the most frequent site of damage in patients who have deficits in verbal working memory is posterior parietal cortex (see e.g. McCarthy & Warrington 1990). Thus, it seems reasonable to conclude that the activation in this region reflects the storage of verbal material.

The other major site of activation found in this experiment included a trio of locations in left prefrontal cortex: one in the inferior frontal gyrus (in the area called Broca's region, after the neurophysiologist who is famous for documenting its function in language), one posterior to this in premotor cortex, and one more superior in the supplementary motor area (SMA). These sites have been implicated in the production of speech (see e.g. Hinke et al. 1993, Paulesu et al. 1993). Thus, it seems reasonable to infer that their function in this task is the production of an internal speech code of the sort required for rehearsal.

The other control condition included in this experiment confirms that rehearsal in the form of internal speech is involved in the two-back task. In this control condition, subjects were presented with a stream of letters, just as in the two-back task, but they were required only to emit a manual response upon presentation of each letter and then silently rehearse the letter to themselves until the next one appeared. Thus, this condition duplicated the perceptual and response requirements of the two-back condition, but required only rehearsal with virtually no memory load compared with the two-back task. So, subtraction of the activations in this "rehearsal" control from those in the two-back task should have yielded left-hemisphere posterior activations if these activations represent storage, but it should have eliminated left-hemisphere anterior activations if these represent rehearsal. We did find that the posterior parietal activation was still reliable in this subtraction. We also found that the anterior activations in Broca's area and premotor cortex were no longer statistically significant, also consistent with predictions. All in all, the results of our experiment confirm nicely the involvement of left posterior parietal cortex in storage and left prefrontal cortex in rehearsal processes.

Finding that storage and rehearsal are dissociable in terms of the neural circuitry suggests that there may be patients with damage to one mechanism with the other mechanism spared. Indeed, this is so. We have already alluded to the fact that there are many cases of patients with left-hemisphere posterior brain damage who show deficits in verbal working memory tasks (Shallice 1988). One such patient, for example, cannot recall more than a single item when presented with a string of letters in random order and asked to repeat them back. There is also evidence that patients with damage to their speech production centres in anterior parts of the brain show impaired working memory performance (Swinney & Taylor 1971). Their retrieval of verbal information is markedly slowed compared with control subjects. These patients presumably have damage to the structures that are involved in rehearsal.[1]

All in all, the case is compelling that verbal working memory consists of two components. One component is responsible for storing information, and the evidence points to a posterior brain location for this component. The other component is responsible for recirculating information, and the circuit responsible for this component seems best characterized as a frontal one. To summarize this part of the architecture of working memory visually, a flow diagram of the processes that would be engaged by visual presentation of verbal information that had to be

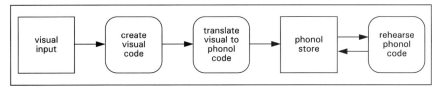

FIG. 8.2.   A schematic flow diagram of processes involved in verbal working memory when the input to memory is visual. Note that the diagram includes different sorts of internal representational codes that need to be created, as well as storage and rehearsal processes.

stored in working memory is given in Figure 8.2. First, this information would be encoded visually, using mechanisms of the inferior temporal lobe that are beyond the scope of this chapter. This visual code would then be translated into a phonological one. The brain areas responsible for this translation are not well understood; however, various investigators attribute this step to posterior mechanisms (see e.g. Posner & Raichle 1994). This code would then be entered into a verbal storage buffer, which is presumably housed in parietal cortex, and recirculated by rehearsal mechanisms of the frontal cortex.

8.3 MULTIPLE WORKING MEMORIES

8.3.1 Neuropsychological studies of spatial working memory

The foregoing discussion is clearly incomplete. If working memory is to play a central role in cognition, it must be capable of storing and manipulating information in a variety of codes, not just a linguistic one (e.g. Kosslyn 1980, 1981, Byrne and Johnson-Laird 1989). Think about the mental processes involved when you try to comprehend a set of directions for getting from your present location to an unfamiliar destination. For many people, this task involves translating a linguistic representation (the verbal utterance that corresponds to the directions) into a spatial one. Then the spatial representations for various parts of the route are combined to give an overall plan for the itinerary in question. Storing the parts of the route, adding new parts to it, and manipulating the representation mentally constitute a working memory task, one that relies on a spatial representation quite different from the verbal representations we have discussed thus far.

There is compelling evidence that the circuitry for spatial working memory differs from that for verbal working memory. An experiment from our laboratory using positron emission tomography (PET) measurement demonstrates this (Smith et al. 1996). Subjects were presented with a stream of letters during each PET scan, as illustrated in Figure

8.3. Each letter was displayed for 0.5 s, with 2.5 s intervening between successive letters. As shown in the figure, the letters were displayed at seemingly random locations around the perimeter of an imaginary circle, and the letters varied in whether they were upper or lower case. These presentation parameters were used for two separate experimental conditions. In one, subjects were responsible for storing spatial information, and in the other they were responsible for storing verbal information. In the spatial memory condition (shown at the top of Fig. 8.3), for each letter subjects had to decide whether it matched in position the letter that appeared three previously in the series, regardless of identity (this is a "three-back" task, analogous to the two-back task described above). In the verbal memory condition (shown at the bottom of Figure 8.3) subjects had to decide whether each letter matched in identity the one that appeared three previously in the series, regardless of its spatial position. Because the case of the letters was varied, the matching decision had to be made on the basis of letter identities, not visual shapes.

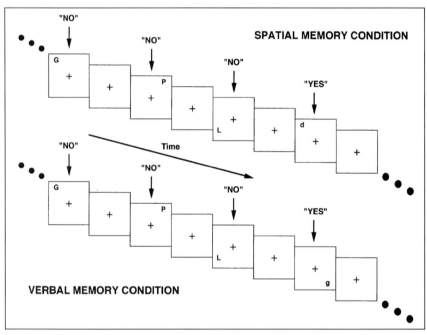

FIG. 8.3.   Schematic diagrams illustrating the procedures in two three-back tasks. The upper panel shows the sequence on a trial in which the subject would have to match each letter-position to the position of the letter that appeared three back. The lower panel illustrates the sequence of letters that would be shown in a trial in which the subject would be responsible for matching each letter to the letter that was shown three back.

In order to remove unwanted processes not directly related to storage, Smith et al. (1996) used two control conditions, one for the verbal memory task and one for the spatial memory task. In the spatial control condition, subjects were shown three target positions (marked by dots) at the beginning of a stimulus sequence that was largely identical to the sequence shown at the top of Figure 8.3. Subjects then had to decide whether each position in the sequence matched one of these three target positions. In a similar way, in the verbal control condition, subjects were shown three target letters at the beginning of each sequence, similar to the sequence shown at the bottom of Figure 8.3. Subjects then had to decide whether each letter in the sequence matched one of these three target letters. The activations from these control conditions were then subtracted from those of their respective memory conditions.

Figure 8.4, which has been reproduced on page 152, displays right, left and superior renderings of brains on which have been superimposed the PET activations from the three-back tasks, separately for the spatial and verbal conditions. The activations are shown as coloured splotches that code increasing activation as yellow and red areas superimposed on the magnetic resonance images of the brains. Although there was clear evidence of bilateral activation in both tasks, in the spatial task there was more activation in posterior and anterior areas in the right than those in the left hemisphere. Conversely, in the verbal task, the activations in the left hemisphere were higher than those in the right hemisphere. This presents us with a double dissociation between spatial and verbal working memory at a global level of analysis.

At a finer level, the verbal task resulted in activation in several regions. As in the two-back verbal task described above, there was activation in posterior parietal cortex in the left hemisphere. As we have argued, this region seems to be associated with the storage of verbal information in working memory (Paulesu et al. 1993, Petrides et al. 1993b, Awh et al. 1996).

In addition to the posterior activation, Broca's area in prefrontal cortex showed reliable activation, as in the two-back task. However, the three-back verbal task did not show evidence of activation in premotor or supplementary motor areas; but this may be because the verbal control task itself may have involved some rehearsal, and some of the activation due to rehearsal may have been subtracted from the verbal memory condition (as argued by Smith et al. 1996). The verbal memory condition also shows evidence of activation in dorsolateral prefrontal cortex in the left hemisphere, an area that has been found in other complex verbal working memory tasks and that may be a signature of the operation of executive processes rather than storage or rehearsal processes (Petrides et al. 1993b, Cohen et al. 1995). We shall return to this point later.

Figure 8.4 shows that the spatial memory condition minus its control also showed activation in posterior parietal cortex, but the activation was largely in the right hemisphere. This is consistent with other PET studies of spatial working memory that have repeatedly found activation in right parietal cortex (Jonides et al. 1993, Petrides et al. 1993b). By analogy to the posterior activation in the verbal task, we attribute this site of activation to spatial storage processes.

Note that the spatial memory subtraction also shows substantial evidence of frontal activation, also concentrated in the right hemisphere. One site of this activation is in premotor cortex. Recall that this is one of the sites which, when activated in the left hemisphere in a verbal memory task, we attributed to part of a verbal rehearsal mechanism. It is tempting to draw an analogy between these two results, and suggest that subjects have the capability of engaging a spatial rehearsal mechanism when they are storing spatial information, just as they can engage verbal rehearsal when storing verbal material. It remains to be seen whether this case can be made empirically (but for some evidence concerning this case see Awh et al. 1995).

The neuroimaging data from our laboratory confirm a division between verbal and spatial working memory that has also been suggested by comparison of the working memory deficits of two patients. Consider first patient P.V. At the time of the report by Basso et al. (1982), P.V. was a 28-year-old, right-handed woman who had had a stroke, with subsequent commissurotomy. Her lesion was quite large, extending over the full anterior–posterior extent of language areas in the left hemisphere. Given the size of her lesion, her language functions were remarkably intact. However, she had a noticeable inability to comprehend auditorally presented sequences of digits. This observation was documented by Basso et al. (1982), who showed that on memory-span tests with digits, letters or words, P.V.'s memory span was worse than would be shown by normals. For example, when tested on ten digit strings each string being 5 digits long, she was able to recall only one string completely correctly; normal subjects typically get all ten strings completely correct. This performance is to be contrasted to P.V.'s perfectly normal spatial working memory. This was tested using a standard neuropsychological task called the "Corsi blocks" test. In this task, the experimenter touches a set of randomly arrayed blocks one at a time, and then the patient repeats the order by touching the blocks one at a time. For this test, P.V. was given strings of span-plus-two in length with repeated presentations of each string until she was able to repeat each string three times perfectly. She needed 11 attempts to reach this criterion, compared with a group of normal controls who needed 11.8 attempts on average. These results indicate that P.V.'s verbal working memory span is considerably worse than her spatial span, which appears normal.

Contrast P.V.'s performance on these tasks with that of patient E.L.D., studied by Hanley et al. (1991).At the time of their study, E. L. D. was a 55-year-old, right-handed woman who had suffered an aneurysm of the middle cerebral artery in the right hemisphere which had led to a haematoma in the area of the Sylvian fissure some 6 years previously. Her major cognitive deficit was an anterograde amnesia for spatial and visual information with which she was unfamiliar prior to her trauma. When tested on the Corsi blocks task, she was noticeably worse than normals, indicating a deficit in spatial working memory. For example, E.L.D. correctly recalled no sequences of length 5, compared with a group of normals who recalled 70% of sequences of this length perfectly. E. L. D. showed no deficit in verbal working memory, however, performing comparably with normal controls. When given three sequences of six phonologically different letters to recall, E.L.D. recalled all sequences perfectly, in contrast to controls who recalled only 1.4 sequences on average.

It thus appears that the circuitry for verbal and spatial working memory are differentiable. This accords well with behavioural evidence, indicating that one can identify experimental variables that selectively affect verbal or spatial working memory differently (Brooks 1968, Logie et al. 1990). The model shown in Figure 8.2 needs to be amended to recognize this evidence. If we assume, as the evidence

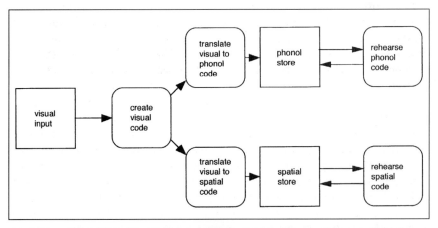

FIG. 8.5.   An elaboration of the model shown in Figure 8.2 to include processes responsible for creating a spatial code and for storing and rehearsing that code in working memory.

indicates, that spatial storage may be accompanied by spatial re-hearsal, then we can summarize our model as shown in Figure 8.5. This figure shows that, when visual information is presented to a subject, depending on the kind of information and task demands, the subject can create a visual code to be translated into a phonological or a spatial code for storage and manipulation in working memory.

8.3.2 Spatial working memory in monkeys

Verbal working memory must be a uniquely human capacity, humans being the only animals with a fully developed language system. How-ever, the same need not be true of spatial working memory. In fact, some of the most detailed evidence about spatial working memory comes from experiments that have used monkeys as subjects.

For some time, it has been known that lesions to the dorsolateral pre-frontal cortex cause deficits in monkeys' spatial working memory. For example, examine the pair of tasks illustrated in Figure 8.6, taken from Goldman-Rakic (1993). In the left panel, the animal is engaged in a working memory task called the "delayed response" task. The monkey is shown two locations in one of which food is placed. It cannot reach for the food immediately, however; rather, an enforced delay of several sec-onds is introduced so that the animal must rely on its memory of the baited location, as shown in the second row of the left panel in the fig-ure. Then, in the third row, the monkey is allowed to reach for the food. In this task, the location of the food is changed from trial to trial, and so the animal must remember the relevant location in each particular trial in order to be rewarded. Performance in this delayed response task is dramatically degraded if an animal has lesions in the dorsolateral area of prefrontal cortex. By contrast, if the same lesioned animal is given another delayed response task, but one that does not require working memory, it performs normally. This is shown on the right in Figure 8.6, which illustrates what is sometimes called an "associative memory" task. Again, one of two locations in the stimulus array is baited, but this time the location is marked by a unique stimulus, as shown by the "plus" sign in the figure. Then the animal has a forced delay, following which it can reach for the food. The food is marked by the "plus" sign, re-gardless of the side on which it appears, and the animal, even though lesioned, can learn to use this associative cue to find the reward. This experiment illustrates that, in monkeys, dorsolateral prefrontal cortex is critical to the maintenance of spatial information in working memory, but it is not necessary for all memory, as the associative memory task shows.

Further studies of spatial working memory in monkeys reveal a remarkable finding. Not only can one identify working memory with a

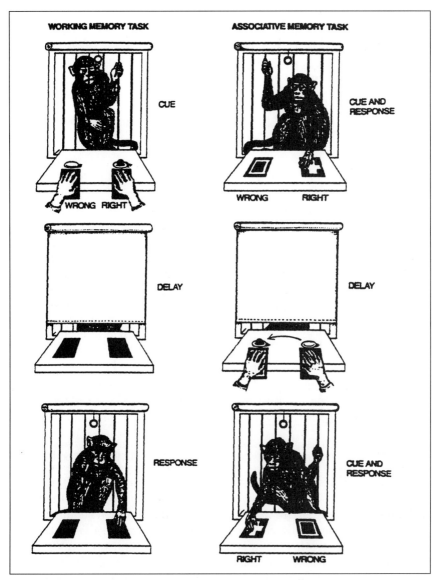

FIG. 8.6.   Illustrations of a delayed response task and an associative memory task that have been used to test memory in monkeys. Adapted from Goldman-Rakic (1993).

particular region of prefrontal cortex, but one can also show that individual nerve cells in this region behave as if they themselves are the mechanism of the memory storage. This is most impressively illustrated by considering an experiment by Funahashi et al. (1989). Three

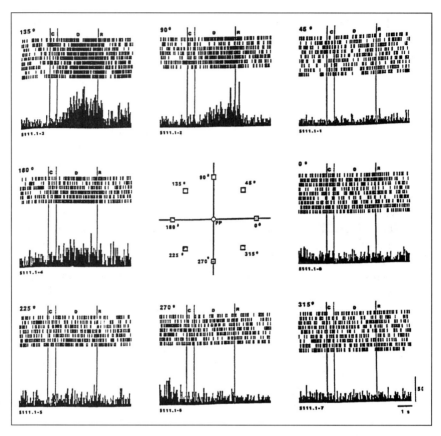

FIG. 8.7.   Illustration of a task used to test spatial working memory in monkeys together with illustrative recordings from a single neuron from which recordings were taken on this task. From Funahashi et al. (1989).

monkeys were taught the working memory task shown schematically in Figure 8.7. The monkeys learned to fixate a spot in the centre of a screen to begin a trial. This is marked by "FP" ("fixation point") in the figure, in the centre of the schematized display. After fixation was achieved, a monkey would be shown a small square that could appear unpredictably at one of eight locations surrounding the fixation point. The animals were trained to maintain their fixation while this square was presented and to continue fixation during a 3-s retention interval that followed presentation of the square. Following this period, the fixation point disappeared, which served as a signal to the subject to shift its gaze to the location that had contained the square on that trial. The design of this procedure requires the animals to maintain a memory of the location of the stimulus on each trial. Since the relevant location changed from trial to trial, presumably the spatial information was being stored in working memory. The experimenters recorded the responses of individual neurons in the region of the principal sulcus in dorsolateral prefrontal cortex while the monkeys performed the task.

The experimenters found a number of neurons with responses similar to the ones shown in Figure 8.7. The figure includes data from a single neuron when the animal was shown stimuli at each of the eight locations used in the task. Each of the graphs plots the responsiveness of the neuron as the number of spikes per second during each of the epochs of a trial: before a stimulus cue was presented (the first period in each graph); during presentation of the cue (denoted by "C"); during the delay interval, while the animal presumably retained the location of the cue (denoted by "D"); and during the response interval, when the animal shifted its gaze to the cued location (denoted by "R"). Focus on the responsiveness of the neuron when the cue was presented at the location labelled "315°". You can see that the cell did not change its basal level of responsiveness during the entire trial, indicating that it was not sensitive to the presentation of this cue. By contrast, consider the responsiveness when the cue was presented at the 135° position. While the cell did not discharge with any greater frequency than during the pre-trial baseline, during the delay interval the responsiveness increased dramatically, and then it dropped off again during the interval when a response was required. This pattern is quite different from that when the cue was presented at the 315° position. Note also, that the responsiveness of the cell when a cue was presented at either 90° or 180° was quite similar to that when the cue was presented at the 135-degree position, although with a somewhat lower spike frequency.

What can we make of this pattern of activity by this neuron? One thing to note is that this cell (and others recorded in this region of prefrontal cortex) was selectively responsive during the retention interval of the task; this suggests that these cells have a memory function. Secondly, the activity of the cell was in response to only some of the locations that could be shown, and not to others. These two facts lead to the conclusion that the cell in question encoded and retained the location of the stimulus for a brief period of time, just what would be required of a working memory system. Goldman-Rakic and her colleagues have also shown that cells in this region are connected closely with cells in posterior parietal cortex (Chafee & Goldman-Rakic 1994, Goldman-Rakic & Chafee 1994), in a region similar to the one that is activated in human studies of working memory for spatial information. Furthermore, cells in parietal cortex show the same kind of location-specific and delay-specific responsiveness as cells in prefrontal cortex. In short, it appears that there is a circuitry including parietal and prefrontal cortex that is specialized for briefly storing information about spatial location in monkeys.

One question that arises from these studies is: What is the nature of the memory that is stored by these cells? Two possibilities present themselves. One is a straightforward conclusion from the obvious details of the experiment: The cells store a representation of the spatial locations themselves. Another possibility is that the cells store not spatial location *per se*, but rather a representation of the eye movement that the animal must make in order to respond properly after the delay interval has passed. According to the first interpretation, the working memory is for spatial location; according to the second, it is for a motor programme that is executed shortly afterwards.

A direct test of these two alternatives comes from an experiment by Funahashi et al. (1993). They trained monkeys on a delayed response task that was a bit more complex than the oculomotor task described above. In this case, the stimuli appeared only to the left or right of fixation point (as opposed to appearing at one of eight locations), but again there was a 3-s delay before the animal could respond with an eye movement. The eye movement varied as a function of the kind of fixation point the animal was given. If the fixation point was a spot, this was a signal to the animal that it should move its eyes to the stimulus cue after the delay period terminated. If the fixation point was a plus sign, however, this was a signal that the animal should move its eyes diametrically away from the stimulus cue after the delay interval. Again, the investigators recorded the responses of neurons in the region of the principal sulcus of dorsolateral prefrontal cortex. Interestingly, they found cells of two types. Some responded during the delay interval to stimuli in a particular location, regardless of whether the animal had to move its eyes to the target or away from it. Other cells responded specifically to the direction of the eye movement, regardless of whether the stimulus cue appeared in one location or another. This pattern of results indicates that there may be at least two different representations stored in the prefrontal cortex of monkeys during a working memory task. One is for spatial position and the other is for a motor programme of an oculomotor response (for a related description, see also Fuster 1995). These results raise the possibility that the representation of spatial location that may be stored in working memory may be a complex mixture of a representation of space *per se* and a representation of motor actions that accompany responding to stimuli in space. Further research is needed to uncover more details of this representation.

8.3.3 Working memory for objects

The evidence we have reviewed presents a case that the working memory system is composed of more than one module. A combination of behavioural, neuropsychological, neuroimaging and electrophysiological data convince us that working memory for verbal information is mediated by a different set of brain circuits than for spatial information. This is the case presented by Baddeley and his colleagues in first proposing the idea of a working memory (Baddeley & Hitch 1974, Baddeley 1986, 1992). However, the architecture of working memory storage buffers is still more complex. There is neuropsychological and neuroimaging evidence that a pathway exists in humans and in other animals for the short-term storage of visual information about objects and their characteristics that is different from the pathways for verbal and spatial information. As such, a case can be made for a visual storage buffer in addition to a spatial and a phonological buffer.

Early evidence for an object memory pathway comes from studies of animals with lesions in the prefrontal cortex (e.g. Passingham 1975, Mishkin & Manning 1978). Mishkin & Manning (1978), for example, trained three groups of monkeys on one of three non-spatial memory problems: (a) delayed object alternation, in which an animal was rewarded if, after a delay, it chose an object that it had not chosen on the previous trial; (b) delayed colour matching, in which a sample colour patch had to be matched by the monkey after a delay by choosing one of two choice stimuli; or (c) delayed object matching, in which a sample object had to be matched after a delay by selecting one of two choice stimuli. Lesions in the area of the principal sulcus produced few deficits on any of these tasks. However, lesions in an area just inferior to the principal sulcus (called the "inferior convexity" of dorsolateral prefrontal cortex) produced marked deficits in performance in all the tasks. Note that all the tasks share the feature that animals were tested on memory for objects or for features of objects.

These results, taken together with those on spatial working memory in monkeys, suggest the following hypothesis: the region of the principal sulcus is responsible for storing representations of spatial locations, and the inferior convexity of prefrontal cortex is responsible for storing information about object identities. This hypothesis was tested directly in a later experiment by Wilson et al. (1993), in which they recorded from single neurons in either principal sulcus or inferior convexity regions during spatial or object working memory tasks. The spatial task involved stimuli that were presented briefly to the left or right of fixation while the monkeys fixated the centre of a display. As in the experiment by Funahashi et al. (1989), the monkeys learned to shift their gaze to the location of the stimulus after it disappeared and after

a delay had ensued. The object memory task involved a brief presentation of one of two patterns in the centre of the display screen, after
which a delay followed. The monkeys were trained to shift their gaze to
the left or right after the delay, depending on which of the two patterns
they had seen. Thus, in the spatial task the animals produced one of
two oculomotor responses depending on which of two spatial locations
they stored in memory, and in the object task they produced one of two
responses depending on which of two objects they held in memory.

The results of this experiment revealed that working memory for
spatial position and for object shape are the responsibility of different
frontal areas in monkeys. Neurons in the principal sulcus were responsive during the delay interval in the spatial memory task but not in the
object memory task; conversely, neurons in the inferior convexity were
responsive only in the object memory task and not in the spatial
memory task. These results are consistent with the neuroanatomical
connections to each of these regions. The area of the principal sulcus
receives substantial projections from the posterior parietal cortex, a
region that is known to subserve spatial vision among other things
(Ungerleider & Mishkin 1982). The inferior convexity, however, receives many of its projections from the inferior temporal cortex, which
has been implicated in object processing and object memory (e.g. Fuster
& Jervey 1981, Miyashita & Chang 1988, Miller & Desimone 1991).
Based on this pattern of projections and on the selective responsiveness
of the two regions of prefrontal cortex, it seems plausible to hypothesize
that there are two pathways for working memory, one for spatial and
one for object information. The spatial pathway begins with visual input in occipital cortex, then makes use of a spatial processing apparatus in parietal cortex, with the resulting spatial code being stored in
some combination of parietal cortex and dorsolateral prefrontal cortex
in the region of the principal sulcus. The object pathway also begins
with occipital processing, progresses with object coding and recognition
processes in inferotemporal cortex, and continues with storage involving some combination of inferotemporal and inferior prefrontal cortex.

Thus far our inferences about the circuitry of spatial and object
work-ing memory derive from studies of monkeys. The data on human
working memory for these two types of information also suggest two
systems; however, their architecture seems to be somewhat different,
making use of the lateralized specialization of the two hemispheres in
the human brain and, perhaps, relying more on parietal mechanisms
for the storage of information than seems to be the case in monkeys.
The data that support this position come from neuroimaging studies
described by Smith and co-workers (Smith & Jonides 1994, Smith et al.
1995). Subjects engaged in one of two tasks while PET measurements

were made. In one, they had to retain the locations of three dots for a retention interval of 3s, after which they were probed for their memory of one of the dot positions. In the other condition, they had to retain the identity of two unfamiliar, line-drawn objects for 3s after which a probe object was shown and they had to decide whether or not it matched one of the two objects they held in memory. Each of these conditions had appropriate control conditions associated with it to subtract out processes that were not directly related to storage. When these were subtracted, the resulting brain activations revealed different pathways for spatial and object memory. The spatial pathway included largely right-hemisphere processes, including occipital, parietal and prefrontal sites. The object pathway included largely left-hemisphere processes, mainly in the parietal and inferotemporal areas.

These results are consistent with the general view of spatial and object working memory that derives from the data on monkeys, data that implicate a dorsal stream of processing for spatial information and a ventral stream for object information. However, the PET findings lead to the view that parietal mechanisms may play a more prominent role in storage processes in humans than they do in monkeys. These findings also show that the pathways in humans are consistent with the general fact that spatial processing is a skill for which the right hemisphere seems to be specialized.

The human studies of working memory for objects also suggest a parallel to the rehearsal processes that we have proposed for verbal and spatial working memory. In at least one of the object working memory experiments, there was activation in prefrontal cortex, specifically in the premotor area – an area that has consistently shown activation in spatial and verbal working memory studies. This area, as discussed above, may mediate processes that are involved in generating and refreshing an internal representation of stored material so that it can be protected from interference and decay. At this point, it is premature to conclude that rehearsal is an integrated part of the working memory system for objects, but it is certainly a hypothesis that deserves further scrutiny. If we assume for the moment that this hypothesis has some currency, then we can expand our model of working memory for visual input as shown in Figure 8.8. This figure takes what we had determined previously about the circuitry for spatial and verbal working memory and adds to it circuitry for working memory for object representations, including a rehearsal process.

8.3.4 Other working memory modules
While we have focused on verbal, spatial and visual-object working memories, there is reason to believe that there are other memory

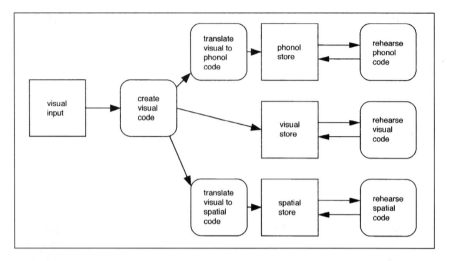

FIG. 8.8.   An elaboration of the model shown in Figure 8.5, recognizing a circuit for the processing and storage of information about visual objects.

modules as well. For one thing, there may be a separate working memory module for each major sensory system, perhaps for use in processing the identities of the inputs to these systems. The visual-object module just discussed may be the working memory buffer for the visual system; similarly, there is some evidence for a comparable short-term buffer for auditory information (e.g. Colombo et al. 1990, Zatorre & Samson 1991). In addition, there may be a working memory system that is specialized for storing motoric representations, as indicated by evidence from studies of monkeys (for some relevant evidence see e.g. Gnadt & Andersen 1988, Georgopoulos et al. 1989). However, the case for these further modules has not yet been established with the variety of evidence in both humans and other animals that characterizes the case for verbal, spatial and object representations. Still, as further studies of working memory continue, there may be reason to elaborate the model shown in Figure 8.8, with further modules for yet other kinds of representation.

Assuming that all the above-mentioned buffers exist, note that there is an important difference between those buffers that are tied to a sensory system and the spatial or verbal buffers. Sensory buffers, by definition, store information only from their own input modality, whereas the spatial and verbal modules can, in principle, accept information from multiple input modalities. In this sense, spatial and verbal working memory are relatively abstract; they are not tied to sensory modality, as a recent experiment from our laboratory demonstrates

(Schumacher et al. 1995). In this experiment, the very same verbal information was presented either auditorally or visually in a working memory task; regardless of input modality, the identical working memory circuit was activated.

Another issue that certainly requires further study is this. The prevailing view of working memory is that it stores verbal, spatial and visual codes. These codes, by assumption, are stored in the service of cognitive processes that are engaged in various tasks that require working memory. For example, one could draw on a spatial code of locational information in building up a representation of a familiar environment while comprehending directions. Or one could draw on a visual code as the basis for making similar judgments from memory about two objects that one has stored. Yet again, one could draw on a phonological code of a set of digits in the service of mental arithmetic processes of the sort we illustrated at the beginning of this chapter. What is lacking, however, is any statement about an even more abstract representation, the sort one would need to use working memory productively in the comprehension of language, in problem-solving, in inductive or deductive reasoning, and so on. The critical point is that there must be some sort, or sorts, of more conceptual or propositional representations that are involved in cognition which have not been captured by current conceptions about working memory.

It is worth noting that there is some behavioural evidence that a conceptual code may be stored in working memory (for a partial review see Shulman 1971). Hintzman (1965) found, for example, that recall of letters and digits was influenced not only by acoustic confusions (as reviewed above), but also by confusions in semantic category, suggesting that the category of the items had been coded in memory in addition to the phonological code. Also, Dale & Gregory (1966) and Wickens et al. (1963), among others, have shown that interference in recall in working memory tasks can be traced to semantic factors in addition to phonological ones. This finding allows one to infer that there is a semantic code used for storage. These bits of evidence lead one to suspect that there may be a working memory code for semantic or conceptual information as well as phonological, spatial, and visual codes. However, this issue remains unsatisfactorily resolved at present and requires further investigation.

8.4 EXECUTIVE PROCESSES

The architecture of working memory proposed thus far is incomplete. It lacks any discussion of the processes that make use of information that is stored in working memory. There are, of course, many such processes. Consider the mental arithmetic task with which we began the chapter. Successful solution of this problem requires ordering of the addition of the three columns in the problem, attending to the number that is carried from one column to another, inhibiting the numbers of a column that has been added when one moves on to the next one, and so forth. The original conception of working memory classed these and other processes under the general heading of a "central executive", but listing them in this way makes clear that there is little reason to view them as a single entity. Rather, it is probably more appropriate to classify these as "executive processes", as we mentioned above, to highlight the fact that there are various such processes used in different task contexts.

Even seemingly simple tasks include some role for executive processes. We introduced one such task above, the "n-back" task, in which a subject is shown a sequence of letters and for each must decide whether it matches the one that appeared n-back in the series (n can vary, and was 2 and 3 in the examples discussed). As emphasized earlier, this task loads heavily on storage processes because subjects must constantly have information stored in working memory in order to perform successfully. Note, though, that the task requires other processes too. One such process is a constant updating of the contents of working memory as each new letter is presented in the sequence. Older letters must be dropped or inhibited and new ones added. The requirement to drop and add letters also introduces a need to keep track of the temporal order in which each letter occurred because it is the "$n + 1$" letter back in the sequence that must be dropped and the newest one that must be added. To accomplish this, there must a time-tagging of which letter occurred when. Also, a response inhibition process plays a role in the typical version of this task. If the task is a three-back task, for example, there will occasionally be matches to the current letter that appear one-back or two-back, and it would be incorrect to respond to these as matches. So the subject must guard against a positive response in these cases, inhibiting what may be a natural tendency to respond because a match has occurred.

This analysis of the n-back task suggests that an examination of brain activations in n-back experiments may provide hints about the locus of executive processes. Indeed it does. Various results from our laboratory, for example, indicate that there is substantial activation in dorsolateral prefrontal cortex; this has also been reported by others for n-back tasks (Cohen et al., in press) as well as for other working memory tasks that extensively involve executive processes (Petrides et al. 1993a,b). Interestingly, we find that the hemispheric site of this dorsolateral prefrontal activation varies depending on whether the task requires the processing of spatial or verbal information. For the former, the predominant site is a right-hemisphere dorsolateral prefrontal one, whereas for the latter it is a homologous area in the left hemisphere (for a similar contrast between right- and left-hemisphere prefrontal activation due to executive processes see also Petrides et al. 1993a,b).

The preceding data suggest that at least some executive processes may be the responsibility of prefrontal cortex. If so, then damage to this area should produce deficits on tasks in which the executive processes of working memory play an important role. A classic example of this comes from study of the Wisconsin card-sorting task (Berg 1948). In this task subjects are first given four target cards, each bearing a design in which shape is one dimension of variation (e.g. cross or triangle), colour is another (e.g. red or blue), and the number of figures on the card is the third (e.g. one or two). Subjects are then given a stack of cards to sort, placing each card in front of one of the four target cards depending on what they think the proper criterion is on which to sort the cards. The experimenter has a sorting criterion in mind (say, colour), but the subject does not know this and is simply given feedback about whether or not the placement of each card is correct, according to the criterion. When the subject begins sorting correctly according to the chosen criterion, the criterion is abruptly changed to another dimension (e.g. shape) without informing the subject. Sorting must then continue until the subject has satisfied this new dimension, at which point the criterion is changed again.

This task has an obvious working memory component. Subjects must keep in mind the current sorting criterion, using it as a guide to place each card. The main executive processes that are engaged by the task come into play at the time of a switch of criterion, at which point subjects use the feedback to determine that the current criterion is no longer correct, suppress or inhibit this criterion, generate a new criterion that is consistent with the current feedback (and with that on any previous trials the subject can remember), hold this new criterion in mind, and assess the feedback that comes when it is used as the basis of sorting. Normal subjects have little difficulty with this task, finding the correct criterion within a few trials, and switching to a new one when it is called for within a few trials. Patients with damage to the prefrontal cortex, however, find this task most difficult (Milner 1964). They can find the first dimension relatively quickly, but they then persevere with it when they are required to switch to another dimension. This pattern of behaviour suggests that the patients have little difficulty storing information about a dimension, but they cannot engage the executive processes necessary to accomplish a switch, including the processes necessary to inhibit a previously correct response as they try out new dimensions.

Consider now a task that is much more demanding of executive processes and of memory as well, a task devised by Shallice (1982) to study frontal lobe functioning. The task is called the Tower of London and is illustrated in Figure 8.9. Subjects are given three pegs of different lengths with three beads of different colours (red, green and blue) placed on the pegs in an initial position, as shown on the left of the figure. Their task is to achieve a goal configuration, three examples of which are shown in Figure 8.9. Subjects are permitted to move only a single bead at a time, keeping all beads on the apparatus when they are not being moved; they are also permitted to stack more than one bead on a peg if necessary. Examination of Figure 8.9 reveals that the problems can be graded in difficulty, with some requiring more moves than others to complete. The figure shows the minimum number of moves necessary to solve each of the three example problems shown.

This task obviously involves mentally planning a number of moves in order to decide how one should begin. It involves a heavy storage component, since a subject mentally simulates a set of moves, and it also involves substantial scheduling processes, often thought to be associated with executive functioning. Scheduling itself involves plotting out subgoals that must be reached as one is trying to achieve the final common goal (for a discussion see Newell and Simon 1972). Shallice (1982) found that patients with lesions in left frontal cortex had great difficulty with this task, as would be expected if frontal cortex is important to executive functioning. By contrast, he found that patients with lesions in posterior cortex performed much like normal control subjects. Baddeley (1986) has reported results from a patient with bilateral dam-

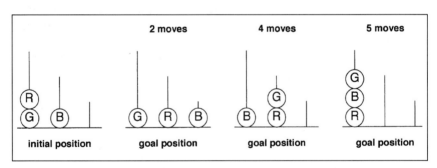

FIG. 8.9.   An illustration of the Tower of London task, after Shallice (1982). The subject is given a starting configuration of three beads (R, red; G, green, and B, Blue), as shown on the left. The task is to use the least number of moves to achieve a final configuration, three examples of which are shown to the right of the starting configuration. Note that the three goal configurations represent problems of varying difficulty, in that two, four, or five moves, respectively, are needed to solve them.

age in frontal cortex who failed on another problem quite similar to this one, the Tower of Hanoi problem. Goel & Grafman (in press), in analysing the problem-solving behaviour of a set of other patients with frontal lesions on the Tower of Hanoi, have noted that the difficulty that frontal patients seem to have with this sort of task is in recognizing the conflict that occurs when the final goal of the task conflicts with a subgoal that must be reached in an intermediate state of the solution. (For example, note that to reach the goal position shown on the right of Figure 8.9, one needs to stack the red bead on the blue one, an intermediate state that conflicts with the final state that has the blue bead on top of the red one.) Patients with lesions in frontal cortex seem to have great difficulty in resolving conflicts of this sort.

The results from patients with frontal lesions on tasks of this sort are confirmed by neuroimaging studies of the Tower of London task. Owen et al. (1994) and Rogers et al. (1994) report PET studies of normal subjects engaged in the Tower of London task. These studies revealed two major sites of activation compared to appropriate control conditions. One site was in posterior parietal cortex, concentrated in the left hemisphere. Our preceding review suggests that this activation may have resulted from the heavy working memory storage requirements of the task. In this context, the fact that the predominant activation in posterior cortex was in the left hemisphere may indicate that subjects in this task rely heavily on language-like representations to conduct their planning of successive moves. The other site of activation was in frontal cortex, agreeing with the results of Shallice (1982) and Baddeley (1986) that frontal mechanisms are important to the planning operations needed to be successful at the Tower of London task. Taken together, the reports of performance in the Tower tasks by patients with frontal damage and the reports of brain activation in the tasks by normal subjects indicate a heavy involvement of working memory, both storage and executive processes.

Finally, let us return to the mental arithmetic task with which we began. It should be clear by now that any task as complex as mental arithmetic recruits a variety of processing components. Hitch (1978) and Logie et al. (1994), among others, have argued that working memory plays a major role in this processing, but we must recognize that there are important contributions of other processes as well: those required to recognize numbers in their arabic form (e.g. 68), those required to comprehend verbal representations of numbers (e.g. sixty-eight), those that assign magnitudes to numerical quantities, those that report a numerical sum, and so forth. Dehaene (1992) has introduced a model of number processing that recognizes various kinds of code for numbers that are necessary to account for our skill in mentally manipulating them.

Given that multiple processes and representations are required to account for our mental skill with numbers, it would not be surprising to discover that there are multiple brain centres involved with number processing. Dehaene & Cohen (1995) have proposed a model of the anatomical representation of number processes that includes structures in occipital, temporal and parietal cortices of the right hemisphere, as well as structures in occipital, temporal, parietal and prefrontal cortices of the left hemisphere. This model makes clear that there is no one centre of numerical representation in the brain, and that elegant co-ordination of processes in multiple brain locations is needed to perform mental arithmetic.

What kinds of numerical representation are created and used by these various anatomical sites? Several possibilities suggest themselves. One is that visual representations of the numbers presented on a page may be created and stored by inferotemporal mechanisms. A second possibility is that these visual representations may be translated into a phonological representation of the problem elements, with this stored by the parietal–prefrontal circuit that we discussed in the context of studies of verbal working memory. A third possibility is that the visual and verbal representations of numbers need to be translated into magnitude representations that can be used for calculation purposes, which may be a function of parietal mechanisms in both hemispheres (Dehaene & Cohen 1995).

The operations involved in mental arithmetic – retrieving number facts, deciding what to carry, sequencing which operations to perform before others, using short-cut strategies that may help with certain problems, etc. – may involve a complex interplay among the neural systems housed in the above-mentioned areas. This seems likely given that the mental operations involve a combination of long-term memory retrieval, short-term storage, sequencing of operations, strategies, and so forth. That multiple mechanisms are involved is suggested by a behavioural study by Logie et al. (1994). Subjects had to keep a running total of a series of two-digit numbers while they engaged in various secondary tasks. The secondary task that caused the most interference on performance was one in which subjects had to produce a series of random letters while doing their arithmetic. Random generation has been shown to require extensive use of dorsolateral prefrontal mechanisms in humans and in other animals (Petrides et al. 1993b, Petrides 1995). Consequently, it is reasonable to suppose that some components of mental arithmetic involve these same mechanisms. In addition, Logie et al. (1994) also found that articulatory suppression also produced interference, although to a lesser extent. As argued above, articulatory suppression has an effect on disrupting verbal rehearsal, thus suggesting that this is another component process in mental arithmetic.

In light of the above, it is natural to predict that lesions in a number of brain sites should affect the ability to perform arithmetic calculations. Indeed, this is the case (Dehaene & Cohen 1995). Lesions in inferior parietal, subcortical, and frontal sites have all been implicated in deficits in arithmetic skill, a syndrome called "anarithmetia" (see e.g. Warrington 1982, Corbett et al. 1988, Lucchelli & De Renzi 1993). Further evidence that multiple regions involving storage and executive processes are involved in mental arithmetic comes from neuroimaging studies (Roland & Friberg 1985, Appolonio et al. 1994). In these studies, subjects had iteratively to subtract 3 from a starting number (e.g. 50, 47, 44, 41). Constrasting the activation from this task with either a rest control condition or a forward-counting control revealed several areas of activation: inferior parietal, prefrontal, premotor and motor cortices. These activations were largely bilateral in locus, but with somewhat higher activation in the left hemisphere. Note that this pattern of activation follows nicely from the activations we have previously identified with storage and executive components of working memory. The parietal and premotor areas are ones that have shown themselves to be prominent in verbal storage tasks, and the prefrontal activation could represent a combination of rehearsal processes and the scheduling and control processes required to conduct the arithmetic operations themselves. Mental arithmetic, in short, is a complex task that seems to recruit fully the storage and executive processes of working memory.

8.5 SUMMARY

As we have shown, current conceptions of working memory identify two general classes of component. One class is devoted to the temporary storage of information. This component is itself not singular in form: evidence leads to the view that different forms of information (verbal, spatial, visual and possibly others) are stored using different mechanisms. The evidence that leads to this view comes from a combination of studies of behaviour in normal individuals, behaviour in brain-injured patients, lesion and single-cell studies of animals performing working memory tasks, and neuroimaging studies of human performance. This evidence converges on a model of storage processes such as that illustrated in Figure 8.8, in which there are processes for creating representations, for transforming these into other codes, for storing information and for rehearsing information in various storage buffers.

The second class of working memory components is devoted to various processes that manipulate and transform information in the storage buffers. Again, this component is not unitary in nature. Rather, it seems best characterized as a set of processes capable of controlling various aspects of processing, such as temporally tagging information, sequencing operations, inhibiting some processes in favour of others, and so on. Again, our knowledge of the workings of executive processes comes from a combination of sources studying behaviour and brain mechanisms in humans and other animals. While our understanding of executive processes lags behind that of our understanding of storage mechanisms in working memory, the available evidence is beginning to reveal the complex architecture of executive processes and their representation in the brain.

No doubt, further understanding of working memory will elaborate on, and possibly change, our current view. Whatever the future development of theory about this fundamental set of psychological mechanisms, our understanding of working memory will continue to be guided by a combination of behavioural and brain evidence. Only by gathering converging evidence from several sources are we likely to unravel the complexities of this critical component in cognition.

ACKNOWLEDGEMENTS

Preparation of this chapter was supported in part by a grant from the Office of Naval Research and in part by a grant from the National Institute on Aging.

NOTE

1. It is not inevitable that lack of speech produces a working memory deficit, however. It has been shown that some patients who are anarthric (see e.g. Vallar & Cappa 1987) – that is, cannot produce speech – nonetheless have reasonably normal verbal working memories. Such patients may not have damage to their cortical circuits for producing speech (such as those described above) so much as damage to more peripheral structures necessary for speech production. Alternatively, they may represent evidence that internal speech is not the result of precisely the same mechanism that results in explicit speech.

REFERENCES

Appolonio, I., L. Rueckert, A. I. Partiot, I. Litvan, J. Sorenson, Le D. Bihan, J. Grafman 1994. functional magnetic resonance imaging (F-MRI) of calculation ability in normal volunteers. *Neurology* **44** (Suppl. 2), 262.

Awh, E., E. E. Smith, J. Jonides 1995. Human rehearsal processes and the frontal lobes: PET evidence. In *Structure and functions of the human prefrontal cortex*, J. Grafman (ed.), 97–118. New York: New York Academy of Science.

Awh, E., J. Jonides, E. E. Smith, E. H. Schumacher, R. Koeppe, S. Katz 1996. Dissociation of storage and rehearsal in verbal working memory: evidence from PET. *Psychological Science* **7**, 25–31.

Baddeley, A. D. 1986. *Working memory*. Oxford: Oxford University Press.

Baddeley, A. D. 1992. Working memory. *Science* **255**, 556–9.

Baddeley, A. D., & G. J. Hitch 1974. Working memory. In *Recent Advances in Learning and Motivation*, vol. VIII, G. Bower (ed.), 647–67. New York: Academic Press.

Baddeley, A. D., N. Thomson, M. Buchanan 1975. Word length and the structure of short-term memory. *Journal of Verbal Learning and Verbal Behaviour* **14**, 575–89.

Baddeley, A. D., V. J. Lewis, G. Vallar 1984. Exploring the articulatory loop. *Quarterly Journal of Experimental Psychology* **36**, 233–52.

Basso, A., H. Spinnler, G. Vallar, E. Zanobio 1982. Left hemisphere damage and selective impairment of auditory verbal short-term memory: a case study. *Neuropsychologia* **20**, 263–74.

Berg, E. A. 1948. A simple objective technique for measuring flexibility in thinking. *Journal of General Psychology* **39**, 15–22.

Brooks, L. R. 1968. Spatial and verbal components of the act of recall. *Canadian Journal of Psychology* **22**, 349–68.

Brown, J. 1958. Some tests of the decay theory of immediate memory. *Quarterly Journal of Experimental Psychology* **10**, 12–21.

Byrne, R. M. J. & P. N. Johnson-Laird 1989. Spatial reasoning. *Journal of Memory and Language* **28**, 564–75.

Chafee, M. & P. S. Goldman-Rakic 1994. Prefrontal cooling dissociates memory- and sensory-duided oculomotor delayed response functions. *Society for Neuroscience Abstracts* **20**, 808.

Cohen, J. D., S. D. Forman, T. S. Braver, B. J. Casey, D. Servan-Schreiber, D. C. Noll (1994). Activation of prefrontal cortex in a non-spatial working-memory task with functional MRI. *Human Brain Mapping*, I, 293–304.

Colombo, M., M. R. D'Amato, H. R. Rodman, C. G. Gross 1990. Auditory association cortex lesions impair auditory short-term memory in monkeys. *Science* **247**, 336–8.

Conrad, R. 1964. Acoustic confusions in immediate memory. *British Journal of Psychology* **55**, 75–84.

Conrad, R. 1970. Short-term memory processes in the deaf. *British Journal of Psychology* **61**, 179–95.

Corbett, A. J., E. A. McCusker, O. R. Davidson 1988. Acalculia following a dominant-hemisphere subcortical infarct. *Archives of Neurology* **43**, 964–6.

Dale, H. C. A. & M. Gregory 1966. Evidence of semantic encoding in short-term memory. *Psychonomic Science* **5**, 153–4.

Dehaene, S. 1992. Varieties of numerical abilities. *Cognition* **44**, 1–42.

Dehaene, S. & L. Cohen 1995. Towards an anatomical and functional model of number processing. *Mathematical Cognition* **1**, 83–120.

Funahashi, S., C. J. Bruce, P. S. Goldman-Rakic 1989. Mnemonic coding of visual space in the monkey's dorsolateral prefrontal cortex. *Journal of Neurophysiology* **61**, 331–49.

Funahashi, S., M. V. Chafee, P. S. Goldman-Rakic 1993. Prefrontal neuronal activity in rhesus monkeys performing a delayed anti-saccade task. *Nature* **365**, 753–6.

Fuster, J. M. 1995. *Memory in the cerebral cortex*. Cambridge, MA: MIT Press.

Fuster, J. M. & J. P. Jervey 1981. Inferotemporal neurons distinguish and retain behaviourally relevant features of visual stimuli. *Science* **212**, 952–5.

Garner, W. R., H. W. Hake, C. W. Ericsen 1956. Operationism and the concept of perception. *Psychological Review* **63**, 149–59.

Georgopoulos, A. P., J. T. Lurito, M. Petrides, A. B. Schwartz, J. T. Massey 1989. Mental rotation of the neuronal population vector. *Science* **243**, 234–6.

Gnadt, J. W. & R. A. Andersen 1988. Memory related motor planning activity in posterior parietal cortex of macaque. *Experimental Brain Research* **70**, 216–20.

Goel, V. & J. Grafman 1995. Are the frontal lobes implicated in "planning" functions? Interpreting data from the Tower of Hanoi. *Neuropsychologia* **33**, 623–42.

Goldman-Rakic, P. S. 1993. Working memory and the mind. *Scientific American* **267**, 110–17.

Goldman-Rakic, P. S. & M. Chafee 1994. Feedback processing in prefronto-parietal circuits during memory-guided saccades. *Society for Neuroscience Abstracts* **20**, 808.

Hanley, J. R., A. W. Young, N. A. Pearson 1991. Impairment of the visuospatial sketch pad. *Quarterly Journal of Experimental Psychology: Human Experimental Psychology* **43A**, 101–25.

Hinke, R. M., X. Hu, A. E. Stillman, S. Kim, H. Merkle, R. Salmi, K. Ugurbil 1993. Functional magnetic resonance imaging of Broca's area during internal speech. *Neuroreport* **4**, 675–8.

Hintzman, D. L. 1965. Classification and aural coding in STM. *Psychonomic Science* **3**, 161–2.

Hitch, G. J. 1978. The role of short-term working memory in mental arithmetic. *Cognitive Psychology* **10**, 302–23.

Jonides, J., E. E. Smith, R. A. Koeppe, E. Awh, S. Minoshima, M. A. Mintun 1993. Spatial working memory in humans as revealed by PET. *Nature* **363**, 623–5.

Kosslyn, S. M. 1980. *Image and mind*. Cambridge, MA: Harvard University Press.

Kosslyn, S. M. 1981. The medium and the message in mental imagery: a theory. *Psychological Review* **88**, 46–66.

Logie, R. H., G. M. Zucco, A. D. Baddeley 1990. Interference with visual short-term memory. *Acta Psychologica* **75**, 55.

Logie, R. H., K. J. Gilhooly, V. Wynn 1994. Counting on working memory in arithmetic problem solving. *Memory and Cognition* **22**, 395–410.

Longoni, A. M., J. T. E. Richardson, A. Aiello 1993. Articulatory rehearsal and phonological storage in working memory. *Memory and Cognition* **21**, 11–22.

Lucchelli, F. & E. De Renzi 1993. Primary dyscalculia after a medial frontal lesion of the left hemisphere. *Journal of Neurology, Neurosurgery, and Psychiatry* **56**, 304–7.

McCarthy, R. A. & E. K. Warrington 1990. *Cognitive neuropsychology: a clinical introduction*. San Diego, CA: Academic Press.

Miller, E. K. & R. Desimone 1991. A neural mechanism for working and recognition memory in inferior temporal cortex. *Science* **254**, 1377–9.

Miller, G. A. 1956. The magical number seven, plus or minus two: some limits on our capacity for processing information. *Psychological Review* **63**, 81–97.

Milner, B. 1964. Some effects of frontal lobectomy in man. In *The frontal granular cortex and Behaviour*, J. M. Warren & K. Akert (eds), 313–31. New York: McGraw-Hill.

Mishkin, M. & F. J. Manning 1978. Non-spatial memory after selective prefrontal lesions in monkeys. *Brain Research* **143**, 313–23.

Miyashita, Y. & H. Chang 1988. Neuronal correlate of pictorial short-term memory in primate temporal cortex. *Nature* **331**, 68–70.

Newell, A. & H. A. Simon 1972. *Human problem solving*. Englewood Cliffs, NJ: Prentice-Hall.

Owen, A. M., J. Doyon, M. Petrides, A. C. Evans, A. Gjedde 1994. The neural mediation of high level planning examined using positron emission tomography (PET). *Society for Neuroscience Abstracts* **20**, 353.

Passingham, R. E. 1975. Delayed matching after selective prefrontal lesions in monkeys (*Macaca mulatta*). *Brain Research* **92**, 89–102.

Paulesu, E., C. D. Frith, R. S. J. Frackowiak 1993. The neural correlates of the verbal component of working memory. *Nature* **362**, 342–44.

Peterson, L. R. & M. J. Peterson 1959. Short-term retention of individual verbal items. *Journal of Experimental Psychology* **58**, 193–8.

Petrides, M. 1995. Impairments on nonspatial self-ordered and externally ordered working memory tasks after lesions of the mid-dorsal part of the lateral frontal cortex in the monkey. *The Journal of Neuroscience* **15**, 359–75.

Petrides, M., B. Alivisatos, A. C. Evans, E. Meyer 1993a. Dissociation of human mid-dorsolateral from posterior dorsolateral frontal cortex in memory processing. *Proceedings of the National Academy of Science, USA* **90**, 873–7.

Petrides, M., B. Alivisatos, E. Meyer, A. C. Evans 1993b. Functional activation of the human frontal cortex during performance of verbal working memory tasks. *Proceedings of the National Academy of Science, USA* **90**, 878–82.

Posner, M. I. & M. E. Raichle 1994. *Images of mind*. New York: W. H. Freeman.

Rogers, R. D., S. C. Baker, A. M. Owen, C. D. Frith, R. J. Dolan, S. J. Frackowiak, T. W. Robbins 1994. Frontal and parietal activations in a test of planning: a PET study with the Tower of London. *Society for Neuroscience Abstracts* **20**, 353.

Roland, P. E. & L. Friberg 1985. Localization of cortical areas activated by thinking. *Journal of Neurophysiology* **53**, 1219–43.

Schumacher, E. H., E. Lauber, E. Awh, J. Jonides, E. E. Smith, R. A. Koeppe 1996. PET evidence for an amodal verbal working memory system. *Neuroimage* **3**, 79–88.

Shallice, T. 1982. Specific impairments of planning. *Philosophical Transactions of the Royal Society of London, Part B* **298**, 199–209.

Shallice, T. 1988. *From neuropsychology to mental structure*. Cambridge: Cambridge University Press.

Shulman, H. G. 1971. Similarity effects in short-term memory. *Psychological Bulletin* **75**, 399–415.

Smith, E. E. & J. Jonides 1994. Working memory in humans: neuropsychological evidence. In *The cognitive neurosciences*, M. Gazzaniga (ed.), 1009–20. Cambridge, MA: MIT Press.

Smith, E. E., J. Jonides, R. A. Koeppe, E. Awh, E. H. Schumacher, S. Minoshima 1995. Spatial vs. object working memory: PET investigations. *Journal of Cognitive Neuroscience* **7**, 337–56.

Smith, E. E., J. Jonides, R. A. Koeppe 1996. Dissociating verbal and spatial working memory using PET. *Cerebral Cortex* **6**, 11–20.

Sternberg, S. 1966. High speed scanning in human memory. *Science* **153**, 652–4.

Sternberg, S. 1975. Memory scanning: new findings and current controversies. *Quarterly Journal of Experimental Psychology* **27**, 1–32.

Swinney, D. A. & O. L. Taylor 1971. Short-term memory recognition search in aphasics. *Journal of Speech and Hearing Research* **14**, 578–88.

Ungerleider, L. G. & M. Mishkin 1982. Two cortical visual systems. In *Analysis of visual behaviour*, D. J. Ingle, M. A. Goodale, R. J. Mansfield (eds), 549–86. Cambridge, MA: MIT Press.

Vallar, G. & S. F. Cappa, 1987. Articulation and verbal short-term memory: evidence from anarthria. *Cognitive Neuropsychology* **4**, 55–78.

Warrington, E. K. 1982. The fractionation of arithmetical skills: a single case study. *Quarterly Journal of Experimental Psychology* **34A**, 31–51.

Wickens, D. D., D. G. Born, C. K. Allen 1963. Proactive inhibition and item similarity in short-term memory. *Journal of Verbal Learning and Verbal Behaviour* **2**, 440–5.

Wilson, F. A. W., S. P. O'Scalaidhe, P. S. Goldman-Rakic 1993. Dissociation of object and spatial processing domains in primate prefrontal cortex. *Science* **260**, 1955–8.

Zatorre, R. J. & S. Samson 1991. Role of the right temporal neocortex in retention of pitch in auditory short-term memory. *Brain* **114**, 2403–417.

CHAPTER 9

Language in the human brain

David Howard

Language is a uniquely human ability. Investigators of how language is represented in the human brain cannot, therefore, use animal models to aid their research (see Walker 1987). As a consequence, there is considerable uncertainty about the neuroanatomy of the regions involved. For instance, the classical, textbook view of organization of language postulates two areas – Wernicke's area in the left posterior superior temporal gyrus, and Broca's area at the foot of the left frontal lobe – and suggests that they are joined by a bundle of fibres called the arcuate fasciculus. However, because these structures only exist in humans, we cannot easily establish whether the arcuate fasciculus really joins these regions. Standard ways of showing where fibres run to and from involves injection of tracers into living brains followed by detailed anatomical work on the dead brain: a procedure which is impossible to carry out with human subjects.

The primary source of evidence on language in the brain has been from people, with previously normal language abilities, who have damage to the brain and suffer impairment of language – aphasia. In these so-called "experiments of nature", damage can result from stroke, head injury (including both road accidents, and blows from axes, bullets and a range of other implements), and other neurological disease. While some aphasic patients – typically those with very large brain lesions – have global impairment of all aspects of comprehension and production of spoken and written language, the more typical pattern of aphasia is for some aspects of language to be relatively well preserved while others are severely affected. Some very selective deficits can be observed. For instance, spoken-word recognition can be profoundly impaired, when the patient's hearing is normal, and all other language functions are intact ("pure word deafness"; e.g. Albert & Bear 1974). Patients can have selective difficulties with written word recognition ("pure alexia"; e.g. Dejerine 1891), or with spoken word production (e.g. Mohr et al. 1978). There are selective impairments of knowledge of word meanings (e.g. Hodges et al. 1994), of the syntactic aspects of speech production (e.g. Kolk et al. 1985), or of the ability to produce proper names (e.g. Semenza & Zettin 1988). Such selective deficits following localized damage to the brain suggest that there is specialization of parts of the brain for specific aspects of language.

While the study of language disorders following brain lesions has been the principal source of evidence on how language is organized in the brain, this has more recently been supplemented by other techniques. Evidence has come from the effects of electrical stimulation of the exposed cortex in conscious patients undergoing neurosurgery (e.g. Penfield & Roberts 1959), from recording activity from electrodes planted on the surface of the brain while subjects perform language tasks (e.g. Lesser et al. 1994) and from analysing changes in blood flow in the brain when language is being used (e.g. Petersen et al. 1988; see Ch. 6).

This chapter reviews how these sources of evidence have been used to build up our knowledge of how language is organized in the brain. First, I return to the roots in the latter half of the nineteenth century of the current textbook conception of language representation. This account is then examined critically in the light of modern knowledge from the effects of cerebral lesions and other more recent evidence obtained using other techniques.

9.1 CLASSICAL CONNECTIONISM

In 1861, Paul Broca examined a patient, Leborgne, who had been resident at the Bicêtre Hospital in Paris for more than 20 years. He had initially been admitted to the hospital because he was almost mute – his speech was limited to the repetitive utterance "tantan". He could, however, understand all that was said to him, and used varied gestures to communicate. When he was not understood, he could become quite angry, and then would also say "Sacré nom de Dieu". After 10 years, his conditioned worsened and he became paralysed in the right arm. The paresis spread to his right leg, and gradually his intellectual functioning was affected. His paralysed leg became infected, and general sepsis set in. Three days after Broca examined him, Leborgne died.

During his examination, Broca was careful to show that Leborgne's difficulty in speech was not due to any impairment of articulation. His control of his mouth and larynx was good, and what he did say was well articulated. In the post mortem, Broca found an extensive lesion of the posterior inferior regions of the left frontal lobe. The earliest part affected was, in Broca's opinion, one of the frontal gyri, most probably the third (Broca 1861). This lesion was responsible for Leborgne's long-standing language deficit, which Broca described as the loss of the faculty to articulate language.

Over the next few years, Broca observed a number of patients with the same disorder. In 1863 he reported ten subjects, all of whom had lesions of the third frontal gyrus, and in 1865, bolstered by his finding that patients with autopsy lesions of the same area in the right hemisphere were not aphasic, he proposed that the faculty to articulate language was localized to the left hemisphere.

In 1874, Carl Wernicke, a young neuropsychiatrist in Breslau, published a monograph in which he argued that there were different forms of aphasia which could be found after lesions to the left hemisphere. He described two patients who had prominent difficulties in understanding spoken language. Unlike patients with lesions in Broca's area, whose speech was, as in Leborgne's case, limited to recurrent utterances, or, in other patients, restricted to single words and short phrases uttered with effort, Wernicke's two patients had fluent, paraphasic speech – with frequent errors, with both sounds and words substituted – so that the result made little sense. When one of these two patients died, Wernicke was able to do an autopsy. The lesion found involved the posterior half of the left superior temporal gyrus as well as neighbouring regions. Influenced by his teacher Meynert, Wernicke argued that the centre for acoustic speech imagery should lie in association cortex adjacent to primary auditory cortex; he suggested, therefore, that spoken-word comprehension was a function of the posterior part of the superior temporal gyrus.

The process of language acquisition depended, in Wernicke's view, on the ability to repeat words. He therefore suggested that association fibres should link the centre for motor speech images in Broca's area to the superior temporal gyrus, and in dissection he found a tract which he believed connected the two areas.

A lesion of the centre for auditory word images lying in superior temporal cortex could account for his patients' difficulty in comprehension, but it left unexplained why they showed fluent, but paraphasic speech. Wernicke accounted for this by postulating that fluent speech production required the simultaneous activity of both centres for acoustic and motor word images where the acoustic centre monitored the imagery of the spoken sound.

This schema, with the two centres linked by a fibre tract subsequently identified as the arcuate fasciculus, predicted a third form of aphasia, in which both centres were intact but the linking pathway was damaged. In this condition – conduction aphasia – repetition should be impossible, but comprehension of speech should be intact. Speech production would not be monitored by the interaction of motor and acoustic speech centres, and so should be fluent and paraphasic like the patients with lesions in Wernicke's area. In his 1874 monograph Wernicke described two patients, who, he believed, had this disorder. Both had good comprehension and fluent, paraphasic speech; unfortunately (and surprisingly), repetition was not tested.

Wernicke therefore recognized two localized centres: one responsible for spoken-word recognition and one for spoken-word production. Word meanings, on the other hand, were not localized. The meaning of a word consisted of evocation of the visual, auditory, tactile and other sensory images widely distributed across the cortex and linked by association

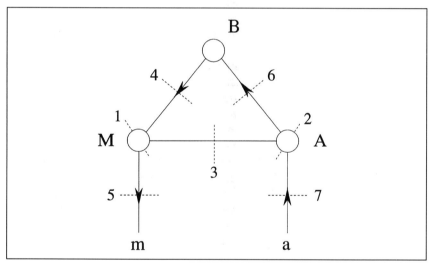

FIG. 9.1.   The Wernicke–Lichtheim model. A, the centre of acoustic word images located in Wernicke's area in the posterior part of the superior temporal gyrus; M, the centre for motor word images in Broca's area in the third frontal gyrus; B, represents word meanings which are distributed across cortex; a, input to A from subcortical regions; m, the output from M to the motor nuclei controlling speech. The seven basic forms of aphasia are indicated by dotted lines indicating the location of the lesion. (The directions of information flow (arrows) are as in the original schema. It should be noted that the M–A link should have a bidirectional arrow to account for the simultaneous evocation of both motor and sensory images in spontaneous speech.)

fibres. Fibres radiating from the motor and sensory word centres linked these non-linguistic representations of meaning to the language centres.

In 1885, Lichtheim, published a paper which systematized much of Wernicke's work and distinguished seven simple forms of aphasia; in 1886, Wernicke indicated his substantial support for the schema (Fig. 9.1). Lichtheim emphasized how this schema was a falsifiable theory which could explain seven forms of aphasia from damage to the two localized language centres and the tracts linking them (Table 9.1); he provided brief, but unsatisfyingly sketchy accounts of patients with all seven of his postulated syndromes. Other more complicated forms of aphasia could be acquired by multiple lesions. This model (and its variants) became a standard way of describing forms of aphasia in the latter part of the nineteenth century, and the early part of the twentieth.

Table 9.1
The seven basic forms of aphasia in the Wernicke–Lichtheim model.

Lesion in Fig. 9.1	Wernicke's name	Modern name	Symptoms
1	Cortical motor aphasia	Broca's aphasia	Comprehension is intact. Repetition and spontaneous speech are impaired and non-fluent
2	Cortical sensory aphasia	Wernicke's aphasia	Comprehension and repetition are impaired. spontaneous speech is fluent and paraphasic
3	Conduction aphasia	Conduction aphasia	Repetition is impaired. Spontaneous speech is fluent and paraphasic. Comprehension is intact
4	Transcortical motor aphasia	Transcortical motor aphasia	Repetition and comprehension are intact. Spontaneous speech is impaired and non-fluent
5	Subcortical motor aphasia	Aphemia	Comprehension is intact. Both spontaneous speech and repetition are very limited, but the word concept is intact. The patient can indicate the number of syllables in a word
6	Transcortical sensory aphasia	Transcortical sensory aphasia	Repetition is intact. Comprehension is impaired, and spontaneous speech is fluent and paraphasic
7	Subcortical sensory aphasia	Pure word deafness	Both repetition and comprehension are impaired, but spontaneous speech is normal. Auditory acuity is normal

A growing dissatisfaction with the schema developed in the first quarter of the twentieth century. This was for a number of different reasons. One of these was the realization that there were some kinds of aphasic disorder which could not be accommodated within the schema. For instance, in 1885 Grashey described a patient with anomic aphasia. His speech was lacking in nouns and specific verbs and adjectives, and he was unable to name objects. However, he had no difficulty in understanding the same words when they were spoken to him, and no difficulty in repetition. This indicated that both auditory word images and object concepts were intact. The only plausible explanation was that there was damage to the tract linking concepts to Broca's area, which, in the Wernicke–Lichtheim schema, results in transcortical motor aphasia. The difficulty was that his spontaneous speech was quite unlike that found in transcortical motor aphasia; these patients had the halting, sparse and effortful speech of Broca's aphasic. Grashey's patient, in contrast, had fluent, easily articulated speech lacking in substantive nouns and verbs.

A second kind of problem that increasingly emerged was that the model provided no obvious account of the characteristics of impaired functions; it could deal only with loss of ability to perform a task. For instance, it became increasingly clear that Broca's aphasics had not typically lost articulatory images of all words. In fact their speech was typically agrammatic: free-standing function words were omitted and inflections were omitted or reduced to the unmarked form. Nouns were, by comparison, relatively freely available. The Wernicke–Lichtheim model simply did not speak to such issues; it had no way of accounting for the qualitative features of the disorders. Similarly, as Head (1926) pointed out, it did not have any way of dealing with performance which varied from time to time or which depended on the context of the task (as in the famous example of the patient asked to repeat the word "no" who replied, after some struggle "no doctor, I can't say no"), or with the availability of "emotional" language, such as swearing, in otherwise severely affected patients.

There was also a growing disenchantment with the underpinnings of localizationism. Wernicke had been clear on his underlying assumption: "the basic elementary hypothesis which now can hardly be seriously challenged [is] that the central nerve endings are invested with the role of psychic elements" (Wernicke 1874: 143). Freud (1891) was worried by this: "Is it justified to immerse a nerve fibre, which over the whole of its course has been only a physiological structure subject to physiological modifications with its end in the psyche and furnish this end with an idea or memory?" Marie (1907: 249) was more scathing: "To claim to translate psychology into diagrams of an anatomical order when we are completely ignorant of the physiology and even of the fine anatomy of the brain, this we cannot allow".

Under the criticisms of Head (1926), Marie (1906a,b) and Goldstein (1948), amongst others, the localizationist position lost its dynamism, and was replaced by a variety of aphasiological traditions which did not accept the classical aphasic syndromes of the Wernicke–Lichtheim model (e.g. Weisenberg & McBride 1935, Luria 1947, Schuell et al. 1964).

9.2 NEOCLASSICAL CONNECTIONISM

In the early 1960s, Norman Geschwind revived the approaches of the Wernicke–Lichtheim schema. In his monumental paper on "Disconnexion syndromes" in 1965, he argued that a variety of disorders could best be understood as lesions to localized cortical centres and the fibre tracts connecting them. With Harold Goodglass he reintroduced the syndromes of the classical Wernicke–Lichtheim schema, – without, however, its diagram (Geschwind 1965b, Goodglass & Geschwind 1976), and they gathered a prolific and influential group of workers in Boston. The syndromes adopted by Geschwind and Goodglass were essentially the seven proposed by the Wernicke–Lichtheim schema, with two additions. Anomic aphasia was a difficulty in word retrieval accompanied by fluent, if circumlocutory and empty, spontaneous speech and good comprehension and repetition. For this Geschwind proposed a lesion localization in the angular gyrus, arguing that this was where fibres from different sensory domains converged onto the language system. The second addition was comparatively minor; in recognition of its frequency, global aphasia with severe impairment in all language modalities was recognized, with a large lesion encompassing both Broca's and Wernicke's areas. They also developed an aphasia test which could be used to identify the basic aphasic syndromes. The syndromes are identified primarily on the basis of their characteristics in spontaneous speech, although repetition and comprehension scores are also important. The localizations as proposed by Geschwind (1965b, 1979) are summarized in Figure 9.2.

This group (often called the Boston School), also brought a linguistic sophistication, absent from the Wernicke–Lichtheim schema, to the investigation of the patterns of performance of aphasic patients. For instance, in a series of studies it was demonstrated that, in addition to their non-fluent, laboured speech, many Broca's aphasics had particular difficulty in producing function words and appropriate inflections, and many of them also showed use of a very limited range of syntactic structures (see e.g. Goodglass 1976). Moreover, it became clear that this

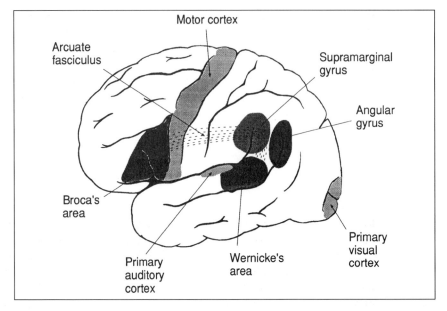

FIG. 9.2.   Areas critical for language in Geschwind's (1965b, 1979) adaptation of the Wernicke–Lichtheim model. Word repetition involves activation in turn of primary auditory cortex and Wernicke's area; transmission to Broca's area via the arcuate fasciculus, generation of a spoken response in Broca's area and articulatory production from motor cortex. Reading aloud involves visual processing in primary visual (striate) cortex, visual word recognition in the angular gyrus, activation of Wernicke's area, Broca's area and, finally, motor cortex. The angular gyrus region is involved in cross-modal association and is particularly involved in naming.

difficulty in the production of syntax was often accompanied by a difficulty in sentence comprehension, when this was assessed by methods which ensured that the syntactic and morphological structure of the sentence was understood (Caramazza & Zurif 1976). Studies of groups of aphasics thus were able to enumerate a number of domains in which such patients were, on average, impaired.

However, it also became clear that, within the group of non-fluent Broca's aphasics, the speech production problems could dissociate. Some patients showed dysfluency and laboured non-fluent speech without any agrammatic symptoms. Other patients could have difficulties in producing appropriate inflectional morphology, although they could produce otherwise normal syntactic structures. Yet other patients had selective difficulties with syntactic structures (Tissot et al. 1973, Howard 1985). Patients, then, could be diagnosed as showing the syndrome of Broca's aphasia when their language showed a subset of a set of possible features. No symptoms were necessary or sufficient for the diagnosis. This leaves the problem that, since the symptoms can dissociate, there can be no single functional disorder underlying all the surface symptoms (see Coltheart 1984, Marshall 1986). In this sense Broca's aphasia as employed by the Boston School is defined in a very different way to the Broca's aphasia in the Wernicke–Lichtheim schema. In the first case it is a fuzzy set of patients whose surface symptoms bear a family resemblance with no defining features. For Wernicke, in contrast, a patient with Broca's aphasia was one who had impairment to words' articulatory images – a definition in terms of an underlying functional deficit.

9.3 SCANNING OF LESIONS IN THE LIVING BRAIN

Until the 1970s the only reliable way of establishing the location of a cortical lesion was by post mortem. Very few were done, and in the majority of cases which did come to post mortem the language performance was poorly described. In the classical localizationist schema, correlations between linguistic impairments and brain lesions were established on the basis of quite limited information. In the 1970s, development of the computed tomography (CT) scan, in which X rays are used to build up a three-dimensional picture of brain density, made possible the investigation of the lesions corresponding to aphasic syndromes in much larger numbers of patients.

The initial studies using this technique were encouraging. There was a substantial relationship between CT scan lesion location and aphasic syndromes. Broca's aphasics tended to have lesions primarily involving the frontal lobes and Wernicke's aphasics had lesions which were much more likely to involve temporal structures; global aphasics typically had larger lesions involving both pre- and post-rolandic language areas (e.g. Naeser & Hayward 1978, Blunk et al. 1981). More detailed studies suggested that matters were not quite so simple. Mohr et al. (1978) demonstrated that lesions confined to Broca's area did not result in Broca's aphasia. Instead, these patients had a transient non-fluent aphasia with initial apraxia, which resolved rather rapidly and, unlike the Broca's aphasics, writing was much less severely disturbed than speech. The syndrome of Broca's aphasia was associated with much more extensive frontal lesions including Broca's area, which frequently also extended into the parietal lobes. Worse, when larger numbers of patients were considered, a rather substantial proportion of patients did not, in their CT scans, have the lesions that their language performance should predict. Basso et al. (1985) document such exceptions. They concluded that around 10–15% of patients have lesions discordant with their aphasic syndrome. However, as de Bleser (1988) points out, they do so by discounting many of the exceptions. For instance, Basso et al.

considered 77 patients with Wernicke's aphasia who would be expected to have posterior temporal lesions, which might also extend into the inferior parietal region. Within this group, Basso et al. recognized 14 exceptions. One patient had a lesion exclusively in the occipital lobe. Eight had extensive lesions involving both Broca's and Wernicke's area, which should have resulted in global aphasia. Five had exclusively frontal lesions (expected to result in Broca's aphasia). There were, however, further patients who did not show exclusively temporal lesions: 12 patients had exclusively deep lesions with no cortical involvement, and 13 had lesions which extended from the temporal lobe into the frontal lobe (although the frontal involvement was less severe than in the other ten patients with temporofrontal lesions). Only 38 of the 77 subjects had lesions in the expected area. The Basso et al. findings show both that there are patients with the same aphasic syndrome with lesions to very different and wholly non-overlapping regions, and that it is possible to have patients with very similar lesions as seen in a CT scan with very different language disorders.

One possible reaction to this would be to argue that many of the patients called "Wernicke's aphasics" in this study were not truly Wernicke's aphasics and had, instead, mixed aphasic disorders. De Bleser (1988) included in her study a group of Broca's aphasics (seven from a pool of 72 non-fluents) and a group of Wernicke's aphasics (six from a pool of 47 fluent patients) who were very clear examples of the syndromes. The CT scan lesions of these subjects together with a further 33 other aphasic subjects were partitioned, using cluster analysis, into groups with similar spatial lesions. The simplest clustering solution divided the patients into three groups: those with pre-rolandic (frontal) lesions which included Broca's area, those with post-rolandic (temporo-parietal lesions) which included Wernicke's area, and those with large frontotemporal lesions including both Broca's and Wernicke's area. Four of the Broca's aphasics fell, as should be predicted, into the pre-rolandic cluster, but three were in the post-rolandic group. Four of the Wernicke's were post-rolandic, but two had large lesions including both Broca's and Wernicke's areas. Thus, even with patients chosen to be paradigmatic examples of the classical syndromes, there is at best a very weak relationship between lesion localization and form of aphasia.

A larger scale study by Willmes & Poeck (1993) confirms this view. While 90% of patients with Wernicke's aphasia had lesions affecting Wernicke's area, only 48% of patients with lesions in Wernicke's area had Wernicke's aphasia. Similarly, 59% of patients with Broca's aphasia had lesions affecting Broca's area, but only 35% of patients with lesions involving Broca's area actually had Broca's aphasia. This confirms the view that destruction of Broca's and Wernicke's areas does not lead to the aphasia syndromes that one might predict. A study by Selnes et al. (1984) suggests that Wernicke's area plays no essential role in word recognition. Eight out of 22 patients whose word comprehension scores had recovered to within the normal range 6 months after the aphasia onset had lesions involving Wernicke's area. Chronic difficulties in comprehension not of single words but of sentences, are, however, associated with lesions involving Wernicke's area (Selnes et al. 1983, Naeser et al. 1987). The poor correspondence between localized lesions and deficits may be even worse than these studies report. This is because almost all of these studies are of lesion localization in patients who show aphasic language disorders. The incidence of patients who acquire lesions to supposedly critical language areas and yet never show any language impairment is currently unknown.

Clearly, such results are difficult to accommodate within any localizationist position. Yet, clearly some quite selective impairments of language processes can be observed in patients with perisylvian lesions in the dominant hemisphere. What responses can be made?

One possibility is that the wrong disorders are being localized. As pointed out above, the aphasic syndromes are clearly heterogeneous, and the patients categorized as belonging to one syndrome must have a set of different processing deficits. If it is the processing modules corresponding to the underlying deficits that are localized, one would not predict consistent localization of the syndromes which correspond to a number of different possible causes. Indeed, there is quite substantial evidence that the aphasic syndromes do not effectively pick up functional disorders. For instance, a patient with a difficulty in auditory word recognition (which is classically a function of Wernicke's area) should make errors in matching words to pictures where there are distractors which are phonologically related to the distractor (for instance choosing a picture of a cap to go with the spoken word "cat"). The prediction, then, is that these errors will be characteristic of Wernicke's aphasics and not Broca's aphasics. However, comparisons of Broca's and Wernicke's aphasics on such tasks show that very similar proportions of word-to-picture matching errors are phonological for the two groups of subjects (e.g. Gainotti et al. 1975, Baker et al. 1981). One possibility, then, is that the symptom of phonological errors in comprehension, for instance, is related to a specific lesion site, while neither the syndrome of Wernicke's nor of Broca's aphasia – both of which may include this symptom – can be localized.

A second way of dealing with these conflicting results is to argue that CT scans give the wrong neurological information. The CT scan shows (with reasonable accuracy) the extent of dead tissue in the brain. What it does not show is whether the remaining, apparently intact areas are working normally. Structurally intact areas may be unable to function because they are deprived of their normal inputs or are unable to produce their outputs, or they may be physiologically unable to support the changes in blood flow needed for normal processing. Thus there is poor correspondence between structural lesions as visualized by CT and the functional lesion. Furthermore, because little is reliably known of the interconnections of brain areas involved with language, it is impossible to establish from the CT lesion whether connections are intact.

Both these responses run into some serious difficulties, however, if one takes the strong view (espoused by the classical model of Wernicke–Lichtheim–Geschwind) that Broca's area and Wernicke's area are necessary for word production and word recognition, respectively. As we have seen, Mohr et al. (1979) showed that lesions confined to Broca's area result only in transitory difficulties in spoken word production, and Selnes et al. (1984) demonstrated that a substantial proportion of patients with lesions involving Wernicke's area show recovery of word comprehension to normal levels. One has to conclude either that these areas only play these roles in some – perhaps the majority – of people, or that other areas of the cortex are capable of taking over the functions normally carried out in these regions.

The third possibility, then, is that language functions, while localized in individual subjects, are not consistently localized in different individuals. While primary motor and sensory areas may be strongly constrained in their localization by the afferent and efferent fibres, higher cortical functions such as language may have a certain amount of freedom in the areas of cortex devoted to them (Caplan 1987).

Studies on electrical stimulation of exposed cortex with conscious subjects in the course of surgery for chronic epilepsy suggest that, while language functions are highly localized, there is great variability in where they are localized. In a series of papers, Ojemann has mapped the areas involved in picture naming using electrical stimulation (Ojemann & Whitaker 1978, Ojemann et al. 1989, Ojemann 1991, Ojemann 1994). In this paradigm, the patient names pictures while small electric currents are applied to individual locations on the exposed cortex; these result in interference with the activity of the underlying cortex. In effect, the stimulation results in a temporary, reversible, localized cortical lesion, which can be used to identify areas essential to picture naming. Ojemann draws a number of general conclusions. First, sites where there was interference with naming are typically quite small and localized; in more than 60% of subjects no area was larger than 2.25cm^2. Secondly, in 67% of patients there was more than one site essential for naming; typically there was one site in the frontal cortex and one in the temporoparietal cortex. Thirdly, these sites were separated with wide areas of cortex where no interference with naming was found from stimulation. Fourthly, there was great variation across individual subjects in the sites that interfere with naming. The results from the whole series of 117 subjects are summarized in Figure 9.3. The area with the highest proportion of subjects with affected naming (79%) was the foot of the pre-central gyrus (the area of motor cortex traditionally associated with control of articulation). Sites throughout the superior, middle and inferior frontal gyri resulted in interference with naming in a substantial proportion – but a minority – of subjects. Stimulation of Broca's area was not associated with high rates of naming interference. A variety of sites in the superior temporal gyrus, middle temporal gyrus and the inferior parietal lobe were associated with induced naming impairment, but no more than 36% of subjects are affected at any location. While there is a small tendency for more subjects to be affected by stimulation in the posterior part of the superior temporal gyrus (i.e. Wernicke's area), there is no strong support for Geschwind's suggestion that naming particularly involves the cortex of the angular gyrus (only 8% naming impairment).

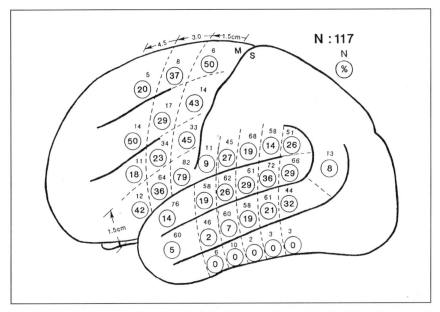

FIG. 9.3.   Areas in the brain where Ojemann (1991) found that electrical stimulation of the exposed cortex interferes with picture naming. Data are from a total of 117 subjects. In each region the circled figure shows the percentage of subjects who, when stimulated there, showed interference in naming. The small figure above shows the number of subjects stimulated in that location.

A fourth, related, possibility is that regions in the non-dominant (and usually undamaged) hemisphere have developed some linguistic abilities. The extent to which this happens may vary from person to person. After loss of language areas in the left hemisphere the clinical aphasia pattern will depend on both the remaining left hemisphere areas and the extent to which the right hemisphere language system is able to take over. There is some evidence that in aphasic subjects language functions may reflect right hemisphere processing; for instance, language can be abolished by right intracarotid sodium amytal injection, which temporarily disables the right hemisphere (Czopf 1972; for a review see Gainotti 1993). However, what is puzzling in this account is why a right hemisphere language system might develop (and variably so), as it apparently plays no essential role in normal people. Lesions of the non-dominant hemisphere do not result in classical aphasia, and injection of sodium amytal into the right internal carotid artery (temporarily anaesthetizing and disabling the right hemisphere) does not affect language in normal subjects.

A fifth reaction is that attempts to correlate language impairments to lesion sites are hopelessly premature. Mehler et al. (1984: 99) argue that:

> To attempt a mapping between the underlying neurophysiological structures and basic psychological processes, prior to determining what the key elements are that must enter into a correct description of each level, is haphazard at least. In the long run, premature assumptions about the mapping between neurophysiological substrate and specific psychological process could actually impede scientific progress ... If a mapping between psychological process and neurophysiological structures is possible, it will only come about after the key theoretical constructs are established for each level of explanation.

Under this view we simply know far too little about either the nature of the brain systems in humans related to language and the nature of the psychological processes to attempt any sensible mapping between the two.

Overall, it is clear that the lesion data are incompatible with a strong localizationist position, where specific language functions are located in localized areas of cortex in all individuals. Yet, the consistent observation of a great variety of selective disorders does appear to indicate that functions are localized in individual patients, but not, presumably in the same location in each individual.

9.4 CEREBRAL BLOOD FLOW ACTIVATION STUDIES

A second major advance for the understanding of the relationships between brain and language came in the 1980s with the development of positron emission tomography (PET)(see Ch. 6).

While the advent of CT scans failed to find persuasive support for the essential elements of the classical localizationist schema, investigations using PET in normal subjects have provided results which are slightly more easily reconciled. A number of studies have shown that auditory stimulation, relative to a resting control condition, results in large increases in regional cerebral blood flow (rCBF) bilaterally in superior temporal cortex with the peak activation lying, typically, in Heschl's gyrus (primary auditory cortex) (e.g. Petersen et al. 1988, Wise et al. 1991, Howard et al. 1992, Zatorre et al. 1992). Zatorre et al. (1992) compared the activation produced by speech sounds (nonsense syllables) to that from bursts of white noise, and found bilateral activation of superior temporal gyrus. This suggests that phonemes may be processed bilaterally, which is in accordance with the claim that pure word deafness, characterized by difficulties in phoneme perception in the absence of otherwise impaired language, is often associated with bilateral superior temporal lesions (Auerbach et al. 1982). Hearing real words, however, results in activation of posterior superior temporal gyrus (Wernicke's area as narrowly defined) only on the left. For instance, Howard et al. (1992) showed activation in this region when subjects repeated real words relative to a condition where they heard reversed words (equivalent in noise spectrum to the real words) and said the same word in response to each stimulus. Investigations of the effects of rate of presentation of spoken words confirm that Wernicke's area has a specialized functional role. Price et al. (1992) asked subjects to listen to spoken words presented at a variety of rates from 0 to 90 words per minute. rCBF increased linearly with rate of word presentation over anterior and middle superior temporal gyrus on the left, and in the whole of the superior temporal gyrus on the right. Left posterior superior temporal gyrus, in contrast, was strongly activated when words were presented (i.e. relative to rest), but rCBF in this region was insensitive to changes in the rate of auditory presentation.

Localization of semantic functions proved more controversial. Wernicke and Lichtheim had emphasized that semantic representations were widely distributed sensory features. Geschwind emphasized the importance of the left angular gyrus as a cross-modal association area probably involved in the mappings between semantics and Broca's and Wernicke's areas. More recent evidence on the localization of lesions in patients with conspicuous semantic disorders (e.g. "semantic dementia"), where other linguistic functions such as repetition and syntax are relatively intact, have typically shown atrophy confined to lateral temporal regions, often particularly pronounced in left temporal neocortex (Hodges et al. 1992). The earliest studies of semantic processing in PET by Petersen et al. (1988, 1989) compared rCBF in a task where subjects had to generate verbs as uses for nouns presented as auditory or visual stimuli (e.g. for CAR generate "drive, crash"), compared with repetition or reading aloud of the same stimuli. With both auditory and visual input this comparison yielded an area of increased rCBF in inferior prefrontal cortex. They confirm this finding by showing that there is also activation in this region when subjects have to silently monitor a list of visually presented nouns for the presence of animal names. Evidence in support of involvement of prefrontal cortex in semantic tasks comes from Kapur et al. (1994), who showed significant increases in rCBF in left lateral prefrontal cortex for categorizing visually presented nouns as living or non-living relative to a task where subjects had to judge if a noun contained the letter "A".

Other semantic tasks have not resulted in clear evidence for a role of lateral prefrontal cortex in semantic processing. Wise et al. (1991) used a variety of semantic tasks, including judging whether pairs of nouns described a category and a member (e.g. "fruit orange" or "furniture shirt"), whether a verb and a noun were related (e.g. "eat orange" or "knit glasses"), and generating a set of verbs as uses for a noun. All the tasks were performed silently. When compared with rest, none of these tasks resulted in significant prefrontal or frontal activation. The only area involved in all the semantic tasks was left posterior superior temporal gyrus (Wernicke's area), and Wise et al. speculate that this region is involved in semantic processing as well as spoken-word recognition. Verb generation was the only task which activated Broca's area on the left as well as left posterior middle frontal gyrus and the supplementary motor area. Wise et al. argue that, although it requires no overt output, this task involves covert generation of spoken words, and this is responsible for these regions of activation.

Other, relatively complex semantic tasks have been used in PET activation studies. Demonet et al. (1992) carried out a study in which subjects listened for particular combinations of properties in spoken stimuli. The authors compared a task where subjects had to monitor for sequences of phonemes (specifically whether /b/ preceded /d/ in a nonword), with a task where subjects had to decide if an adjective noun combination had a pleasant adjective and referred to an animal smaller than a chicken. The semantic task relative to the phoneme task resulted in significant increases in blood flow in three locations – posterior left inferior temporal gyrus, the left supramarginal and angular gyri and deep in left prefrontal cortex – which Demonet et al. suggest together make up a semantic network. Chertkow & Bub (1994) also report that, in a task where subjects had to judge whether animals had horns, tusks or antlers, activation was found in a posterior left temporal region. Visual imagery tasks, on the other hand, resulted in activation in a separate area inferiorly at the left occipitoparietal junction.

It is clear that these semantic tasks vary radically in the kinds of semantic operation performed on the words, and it is possible different aspects of these tasks are related to the frontal and temporal activations. All of these tasks, however, involve complex semantic judgments, and this is different from the activation of word meanings that happens automatically when subjects listen to or see words. Wise et al. (1996) measured rCBF while subjects listened to words; the word sets varied in imageability from very abstract to very concrete words. They found a linear increase in blood flow with decreasing word imageability in the middle part of the left superior temporal sulcus, and argue that this is either where abstract aspects of word semantics are represented or an area which is particularly involved in semantic access for abstract words. No areas showed linear increases in blood flow with increasing imageability, and they argue that this is because the sensory properties which characterize the meanings of more concrete words may be, as Wernicke (1874) and Allport (1985) suggested, represented as widely distributed networks across the cortex. They point out that a left temporal lobe locus for abstract word semantics fits reasonably well with the neuropsychological data; difficulties with abstract-word semantics are characteristic of fluent aphasic subjects whose lesions are predominantly posterior (Franklin 1989).

Tasks involving overt or covert generation of articulation suggest that a complex of areas in the cortex are involved in the generation of spoken words. Petersen et al. (1988) contrasted reading aloud and word repetition with passive input of spoken and written words, respectively. Activation associated with output was found in the supplementary motor area on the midline, in the mouth sensorimotor cortex and in the perisylvian cortex rather posterior to Broca's area bilaterally. Activation of Broca's area on the left has been found in tasks involving silent verb generation (Wise et al. 1991), in Demonet's task where subjects had to decide the order of phonemes in non-words (Demonet et al. 1992), in rhyme judgment tasks (Zatorre et al. 1992, Paulesu et al. 1993), and in silent picture naming (Chertkow et al. 1993a). Activation of the supplementary motor area, left Broca's area and bilateral middle frontal gyrus are also found in lexical decision tasks with written words (Price et al. 1994), suggesting that phonology may be covertly generated by subjects during this task. Lesions to the supplementary motor area are typically followed by a period of mutism with no impairment of comprehension (Masdeu et al. 1978), and lesions confined to Broca's area also cause a temporary, and selective articulatory disturbance (Mohr et al. 1978), suggesting that both these areas are involved in speech production (although neither is necessary for good recovery of speech). Activations of Broca's area seem less frequently found in tasks involving overt speech production, possibly because activation in this region is masked by the bilateral activation of the adjacent articulatory motor cortex. Although most tasks involving covert speech production appear to activate left frontal structures more than right, in a silent short-term memory task, Paulesu et al. (1993) found activation bilaterally of the whole perisylvian region. They suggest that the bilateral activation of Broca's area and supplementary motor area represent the processes of articulatory rehearsal, while activations bilaterally in the superior temporal gyrus and the supramarginal gyrus may represent non-articulatory phonological short-term storage (Baddeley 1987).

Attempts to locate the brain areas activated in visual word recognition have resulted in rather conflicting results. Dejerine (1891) and Geschwind (1965a,b) argued that word recognition was a function of the left angular gyrus. Pure alexia was caused by lesions which prevent visual information from reaching this area (see Greenblatt 1973, 1983). Petersen et al. (1990) compared passive viewing of false fonts (letters from an imaginary alphabet), consonant strings (e.g. JVFCR), pronounceable non-words (e.g. TWEAL) and real words with viewing of a fixation point. They found a region in left medial extrastriate cortex which appeared to be most activated by real words and pseudo-words, and suggest that visual word forms are processed in this area. Howard et al. (1992) compared reading words aloud with saying a single word to every presentation of a stimulus in false font. There was a significant increase with word reading in rCBF in the left posterior middle temporal gyrus posterior to Wernicke's area. Howard et al. argue that this location is more consistent with recent lesion evidence. Patients with "surface dyslexia" frequently regularize irregular words (e.g. reading "pint" to rhyme with "mint", or reading "yacht" as "yatched"), and appear to have damage to a lexicon for visual word recognition (Patterson et al. 1985). These patients typically have lesions involving the posterior temporal lobe (Vanier & Caplan 1985).

The contradiction between the results of Petersen et al. and Howard et al. may, in part, be explained by some apparently trivial methodological differences. Petersen et al. presented words every second, but each word was only seen for 150ms. Howard et al. presented words every 1500ms but presented them for 1s. Price et al. (1994) directly contrast the effects of exposure for 150 and 1000ms. At

150ms exposure, comparing real words and false fonts, they found a focus of activation close to that found in the left middle temporal cortex by Howard et al. There was also activation in the posterior superior temporal gyrus, right middle and superior temporal gyrus, bilateral perisylvian regions, left inferior frontal cortex and supplementary motor area, among others. At 1000ms exposure there were much smaller overall changes in rCBF. Significant increases were still found in the left middle temporal gyrus, as well as the right middle temporal gyrus, frontal cortex and elsewhere. Further experiments confirmed: (a) that tasks involving visually presented real words and pseudo-words consistently activated left posterior middle temporal gyrus, but this was only one among many regions involved; and (b) that changes in rCBF were consistently much greater with 150 than 1000ms exposure of words. With the short exposure durations there was no significant increase in the left medial extrastriate region for words or pseudo-words relative to false fonts. Medial extrastriate activation was only found in the comparison of silent reading of words relative to viewing of false fonts and the location was about 25mm posterior to the location found by Peterson et al.

Price et al. found very much more extensive activations than did Petersen et al. (1988) or Howard et al. (1992) from very similar tasks. This is principally a result of a number of improvements in PET technology over the last decade. New generation PET scanners are more sensitive, algorithms for fitting subjects' brains to a standard shape have improved and statistical processing programs have become more sensitive. In the early PET studies of language, typically only one or two foci of activation would appear in a comparison of two tasks; investigators would then argue that these loci were the cortical regions responsible for the psychological processes that differentiate the experimental and control task. The increases in sensitivity can be imagined as a flood (of noise) subsiding over a mountain range (of changes in rCBF); as more peaks and hills emerge, it becomes clear that there is no single localization of the differences between two tasks. It then becomes very much harder to draw strong conclusions from PET data alone about the functional roles played by specific cortical areas. In general, with newer and more sensitive techniques, word stimuli produce extensive automatic activation of large areas of the left hemisphere which appear to represent a whole language region (Fig. 9.4).

The consistent and large differences between 1000 and 150ms exposure of words are also important. Subjects can comfortably read aloud or perform lexical decisions with unmasked stimuli in either condition. Current accounts of word recognition suggest that visual stimulus processing should take 100–200ms, and there is no psychological

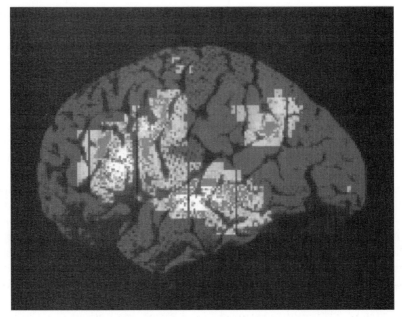

FIG. 9.4.   The language areas in the cortex activated when subjects decide whether a real word contains an ascender (a letter such as b, d, f or l) compared with making the same decision about a false font (non-existent but letter-like forms). Although the task involves only a decision about a physical attribute of the stimulus, large areas of the language cortex are automatically activated when the stimuli are words. There is: extensive activation in the posterior part of the temporal lobe, including Wernicke's area but extending into the middle and inferior temporal gyrus; extensive activation in the frontal lobe, including Broca's area and articulatory motor cortex, but extending to include surrounding areas and the middle frontal gyrus; and activation of a large region of the posterior parietooccipital junction. From Price et al. (1996).

evidence to suggest that different processes would be involved in the two conditions. Yet the difference in exposure modulates rCBF to a marked degree. Price et al. speculate that with words presented for 1000 ms, where the word remains in vision after visual processing of it is complete, changes in rCBF may be reduced because areas are actively prevented from operating. Thus, on this hypothesis, on each stimulus presentation some regions have increases in blood flow while they are engaged in processing, followed by active decreases. PET, which can only measure rCBF averaged over a period of around 30 s, would not be able to follow such rapid changes. Investigations using functional magnetic resonance imaging (fMRI), which can examine rCBF over time windows as short as 100–200 ms, may be able to resolve such issues in the future.

All these PET studies depend on comparing rCBF in two conditions. Clearly, the conclusions that can be drawn will depend on both the activation and the baseline tasks. Two complications arise: first it is impossible to distinguish increases in rCBF in one condition from decreases in another. It is clear that tasks can cause substantial and significant decreases in blood flow: for instance, in the Howard et al. (1992) study, both word repetition and word reading resulted in significant decreases in rCBF over large areas in the right hemisphere. Recording rCBF while subjects are at rest appears initially attractive as a baseline condition; however, even in this state subjects are thinking, and carrying out a variety of cortical activities which will presumably result in a particular pattern of rCBF for each subject. Secondly, it is often assumed when making subtractions that a subject only performs the cognitive functions necessary for the task. For instance, Petersen et al. (1988) compared passive viewing of words with viewing of a fixation cross and assumed that the difference between the tasks lay only in passive sensory processing, and the involvement of visual word recognition systems. However, it is impossible to see a real, known word without understanding it, so some semantic processes are almost certainly involved, and it is also likely that subjects internally compute a phonological representation of the word (Price et al. 1996). Certainly one cannot assume, without good evidence, that linguistic materials do not get processed automatically at a number of levels, irrespective of the surface requirements of the task in which the subject is engaged.

PET studies of language also vary in how "natural" and well practised the tasks involved are. Listening to and repeating words are obviously part of normal people's standard linguistic repertoire, whereas generating verbs to go with a noun or judging whether an animal has tusks, antlers or horns are not part of day-to-day experience. Some data suggest that, with practice at these relatively novel tasks, the pattern of rCBF alters (Raichle et al. 1991), raising the question of whether the relevant comparisons should involve naive or well-practised subjects. Another potential problem is that simply preparing to perform a task also results in rCBF changes. Chertkow et al. (1993b) reported changes in rCBF in subjects who were scanned while performing the antlers/ tusks/horns task relative to two baseline conditions: one was a rest state, and in the other the subjects were given instructions for the semantic task and were prepared to do it, but no stimuli were actually presented during the scan. The significant changes in rCBF were radically different depending on which of these two tasks was used as the baseline for comparison with the semantic task.

Despite these methodological complexities, the evidence from PET provides some support for at least parts of the Wernicke–Lichtheim–Geschwind model. Increases in rCBF in spoken word recognition are consistently found in left superior temporal gyrus, and particularly

Wernicke's area. Broca's area and the supplementary motor area seem to be activated by both overt and internal generation of speech representations. Semantic processing appears to involve regions in either the left lateral frontal cortex or the left temporal lobes, or both. Visual word recognition probably involves either posterior parts of the left temporal lobe or left medial extrastriate cortex.

Why should PET studies provide relatively good support for a localizationist position when the lesion studies do not? There are two important differences between the techniques. First, PET will show the areas which are active in a task, irrespective of whether they play an essential role, and will include areas which are automatically activated. Lesions, on the other hand, will result in deficits only where the affected area is essential for the task, and, if the unaffected parts of the cortex can take over the function, no long-term effects will be found. Secondly, studies of groups of subjects in PET may result in significant changes in a specific area when only some of the subjects are actually processing in the area. If, for instance, some 50% of subjects recognize spoken words in Wernicke's area (a plausible guess given both the Willmes & Poeck lesion data, and the Ojemann stimulation studies), and show increased rCBF there in a task, while the other 50% show no change, over the whole group there will probably be a significant increase. The possibility that there is inconsistent localization of language functions between subjects would account for the relatively small changes in rCBF found in PET studies of language functions. While studies of motor and sensory processes produce changes in rCBF across a group of subjects of up to 30% in specific locations, language studies typically find significant changes of only 5–10%. This is exactly the pattern which one would predict if sensory and motor processes show very consistent localization across subjects, while there is a great deal of variability in localization of language functions.[1]

9.5 CONCLUSION

The Wernicke–Lichtheim–Geschwind model of cortical localization of language functions in its strong version postulates that specific areas of left cerebral cortex are involved in identifiable language functions, such as word recognition and production, and that these areas are the same in all individuals. As we have seen, the lesion data are simply incompatible with this strong view, although both the lesion and the PET data seem to indicate that, despite variability between subjects when specific functions are carried out, there is a statistical tendency for particular regions to be involved in a function for a substantial proportion of subjects.

Recent work on the motor and sensory cortex in primates indicates that, while functions within these regions are localized, the exact localization varies from individual to individual, and furthermore that the areas devoted to specific parts of the body are in a process of continual dynamic reorganization in response to learning and stimulation (see Jenkins & Merzenich 1992). For instance, Nudo et al. (1992) showed that individual forelimb movements are localized to particular regions in squirrel monkey motor cortex, and the localization of the movements are organized in a mosaic-like way which varies from monkey to monkey. Sensory stimulation can enlarge the areas devoted to that sensation; for instance, in rats, nursing results in a three-fold increase in the sensory cortex devoted to the nipple regions (Xerri et al. 1994). In squirrel monkeys, training on auditory discrimination of tones results in an increase in the cortical areas within primary auditory cortex devoted to the trained tones (Recanzone et al. 1993). Stimulation of parts of the fingers in the owl monkey results in increases in the sensory cortex devoted to the stimulated areas (Jenkins et al. 1990). After lesions, cortex can reorganize sensory representations, so that the affected function is re-represented in the remaining cortex. For instance, in the owl monkey, if the sensory cortex devoted to one digit is lesioned, 3 months later areas specialized for sensation from all of the digits are found in the remaining cortex, although the areas devoted to individual digits can be completely changed (Jenkins & Merzenich 1987).

One may, of course, question the extent to which these results concerning the organization of function within motor and sensory cortex can be extrapolated to human language cortex. However, a view of the language cortex in which specific localized areas are devoted to a function, interspersed with cortex which, presumably, has other unknown functions, also emerges from the stimulation studies of Ojemann. It is at least plausible that the whole of the peri-insular region in the temporal, parietal and frontal lobes is potentially involved in language, but that within this region there is a mosaic of relatively localized modules which subserve different functions (see Caplan 1987). There is probably also continual dynamic reorganization of function within these areas throughout life.

As Mohr (1976) notes, the Wernicke–Lichtheim–Geschwind model has shown a remarkable longevity, not because it deals adequately with the available evidence, but more because contrary evidence is simply ignored. From this review it is clear that this model can no longer be sustained. We are still far from understanding the principles that govern and constrain how language is represented in the brain; adherence to a strict, classical, localizationist doctrine will only hinder this search.

ACKNOWLEDGEMENTS

I am grateful to David Caplan, Karalyn Patterson, Cathy Price, Mick Rugg and Richard Wise for their helpful comments on this chapter. This work was supported in part by the Medical Research Council.

NOTE

1. This difference could, of course, be for other reasons. For instance, motor and sensory processes might be more demanding of processing, with more synaptic activity, than language functions.

REFERENCES

Albert, M. L. & D. Bear 1974. Time to understand: a case study of word deafness with reference to the role of time in auditory comprehension. *Brain* **97**, 383–94.

Allport, D. A. 1985. Distributed memory, modular subsystems and dysphasia. In *Current perspectives in dysphasia*, S. K. Newman & R. Epstein (eds). Edinburgh: Churchill Livingstone.

Auerbach, S. H., A. Allard, M. A. Naeser, M. P. Alexander, M. L. Albert 1982. Pure word deafness: analysis of a case with bilateral lesions and a defect at the prephonemic level. *Brain* **105**, 271–300.

Baddeley, A. D. 1987. *Working memory*. Oxford: Oxford University Press.

Baker, E., S. E. Blumstein, H. Goodglass 1981. Interaction between phonological and semantic factors in auditory comprehension. *Neuropsychologia* **19**, 1–15.

Basso, A., A. R. Lecours, S. Moraschini, M. Vanier 1985. Anatomoclinical correlations of the aphasias as defined through computerised tomography: exceptions. *Brain and Language* **26**, 201–29.

Blunk, R., R. De Bleser, K. Willmes, H. Zeumer 1981. A refined method to relate morphological and functional aspects of aphasia. *European Neurology* **20**, 69–79.

Broca, P. 1861. Remarques sur le siège de la faculté de langage suivies d'une observation d'aphemie. *Bulletin de la Société d'Anatomie* **6**, 330–57.

Broca, P. 1863. Localisation des fonctions cérébrales: siège de langage articulé. *Bulletin de la Société d'Anthropologie de Paris* **4**, 200–8.

Broca, P. 1865. Remarques sur le siège de la faculté du langage articulé. *Bulletin de la Société d'Anthropologie de Paris* **6**, 330–57. [Edited version reprinted in H. Hécaen and J. Dubois (eds) 1969. *La naissance de la neuropsychologie du langage 1825–65*. Paris: Flammarion.]

Caplan, D. 1987. *Neurolinguistics and linguistic aphasiology: an introduction*. Cambridge: Cambridge University Press.

Caramazza, A. & E. B. Zurif 1976. Dissociation of algorithmic and heuristic processes in language comprehension: evidence from aphasia. *Brain and Language* **3**, 572–82.

Chertkow, H. & D. Bub 1994. Functional activation and cognition: the [15]O PET subtraction method. In *Localization and neuroimaging in neuropsychology*, A. Kertesz (ed.), 151–84. New York: Academic Press.

Chertkow, H., D. Bub, A. Evans, E. Meyer, S. Marrett 1993a. Neural correlates of picture processing studied with positron emission tomography. *Brain and Language* **44**, 460.

Chertkow, H., D. Bub, G. Waters, A. Evans, V. Whitehead, C. Hosein 1993b. Separate effects of instructions and stimuli on cerebral blood flow: a ^{15}O positron emission tomography study. *Neurology* **43**, A189.

Coltheart, M. 1984. Editorial. *Cognitive Neuropsychology* **1**, 1–8.

Czopf, J. 1972. Ueber die rolle der nicht dominanten Hemisphäre in der Restitution der Sprache der Aphasischen. *Archiv für Psychiatrie und Nervenkrankheiten* **216**, 162–71.

de Bleser, R. 1988. Localisation of aphasia: science or fiction? In *Perspectives on cognitive neuropsychology*, G. Denes, C. Semenza, P. Bisiacchi (eds). Hove, UK: Lawrence Erlbaum Associates Ltd.

Dejerine, J. 1891 Sur un cas de cécité verbale avec agraphie, suivi d'autopsie. *Mémoires de la Société de Biologie* **3**, 197–201.

Demonet, J.-F., F. Chollet, S. Ramsay, D. Cardebat, J.-L. Nespoulous, R. J. S. Wise et al. 1992. The anatomy of phonological and semantic processing in normal subjects. *Brain* **115**, 1753–68.

Franklin, S. 1989. Dissociations in auditory word comprehension: evidence from nine "fluent" aphasic patients. *Aphasiology* **3**, 189–207.

Freud, S. 1891. Zur Auffassung der Aphasien. Vienna: Deuticke. [In E. Stengel (trans.) 1953. *On aphasia*. New York: International Universities Press.]

Gainotti, G. 1993. The riddle of the right hemisphere's contribution to the recovery of language. *Eurpoean Journal of Disorders of Communication* **28**, 227–46.

Gainotti, G., C. Caltagirone, A. Ibba 1975. Semantic and phonemic aspects of auditory language comprehension in aphasia. *Linguistics* **154/155**, 15–29.

Geschwind, N. 1965a. Disconnexion syndromes in animals and man. *Brain* **88**, 237–94, 585–644.

Geschwind, N. 1965b. The organization of language and the brain. *Science* **170**, 940–44.

Geschwind N. 1979. Specializations of the human brain. In *The brain*. San Francisco, CA: W. H. Freeman.

Goldstein, K. 1948. *Language and language disturbances*. New York: Grune & Stratton.

Goodglass, H. 1976. Agrammatism. In *Studies in neurolinguistics*, vol. 1, H. Whitaker & H. A. Whitaker (eds). New York: Academic Press.

Goodglass, H. & N. Geschwind, N. 1976. Language disorders (aphasia). In *Handbook of perception*, vol. 7, E. C. Carterette & M. P. Friedman (eds), 389–428. New York: Academic Press.

Grashey, M. 1885. Über Aphasie und ihre Beziehung zur Wahrnehmung. *Archiv für Psychiatrie und Nervenkrankheiten* **16**, 654–88. [In R. De Bleser (trans.) 1988. On Aphasia and its relations to perception. *Cognitive Neuropsychology* **6**, 515–46.]

Greenblatt, S. H. 1973. Alexia without agraphia or hemianopsia. *Brain* **96**, 307–16.

Greenblatt, S. H. 1983. Localization of lesions in alexia. In *Localization in neuropsychology*, A. Kertesz (ed.). New York: Academic Press.

Head, H. 1926. *Aphasia and kindred disorders of speech*. Cambridge: Cambridge University Press.

Hodges, J. R., K. E. Patterson, S. M. Oxbury & E. Funnell 1992. Semantic dementia: progressive fluent aphasia with temporal lobe atrophy. *Brain* **115**, 1783–806.

Hodges, J. R., K. E. Patterson, L. K. Tyler 1994. Loss of semantic memory: implications for the modularity of mind. *Cognitive Neuropsycholgy* **11**, 505–42.

Howard, D. 1985 Agrammatism. In *Current perspectives in dysphasia*, S. K. Newman & R. Epstein (eds). Edinburgh: Churchill Livingstone.

Howard, D., K. E. Patterson, R. J. S. Wise, W. D. Brown, K. Friston, C. Weiller, R. S. J. Frackowiak 1992. The cortical localization of the lexicons; positron emission tomography evidence. *Brain* **115**, 1769–82.

Jenkins, W. M. & M. M. Merzenich 1987. Reorganization of neocortical representations after brain injury: a neurophysiological model of the bases of recovery from stroke. *Progress in Brain Research* **71**, 249–66.

Jenkins, W. M. & M. M. Merzenich 1992. Cortical representational plasticity: some implications for the bases of recovery from brain damage. In *Neuropsychological rehabilitation*, N. von Steinbuechel, D. Y. von Cramon, E. Poeppel (eds), 20–35. Berlin: Springer-Verlag.

Jenkins, W. M., M. M. Merzenich, M. T. Ochs, T. Allard, E. Guic-Robles 1990. Functional reorganization of primary somatosensory cortex in adult owl monkeys after behaviourally-controlled tactile stimulation. *Journal of Neurophysiology* **63**, 82–104.

Kapur, S., R. Rose, P. F. Liddle, R. B. Zipursky, G. M. Brown, D. Stuss, D., S. Houle et al. 1994. The role of the left prefrontal cortex in verbal processing: semantic processing or willed action? *Neuroreport* **5**, 2193–6.

Kolk, H. H. J., M. J. F. van Grunsven, A. Keyser 1985. On parallelism between production and comprehension in agrammatism. In *Agrammatism*, M.-L. Kean (ed.). New York: Academic Press.

Lesser, R. P. S. Arroyo, J. R. Hart, B. Gordon 1994. Use of subdural electrodes for the study of language functions. In *Localization and neuroimaging in neuropsychology*, A. Kertesz (ed.), 57–72. New York: Academic Press.

Lichtheim, L. 1885. Ueber Aphasie. *Deutsches Archiv für klinisher Medizin* **36**, 204–68. [Translated as: On aphasia 1885. *Brain* **7**, 433–85.]

Luria, A. R. 1947. *Traumatic aphasia*, D. Bowden (trans. 1970). The Hague: Mouton.

Marie, P. 1906a. La troisième circonvolution ne joue aucun rôle spécial dans la fonction du langage. *Semaine Médicale* **26**, 241–7.

Marie, P. 1906b. Revision de la question de l'aphasie: la troisième circonvolution frontale gauche ne joue aucun rôle spécial dans la fonction du langage. *Semaine Médicale* **26**, 241–7.

Marie, P. 1907. Sur la fonction de langage. Rectifications à propos l'article de M. Grasset. Revue de Philosophie. In *Reader in the history of aphasia*, P. Eling (trans., ed.), 242–50. Amsterdam: John Benjamins.

Marshall, J. C. 1986. The description and interpretation of aphasic language disorder. *Neuropsychologia* **24**, 5–24.

Masdeu, J. C., W. C. Schoene, H. Funkenstein 1978. Aphasia following infarction of the left supplementary motor area: a clinicopathological study. *Neurology* **28**, 1220–3.

Mehler, J., J. Morton, P. W. Jusczyk 1984. On reducing language to biology. *Cognitive Neuropsychology* **1**, 83–116.

Mohr, J. P. 1976. Broca's area and Broca's aphasia. In *Studies in neurolinguistics*, vol. 1, H. Whitaker & H. A. Whitaker (eds), 201–35. New York: Academic Press.

Mohr, J. P., M. S. Pessin, S. Finkelstein, H. H. Funkenstein, G. W. Duncan, K. R. Davis 1978. Broca's aphasia: pathologic and clinical aspects. *Neurology* **28**, 311–24.

Naeser, M. A. & R. W. Hayward 1978. Lesion localization in aphasia with cranial computed tomography and the Boston Diagnostic Aphasia Examination. *Neurology* **28**, 545–51.

Naeser, M. A., N. Helm-Estabrooks, G. Haas, S. Auerbach, M. Srinivasan 1987. Relationship between lesion extent in "Wernicke"s area" on CT scan and predicting recovery of comprehension in Wernicke's aphasia. *Archives of Neurology* **44**, 73–82.

Nudo, R. J., W. M. Jenkins, M. M. Merzenich, T. Prejean, R. Grenda 1992. Neurophysiological correlates of hand preference in primary motor cortex of adult squirrel monkeys. *Journal of Neuroscience* **12**, 2918–47.

Ojemann, G. A. 1991. Cortical organization of language. *Journal of Neuroscience* **11**, 2281–7.

Ojemann, G. A. 1994. Cortical stimulation and recording in language. In *Localization and neuroimaging in neuropsychology*, A. Kertesz (ed.), 35–55. New York: Academic Press.

Ojemann, G. A., J. Ojemann, E. Lettich, M. Berger 1989. Cortical language localization in left, dominant hemisphere. *Journal of Neurosurgery* **71**, 316–26.

Ojemann, G. A. & H. A. Whitaker 1978. Language localization and variability. *Brain and Language* **6**, 239–60.

Patterson, K. E., J. C. Marshal, M. Coltheart (eds) 1985. *Surface dyslexia: neuropsychological and cognitive studies of phonological reading*. London: Lawrence Erlbaum.

Paulesu, E., C. D. Frith, K. Friston 1993. The neural correlates of the verbal component of working memory. *Nature* **362**, 342–5.

Penfield, W. & L. Roberts 1959. *Speech and brain mechanisms*. Princeton, NJ: Princeton University Press.

Petersen, S. E., P. T. Fox, M. I. Posner, M. Mintun, M. E. Raichle 1988. Positron emission tomographic studies of the cortical anatomy of single word processing. *Nature* **331**, 585–9.

Petersen, S. E., P. T. Fox, M. I. Posner, M. Mintun, M. E. Raichle 1989. Positron emission tomographic studies of the processing of single words. *Journal of Cognitive Neuroscience* **1**, 153–70.

Petersen, S. E., P. T. Fox, A. Z. Snyder, M. E. Raichle 1990. Activation of extrastriate and frontal cortical areas by visual words and word-like stimuli. *Science* **249**, 1041–4.

Price, C. J., R. J. S. Wise, S. Ramsay, K. Friston, D. Howard, K. E. Patterson, R. S. J. Frackowiak 1992. Regional response differences within the human auditory cortex when listening to words. *Neuroscience Letters* **146**, 179–82.

Price, C. J., R. J. S. Wise, J. D. G. Watson, K. E. Patterson, D. Howard, R. S. J. Frackowiak 1994. Brain activity during reading – the effects of exposure duration and task. *Brain* **117**, 1255–69.

Price, C. J., R. J. S. Wise, R. S. J. Frackowiak 1996. Obligatory word processing: a direct demonstration. *Cerebral Cortex*, **6**, 62–70.

Raichle, M. E., J. Fiez, T. O. Videen, P. T. Fox, J. V. Pardo, S. E. Petersen 1991. Practice related changes in human functional brain anatomy. *Society for Neuroscience Abstracts* **17**, 21.

Recanzone, G. H., C. E. Schreiner, M. M. Merzenich 1993. Plasticity in the frequency representation of primary auditory cortex following discrimination training in adult owl monkeys. *Journal of Neuroscience* **13**, 87–103.

Schuell, H. M., J. J. Jenkins, E. Jimenez-Pabon 1964. *Aphasia in adults: diagnosis, prognosis and treatment*. New York: Harper & Row.

Selnes, O.A., D. S. Knopman, N. Niccum, A. B. Rubens 1983. CT-scan correlates of auditory comprehension deficits in aphasia: a prospective recovery study. *Annals of Neurology* **13**, 558–66.

Selnes, O.A., N. Niccum, D. S. Knopman, A. B. Rubens 1984. Recovery of single word comprehension: CT-scan correlates. *Brain and Language* **21**, 72–84.

Semenza, C. & M. Zettin 1988. Generating proper names: a case of selective inability. *Cognitive Neuropsychology* **5**, 711–21.

Tissot, R., G. Mounin, F. Lhermitte 1973. *L'agrammatisme: étude neuro-linguistique*. Brussels: Dessart.

Vanier, M. & Caplan, D. 1985 CT scan correlates of surface dyslexia. In *Surface dyslexia: neuropsychological and cognitive studies of phonological reading*, K. E. Patterson, J. C. Marshall, M. Coltheart (eds). London: Lawrence Erlbaum.

Walker, S. F. 1987. The evolution and dissolution of language. In *Progress in the psychology of language*, vol. 3, A. W. Ellis (ed.), 5–48. London: Lawrence Erlbaum

Weisenburg, T. H. & K. E. McBride 1935. *Aphasia: a clinical and psychological study*. New York: The Commonwealth Fund.

Wernicke, C. 1874. Der aphasischer Symptomkomplex: eine psychologische Studie auf anatomischer Basis. Breslau: Cohn & Weigert. [English translation: G. H. Eggert, 1977. In *Wernicke's works on aphasia: a sourcebook and review*, 91–145. The Hague: Mouton.]

Wernicke, C. 1885/86. Einige neure arbeiten über Aphasie. *Forschritte der Medizin* **3**, 824–30, **4**, 371–7, 463–9. [English translation as preceding reference.]

Willmes, K. & K. Poeck 1993. To what extent can aphasic syndromes be localized? *Brain* **116**, 1527–40.

Wise, R. J. S., F. Chollet, U. Hadar, K. Friston, E. Hoffner, R. S. J. Frackowiak 1991. Distribution of cortical neural networks involved in word comprehension and word retrieval. *Brain* **114**, 1803–17.

Wise, R. J. S., D. Howard, A. P. Holmes, K. J. Friston 1996. A physiological correlate of the meaning of words. *Neuroimage* **3**, 8467.

Xerri, C., J. M. Stern, M. M. Merzenich 1994. Alterations of the cortical representation of the rat ventrum induced by nursing behaviour. *Journal of Neuroscience* **14**, 1710–21.

Zatorre, R. J., A. C. Evans, E. Meyer, A. Gjedde 1992. Lateralization of phonetic and pitch discrimination in speech processing. *Science* **256**, 846–9.

CHAPTER 10

Unconscious visual processing in neuropsychological syndromes: a survey of the literature and evaluation of models of consciousness

Stefan Köhler & Morris Moscovitch

10.1 INTRODUCTION

After being rejected and abandoned by experimental psychology, consciousness has once again become a legitimate topic of investigation. Consciousness was central to the rise of scientific investigation of mental phenomena and played an important role in the work of such diverse theorists as Wundt, Freud and James. Critiques of introspectionism and psychoanalytic theory that relied on consciousness as a central construct led to a militant behaviourism in which all mental concepts were forsworn. The study of consciousness in experimental psychology, however, never lost all its adherents, and occasionally, as in the "new look" of the 1950s, it even captured a large following. Moreover, even when experimental psychologists denied the relevance of consciousness in their theoretical and empirical work, their choices of topics for study and their tools were, nonetheless, influenced by those aspects of mental life of which they were conscious through introspection.

It was not until the 1980s that consciousness was admitted once again into mainstream experimental psychology. Although the groundwork was laid by the cognitive revolution that began in the 1960s, the real breakthrough in the 1980s came with neuropsychological studies of individual cases. The studies of patients with striking neuropsychological syndromes demanded consciousness as an explanation both of the deficits that were observed and of normal behaviour. Among these cases were patients with cortical blindness who could respond to visual stimuli although they lacked the (conscious) experience of sight, and patients who, despite being densely amnesic, could acquire, retain and recover information from memory without being consciously aware that they remembered. In the case of amnesia, the prevailing focus on conscious forms of memory that coincided with a lack of an appreciation of unconscious processing in mental life, prevented investigators initially from recognizing the significance of the events that they had discovered. Instead of being interpreted as reflections of unconscious cognition, the retained abilities of amnesic patients on a variety of memory tasks were interpreted as reflecting memory that was limited to the motor domain (Milner 1966), as reflecting intact procedural memory (Cohen & Squire 1980), or as reflecting benefits of retrieval cues for conscious recollection (Warrington & Weiskrantz 1970). Since the early discoveries, the literature on these and related neuropsychological phenomena has grown significantly, especially in the area of memory and visual perception. A review of studies conducted up to the middle of the 1980s that linked these phenomena to each other and to consciousness appeared in 1988 (Schacter et al. 1988) and was followed by a briefer update in 1992 (Schacter 1992a). We restrict the focus of the present review to the neuropsychological investigation of conscious and unconscious processes in visual perception and attention. The literature on memory has recently been surveyed extensively by Moscovitch et al. (1993).

The major purpose of the present chapter is to review evidence concerning dissociations between preserved implicit and impaired explicit knowledge in various neuropsychological disorders of visual perception and attention. *Explicit knowledge* may be defined as knowledge of a particular aspect of external or internal stimulation that can be expressed as conscious experience (i.e. it can be the object of phenomenological awareness) and on which the person who possesses it can reflect. In operational terms, one is conscious of something when a verbal or non-verbal description can be provided of the particular object of that experience or a voluntary response can be made that comments on it (Moscovitch 1995; see also Allport 1988, Schacter 1992a). In contrast, *implicit knowledge* refers to knowledge of a particular aspect of external or internal stimulation that is revealed in task performance but that is not accompanied by a corresponding conscious experience and that cannot be the object of reflection for the person who possesses it.

It is important to distinguish the type of knowledge from the type of test, implicit or explicit, used to probe this knowledge. Implicit knowledge in patients with neuropsychological disorders may be tapped with implicit or explicit tests. With both types of test, the patients' responses are considered to reflect implicit knowledge if the patients disclaim conscious awareness of the specific knowledge that is revealed in their task performance. On *implicit tests*, patients are not required to reflect on, or to report knowledge from the domain under study, but rather their knowledge is tapped indirectly from performance on a seemingly irrelevant task. For example, to measure implicit familiarity of faces, subjects are asked to reflect on names rather than on the faces themselves (e.g. De Haan et al. 1992). Subjects have to judge printed names as being familiar or unfamiliar to them without regard to the faces that accompany the names. If the name is primed with the face of the corresponding individual, i.e. if this face is presented briefly before the name, response times to the name are faster than if the face of a noncorresponding or unfamiliar face is presented instead. This priming effect indicates that the familiarity of the face is processed on some level.

On implicit tests, preserved implicit knowledge may affect and modify a response without the person taking voluntary control over the expression of this knowledge. In fact, testing may proceed without the subject's awareness that this knowledge domain is being probed. In other cases, however, *explicit tests* may serve to obtain evidence for preserved implicit knowledge in the various neuropsychological disorders. Explicit tests require patients to reflect directly on knowledge from the domain under study. For example, in some of the studies on preserved visual knowledge in patients with cortical blindness, patients were asked to make a judgement on whether they saw something in the blind part of their visual field (e.g. Weiskrantz 1986, 1990).Although the subjective report of the patients may indicate a complete lack of knowledge in the specific domain (they may deny seeing anything and think that they are guessing randomly), their performance measures for the task may reveal that their explicit judgements are indeed affected by knowledge from that domain (e.g. they perform above chance in their detection judgements).

The preceding introduction to the relevant terminology makes it clear that the type of test that is administered should be distinguished from the type of knowledge that drives performance on the test (Richardson-Klavehn & Bjork 1988; for a discussion see Reingold & Toth 1996). A test may ostensibly (or purportedly) be implicit, yet performance on it may be contaminated by explicit knowledge (e.g. Toth et al. 1994). Alternatively, unconscious implicit knowledge may influence performance on what is ostensibly an explicit test of explicit knowledge (e.g. Jacoby et al. 1993). Ultimately, we are interested in the knowledge that a person possesses, not the performance on a particular type of test. The realization that few tests are process-pure forms the basis of the process-dissociation framework, which attempts to separate explicit from implicit knowledge in memory, perception and attention by providing a theoretical model and a clever methodological tool (Jacoby 1991, Merikle et al. 1995, Toth et al. 1995). Although this framework has been applied to neuropsychological research on memory and amnesia (Verfaellie & Treadwell 1993, Mayes et al. 1995), it has not been introduced yet to neuropsychological studies of visual perception and attention. To distinguish between tasks and processes in the ensuing survey, we will refer to tasks that aim to probe conscious and unconscious knowledge as direct and indirect tests, respectively. In contrast, when we make reference to processes, we will use the terms implicit and explicit knowledge.

The survey of the literature focuses on dissociations between implicit and explicit knowledge in six neurospychological syndromes that affect distinct aspects of visual perception and attention. The syndromes include cortical blindness, achromatopsia, object agnosia, pure alexia, prosopagnosia and neglect. Research on similar dissociations in patients with non-focal brain lesions, such as patients with dementia, whose cognitive impairments extend beyond deficits in visual perception, will not be included. The literature review is organized and guided by the question as to what type of implicit knowledge has been revealed. Thus, for each of these syndromes, we review what type of information has been shown to be processed implicitly and compare it with the type of information that has been shown to be processed explicitly. In this way, we are able to ask whether the information that is processed implicitly is of the same kind as the information that these patients cannot express explicitly. For example, it may be revealed that implicit knowledge is pre-semantic in nature and does not extend beyond perceptual or motor information, whereas explicit knowledge extends beyond it and includes semantic information.Alternatively, it may be the case that both implicit and explicit knowledge encompass semantic information but that this information differs qualitatively one from the other. Some of the research findings presented may not be entirely compelling instances of dissociations between implicit and explicit knowledge. We decided to include them here in order to provide the reader with as broad a survey as possible of potentially relevant findings.

In addition to reviewing the literature, the purpose of this chapter is to relate the presented findings to models of consciousness. It is our contention that the dissociations to be discussed have important implications for understanding the relations among perception, cognition and consciousness in both normal and brain-damaged populations.

We begin by describing three classes of models of consciousness that have been proposed to account for the preservation of implicit knowledge in neuropsychological syndromes. We then review the evidence concerning dissociations between implicit and explicit knowledge. For each syndrome, having reviewed the evidence, we evaluate how the three models of consciousness can account for the presented findings. We end with a conclusion section, in which we consider the relations among the phenomena described in the individual sections, adjudicate among the three classes of models of consciousness on a more general level, and present a hypothesis regarding the neuroanatomical basis of consciousness.

10.2 MODELS OF CONSCIOUSNESS[1]

10.2.1 Disconnection models

In a previous survey of dissociations between implicit and explicit knowledge in various neuropsychological syndromes (Schacter et al. 1988), the findings were discussed in the context of a model which consists of modules that mediate processing of information in restricted domains and of a conscious awareness system that supports conscious awareness (i.e. explicit knowledge) of information that is processed in any of these modules (Fig. 10.1). According to the model, the distinct syndromes reflect specific functional disconnections between these modules and the awareness mechanism. This model was later elaborated independently by Moscovitch (Moscovitch 1989, Moscovitch & Umiltà 1990, 1991) and Schacter (1989, 1990). Moscovitch & Umiltà (1990, 1991) proposed that the perceptual analysis of external stimulation is mediated by multiple input modules. Each module processes information from only a restricted domain. For example, a face recognition module would be devoted to processing information about faces but not about other visual stimuli such as words. In contrast, a visual word form system would be devoted to identifying words based on their visual appearance but not to identifying faces. Moscovitch & Umiltà (1991: 233) suggested that "the information represented in modules and the operations performed on that information are not subject to conscious inspection". Instead, only the output of the input modules is accessible to conscious awareness. The mechanism that supports conscious awareness is proposed to be a common one that accepts the ouput from each of the input modules. According to the model, neuropsychological syndromes with dissociations between implicit and explicit knowledge "can be viewed as arising from a disconnection of the module's shallow output from conscious awareness, while at the same time the output is made available to other systems that can affect behaviour" (Moscovitch & Umiltà 1991: 233). In other words, it is suggested that these

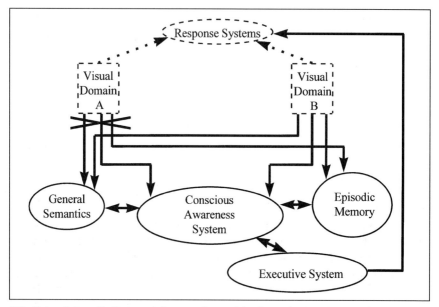

FIG. 10.1.   Schematic diagram of disconnection models of consciousness proposed to account for unconscious and conscious visual processing in various neuropsychological syndromes. Structures with solid outlines and connections shown as solid lines are involved in processing of explicit knowledge. Structures and connections with dashed lines are involved in processing of implicit knowledge. Domain-specific modules are represented by rectangles, while systems operating across different input domains are represented by ellipses. The large X symbolizes the locus of damage. Note that perceptual modules only process implicit knowledge.

syndromes reflect disorders of conscious access to preserved knowledge that is accessible unconsciously. Although not stated explicitly in the model, its description implies that the information that can be expressed as implicit knowledge is identical to the information about which the subject can reflect explicitly when the central awareness system is not disconnected from the input modules.

10.2.2 Distinct knowledge models

An alternative interpretation considered by Schacter et al. (1988), but not endorsed or incorporated into their model, was that distinct mechanisms and representations support implicit and explicit knowledge (Fig. 10.2). According to this view, implicit and explicit knowledge are different so that, even in normal people, implicit knowledge is not available to consciousness but co-exists with the explicit knowledge that is consciously accessible. This view has found acceptance in current work on memory (Tulving & Schacter 1990), blindsight (Weiskrantz 1995) and most recently on higher order vision (Milner 1995). For example,

Milner (1995) proposed for visual object perception that conscious awareness of object characteristics may only be attainable with object-centred representations which are mediated by one of the two major cortical visual pathways, the so-called ventral pathway (Ungerleider & Mishkin 1982). This pathway includes the inferior occipitotemporal cortex and is implicated in object identification and conscious awareness of objects. In contrast, the dorsal pathway, which includes more superior occipitoparietal regions, is, according to Milner (1995), part of an action system that computes viewer-centred representations which are necessary for the manipulation and movement of objects. Object information that is processed in the dorsal pathway is genuinely implicit knowledge in normal people and in patients with neuropsychological syndromes. The knowledge can be expressed in actions, such as the visually guided grasping of an object where the hand aperture has to be adjusted to the size of the object before it can be picked up. Yet, that knowledge is never accessible to conscious reflection. The model would predict that if the ventral pathway is damaged, the conscious appreciation of particular object qualities will be impaired or lacking entirely. Nevertheless, implicit knowledge about these object qualities may still be available

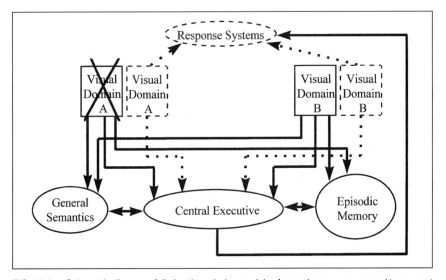

FIG. 10.2.   Schematic diagram of distinct knowledge models of consciousness proposed to account for unconscious and conscious visual processing in various neuropsychological syndromes. Structures with solid outlines and connections shown as solid lines are involved in processing of explicit knowledge. Structures and connections with dashed line are involved in processing of implicit knowledge. Domain-specific modules are represented by rectangles, while systems operating across different input domains are represented by ellipses. The large X symbolizes the locus of damage. Note that distinct perceptual modules process implicit and explicit knowledge in a given domain.

for action control. The neuropsychological support for this model is discussed in Section 10.5. In the current context, it only serves as a specific instance of a class of models that have in common the proposition that implicit and explicit knowledge are different in kind and involve different cognitive and neural mechanisms.

10.2.3 Degraded representation or threshold models

According to a third class of models, implicit knowledge is a degraded form of explicit knowledge (Fig. 10.3). Farah (Farah et al. 1993, Farah 1994) formulated a model of this type for higher order vision. In this model, it is proposed that the information needed to support performance on tests of implicit knowledge is lower in quality but of the same type as that needed to support performance on tests of explicit knowledge. The model suggests a correlation between the quality of the perceptual representation and the likelihood that the information contained therein would reach conscious awareness. The dissociation between preserved implicit knowledge and impaired explicit knowledge in neuropsychological disorders of vision is explained by proposing that

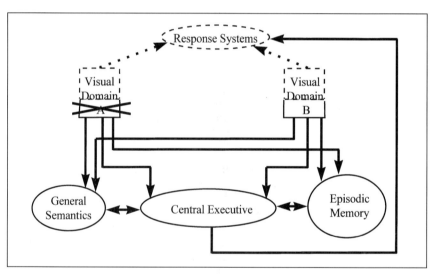

FIG. 10.3.   Schematic diagram of degraded representation models of consciousness proposed to account for unconscious and conscious visual processing in various neuropsychological syndromes. Structures with solid outlines and connections as solid lines are involved in processing of explicit knowledge. Structures and connections with dashed lines are involved in processing of implicit knowledge. Shaded structures are involved in processing explicit and implicit knowledge. Domain-specific modules are represented by rectangles, while systems operating across different input domains are represented by ellipses. The large X symbolizes the locus of damage. Note that only information that passes a certain threshold in the perceptual modules (as indicated by a vertical line) becomes explicit knowledge.

perceptual processes operating on higher quality visual representations are impaired. The fact that this impairment leads to deficits in explicit but not implicit knowledge is seen as a consequence of the probabilistic relation between high-quality representations and consciousness rather than as a reflection of damage to mechanisms of conscious visual awareness or a disconnection from them.

10.3 CORTICAL BLINDNESS

10.3.1 Representative findings

Cortical blindness is a neurological condition in which damage to the geniculostriate visual pathway, in particular to the striate visual cortex, causes a loss of vision in the topographically corresponding parts of the visual field. The visual defect may affect limited parts of the visual fields (i.e. produce a scotoma, hemianopia) or may be complete. The disorder can be revealed by using standard clinical tests and laboratory perimetry. The sensitivity to visual stimuli is determined by asking people to report what they see under controlled visual stimulation of distinct regions of the visual field. Patients with cortical blindness usually report a complete lack of conscious visual experience when stimulated in the blind parts of their visual field (Weiskrantz 1986). However, it is now well established that some of these patients possess preserved implicit knowledge about visual stimulation in their scotoma. This preserved implicit knowledge has been referred to as "blindsight". A variety of methods have been used to provide behavioural and psychophysiological evidence for blindsight (for a review see Weiskrantz 1986, 1990; for evidence in non-human primates see Cowey & Stoerig 1995).

10.3.1.1 Psychophysiological evidence for implicit knowledge

There is evidence from psychophysiological studies that reflexes of the visual and the autonomic system in response to visual stimulation can be preserved in patients with partial or complete cortical blindness. Ter Braak et al. (1971) reported that the optokinetic nystagmus reflex could be elicited by slow movements of a large field of optical contrasts in a patient with complete cortical blindness (see also Heide et al. 1990). Yet, when asked during the testing procedure whether he saw any movement the patient denied seeing anything, demonstrating a deficit in conscious awareness of visual stimulation. Preserved reflexes in response to movement stimulation have also been demonstrated by Zihl et al. (1980). Zihl et al. studied two hemianopic patients and observed significant electrodermal skin-conductance responses in response to moving light stimuli that were presented briefly to the patients' scotoma.

These autonomic responses occurred although the patients reported no awareness of the stimuli. Finally, Weiskrantz (1990) reported that every patient of a group of hemianopic patients had preserved pupillary reflexes, i.e. all patients exhibited changes in pupil diameter in response to changes in light flux in their scotoma.

10.3.1.2 Implicit knowledge revealed with forced-choice guessing

The most extensively used method to demonstrate blindsight is the forced-choice guessing procedure which was adapted from animal research. This procedure can be classified as a direct test of visual processing in the scotoma because it requires patients to comment on stimuli that are presented to the blind portion of their visual fields. It has, for example, been applied to demonstrate preserved visual localization abilities in patients with cortical blindness. To examine these abilities, a briefly flashed stimulus is presented to one of several regions of the scotoma along a chosen meridian. The patients are asked to guess where the target has been presented after an acoustic cue is given to initiate a response. Under these conditions, hemianopic patients have been shown to make surprisingly accurate localization judgements by moving their gaze towards the target positions (Pöppel et al. 1973), by pointing or reaching towards it manually (Perenin & Jeannerod 1975, 1978) or by making a verbal response such as "top" or "bottom" (Barbur et al. 1980, Weiskrantz 1980). Although the accuracy is usually reduced in comparison to judgements for the intact part of the visual field, highly significant correlations have been found between "guessed" location and target eccentricity in the scotoma. This visual discrimination ability may be preserved in the absence of any reported conscious awareness of the stimuli that the patients are able to discriminate. Patients may have to be convinced with much effort to try guessing because, from their perspective, it appears to be a silly request to follow. In addition, they may show a high degree of surprise when they are given feedback about the accuracy of their discriminations (see Weiskrantz 1986, 1990). Thus, preserved localization can be interpreted to reflect implicit visual knowledge.

The forced-choice guessing procedure has also been used to uncover other preserved visual discrimination and detection abilities that reflect implicit visual knowledge in cortical blindness. It has been demonstrated that some patients are able to detect flashing stationary (Barbur et al. 1980, Stoerig et al. 1985) or moving stimuli (Barbur et al. 1980, Blythe et al. 1987), to discriminate the direction of movement (Blythe et al. 1986) and to discriminate between forms based on orientation differences in components of the forms (Weiskrantz 1986). Most recently, preserved discrimination between different stimulus wavelengths has been demonstrated (Stoerig 1987, Stoerig & Cowey 1991, 1992). Stoerig & Cowey (1992) measured wavelength discrimination in three patients with cortical blindness. They first determined spectral sensitivity curves in the normal and blind portions of the visual field. The patients were asked to guess whether a visual stimulus had been presented while they were tested with stimuli that varied in wavelength and stimulus intensity. At each tested wavelength, the stimulus intensity was increased incrementally until forced-choice guessing scores were above chance. On the basis of the resulting spectral sensitivity curves, five stimuli were selected that varied in wavelength but were matched in terms of luminous efficiency. When the patients were subsequently asked to make discriminations between various pairings of these stimuli in a forced-choice guessing situation, all of them discriminated some of these pairings at a level significantly above chance. However, they denied being aware of any type of visual stimulation in the scotoma during testing. These results suggest that some residual (though not normal) wavelength sensitivity and discrimination abilities may be observed in the scotoma of patients with cortical blindness. Because these preserved wavelength processing abilities may occur in the absence of any conscious awareness of visual stimulation, they can be classified as implicit knowledge of colour information.

The utility of the forced-choice guessing procedure to uncover implicit visual processing in cortically blind patients has been criticized for a number of reasons (for a discussion see Weiskrantz 1990). From a practical perspective, it is important to note that the method is extremely time consuming and can only be used with well-practised subjects who show some confidence in the usefulness of the procedure despite their subjective impression of engaging in random guessing. This issue of practicality has important conceptual implications in that it makes it difficult to interpret negative results (Weiskrantz 1990). Positive results (i.e. evidence for blindsight) may only be achieved with an experimenter who exhibits a high degree of persistence and an ability to encourage cortically blind patients to continue with their participation.

Other criticisms that relate more directly to conceptual issues implicated in this research have been raised by Campion et al. (1983). Campion et al. argued that positive findings with the forced-choice procedure may not reflect unconscious visual processing but rather could be due to diffusion of light into intact regions of the visual field during scotoma stimulation. Limitations in space do not allow us to discuss this criticism in detail, but it is worth noting that several studies have convincingly shown that this alternative interpretation does not hold for the majority of data (see Weiskrantz 1986, 1988, Barbur et al. 1994).

As a final point of criticism, the issue has been raised that blindsight as revealed by forced-choice guessing performance may reflect residual conscious awareness of visual stimulation in the scotoma (Campion et al. 1983; for a discussion see Weiskrantz 1988). There are subjective reports of individual patients which indicate that they experience some form of conscious visual awareness under forced-choice testing conditions, in particular when high-contrast and very salient stimuli are used (see Weiskrantz 1986, 1988, Weiskrantz et al. 1995). Weiskrantz et al. (1995) suggest that this residual conscious vision may be qualitatively different from conscious vision in normal subjects in that it is characterized by a "contentless kind of awareness, a feeling of something happening, albeit not normal seeing" (p.6122). Moreover, Weiskrantz (1988) observed that forced-choice guessing performance may actually be better if stimulus conditions are such that stimulation is not accompanied by any residual conscious experience and patients are performing the task in a pure "guessing-mode". Marcel (1993) replicated these observations in a case study in which he showed that forced-choice performance in a stimulus detection task improved when the hemianopic patient was strongly encouraged to guess rather than being instructed to base the decision on any subjective conscious impression of whether a stimulus was present.

Weiskrantz et al. (1995) investigated the relation between discrimination performance in a conscious mode with performance in an unconscious mode in the same hemianopic patient with a psychophysical procedure. They asked whether the two modes of discrimination "are just different portions of the same psychometric function or whether they reflect different and possibly independent processes" (Weiskrantz et al. 1995: 6122). To address this issue, the investigators examined how stimulus parameters such as speed, luminance contrast of the stimulus, orientation of motion trajectory and length of excursion affected the conscious and unconscious discrimination of motion direction and motion orientation in their patient. To distinguish between trials in the two modes of responding, the patient was not only asked to make the conventional psychophysical choice (e.g. to discriminate between two directions in which a stimulus could move) but also to indicate whether he had any awareness of the event in every given trial. Overall, Weiskrantz et al. found that the patient's discrimination performance followed different psychometric functions for the two response modes. One of the parameters that strongly affected visual awareness was the speed of movement of the stimulus. With slow speeds, he had no conscious awareness of the events, although he was able to guess with high accuracy whether the movement was horizontal or not. As speed increased above approximately 10° per second, the number of "aware" responses increased. The most important differences between the two response modes were observed in the range of speed from 10° to 15° per second. Whereas the patient's discrimination performance on trials in which he indicated awareness of the stimuli increased dramatically across this range (starting at chance level), performance on trials in which he indicated a lack of awareness varied little across this range and was always at a level of at least 85% accuracy. These results suggest that the patient's "unaware mode is not just a pale shadow of his aware mode" (Weiskrantz 1995: 149). Rather, they indicate that preserved visual processing in the scotoma may truly reflect implicit knowledge that is not based on any residual visual conscious experience and that is qualitatively different from explicit knowledge. At the same time, the controversial discussion of residual conscious vision in the literature on blindsight clearly shows the difficulties that arise for revealing implicit knowledge when direct methods are used in which a comment on the stimulation in the scotoma is required.

10.3.1.3 Implicit knowledge revealed with indirect tests

Within the last decade, a number of indirect tests have been introduced that are not prone to the specific problems associated with the use of the forced-choice guessing procedure in revealing blindsight. These tests all have in common that they allow investigators to examine interactions between the intact part of the visual field and the scotoma. Evidence for impaired explicit knowledge in the scotoma is obtained by demonstrating that visual stimulation limited to the scotoma leads to chance performance when patients are asked to respond to it directly. In contrast, evidence for preserved implicit knowledge in the scotoma is obtained by showing that combined stimulation of the intact field and the scotoma evokes different responses regarding visual experiences in the intact field than stimulation limited to the intact field. The elegance of these indirect tests lies in the fact that, in order to demonstrate preserved implicit knowledge in the scotoma, patients are required to respond to visual stimuli in the intact part of their visual field and not to stimuli in their scotoma (as required, for example, during forced-choice guessing). This feature has the advantage that patients are likely to engage in the same conscious decision processes and apply the same response criteria regardless of whether their implicit or explicit knowledge is examined.

Marzi et al. (1986) explored the effect of spatial summation in hemianopic patients. Normal people show faster reaction times (RTs) to pairs of flashes presented simultaneously than to single flashes in a simple RT task which requires them to respond as quickly as possible to any presentation of a flash. Such a summation effect also occurs when one stimulus is presented to one hemifield and the other one is presented simultaneously to the other hemifield (interfield summation). The question of interest in Marzi et al.'s study was whether hemianopic patients would show interfield summation when asked to respond to the stimulus in the intact hemifield. A subgroup of patients was found to show this effect. In contrast, none of the patients responded to any stimuli when they were presented only in the scotoma. This pattern of results suggests that interfield summation in cortical blindness may reflect implicit knowledge about visual information in the scotoma. Only a minority of patients, however, showed signs of implicit knowledge. Marzi et al. attribute the observed lack of interfield summation in some of their patients to the patients' marked variability of performance. Nevertheless, the effect was replicated in another subsample of hemianopic patients (Corbetta et al. 1990).

Corbetta et al. (1990) also introduced another simple RT task in order to investigate preserved processing capacities in their patients' scotoma. When a pair of flashes is presented in rapid succession to normal people who are asked to respond to the second flash as quickly as possible, RTs are slower than when only a single flash is presented. This temporal inhibition effect occurs even when the two flashes are presented in different locations of the visual field. Corbetta et al. found this effect to be present in one of their hemianopic patients under conditions in which the first flash was presented to the scotoma and the second one to the intact part of the visual fields. In other words, this patient's RTs were slower when the stimulus presented to the intact part of the visual field was preceded by a stimulus in the scotoma than when it was presented in isolation. Yet, the patient never reported being aware of any additional stimulation under double stimulation conditions. In combination with the findings of Marzi et al.'s study, these results suggest that implicit knowledge about the onset of light stimulation can be preserved in patients with cortical blindness.

Rafal et al. (1990) evaluated how distractor signals presented to the scotoma affect the latency of saccades to target signals in the intact part of the visual field in a small group of hemianopic patients. They were asked to fixate on the centre of a display and were instructed to make a saccade to a target box in the intact part of their visual fields as soon as they saw it brighten. The distractor signal, the brightening of a box in the scotoma, was presented with varying SOAs before and after the target signal. When the distractor signal was presented simultaneously with or 50ms preceding the target, all hemianopic patients showed an increase in saccade latency relative to a condition in which no distractor preceded the target. In contrast, when tested directly for the detection of distractor signals on a presence–absence task, patients performed at chance. This pattern of results suggests that the distractor signal in the scotoma affected saccade latencies in the absence of any conscious awareness of that signal. Inhibition from the distractors on the saccade task was observed only in hemianopic patients, and not in normal people, who detected the distractor signals easily on the presence–absence task. Rafal et al., therefore, suggest that the inhibitory effect may be critically dependent on the absence of conscious awareness of the distractor stimulus. Even in patients, however, the effect was highly constrained. It occurred when distractors were presented to the temporal portion of the blind visual hemifield but not when they were presented to the nasal portion. In addition, it was observed with occulomotor responses only. Rafal et al. interpret this specificity in terms of physiological properties of the retinotectal visual pathway. This pathway may operate in isolation in patients with damage to the geniculostriate pathway.

A further study demonstrating effects of stimulation in the scotoma on responses to stimulation in intact parts of the visual field was reported by Singer et al. (1977). Using a perimeter, Singer et al. determined detection thresholds for briefly flashed stationary lightspots to various locations of the visual fields in hemianopic patients. Curiously, they found that, when the detection threshold for a point in the intact part of the visual field had been elevated as a result of adaptation during multiple testing trials, it could subsequently be reset by adapting a mirror-reversed region in the scotoma. As in normal people, this threshold resetting was location specific in that it was ineffective if the target of the second adaptation was not presented to the mirror-reversed region of the first adaptation but 30° away. Unlike in normal people, however, resetting occurred in hemianopic patients under conditions in which they had no conscious awareness of stimulation in the scotoma. The location specificity of the interaction effect observed by Singer et al. suggests that the signal processed implicitly in the scotoma contains some information about retinal location.

The outcome of three further studies on interaction effects between the scotoma and the intact part of the visual field is of special interest because it provides evidence that implicit visual knowledge may not be limited to stimulus detection but may also encompass processing of specific visual stimulus attributes in the scotoma. Pizzamiglio et al. (1984) designed a study by exploiting the observation that viewing of a rotating visual scene, i.e. a large disc covered by random dots, induces a tilt of the subjective vertical in the direction of the rotating stimulus in normal people. The size of this effect varies in normal people, depending on whether a single hemifield or both hemifields are stimulated. The effect is larger under bilateral than unilateral stimulation. Pizzamiglio et al. hypothesized that, if it could be shown that the size of the tilting effect varied in hemianopic patients depending on whether the scotoma was or was not stimulated in addition to the intact part of the visual fields, this could be taken as evidence for preserved visual processing of motion in the scotoma. All seven hemianopic patients who were tested by Pizzamiglio et al. exhibited a larger subjective tilt when both hemifields were stimulated than when only the intact one was. At the same time, all except one of the patients reported not being aware of any stimulation in their scotoma during testing.

Pöppel (1986) investigated colour-related after-images and demonstrated that the perception of colour of stimuli presented to the intact part of the visual field is affected by residual processing of colour in the scotoma. If normal people fixate the white centre of a round target long enough, it takes on the colour of the surround in the resulting after-image. If the surround consists of two separate subsections in complementary colours (e.g. green and red), the resulting after-image of the centre will appear considerably darker and greyish as compared with the centre of a single-colour surround target. Pöppel showed residual colour processing in the scotoma of his hemianopic patient by observing this subjective difference between a single and a two-colour surround condition in an experimental set-up in which one of the two colours in the two-colour surround condition was presented to the scotoma only. Yet, when tested explicitly to discriminate the single-colour surround and the two-colour surround targets, the patient was unable to perform the task.

Data reported by Torjussen (1976, 1978) raise the possibility that implicit knowledge in the scotoma may also include rudimentary shape information. Torjussen investigated the presence of perceptual completion across the scotoma in hemianopic patients. He asked three patients to reproduce simple shapes to which they had been exposed by means of a very bright photoflash that generated after-images of these shapes (Torjussen 1978). If an incomplete circle was presented to the intact part of the visual field, patients correctly reproduced it as a half-circle. In contrast, if an incomplete circle was presented to the scotoma, patients reported seeing nothing, confirming their lack of explicit knowledge about visual stimulation in the scotoma. Most interestingly, if a complete circle was presented that extended across both the scotoma and the intact part of the visual field, patients reproduced it as a complete circle, revealing the presence of perceptual completion processes across the scotoma. Because the observed completion process occurred despite the absence of conscious visual awareness for stimuli in the scotoma, this finding suggests that visual information in the scotoma was processed implicitly under bilateral stimulation. Implicit knowledge, however, was found to be present only for figures that were mirror symmetrical across the border between the scotoma and the intact portion of the visual field. Therefore, it remains unclear whether the patients' implicit knowledge reflected the detection of non-specific stimulation or rudimentary processing of shape information. Furthermore, even though further evidence for perceptual completion in hemianopic patients has been reported (see Weiskrantz 1986, 1990), other investigators were only marginally successful in eliciting perceptual completion processes (Sergent 1988). Taken together, the findings from Pöppel (1986), Pizzamiglio et al. (1984) and Torjussen (1976, 1978) confirm those from studies with the forced-choice guessing procedure by suggesting that hemianopic patients may process colour, movement and possibly shape in their scotoma in the absence of any conscious awareness of the stimulus attribute or even the stimulation as such.

What is the neuroanatomical basis of blindsight? It has been argued that blindsight may be mediated by islands of intact striate cortex (V1) in the otherwise damaged part of V1 (Fendrich et al. 1992). Although this interpretation may explain the findings observed with the particular patient studied by Fendrich et al., it is highly unlikely that it could account for the majority of data observed in other patients with blindsight. For example, Weiskrantz (1995) showed that the well-studied blindsight patient G.Y., who is clinically blind in the right half of his visual field, had implicit visual knowledge that allowed him to mimic with his arm movement the path of a moving spot of light projected onto a screen. The spot moved on straight and curved trajectories through widely distributed parts of his affected visual hemifield. At the same time, G.Y. maintained fixation on the centre of the screen, as documented by data from an eye tracker. This finding could only be explained by Fendrich et al.'s hypothesis if G.Y. had islands of intact tissue distributed across large portions of his left striate cortex. However, magnetic resonance imaging data for the patient obtained by Barbur et al. (1993) show that this is not the case.

Even stronger evidence against the hypothesis that residual islands of striate cortex mediate blindsight comes from studies of patients who had undergone hemispherectomy. In these patients, a complete hemisphere, including all striate and extrastriate visual cortex, had been removed, thus producing, among other symptoms, blindness in the hemifield opposite to the removed hemisphere. Significantly, hemispherectomy patients have also been reported to show implicit knowledge of stimulation in their affected hemifield. Studies in which the forced-choice guessing procedure was applied have found evidence for blindsight on tasks that require stimulus detection (Ptito et al. 1991), stimulus localization (Perenin & Jeannerod 1978), motion detection (Perenin 1991) and form discrimination (Ptito et al. 1987).

The results of the hemispherectomy studies suggest that subcortical rather than cortical regions may mediate blindsight on tasks that involve these visual functions. They suggest that blindsight as such may depend neither on islands of intact striate visual cortex nor on intact extrastriate cortex. However, it is possible that some blindsight phenomena may require intact extrastriate cortex. For example, implicit motion direction discrimination has been shown to be present in patients with striate cortex damage (that spares at least parts of extrastriate visual cortex) but not in patients who have undergone hemispherectomy (Barbur et al. 1980, Perenin 1991).

10.3.2 Evaluation of the three models

10.3.2.1 Degraded representation model

The basic assumptions of this model are that the same type of processes, mediated by the same neural substrates, are involved in the expression of implicit and explicit knowledge. The only difference between the two types of knowledge is that the former can survive when their shared neural substrate is partially damaged, whereas the latter cannot. It is assumed that the representations necessary to support explicit knowledge are more detailed and refined than are those necessary to support implicit knowledge.

At first glance, this model may seem to account for the evidence from blindsight because degraded representations may be sufficient to support performance on those tasks on which implicit knolwedge was demonstrated.All of these tasks required only simple responses to primitive visual features, such as brightness and motion. A closer inspection, however, suggests that important aspects of the presented data cannot be explained by the model:

(a) The visual stimulation about which one may have explicit knowledge is not necessarily more complex or detailed than that about which one may have implicit knowledge. For example, information about the direction of motion that led to conscious experience was not more complex than the one that allowed for discrimination without awareness in Weiskrantz et al.'s (1995) patient. Similarly, it is not apparent on the surface that changes in brightness that alter the size of the pupil are inherently less complex than the ones that are involved in the conscious appreciation of these changes. Furthermore, it would be difficult to argue that the stimulus onset in the blind field that affected RT performance implicitly in Marzi et al.'s (1986) and Corbetta et al.'s (1990) studies is less complex than the same signal which gave rise to conscious awareness in the intact field.

(b) The neuroanatomical substrate that is necessary for the expression of implicit and explicit knowledge (if not the knowledge itself) can be different in each case, rather than the first being a damaged version of the second. Although loss of conscious awareness of stimulus onset, motion and location is caused by damage to visual cortex, implicit knowledge of each of these attributes is not dependent on the remaining cortical tissue. The presented findings from studies with hemispherectomy patients suggest, instead, that it depends on subcortical regions that can function independently.

(c) Performance based on implicit knowledge may be superior to that based on conscious experience. This outcome can be expected if implicit and explicit knowledge are dependent on different systems, whereas this is an unlikely outcome if implicit knowledge reflects the workings of the system that supports explicit knowledge. A case in point are data reported by Weiskrantz et al. (1995) showing better motion detection when conscious awareness was absent than when it was present.

(d) Consciousness may prevent the expression of implicit knowledge. The release of implicit functions that may occur with the loss of conscious awareness is not an emergent function of a single damaged system, as the degraded representation model would predict, but rather it arises from a loss of inhibitory control of one system by another. This point is supported most clearly by Rafal et al.'s (1990) demonstration that distractor signals in the scotoma inhibit saccades towards targets in the intact part of the visual field only if the distractors are not perceived consciously.

Having specified those aspects of the evidence on blindsight that are inconsistent with a degraded representation model, we now examine to what extent they can be accounted for by the other two models.

10.3.2.2 Disconnection model and distinct knowledge model

The core assumption of the disconnection model is that the processes of visual modules and their representations are intact but that their output does not gain access to consciousness. The model is not susceptible to the objections formulated in (a) against the degraded representation model. According to the disconnection model, the knowledge that can be expressed implicitly is not necessarily less complex or of a lower quality than explicit knowledge.

To accommodate the objections in (b) regarding neuroanatomical evidence, the model would have to assume that some of the neural systems that mediate implicit knowledge are distinct from those that feed into the conscious system. The existence of independent systems whose operations and output are never accessible to consciousness was acknowledged by proponents of the disconnection model (e.g. Schacter et al. 1988) but with little concern about elaborating this aspect of the model and appreciating its implications. One possibility is that, although the systems that mediate the expression of implicit and explicit knowledge are neuroanatomically distinct, they operate on essentially common information or representations. It may simply be the case that the output of one system leads to consciousness, whereas the output of the other feeds into unconscious action or procedural systems. Accordingly, for example, the subcortical neural circuit that drives pupillary reflexes may make use of the same information about brightness that is used by the cortical system which is involved in making conscious judgements about brightness. Alternatively, the conscious and the unconscious systems may be neuroanatomically distinct and may operate on different types of information. Once the second view is endorsed, however, it becomes difficult to distinguish between the disconnection model and the distinct knowledge model. For the sake of clarity in the ensuing discussions, we differentiate between the two models by accepting for the time being that in the disconnection model, but not in the distinct knowledge model, conscious and unconscious systems process the same information.

Even if a disconnection model can be salvaged to accommodate point (b), it would have difficulty with point (c). If only the output is disconnected from consciousness but the representations and processes that give rise to that output are intact, it is difficult to see how performance based on implicit knowledge can exceed performance based on explicit knowledge as was shown by Marcel (1993) and Weiskrantz (1988). Even more serious problems are caused by Weiskrantz et al.'s (1995) finding that the expression of explicit and implicit knowledge on tests of motion perception obey different psychophysical functions. Thus, it is difficult not to reach the conclusion that, at least in some cases, the systems mediating implicit and explicit knowledge are neuroanatomically distinct and process different types of information. This conclusion reflects the core assumption of the distinct knowledge model which, therefore, seems to be favoured by the evidence.

In summary, the degraded representation model appears to be discredited for blindsight. Although the disconnection model can accommodate some of the findings, it too has difficulty accounting for all the evidence. The distinct knowledge model fares best. However, more research along the lines of Weiskrantz et al.'s (1995) study is required to determine what distinguishes the systems and types of information that have privileged access to consciousness from those that do not.

10.4 ACHROMATOPSIA

10.4.1 Representative findings

Achromatopsia is a selective loss of the perception of colour caused by cortical damage to ventromedial occipitotemporal regions (Meadows 1974, Damasio et al. 1980). In its most extreme form, all sensation of colour is lost and patients complain that the world looks drained of colour. There is evidence to suggest that cortical achromatopsia can appear without associated deficits in the visual perception of other attributes such as brightness, depth, form or movement, although the disorder is often accompanied by apperceptive visual object agnosia. Patients with cortical achromatopsia are severely impaired on tests that involve conscious colour perception (for a review, see Zeki 1990). As a core feature, patients are unable to identify colours by name. In addition, they are impaired at classifying colours according to broad hue categories and perform at chance when asked to sort a group of hues so that there is an orderly progression of hues along a row between the predetermined anchor hues at each end (Farnsworth–Munsell 100 Hue Test).

A small number of studies provides evidence for preserved implicit knowledge of colour information in patients with cortical achromatopsia (Mollon et al. 1980, Victor et al. 1989, Heywood et al. 1987, 1991, Heywood et al. 1994). Evidence comes predominantly from studies in which tests of form perception were used to probe knowledge of colour indirectly. All but one (Victor et al. 1989) of these studies were conducted with the same patient, M.S., who exhibits a complete achromatopsia.

Mollon et al. (1980) provided evidence for preserved colour processing in M.S. by showing that the patient was able to identify the shapes of hidden figures in pseudo-isochromatic patterns (Ishihara plates) when seen at a distance. These shapes can only be identified at a distance by processing the chromatic borders between the figure and the surround. M.S.'s ability to use colour information in order to extract shape contrasted with his lack of awareness of any colour difference between figure and surround and with his inability to identify any colours of the patterns used.

More recent studies with M.S. have replicated and extended this basic pattern of findings (Heywood et al. 1991, 1994). The results of these studies provide direct support for the notion that M.S. is able to process information about chromatic borders implicitly but does not show any conscious appreciation of the hues that make up the border and is unable to discriminate between these hues on direct tests of colour perception. Heywood et al. (1994) found that M.S. could readily locate a desaturated coloured form that was embedded in a dynamic or static grey checkerboard of small squares that varied in brightness. For example, a coloured cross was created by replacing nine out of 38 × 28 squares of a grey checkerboard by a colour. The cross randomly changed position from trial to trial. M.S. was not only able to locate the target but was also able to report its form correctly by drawing it. In addition, M.S. was unimpaired in performing a form discrimination task in which the forms were again composed of multiple small squares of the same colour and were presented against a surround of greys of variable luminance. M.S. could discriminate between squares and crosses when given the instructions to select the odd form out of a group of forms (e.g. two squares and a cross). The nearly flawless performance on these indirect tests that involve processing of colour in the context of form detection and form discrimination, contrasted sharply with his grossly impaired performance on an oddity task that is a direct test of colour perception. This task required him to select the odd colour from a group of stimuli with different isoluminant colours but equal shapes. Good performance on the indirect tests also contrasted with his impairment on a task which required the detection of a single coloured square in a group of grey squares of the same size as the coloured square.

Heywood et al. (1994) explain the pattern of results across the checkerboard tasks as indicating that M.S. confuses chromatic and luminance borders when their outlines are identical (e.g. all squares of the same size). In contrast, he is able to discriminate between them to segregate figure from ground when their outlines are different (e.g. a coloured cross on a grey surround). For the present discussion, these findings can be interpreted to suggest that M.S. is able to process information about colour implicitly when the actual perceptual judgement concerns form, but is unable to use this information explicitly when the judgement concerns colour.

Heywood et al. (1991, 1994) have also shown that M. S. can use colour information implicitly when making a perceptual judgement regarding apparent motion and orientation. Despite his absence of conscious colour perception, he performed well when asked to pick the odd grating from a group of three gratings (i.e. a vertical grating among two horizontal gratings, or vice versa). In this task, he detected the orientation of a square wave grating which was composed of two isoluminant colours that were indistinguishable to M.S. in isolation (Heywood et al. 1991). M.S. could report the direction of apparent motion which was produced by a 90° phase shift for a red/green chromatic grating (Heywood et al. 1994), showing that he has access to the sign of colours which he is unable to report explicitly. Finally, Heywood et al. (1991) found that M.S. could discriminate between series of isoluminant colours which were either jumbled or ordered in their chromaticity when he was asked to indicate which was the ordered series. Because this latter ability could only be observed as long as adjacent patches of the series abutted one another directly but not when a 2mm gap was introduced between patches, the finding supports the interpretation that the type of colour information which is accessible to M.S. in the absence of conscious colour perception is about isoluminant chromatic borders.

Suggestive evidence for implicit colour processing in another achromatopsic person comes from a study in which chromatic contrast sensitivity and evoked potientials to isoluminant chromatic checkerboards were found to be normal (Victor et al. 1989). Victor et al. examined a patient with a right homonymous hemianopia and a cortical achromatopsia in his otherwise spared left visual field. Whereas the patient was severely impaired in naming colours, sorting colours into categories and putting colours into sequence in colour space, he exhibited a normal psychophysical threshold for the detection of chromatic gratings, as determined by flicker photometry. This test involves making fine discriminations between regions of different chromaticity but equal luminance, while no explicit identification of the grating components is necessary. Unlike Heywood et al.'s patient M.S., Victor et al.'s patient could also detect colour differences in an oddity task that required him to select the unique patch in a group of patches of one colour and a single patch of the opponent colour. However, the achromatopsia of Victor et al.'s patient was incomplete in that informal observations and formal tests of conscious colour perception showed more accurate performance in the red–purple region than in other regions of colour space. This residual explicit knowledge about colour may have contributed to correct performance on the implicit tasks. Therefore, with respect to revealing implicit knowledge, the data from Victor et al.'s patient must be treated with more interpretive caution than the data reported on M.S.

10.4.2 Evaluation of the three models

The strongest evidence for implicit knowledge of colour in achromatopsia is based on studies showing that a patient may be capable of using information about chromatic borders without awareness of the hues that constitute the borders. This evidence can be accommodated by both the degraded representation and the distinct representation models.

According to the degraded representation model, a damaged colour system could still support the expression of implicit knowledge about chromatic borders but not about richer and more complex colour information at a conscious level. By comparison, the distinct knowledge model could account for this evidence by stating that information about chromatic borders is handled by a separate system from the one involved in conscious perception of colour. As for the disconnection model, the observed limitations of preserved implicit knowledge do not provide support for the hypothesis that all processing of colour information proceeds normally and that only the output from the system that subserves colour processing is disconnected from consciousness.

Neurophysiological considerations may eventually be used to decide between the degraded representation and the distinct knowledge model. Heywood et al. (1991) proposed that information about chromatic borders is processed by neurons in the magnocellular visual pathway, whereas other information about colour depends on the parvocellular pathway. Although initial evidence supported Heywood et al.'s hypothesis and with it the distinct knowledge model, more recent evidence indicates that the patient's sensitivity to colour goes beyond that which would be expected if only the broad-band magnocellular system were involved (Heywood et al. 1994). This is not to say that the patient's performance depends on the impaired functions of a single degraded system. It is possible, as Heywood et al. suggest, that the parvocellular system is itself subdivided into different pathways or subsystems, only some of which can support the expression of explicit knowledge. Accordingly, some of the patient's implicit knowledge could be subserved by those subsystems of the parvocellular system that do not support explicit knowledge. Although refined knowledge of neurophysiological properties of different visual systems can suggest ways to test the degraded representation and the distinct knowledge model, as yet the evidence is inconclusive.

Findings on colour processing in patients with cortical blindness may also help to evaluate the models, even though these patients' deficit extends beyond the perception of colour. For example, Pöppel's (1986) demonstration that colour in the blind field can influence the colour of after-images seen in the intact field suggests that colour information other than about chromatic borders can be processed implicitly in patients with damage to the visual system. Pöppel's procedure, however, cannot be used in patients with achromatopsia because it depends on a preserved ability to make explicit reports about colour in some part of the visual field. A more appropriate method to evaluate the limitations of implicit knowledge in achromatopsia may be the forced-choice guessing procedure used by Stoerig & Cowey (1992). As described above, Stoerig & Cowey demonstrated that patients with cortical blindness performed above chance on a forced-choice test of narrow-band wavelength discriminations without showing conscious awareness of the stimuli. Because only a single stimulus was presented for each decision, performance on this task could not be based on information about chromatic borders. It would be important to know whether patients with achromatopsia could also succeed at this task. Evidence of this sort would be consistent with the disconnection model. It would be strongly supportive of the model if it could be shown that the patients' guessing rate approaches the level of performance of normal people.

Although provocative, research on implicit knowledge in achromatopsia has not advanced as far as that on blindsight. There have been fewer studies and all the evidence is based on an investigation of one, and in some cases two, patients. Based on this limited evidence, the disconnection model fares least well, whereas there is little to favour the distinct knowledge model over the degraded representation one.

10.5 VISUAL OBJECT AGNOSIA

10.5.1 Representative findings

Visual object agnosia is defined as a modality-specific impairment in the higher visual processes necessary for the recognition of objects, with relative preservation of elementary visual functions (for a review, see Farah 1990). Within the syndrome, a broad distinction has been drawn between cases who exhibit deficits that affect the perceptual analysis of known objects (apperceptive agnosia) and other cases who exhibit deficits in deriving the meaning of objects (associative agnosia). Both groups of patients show a severe deficit in naming objects. Unlike patients with associative agnosia, patients with apperceptive agnosia are also severely impaired at matching and copying objects that they cannot name. The focus of the present discussion is on apperceptive agnosia because, to our knowledge, there are no studies on implicit knowledge in associative agnosia (for evidence on implicit processing in a patient with semantic dementia who exhibits symptoms similar to those observed in associative agnosia, see Srinivas et al. in press). The lesions in patients with apperceptive agnosia who have radiologically confirmed diagnoses vary considerably. There is, however, evidence showing that regions bordering around the temporoparietal junction in the right hemisphere are frequently implicated (McCarthy & Warrington 1990).

Today, evidence for preserved implicit processing of visual information related to objects comes exclusively from single-case studies conducted by Goodale, Milner and their colleagues with indirect tests of object processing in their agnosic patient D.F. (Goodale et al. 1991, Humphrey et al. 1991, Milner et al. 1991, Goodale et al. 1994a,b,c). Owing to carbon monoxide intoxication, D.F. sustained a lesion to the occipital poles bilaterally that extends into ventral occipital and dorsal occipitoparietal regions while sparing medial aspects of primary visual cortex (V1). She suffers from a severe apperceptive agnosia. Whereas many of her low-level visual functions remain essentially normal, D.F. shows a profound deficit in recognizing objects on tests that involve naming and copying of objects, matching pictures of objects to a given name and making same–different judgements for pairs of simple objects that differ in shape (e.g. square versus rectangle) (Milner et al. 1991). D.F.'s impairment in object recognition is further characterized by severe discrimination deficits on tasks that involve the conscious visual perception of single attributes such as orientation, size and shape. These deficits, however, contrast sharply with her intact performance on indirect tests of implicit knowledge of these attributes.

To evaluate orientation discrimination, Milner et al. (1991) presented D. F. with an upright disk containing a large slot, the orientation of which could be varied. When asked to judge the orientation of the slot verbally, D.F. performed poorly. This explicit orientation discrimination deficit could also be seen when the judgement was elicited non-verbally by asking the patient to choose which of four line orientations matched the orientation of the target slot or to orient her hand in accordance with the tilt. In contrast, D.F. showed intact implicit knowledge about the orientation of the slot when she was asked to reach out and post a hand-held card through the slot of the disc. Well ahead of arrival at the slot, D.F. matched the card orientation to that of the target slot, indicating her well-preserved capacity to co-ordinate motor behaviour in direct relation to the orienation of a visually presented object. Similar observations were made when D.F.'s size discrimination abilities were evaluated. For this purpose, Goodale et al. (1991) constructed rectangular white plaques of equal area but different length and width ratios, ranging from a square to an elongated rectangle. In a perceptual estimation task, D.F. showed a severe deficit when she was asked to indicate with the index finger and thumb of her hand the width of the plaques placed in front of her. Unlike control subjects' estimates, D.F.'s estimates did not change systematically as a function of the width of the objects. However, Goodale et al. showed that D.F. could process visually perceived information about size in a prehension task which does not require an explicit judgement of size. When asked to reach out and pick up the objects whose width she could not estimate, the aperture between the index finger and thumb was scaled to the actual size of the particular object she was going to pick up, well before contact with the object was made.

In a related study, Goodale et al. (1994a) compared D.F.'s ability to make perceptual judgements about objects that vary in shape with her ability to express implicit knowledge of shape by positioning her fingers correctly on the boundaries of objects for the purpose of grasping them.

The shapes used in this study had smoothly bounded contours and lacked clear symmetry. Therefore, in order to pick up the object, the entire contour envelope of the shape has to be analysed to determine stable grasp points. D.F. had no difficulty in determining stable grasp points and picking up the objects by directly placing her finger and thumb on the appropriate grasp points. In sharp contrast, D.F. failed to apprehend information consciously about the shape of these objects. When asked to judge whether two shapes were either the same or different, she scored very poorly in comparison with normal controls. Taken together, the findings obtained with D.F. indicate that deficits in consciously apprehending visual information about the orientation, size and shape of objects, as assessed in verbal or manual reports about the perceived stimulus attributes, can co-occur with a preserved ability to express implicit knowledge about these stimulus attributes during aiming and prehension movements.

However, research by Goodale and his colleagues (Goodale et al. 1994b,c) provides evidence to suggest that the preserved processing abilities are limited in certain ways. Goodale et al. (1994b) reported that sensitivity to the size of objects in manual prehension was only observed in D.F. when she was allowed to grasp objects in direct response to perceiving them. Unlike normal subjects, D.F. did not show scaling of her hand aperture for object size in pantomimed movements when a delay of 2s or more was introduced between viewing the object and grasping it. In other words, no signs of preserved processing of object size was observed when D.F. had to direct movements to remembered rather than physically present objects. Also, unlike normal subjects, D.F. did not show anticipatory scaling of her grasp when she was asked to pantomime a grasping movement beside a continuously visible object.

In another study, Goodale et al. (1994c) focused on the limits of orientation and pattern processing in D.F. Using modifications of the previously described task, that requires guiding simply shaped objects into slots of varying orientation, it was found that D.F. could not process information about the orientation of objects implicitly when the shape of an object is defined by more than one orientation (e.g. shape of the letter T) and these multiple orientations have to be conjoined in order to perform the goal-directed movements successfully. In addition, Goodale et al. found that D.F.'s ability to process orientation information was limited in that it only occurred when orientation had to be extracted from differences in luminance contrasts, but not when it had to be extracted from differences in texture or spatial frequency. In those conditions in which she failed, succcessful performance is dependent on constructing the orientation of objects perceptually by applying the

Gestalt principle of good continuity. Taken together, these findings suggest that D.F.'s preserved abilities to process object attributes implicitly are highly constrained. Goodale et al. suggest that the observed constraints reflect limitations of an action system that computes viewer-centred object representations, which are necessary for the manipulation and movement of objects, and that operates without conscious awareness. We elaborate on Goodale et al.'s interpretation of these findings in the following section on the evaluation of models.

Importantly, there is also evidence showing that D.F. exhibits implicit knowledge of object attributes when the knowledge is probed with indirect perceptual tasks that do not have a visuomotor component. Humphrey et al. (1991) investigated the McCollough effect in D.F. The McCollough effect is a colour after-effect that is contingent on the specific orientation of grating patterns. The procedure which Humphrey et al. used to investigate this effect in D.F. consisted of three phases. In the first phase, D.F. was exposed to test patterns composed of black-and-white horizontal and black-and-white vertical gratings. When D.F. was asked to specify the orientation of the subcomponents of the gratings explicitly she was seriously impaired in making these judgements. In the second phase, D.F. was adapted to a green-and-black vertical grating which alternated with a red-and-black horizontal grating for a total presentation time of 10 min. In the third phase, the colour after-effect induced by the adaptation phase was tested. The black-and-white test patterns used in the first phase were presented again. They subtended the same visual angle as the gratings used in the adaptation phase. D.F. was asked to indicate whether she saw any colours. Like normal people, she reported seeing colour after-effects on all composite test patterns with the horizontal subcomponent of each pattern looking greenish and the vertical one looking pinkish. As in normal people, the presence of the after-effect was strongly dependent on the congruency of the angles of the subcomponents used in the adaptation and the test phase. In a second experiment, Humphrey et al. (1991) demonstrated a preserved McCollough after-effect in an orientation discrimination task with oblique gratings. These gratings are more difficult to discriminate than horizontal–vertical gratings. The observation that D.F. reported a segregation of colours in both experiments indicates that orientation information was processed to an extent that allowed her to tag colours to different orientations.

In summary, the studies on D.F. show that implicit knowledge of visual attributes that are crucial for object identification can be preserved in a patient with apperceptive agnosia. The processed information may be used to guide visuomotor responses as well as perceptual judgements if the judgements are not on the attribute in question. It must be kept in mind, however, that the evidence supporting this conclusion is based on studies with the same single patient. Replications in other patients with a comparable impairment in object recognition are necessary to ensure that the evidence is reliable and strongly supports the conclusions regarding the characteristics and boundaries of processing object information without conscious awareness. Evidence from studies in normal people, which will be exemplified in the evaluation section, can provide additional insights towards this end.

10.5.2 Evaluation of the three models

10.5.2.1 Distinct knowledge model

The findings on implicit knowledge about visually perceived object attributes in apperceptive object agnosia currently provides the strongest support for the distinct knowledge model. Goodale & Milner (1992) have argued that the two cortical visual pathways are differentially involved in expressing implicit and explicit knowledge about object attributes. They suggest that the ventral pathway mediates the conscious visual identification of objects, whereas the dorsal pathway mediates "the required sensorimotor transformations for visually guided actions directed at such objects" (Goodale & Milner 1992: 20). It is not the case that the ventral pathway is the conscious repository of output from the dorsal pathway, as the disconnection model might suggest. Rather, the types of visual information or representations that are computed by the two pathways are qualitatively different. Milner (Milner 1995, Milner & Goodale 1995) proposed that object representations are viewer-centred in the dorsal pathway to allow for fine and rapid visuomotor co-ordination. In contrast, the representations are object-centred in the ventral pathway to permit identification that is not hampered by changes in view, orientation and size. In keeping with this hypothesis, the ventral pathway can form long-lasting memory representations of objects, whereas the dorsal pathway has a rapidly decaying memory of the constantly changing representations that are necessary to support online visuomotor interactions with objects. In the studies by Goodale & Milner that we reviewed, the division of labour between the dorsal and ventral pathways has primarily been shown to hold for information about orientation and size. However, it may be expected to hold for other types of information as well. For example, Milner & Goodale (1995) suggest that information about spatial location is also coded differently in both pathways.

Support for Goodale & Milner's model or, speaking more generally, for the distinct knowledge model, comes not only from studies on visual object processing in patients with lesions in the ventral visual pathway, but also from a study on visual object processing in an optic ataxic patient with bilateral dorsal parietal lobe lesions (Jakobson et al. 1991). This patient's pattern of preserved and impaired functions was opposite to that of the object agnosic D.F.: Whereas this patient had no difficulty in recognizing line drawings of common objects, her ability to use visual information in order to pick up such objects was severely impaired. For example, when asked to reach out for a small block that varied in size from trial to trial, the magnitude of the aperture between her index finger and thumb did not vary systematically with the side of the block as the movement unfolded. In combination with the research on D.F., these findings provide strong support for the distinct knowledge model because they suggest that implicit and explicit knowledge of object information can be double-dissociated.

If the distinct knowledge model is correct, it follows that functional dissociations similar to those observed in neurological patients should also be observed in normal people. Most importantly, information in the dorsal pathway should remain inaccessible to consciousness in normal people and there should be no difference between their behaviour and that of agnosic patients. In an experiment on the Titchener size illusion, Aglioti et al. (1995) showed that an individual's conscious estimate of the size of a central disk, as indicated by their performance on a perceptual matching task, was influenced by the size of the surrounding disks. In contrast, the scaling of grip aperture that was observed when subjects reached for the target disk was not affected by the surround and, thus, was more veridical. In other words, size estimates for the purpose of visuomotor control proved to be immune to the perceptual illusion. In another study, normal subjects were asked to reach for a bulb that could be inflated or deflated slightly during the reach without their knowledge (L. S. Jakobson, personal communication). The subjects modified their grasp aperture in mid-reach to accommodate the changes in bulb size while performing at chance in detecting the changes on a conscious level. This kind of evidence provides further support for the distinct knowledge model. In addition, it underscores the point that visual perception is not unified but can proceed along parallel pathways with one being conscious and the other not.

10.5.2.2 Degraded representation model and disconnection model

The degraded representation model cannot adequately account for the findings on agnosia that we have reviewed. Evidence of double dissociation between implicit and explicit knowledge of object attributes discredits this model with regard to visual object processing. If implicit knowledge reflects degraded explicit knowledge, and if impoverished representations are sufficient to support performance on tests of implicit but not of explicit knowledge, then it cannot be the case that performance on tests of implicit knowledge is impaired while that on tests of explicit knowledge is spared. However, this pattern of performance was seen in the optic ataxic patient investigated by Jakobson et al. (1991).

Evidence of double dissociation is equally troublesome for the disconnection model. Damage to the modules in which implicit knowledge is represented should, by necessity, also affect explicit knowledge. This should be the case because, according to this model, one type of knowledge feeds into the other.

Single dissociations between implicit and explicit knowledge, however, can be accommodated by both the disconnection or degraded representation models. For example, the preserved McCollough effect that was reported by Humphrey et al. (1991) suggests that implicit knowledge about line orientation may be expressed even when it does not guide action. Thus, this effect is not likely to be based on information that is processed in the dorsal pathway. These results can be interpreted in accordance with either the degraded representation or disconnection model. More extensive evidence of this sort would be needed to gain support for the models. Potential supportive evidence may come from studies of patients with associative object agnosia. It is possible that these patients process information about objects to a high level in the ventral pathway, but that they may possess no explicit knowledge of this information. Studies of implicit memory for objects suggest that perceptual information may be retained in perceptual modules or representation systems of the ventral pathway without the subject's awareness (Moscovitch 1992, Schacter et al. 1995, Srinivas et al., in press).

10.6 PURE ALEXIA

10.6.1 Representative findings

Pure alexia (or 'alexia without agraphia') is an acquired reading disorder which occurs in the context of otherwise well-preserved language abilities. The lesion that causes the disorder has most frequently been observed to affect the left inferior occipitotemporal cortex, in particular the projection fibres in the periventricular white matter (Damasio & Damasio 1983, Black & Behrmann 1994). Patients who suffer from this syndrome are unable to recognize whole words when these are presented visually. Because these patients usually retain the ability to identify single letters, they may succeed in reading accurately by relying on a laborious and time-consuming sequential letter-by-letter decoding strategy. A hallmark of the syndrome is that the patients' reading times for words increase monotonically as a function of the number of letters in the words (McCarthy & Warrington 1990). The evidence relevant to the concerns of this chapter comes from studies demonstrating that patients with pure alexia may be able to extract some information from whole words under experimental conditions in which explicit word identification by means of letter-by-letter decoding is impossible.

10.6.1.1 Implicit lexical knowledge

Several studies have shown that patients with pure alexia may be able to engage in lexical processing of letter strings under conditions in which the stimuli are presented too briefly to be identified via letter-by-letter reading. Shallice & Saffran (1986) reported that the lexical decision performance of a pure alexic patient was clearly above chance level for stimuli that he was unable to identify. Performance was found to be sensitive to word frequency in that it was better for high frequency than low frequency words, suggesting that it was mediated by processes that involve lexical access. Coslett & Saffran (1989) (see also Bub & Arguin 1995) extended this finding by showing in a group of four pure alexics that lexical decision performance, in contrast to letter-by-letter reading, was insensitive to word length. Moreover, they found that increasing the exposure duration of the stimuli did not improve performance on the lexical decision task, as would be expected if patients were using their letter-by-letter reading strategy. Coslett & Saffran's results therefore suggest that lexical access may be obtained independently from the "pathological" processes that lead to explicit word identification via letter-by-letter decoding. They further proposed that implicit knowledge in reading may be mediated by the right hemisphere (Moscovitch 1973, 1976, Saffran et al. 1980, Coltheart 1980, Coslett & Saffran 1994). This conjecture is supported by their additional findings that there was no evidence of implicit phonological knowledge, that residual reading was better for nouns than for functors, and that among nouns it was better for those of high than low imagery. Hemispherectomy and commissurotomy patients show a similar pattern of reading performance when the processing capacities of their isolated right hemisphere are examined (Coslett & Saffran 1994).

Further evidence for the preservation of lexical processing in the absence of explicit word identification comes from a study by Bub et al. (1989). These investigators tested the ability of a pure alexic to identify letters in familiar words, orthographically legal pseudo-words and random letter strings. They presented their patient with letter strings for 400 ms, followed by a pattern mask. Subsequently, the target stimulus was presented together with a lure that differed in terms of a single letter from the target. The patient was asked to select the stimulus that matched the masked one. Bub et al. found that their pure alexic, like normal people, exhibited a word superiority effect in that he performed better at identifying letters in real words and pseudo-words as compared with random letter strings. The accuracy of the patient's judgement was not affected by the serial position of the letter that distinguished the target from the lure when it was part of a word. In contrast, accuracy was better for letters in starting positions than in ending positions when they were part of a random letter string. This pattern of results indicates that the pure alexic was able to take advantage of the orthographic context of individual letters and was able to access words as lexical units without relying on the letter-by-letter reading strategy when he performed the letter identification task. Yet, when the words used in the letter identification task were displayed under the same conditions as before but the patient was asked to report the whole words, he failed to identify the majority of them. As expected in sequential letter-by-letter reading, he committed more errors by omitting or replacing letters in ending than in starting positions of the words.

Together, these findings suggest that pure alexics may demonstrate preserved lexical processing under conditions in which whole words do not have to be reported explicitly. It should be noted, however, that not all patients with pure alexia have been reported to show preserved lexical processing on lexical decision or letter identification tasks (Patterson & Kay 1982, Behrmann et al. 1990a).

10.6.1.2 Implicit semantic knowledge

There is also evidence suggesting that pure alexics can process the semantic content of words which they cannot report explicitly. Landis et al. (1980) described a patient with pure alexia who was unable to identify words or even letters that were displayed for 30ms in a tachistoscope. He denied seeing anything under these conditions. In marked contrast, he was successful at matching the majority of the stimulus words to items from an array of objects when asked to provide an intuitive choice. Because the preserved matching ability occurred in the absence of any stimulus awareness, this finding suggests that the patient processed the words' meaning implicitly. However, when tested 4 weeks later, his reading abilities had improved, allowing him to read some words that were presented for only 20ms. Now, he was unable to match more than one word to the corresponding object. Landis et al. concluded that partial letter-by-letter reading, as observed in the later test session, made the demonstration of preserved implicit reading impossible and that a "total functional disconnection" (Landis et al. 1980: 45), as observed initially, is necessary to show implicit reading abilities (for comparable effects in blindsight see Rafal et al. 1990). This finding is also consistent with the hypothesis that implicit processes in reading are mediated by the right hemisphere and that pathological processes in the left hemisphere may prevent or inhibit their expression (Sperry et al. 1969, Moscovitch 1973, 1976).

In a more controlled and more extensive investigation of another pure alexic, Shallice & Saffran (1986) replicated the finding that patients with this syndrome may be able to derive semantic information from words presented too briefly to be identified by the patients explicitly. Their patient was successful at making many but not all binary semantic classifications. For example, he correctly classified more than 80% of the words that he was unable to read at a presentation duration of 2s when the classifications were between living and non-living objects, authors and politicians, places inside and outside of Europe, or pleasant and unpleasant words, but performed worse on distinctions between leisure or work words, and between adjectives describing people or objects. A striking feature of his performance relates to observations which suggest that he may have used different reading strategies on the explicit identification and the semantic classification tasks. Whereas he seemed to use the serial letter-by-letter reading approach on the identification task by focusing on each word for the complete 2s period, he seemed to use an alternative strategy on the classification task by taking only a brief glance at the word and averting his eyes afterwards.

Coslett & Saffran (1989) provide further evidence for preserved semantic processing on classification and matching tasks. All of their four patients could derive some semantic information from rapidly presented words. They were successful in judging whether the referent of a word was edible, whether a word represented an animal name and whether a proper name was appropriate for a man or for a woman. The patients also performed better than chance on a semantic processing task that required the matching of a briefly presented word to one of two pictures of objects. Successful performance was even observed on a version of this task in which the two pictures represented objects from the same category (e.g. a giraffe versus a goat). This particular result suggests that the patients did not only have access to the semantic content of the words on a superordinate level but also to more specific information that allows for the discrimination between members of the same category.

Coslett & Saffran's (1989) findings lend additional support to the notion that semantic processing of briefly presented words may proceed in the absence of explicit word identification in pure alexia. Other studies, however, failed to obtain such evidence with matching and semantic classification tasks (Warrington & Shallice 1980, Patterson & Kay 1982). Coslett & Saffran (1989) suggest that the inconsistency between the latter studies and those with positive results may reflect methodological differences with respect to the task instructions provided. They argue that it may be crucial that patients are actively discouraged from engaging in unsuccessful letter-by-letter reading in order to show semantic processing in the absence of explicit word identification.

The results of a recent investigation by Moscovitch, Harman and Melo (unpublished observations) are consistent with Coslett and Saffran's hypothesis. Moscovitch et al. showed a preserved Stroop interference effect in a letter-by-letter reader. Although he was not required to read the words explicitly, rapid naming of the colour in which colour words were written took longer when the colour and the word were incongruent than when they were congruent. This effect was lost when the words were inverted. The results indicate that the semantic content of the written words affected the patient's responses.

Finally, Howard (1991) and Bub & Arguin (1995) used priming to show that briefly presented words can be processed semantically without awareness in pure alexia. Howard investigated whether the brief presentation of a prime word can bias the patients' definition of a subsequently encountered polysemous word. Howard asked his two patients to read and define a target word (e.g. "match") that was immediately preceded by a brief prime (e.g. the word "flame") which had a meaning closely related to one of the multiple meanings of the target. Although the patients were encouraged to report all the words that they saw, they never reported any of the primes and, after completion of the study, indicated that they were unaware of the fact that any stimuli had preceded the targets. Yet, in contrast to these explicit reports, one of the patients provided definitions of the targets that were in their large majority in accordance with the primed meaning, suggesting that the semantic content of the primes had been processed in the absence of any conscious awareness of the stimuli. Bub & Arguin (1995) reported preserved semantic priming in a patient with pure alexia on a lexical decision task. They showed that the patient's latencies of responses on a lexical decision task were affected by the semantic content of primes that preceded the target word with brief exposure durations (50 and 200ms).

10.6.2 Evaluation of the three models

10.6.2.1 Disconnection model
The findings on implicit knowledge in reading seem to be consistent with the disconnection model. The evidence suggests that subjects

cannot gain conscious access to information that they process implicitly at both a lexical and semantic level. In terms of the terminology used by proponents of these models, the pre-semantic perceptual modules (Moscovitch 1992) or representation systems (Schacter 1992b) in which visual word forms (Warrington & Shallice 1980) are represented are intact. It is only the output of these systems to consciousness that is lacking. Evidence of preserved repetition priming without conscious memory in a pure alexic patient supports the idea that these modules are disconnected from consciousness. Schacter et al. (1990) found that, although their patient could not identify words at short durations and could not remember having studied them, seeing the words in an earlier study phase improved her performance on a perceptual implicit test of memory.

The observation that semantic information can also be processed implicitly in pure alexia indicates that semantic processing is not the privileged domain of consciousness. One interpretation of these findings in light of the disconnection models is that the perceptual modules themselves have some limited propositional, semantic knowledge which accounts for the observed performance (see Fodor 1985 and related commentaries; Moscovitch & Umiltà 1990). Alternatively, it may be the case that the output from perceptual modules automatically activates some limited (associative) semantic information, but that this information does not gain access to consciousness (Moscovitch & Umiltà 1990, Tulving & Schacter 1990).

10.6.2.2 Degraded representation model

The findings are equally (or maybe more) consistent with a degraded representation model which relies on evidence showing that the lexical or semantic information which pure alexics process implicitly is impoverished in comparison with what normal people process during reading. Although pure alexics perform well above chance on lexical decision and some semantic classification tasks, they fall well below the virtually perfect performance that can be expected of normal people. Moreover, the observation that they perform poorly on some simple semantic classification tasks suggests that these patients do not process semantic information, even implicitly, in its entirety. In addition, they cannot derive phonological information from unidentified words. Thus, the preserved implicit reading abilities of pure alexics may reflect the remnants of a damaged conscious reading system.

Similar arguments have been made by Farah (1994) to support the degraded representation model. She also asserts that the preserved abilities of pure alexics to extract information at short exposure durations without conscious awareness is comparable with the pattern of performance that is observed in normal people, although shorter exposure durations and masks are needed to elicit this performance in normal subjects. This assertion receives support from computer simulations (e.g. Plaut & Shallice 1993) and from extensive studies on masked priming in normal people by Forster and his collaborators (Forster et al. 1990).

10.6.2.3 Distinct knowledge model

There is some evidence, however, that cannot be accommodated easily by either of the above models. The most damaging evidence, as Farah (1994) herself admits, is the repeated observation that as subjects become aware of the processed words and rely on conscious reading strategies, their performance may actually deteriorate. This observation is difficult to reconcile with the disconnection model because it states that explicit knowledge arises from making the output of implicit processes accessible to consciousness. Similarly, the degraded representation model would predict that, as knowledge becomes explicit, the quality of the representation should exceed that which supports implicit knowledge.

The above finding, however, can be accommodated by the distinct knowledge model. If knowledge in one system is distinct from the other, then it is reasonable to suppose that interference can arise when the two sources of knowledge are in conflict. One need only make the reasonable assumption that the system involved in explicit reading has privileged access to the control of voluntary responses. Thus, according to the model, as the conscious letter-by-letter strategy gains hold, decisions come to rely on inadequate explicit knowledge rather than reflecting preserved implicit knowledge.

The distinct knowledge model can also account for the dissociations between different types of information that can be processed with and without awareness in pure alexia. For example, in implicit reading, lexical (orthographic) knowledge is preserved but phonological knowledge is not, knowledge of root morphemes is preserved but knowledge about affixes is not, and imageable nouns are easier to read than non-imageable nouns and functors (Coslett & Saffran 1994). The pattern of preserved and impaired knowledge is consistent with the hypothesis that distinct systems, possibly one in the right hemisphere and the other in the left, are involved in processing of implicit and explicit knowledge, respectively. This is not to imply that all right hemisphere processes are unconscious (Eccles 1973), but rather to leave open the possibility that those processes in reading that are implicit may depend on the right hemisphere.

10.7 PROSOPAGNOSIA

10.7.1 Representative findings

Prosopagnosia is a neuropsychological syndrome that is characterized by cognitive impairments in visual processing of faces. Lesions causing the syndrome always include the occipitotemporal region of the right hemisphere (McCarthy & Warrington 1990). Although some evidence suggests that bilateral damage in posterior cortex is necessary for the deficit to occur (Damasio & Damasio 1986), the current consensus is that right hemisphere damage suffices (De Renzi 1986a, Sergent & Signoret 1992a). Most commonly, prosopagnosic patients are able to discriminate a face from a non-face stimulus but have trouble identifying specific individuals. Patients with prosopagnosia show impairments on explicit recognition tasks that involve the identification of famous individuals. They also perform poorly on delayed matching tasks in which they are first presented with unfamiliar faces and subsequently asked to select these from a larger array. Substantial evidence, however, has accumulated over the last decade which indicates that prosopagnosic patients possess implicit knowledge about the familiarity of faces, about face identity and about semantic information (accessed through faces). This evidence has been obtained with psychophysiological as well as behavioural measures.

10.7.1.1 Implicit knowledge of familiarity

Psychophysiological evidence which indicates preserved implicit knowledge of familiarity in prosopagnosia comes from a study in which event-related potential recordings were used to measure variations in electric brain activity in relation to face recognition. Renault et al. (1989) investigated the P300 component (see Ch. 7) of a prosopagnosic patient in a face recognition task. The patient generated higher P300 amplitudes at shorter latencies to familiar faces than to unfamiliar ones, although he was unable to recognize any of the familiar faces explicitly. In line with the widely accepted notion that variations in P300 amplitude reflect the detection of low probability events in categorization or discrimination tasks, larger amplitudes to familiar faces were only found when their probability of occurrence was lower than that of unfamiliar faces. These data indicate that the P300 component reflected the same cognitive processes in the prosopagnosic person as in normal people.

Additional psychophysiological evidence for preserved implicit knowledge of familiarity comes from studies by Tranel & Damasio (1985, 1988). These investigators asked four prosopagnosic patients simply to look at faces and measured skin conductance responses (SCRs) while the patients engaged in this activity. Familiar faces elicited more frequent and significantly larger SCRs than unfamiliar ones. This pattern of results also held for familiar faces to which the patients had been introduced after the onset of their neurological condition.

Greve & Bauer (1990) provide behavioural evidence for preserved implicit knowledge of familiarity in prosopagnosia. They used an indirect perceptual memory test (the mere exposure paradigm) to investigate repetition priming effects for novel faces in the prosopagnosic patient L.F. In an initial study block, L.F. was presented repeatedly with faces to which he had not previously been exposed. Subsequently, a forced-choice recognition test was administered to evaluate explicit memory performance for faces presented at study. In addition, the patient was required to indicate preferences within pairs of previously seen and unseen faces. Despite the fact that L.F. performed at chance when asked to recognize the previously presented faces, like normal control subjects, he showed a preference for target faces from the study block. These data suggest that mere exposure to a novel face can affect later processing of the same face in the absence of conscious recognition. In line with the data reported by Tranel & Damasio (1985, 1988), they suggest that prosopagnosics may acquire new implicit knowledge about the familiarity of faces.

Sergent & Poncet (1990) used an indirect test of familiarity in which they asked a prosopagnosic patient to match photographs of faces of identical individuals that were taken 30 years apart. The faces were from famous persons who were either unknown (coming from a foreign country) or known to her (coming from her domestic country). When asked to find matching faces of identical persons depicted in photographs at different ages, she performed the task faster for known than unknown faces, suggesting that she had implicit knowledge about their familiarity. In sharp contrast, when asked to identify the faces on a direct test of familiarity, she did not recognize any of the faces from persons that she knew by name. This pattern of performance was replicated by Sergent & Signoret (1992b) in another prosopagnosic patient.

10.7.1.2 Implicit knowledge of face identity

Bauer (1984) used SCRs to demonstrate preserved implicit knowledge of face identity in prosopagnosia. He presented faces of famous personalities and family members to a prosopagnosic patient and recorded SCRs while the patient tried to select the name that corresponded to a given face from a group of names in a forced-choice recognition procedure. The choices made by the patient were at chance and indicated no explicit recognition. Yet, he displayed larger electrodermal responses when the names correponded to the target face than when they did not. Bauer & Verfaellie (1988) replicated Bauer's results with a second prosopagnosic patient. In addition, they found no differential electrodermal responses when the familiar faces used came from persons whom the patient had not known pre-morbidly. These data suggest that for face identity, unlike familiarity, prosopagnosics may have implicit knowledge only when pre-morbidly stored face representations are available.

Bruyer et al. (1983) were the first to describe interference effects of preserved implicit knowledge in an indirect test of face identity. They applied a learning procedure in which their patient, Mr W., was asked to associate names with famous faces in multiple learning trials. The patient was severely impaired at identifying famous faces and at discriminating them from unfamiliar ones when asked for a recognition judgement. The crucial experimental manipulation in the learning task concerned the relation between the elements of a face–name pair. It could be either true or false, i.e. a famous face was either paired with the actual corresponding name or it was paired with an arbitrary name. Bruyer et al. observed that Mr W. had more difficulty learning untrue face–name pairs than true ones. Thus, although Mr W. failed to show explicit knowledge about the associations between faces and their corresponding names, preserved implicit face identity information interfered with the learning of incorrect face–name pairings. De Haan et al. (1987a) replicated the interference effect reported by Bruyer et al. with a prosopagnosic patient (P.H.) who could not recognize any familiar faces. De Haan et al. observed interference for faces which were familiar to P.H. pre-morbidly as well as for those of individuals whom he met post-morbidly. These results suggest that prosopagnoics may acquire new implicit knowledge about face identity. They are, however, at odds with the outcome of the psychopysiological study reported by Bauer & Verfaellie (1988).

Implicit knowledge of face identity has also been documented in a priming study in prosopagnosia. De Haan et al. (1992) investigated priming by using an indirect test of face identity. Reaction times were measured while the patient judged printed names as familiar or unfamiliar. Names were preceded by face primes that were either from the same individual or from neutral or unrelated individuals. The patient showed intact priming effects from faces to names in that his responses to names preceded by the face of the same individual were significantly faster than responses to names preceded by unrelated and neutral faces. In contrast, when asked to identify the faces that were used as primes on a direct test of face identity, the patient could not perform the task successfully.

Some researchers have argued that performance on direct forced-choice recognition tests may also reflect implicit knowledge of face identity in prosopagnosia. In three studies (Sergent & Poncet 1990, De

Haan et al. 1991, Sergent & Signoret 1992b), prosopagnosic patients were presented with faces of famous people and were asked to select the corresponding name from a pair consisting of a lure and a target. In each of these studies, it was found that prosopagnosic patients performed this task at a level significantly above chance. Several characteristics of the patients' responses suggest that they performed the task without consciously recognizing the faces. Most importantly, the patients reported experiencing no familiarity with the faces while performing the task. When asked how they performed it, they indicated that they were purely guessing. Furthermore when tested on "deceit trials" in which none of the names corresponded to the faces presented, the patients continued to perform the task without any noticeable change in their behaviour. Taken together, these observations suggest that the prosopagnosic patients performed the forced-choice task on the basis of implicit rather than explicit knowledge of face identity.

10.7.1.3 Implicit semantic knowledge

De Haan et al. (1987a) and Young & De Haan (1988) asked whether the implicit knowledge that is reflected in interference during learning of untrue associations between names and faces is limited to names or whether it includes semantic information as well. De Haan et al. (1987a) observed interference when they asked their prosopagnosic patients to associate untrue or true occupations with the faces of famous people. No interference, however, was observed when learning required associating famous faces with untrue first names (rather than full names as in Bruyer et al. 1983) or with more specific untrue semantic information such as the political parties of famous politicians or the particular sporting categories of famous sportsmen (Young & De Haan 1988). Sergent & Poncet (1990) observed interference in a prosopagnosic during learning of untrue associations between famous faces and occupations. In addition, Sergent & Signoret (1992b) showed that interference may also be observed when patients are required to learn untrue associations between famous faces and residence countries. Taken together, the data on interference effects in learning tasks suggest that some but not all types of semantic information are accessible through faces and can be expressed as implicit knowledge in prosopagnosia.

Interference deriving from semantic information that is associated with familiar faces was also observed by De Haan et al. (1987b). De Haan et al. instructed their prosopagnosic patient P.H. to classify names according to whether they belonged to politicians or not. Simultaneously with each name, a distractor face was presented that P.H. was asked to ignore. Classification responses were slower when the distractor face was drawn from the category that was non-congruent with that of the target name than when it was taken form the congruent category. This pattern of response times parallels the one observed in normal people (Young et al. 1986). Unlike normal people, however, P.H. performed at chance when asked to classify the faces as belonging to politicians or non-politicians. Because P.H. showed interference from faces on the classification task for names but could not classify the faces themselves, these data indicate that he could derive semantic information from the faces only implicitly. A similar dissociation between preserved interference effects and impaired explicit classification abilities has also been reported by De Haan et al. (1992) and by Sergent & Signoret (1992b) using variations of the same paradigm.

There are also studies which have shown intact semantic priming effects for faces in prosopagnosia. Young et al. (1988) investigated cross-domain semantic priming effects in P.H. Reaction times were measured while he judged printed names as familiar or unfamiliar. Names were preceded by primes that were either familiar faces of individuals who were closely related to those referred by the target names or familiar faces of unrelated individuals. Like normal controls, P.H. showed semantic priming effects in that his responses to names preceded by related faces were significantly faster than responses to names preceded by unrelated faces. In a second experiment that included a neutral condition with face primes of unfamiliar individuals, it was shown that the semantic priming effects reflected facilitation of decisions for related prime–target pairs rather than inhibition of decisions for unrelated prime–target pairs. In general, P.H.'s responses across experimental conditions in the priming tasks were influenced by the presence of familiar faces in the same way as normal subjects' responses. In sharp contrast, however, he showed a marked impairment when asked to identify the familiar faces that were used as primes.

Not all studies on implicit knowledge in prosopagnosia have shown positive results. Several investigators found either limited or no evidence for implicit knowledge of familiarity, face identity and semantic information in prosopagnosia (Bauer & Verfaellie 1988, Newcombe et al. 1989, Sergent & Villemure 1989, Etcoff et al. 1991, McNeil & Warrington 1991, Humphreys et al. 1992, Sergent & Signoret 1992c). To interpret the observed inconsistencies across studies, Newcombe et al. (1989) and Sergent & Signoret (1992c) referred to the distinction between mnestic and perceptual deficits that may underlie different forms of prosopagnosia (see De Renzi 1986b). According to Newcombe et al. and Sergent & Signoret, prosopagnosic patients who do not show implicit knowledge are those who have a perceptual impairment in analysing incoming information about the physical characteristics of faces (apperceptive prosopagnosia). Intact perceptual information, however, may be necessary for an expression of implicit knowledge in prosopagnosia. In line with this argument, the prosopagnosic patients who do show signs of preserved implicit knowledge are those who exhibit a mnestic deficit (mnestic or associative prosopagnosia). They exhibit no impairments in the perceptual analysis of faces but rather in recovering face information from memory. This view, therefore, suggests that preserved perceptual abilities are a prerequisite for implicit knowledge in prosopagnosia. However, because implict knowledge has been shown to be preserved in patients with perceptual impairments in other visual domains (e.g. apperceptive object agnosia) (Milner et al. 1991), the evidence indicates that intact perceptual abilities may only be a prerequisite for accessing information about the familiarity, identity and semantic associations of faces.

10.7.2 Evaluation of the three models

10.7.2.1 Disconnection model
The evidence of preserved implicit knowledge about face familiarity and identity is consistent with the disconnection model (for a specific model on face processing see De Haan et al. 1992). In line with the model's predictions, patients with prosopagnosia, in particular of the mnestic or associative type, have preserved knowledge of facial identity despite not being able to access that knowledge consciously. The pre-semantic perceptual module or representation system for faces appears to be intact. The evidence reported by Greve & Bauer (1990) that repetition priming (implicit perceptual memory) for faces is intact and pre-semantic in this type of prosopagnosia, speaks directly in favour of this point. In apperceptive prosoagnosia, the module itself may be damaged, so that even implicit knowledge of faces and implicit memory for them is impaired or lost (for discussions see Moscovitch & Umiltà 1990, 1991, Moscovitch 1992).

As in pure alexia, the preservation of some semantic knowledge related to faces causes difficulties for disconnection models that postulate only access to pre-semantic knowledge in perceptual modules. The models would have to be modified to include some limited types of (associative) semantic information in the perceptual modules or to postulate that some associations between perceptual modules and semantics can be activated automatically without being delivered to consciousness (see Moscovitch & Umiltà 1990).

10.7.2.2 Degraded representation model
Farah (Farah 1994, Farah et al. 1993) has argued that the evidence of implicit knowledge in prosopagnosia is most consistent with a degraded

representation model. To support this claim, Wallace & Farah (1992) trained a group of normal subjects on a set of face–name associations and then allowed them to forget these associations over a period of 6 months. They found that, at the end of this delay, normal subjects could not remember the face–name associations when tested explicitly. In contrast, they showed savings in relearning the previously studied "true" but not "false" face–name associations. According to Farah (1994), these data support the degraded representation model, because the preserved knowledge observed in normal people after forgetting parallels that of patients with prosopagnosia. If normal forgetting involves the degradation of representations, as Farah assumes, then the similarity between the results in normal people and prosopagnosics suggests that residual knowledge in prosopagnosia may reflect the expression of explicit knowledge based on degraded representations. The strongest evidence to support her argument comes, according to Farah, from neural network simulations (Farah et al. 1993). The investigators "lesioned" a simple computational model of face recognition in those parts of the network that subserve the perceptual analysis of incoming face information. They found that the lesioned network behaved similarly to prosopagnosic patients on several tasks that were designed to simulate those that tap implicit knowledge in prosopagnosia (see also Burton et al. 1991).

Not all the data on prosopagnosia, however, are consistent with the degraded representation model. At least for some patients, the perceptual analysis of faces does not seem to be impaired (Sergent & Signoret 1992a, Young 1994), although the degraded model would require that it should be. Also, Young et al. (1988) showed that the size of the priming effect from faces to names was the same as that from names to names, a result that is unexpected if facial representations alone were degraded. As for Wallace & Farah's demonstration of functional deficits resembling prosopagnosia in normal people, its value rests on the assumption that degraded memory representations of faces in normal people are functionally equivalent to degraded perceptual representations of faces in prosopagnosic patients. There is no basis for this assumption other than the comparable effects that Wallace & Farah obtained on their relearning task with two normal subjects. To be convincing, it would be necessary to provide converging evidence that the nature of impaired recognition of forgotten faces in normal people is similar to impaired identification in prosopagnosic patients. In agreement with Farah, we believe that currently the computational model provides the most compelling evidence in favour of the degraded representation model, but we maintain that more direct evidence obtained with human subjects is needed.

10.7.2.3 Distinct knowledge model

The distinct knowledge model receives little support from studies on implicit knowledge in prosopagnosia, but neither is it disconfirmed by the evidence. Thus far, it is not known whether the facial representations underlying explicit and implicit knowledge are qualitatively different from one another. The observation that implicit knowledge of faces is associated with only limited types of semantic information may be a hint that some differences exist. Other evidence that is relevant is the often reported observation that face recognition, at least in some prosopagnosics, is part or feature-based whereas that in normal people is holistic or configural (Farah 1990, Bruce & Humphreys 1994, Carey & Diamond 1994). The question remains as to whether the representation of faces that underlies implicit knowledge is of one type and that which mediates explicit knowledge is of another. In this regard, it would be important to know whether part-based facial representations are found only in apperceptive prosopagnosics who do not possess implicit knowledge, or whether they also occur in mnestic or associative prosopagnosics who do. If the latter is the case, it would provide strong evidence for the distinct knowledge model in that it would suggest that part-based representations are adequate for implicit but not explicit knowledge about familiarity, identity and semantics.

Support for the distinct knowledge model could also come from studies showing that deficits in implicit and explicit face knowledge can be double-dissociated. Tranel et al. (1995) recently reported that patients with ventromedial frontal lobe lesions show a pattern of impairments in facial processing opposite to that seen in prosopagnosia. These patients may recognize the identity of familiar faces normally while they fail to generate corresponding discriminatory SCRs. However, it seems likely that the observed deficit reflects an output-specific impairment in controlling autonomic somatic responses to emotionally significant stimuli, rather than selectively impaired implicit knowledge about the familiarity of faces (see Damasio et al. 1991). Nevertheless, because prosopagnosic patients with damage to the occipitotemporal cortex show normal SCRs to familar faces, the pattern of findings hints that brain regions other than those damaged in prosopagnosia provide input about faces to the ventromedial frontal regions which presumably control SCRs.

10.8 NEGLECT

10.8.1 Representative findings

"Neglect" refers to an impaired ability to attend to and to report objects and events which occur on the side of space contralateral to the lesioned hemisphere (for descriptions see Rafal 1994, Weintraub & Mesulam 1989). Neglect may be demonstrated by asking patients to cancel each item in an array of widely scattered differently oriented lines. Patients with neglect will fail on this task by omitting to cancel lines on the contralesional side of the page on which the array is presented. When asked to bisect a line, neglect patients may behave as if the left side of the line were absent. They may begin reading or writing in the middle of the page and omit the contralesional side of objects when asked to copy them. In less severe cases, the deficit may become evident only under conditions of competing bilateral stimulation. The presentation of a single stimulus anywhere in the visual field may result in an accurate description of it, whereas simultaneous presentation of two stimuli may lead to an accurate description of the ipsilesional but an omission of the contralesional stimulus. This milder form of neglect is referred to as "extinction" (Weintraub & Mesulam 1989). Although neglect often co-occurs with hemianopia, it can clearly be dissociated from it. Neglect for a contralesional stimulus may be observed even when both the ipsilesional and the contralesional stimuli are presented in the intact part of the visual field (Làdavas et al. 1990). Neglect takes its severest form following lesions to the right parietal lobe, but may also occur following left-sided parietal lesions, unilateral lesions to the frontal cortex, and subcortical lesions to the pulvinar (Gainotti et al. 1986, Weintraub & Mesulam 1989, Vallar 1993).

The behaviour of patients with neglect on tests that require an overt report of events in the contralesional field, such as the ones discussed, suggests that they are completely unaware of these events. However, recent research using indirect tests has revealed that patients may process information in the affected field up to a remarkably high level. This research is surveyed in the following section. Because of space limitations, research on neglect dyslexia is not included in this review (see Behrmann 1994, Berti et al. 1994, Wallace 1994).

10.8.1.1 Implicit knowledge of perceptual information

Volpe et al. (1979) were among the first to demonstrate that neglect patients are influenced by information in the neglected field. Four patients with right parietal lobe tumours were shown pairs of pictures of common objects or of familiar words simultaneously to both visual fields and were asked to name the stimuli. The pairs consisted of identical or different stimuli. On the trials, in which the stimuli were different, all patients showed extinction in naming the stimuli in the left field. Two of the patients "felt that something had appeared" (Volpe et al. 1979: 723) in the left visual field, but were strongly impaired in naming it. The two other patients were completely unaware that anything had been presented. In contrast, on a test in which patients were asked to judge whether the stimuli that made up a pair were the same or different, the patients performed at high levels of accuracy, indicating that they had some preserved knowledge about the stimuli, which they could not identify explicitly. Accurate performance was observed, although the patients who were unaware of the stimuli presented to the left visual field asserted "that the task was 'silly', since there was no stimulus in the left visual field with which to compare the right visual field stimulus" (Volpe et al. 1979: 723). This pattern of results was also replicated in other patients with neglect (Karnath & Hartje 1987, Karnath 1988; but see Farah et al. 1991). Milovic-Prelec et al. (1994) showed that neglect patients may be sensitive to the onset of a stimulus in the neglected field although they report not being aware of it. In a speeded simple yes/no detection task for a dot presented to the left or the right visual field, their patient exhibited neglect by incorrectly responding with "no" on the majority of trials on which a dot was presented to the left visual field. Yet, he made these incorrect rejections more quickly than the correct rejections when no stimulus was actually presented. The latency distribution for denied contralesional dots matched the latency distribution for detected ipsilesional dots rather than the slower distribution for true absence trials. Thus, whereas the content of the patient's report indicated no awareness of most of the contralesional stimuli, the response times for these reports indicated that the patient processed these stimuli implicitly. Similar evidence for preserved implicit processing of stimulus onset in neglect was reported by Marzi et al. (1996). These investigators used a simple RT task (described in Section 10.3; Marzi et al. 1986) to demonstrate an intact summation effect across the two hemi-fields.

Driver et al. (1992) demonstrated that perceptual grouping processes which serve to segregate figure from ground in visual images may proceed normally in the neglected field when tested indirectly. Driver et al. explored the effects of symmetry about the vertical axis of shapes on figure–ground segregation in a patient with severe left-sided neglect. It is well documented that, other factors being equal, symmetrical shapes are seen as figures against asymmetrical backgrounds (Rock 1983). Because symmetry depends on the correspondence between reflected sides, sensitivity to symmetry about the vertical requires the processing of both the right and the left sides of shapes at the stage of figure–ground segregation. The patient was presented with displays of pseudo-random shapes that alternated from green to red. Either the green or the red shapes of a display were symmetrical. The patient was asked to decide for each display whether he saw green shapes on a red background or red shapes on a green background. He showed the usual effect of symmetry on figure–ground segregation and no bias towards reporting the rightmost colour, suggesting that the left side of the shapes was processed at the stage of segregation. However, when asked to make a direct symmetry judgement for individual shapes from the displays, he was unable to do so. This impairment was observed when the symmetry was about the vertical axis, and not when it was about the horizontal axis, indicating that it reflected his neglect of left-sided information.

Using a flanker task, Audet et al. (1991) asked patients with neglect to name a target letter as quickly as possible. The letter, either a T or a K, was presented in a cued location. The experimental manipulation concerned the presentation of a flanking letter that served as context to the left or above the target letter. In normal people, it has been shown that the presentation of identical letters as flanker and target (e.g. TT) leads to facilitation of the response to the target in comparison to when a neutral letter (e.g. OT) is used as flanker. This effect has been suggested to occur at the level of letter encoding (Taylor 1977). Audet et al. found that two patients with left-sided neglect did not notice the presence of the flanking letter when it was presented to the left of the target but reported seeing it when it occurred on top of it. Despite his inability to report the left-sided flankers, one of the patients showed a significant facilitatory effect in his naming latencies when the onset of the flanker preceded that of the target by 250 ms.

In a control experiment, Audet et al. showed that the facilitatory effect for the left-sided flanker was not affected by how well the flanker predicted the target. It was not larger when the flanker matched the target in 80% of the trials than when it matched in 50% of the trials as it should have been if the flanker information had been used voluntarily. In combination with the patient's inability to report explicitly the presence of the left-sided flanker, this result suggests that the observed facilitation resulted from implicit processing of information about letter identity in the neglected field.

Implicit processing of letter flankers in the neglected field was also observed in another patient by Fuentes & Humphreys (1996) using a modified version of the flanker task. The investigators showed that flankers affected RTs to target letters even when flankers and targets differed in case, suggesting that letter identity can be processed on an abstract level in the neglected field. Finally, using a colour version of the flanker task as an indirect test, Cohen et al. (1995) showed preserved implicit processing of colour information in the neglected field in two other patients.

10.8.1.2 Implicit knowledge of semantic information

Berti et al. (1992) followed up on Volpe et al.'s (1979) study by examining with a similar matching task to what stage information is processed implicitly in neglect. They asked their patient to judge whether two pictures of common objects presented simultaneously to each visual field depicted objects of the same name. In addition, the patient was asked to name them. On "same" trials, the pictures were either identical, depicted different views of the same object, or depicted different exemplars from the same name category (e.g. two different chairs). On "different" trials, the pictures depicted two objects that did not share a common name. While the patient studied by Berti et al. was always aware that something had been presented to both visual fields, she showed extinction for the left visual field in that she was severely impaired in naming the objects presented there. In contrast, she was highly accurate on the matching task. Her performance was above chance even on "same" trials on which the depicted objects shared the same name but represented different exemplars of the same category, as well as on trials on which they represented different viewpoints of the same object. This pattern of findings indicates that the judgements were not based on low-level, viewpoint-specific information. The finding that even the judgements for two exemplars with the same name were above chance suggests that processing of information about objects in the neglected field extended to a semantic level. Because the same–different judgements did not require any explicit report of information presented in the neglected field and because accurate performance on these judgements occurred in the presence of impaired explicit object identification, the results of Berti et al.'s study may be interpreted to suggest that categorical information about objects can be processed implicitly in the neglected field.

The results of studies by Marshall & Halligan (1988) and Bisiach & Rusconi (1990) suggest that matching judgements for stimuli in the intact and the neglected fields may not always be preserved in neglect. Marshall & Halligan presented a patient with severe neglect for the left field with the drawing of an intact house and that of a burning house. The drawings were presented on top of each other and the features that distinguished the two houses were located on the left side. When asked to tell whether the houses were the same or different, the patient judged them to be the same, indicating that she was unaware of any difference in the neglected field. However, even though she was unable to perform a matching judgement, she demonstrated preserved processing of information in the neglected field on another task. When forced to choose the house in which she would prefer to live she indicated a consistent preference for the intact house. At the same time, she was unable to report the flames as the stimulus features on which her judgement was based.

Bisiach & Rusconi (1990) replicated Marshall & Halligan's study in a group of four neglect patients using an extended set of stimuli. Their patients were also unable to detect left-sided differences in pairs of drawings on the matching task. In their preference judgements, however, the patients chose the drawing of the object that had the preferable features on some trials only. When asked to specify the reasons for making their choices they made no reference to any of the relevant differences but rather to insignificant or non-existing differences, regardless of whether they chose the objectively preferable or non-preferable object. Bisiach & Rusconi's results may be interpreted to suggest that the left-sided differences of which the patients were consciously unaware may have been processed on some level. These processes may then have triggered a more extensive perceptual analysis of stimulus features in the non-neglected side of space or may have triggered confabulations. Together, the results of the two studies indicate that preference judgement in neglect may be affected implicitly by information that is neglected on a matching task. In addition, the data presented by Bisiach & Rusconi suggest that the preference judgements of neglect patients may only be based on an implicit perceptual rather than on a semantic analysis of the stimulus in the neglected field.

More clear-cut evidence supporting the notion that information in the neglected field is processed on a semantic level comes from studies on semantic priming. McGlinchey-Berroth et al. (1993) investigated whether the lateralized presentation of a picture prime facilitates performance for semantically related target words on a lexical decision task. The authors presented individual pictures of common objects which were immediately followed by a letter string that could either be a word or a non-word, and that was presented in a central location. Words were either semantically related to the picture or neutral. Priming on this task is demonstrated by showing that latencies in the lexical-decision task are faster for related than for neutral words. Like normal controls, patients with left-sided neglect showed equivalent priming effects when the primes were presented to the left or to the right visual field. Because there was no physical similarity between primes and targets, the observation of priming in this study indicates that the primes presented in the neglected field underwent semantic processing. This processing occurred when there was no requirement to provide any verbal report or another form of explicit response to the picture primes. In a subsequent experiment, the patients had the same pictures and presentation conditions but were tested with a direct test which required them to provide an explicit response to the lateralized pictures in a delayed matching-to-sample task. After viewing a picture in either visual field, patients had to match it with one of two pictures that were presented centrally on top of each other. In this task, patients had marked difficulty matching pictures presented to the left visual field. Together, these results provide evidence for a dissociation between implicit semantic processing and explicit conscious awareness of information in the neglected field. This type of dissociation was also found in two other studies in which implicit processing of neglected information was examined with a semantic priming paradigm (Berti & Rizzolatti 1992, Làdavas et al. 1993).

Làdavas et al. (1993) extended McGlinchey-Berroth et al.'s findings by showing that semantic priming from a stimulus presented to the neglected field may also be obtained on the lexical decision task if the prime is a semantically related word rather than a picture. Furthermore, Berti & Rizzolatti (1992) showed that pictures presented to the neglected field may also prime performance on a semantic categorization task for target pictures that are presented to the non-neglected field. In both studies, priming was observed even when patients were completely unaware of the primes. Together, the results of the studies on semantic priming suggest that verbal and pictorial information which patients may neglect when asked to provide an explicit report may, nevertheless, be processed up to a semantic level implicitly.

10.8.2 Evaluation of the three models

All of the syndromes discussed in previous sections were concerned with domain-specific disorders. Although there is evidence that neglect also can be domain specific (Rizzolatti et al. 1994), most of the evidence suggests that typically it affects a variety of domains such as processing of words, faces and objects, and may occur in more than one modality. Therefore, unlike for the other syndromes, the loss of explicit knowledge cannot be attributed to damage to a single perceptual module or knowledge. One may assume that there is an attentional module which registers information about any abrupt or salient change in the perceptual world (Moscovitch & Umiltà 1990), but even if this were the case this assumption would be of little use in analysing the pattern of preserved implicit and impaired explicit knowledge in neglect.

In recent years, the deficits in neglect have been viewed as resulting from degraded internal spatial representation of the contralesional side (Bisiach & Luzzatti 1978, Bisiach et al. 1979, Bisiach & Berti 1994), the content of which cannot be apprehended consciously. An alternative interpretation is that the spatial representations are intact but that their contralesional side does not capture attention automatically, as would be necessary for its content to gain access to consciousness.

According to the latter interpretation, if attention is deployed voluntarily to the neglected side, information can be registered at a conscious level (Moscovitch & Umiltà 1990, 1991). These two interpretations correspond to the degraded representation and the disconnection models, respectively.

10.8.2.1 Disconnection model and degraded representation model

The initial formulation of the degraded representation model made no allowance for the possibility that information on the neglected side of space could be preserved as implicit knowledge. Proponents of the disconnection model, in contrast, recognized that the model predicts the existence of such knowledge (see Schacter et al. 1988, Moscovitch & Umiltà 1990). The findings surveyed in this section on implicit knowledge in neglect are consistent with this prediction. To gain strong support for the disconnection model, however, it would be necessary to show that the implicit knowledge that is derived from the neglected field is comparable in quality with that which is available to consciousness. Such evidence is provided by McGlinchey-Berroth et al.'s (1993) finding that primes in the neglected field are as effective as those in the intact field in producing semantic priming on a lexical decision task (but see Farah 1994).

More recently, a number of investigators have shown that even the degraded representation model can accommodate evidence of implicit knowledge in neglect. According to the model, this evidence can be accommodated if it is assumed that the quality of the visual input from the neglected field, although impoverished, is sufficient to support implicit knowledge (Farah et al. 1991, Farah 1994; see also Behrmann et al. 1990b, Mozer & Behrmann 1990). The degraded representation model can account easily for evidence of preserved implicit detection of stimulus onset (Mijovic-Prelec et al. 1994), figure–ground segregation (Driver et al. 1992) and same–different judgements of simple stimuli (Volpe et al. 1979), because impoverished input may be sufficient to support performance. Elaborated high-quality representations may not be required for successful performance on the tasks administered in these studies. The model also deals well with findings of preserved preference judgements that neglect patients may make based on information presented in the neglected field (Marshall & Halligan 1988, Bisiach & Rusconi 1990). Because Bisiach & Rusconi showed that the patients made their judgements based on the detection of some (presumably low-level) perceptual information, it could be argued that impoverished representations were sufficient to allow the neglect patients to make these preference judgements.

More troublesome for the model are findings showing that stimuli in the neglected field can be processed implicitly to a deep semantic level on tests of semantic priming involving words (e.g. McGlinchey-Berroth et al. 1993) and on matching tasks involving objects (Berti et al. 1992). These results could only be accommodated by the degraded representation model if it were assumed that even impoverished perceptual representations can activate related semantic information. Although direct evidence to support such a claim is missing, indirect supporting evidence can be obtained from simulations with neural networks which allow for interactive activation between different levels of representation (Mozer & Behrmann 1990, Farah 1994).

10.8.2.2 Distinct knowledge model

The traditional way of dealing with differences in processing of attended and unattended information in the attention literature is to postulate that the information that has not received attention is processed to a lower level than information that has been attended. These considerations are crucial in controversies between proponents of early and late selection theories of attention (for a review seeAllport 1989).

The neuropsychological distinct knowledge model, in contrast, does not focus on issues of early versus late selection. Instead, it postulates that at roughly the same level of processing, explicit knowledge includes different types of information than implicit knowledge. In the studies that we reviewed, there is no evidence that addresses this issue satisfactorily. However, a general prediction can be made based on evidence from the domain-specific syndromes reviewed in the previous sections. The prediction that follows from the model is that the types of information that can be expressed as implicit knowledge in each of these syndromes should also be part of implicit knowledge in neglect. For example, any information that can be processed implicitly in object agnosia, pure alexia and blindsight should also be available as implicit knowledge in neglect. This general prediction follows from the model because it is assumed that those types of information that are processed implicitly by a distinct neural system should be available in any syndrome (as well as in normal people), as long as the system that supports this implicit knowledge is not itself damaged.

10.9 CONCLUSIONS

It is clear from the evidence that perceptual information is available at an unconscious level, even when ostensibly comparable information about the same material at a conscious level is lacking or grossly deficient. In other words, even though explicit knowledge is impaired or absent, implicit knowledge can be relatively, if not completely, preserved. What is less clear is how dissociations between implicit and explicit knowledge are to be interpreted and what they imply for theories of perception, cognition and brain organization. Although we will not address these issues fully, we hope that the ensuing discussions will elucidate what the problems are and provide a framework for future discussion, research and theory.

10.9.1 Domain specificity

What is striking about the evidence we have reviewed is that the loss of explicit knowledge is domain specific (see also Schacter et al. 1988, Moscovitch & Umiltà 1990). What is lost is not consciousness itself, but rather some aspect of knowledge which is conjoined to consciousness. Moreover, domain specificity implies that at some level of organization, these conjoined knowledge–consciousness elements are independent of one another.

One of the things that distinguishes one type of model from the others, is the way each attempts to deal with domain specificity. The disconnection model assumes a central conscious awareness system (CAS) into which knowledge is fed from independent, domain-specific modules or representation systems (see Fig. 10.1). Knowledge becomes explicit once the CAS is entered. Domain-specific deficits arise when access to this system is lost.

For the degraded representation model, conscious awareness is a by-product of the integrity of domain-specific perceptual systems and the quality of the representations they support (see Fig. 10.3). Knowledge becomes explicit once the quality of the representation reaches or exceeds a certain threshold.

In contrast to the two other models, the distinct knowledge model posits that there is something special about explicit knowledge that distinguishes it from implicit knowledge. To become conscious (or, more correctly, for an individual to become aware of some knowledge), the knowledge has to be of a specific type that is different from knowledge, which is implicit and represented in a different form (see Fig. 10.2). As Weiskrantz (1995) put it, implicit knowledge is not just a shadow of explicit knowledge, as the degraded model would suggest, but a different entity. In a sense, domain specificity applies not only across independent systems of knowledge, but also within each system to explicit and implicit knowledge itself.

10.9.2 Evaluation of the three classes of model

Much of the evidence we reviewed on implicit and explicit knowledge in each of the six syndromes was consistent with all three models. If all the evidence were of this sort, the degraded representation model would be favoured on the principle of parsimony. According to that model, no new structures or processes need to be invoked to account for differences in explicit as compared with implicit knowledge. The model simply posits that implicit knowledge is a degraded form of explicit knowledge. Conscious and unconscious processes are mediated by common structures and representations. However appealing such a model is, and however successful it may be for accounting for some of the data, our review indicates clearly that some findings cannot be accommodated by the model. Rather than recapitulate the evidence, we list here the types of finding that are especially difficult for the degraded representation model to handle:

(a) The information and presumed representation that drives performance on tests of implicit knowledge is not necessarily less complex than that which is associated with consciousness and tests of explicit knowledge (e.g. Weiskrantz et al. 1995, for blindsight; Jakobson et al. 1991, for object agnosia).

(b) Different neural structures may mediate implicit and explicit knowledge, as shown in double dissociations. This condition should not occur if the same structures were implicated in both cases (e.g. Weiskrantz 1995, for blindsight; Milner & Goodale 1995, for object agnosia and optic ataxia; Tranel et al. 1995, for prosopagnosia).

(c) Performance on the same test can be better when conscious awareness is absent, i.e. when knowledge is truly implicit, than when the same test is performed under conditions of conscious awareness (e.g. Weiskrantz 1988, Marcel 1993, for blindsight; Coslett & Saffran 1989, for pure alexia).

(d) Explicit knowledge may prevent the expression of implicit knowledge or interfere with it, a finding that is difficult to reconcile with the view that the latter is only a degraded version of the former (e.g. Rafal et al. 1990, for blindsight).

(e) Implicit knowledge may be qualitatively different from explicit knowledge (Milner & Goodale 1995, for object agnosia and optic ataxia; Weiskrantz et al. 1995, for blindsight).

To salvage the degraded representation model in light of these objections, one could argue that the degraded representation model has only limited applicability, but nonetheless occupies its own special niche in which it accounts for the evidence better than any other model. Alternatively, it could also be argued that degraded representations are not merely lower level versions of intact representations but that the degradation transforms the representation into a different type entirely. Neither solution is satisfactory. The former treats the degraded representation model as a curiosity (but see below), whereas the latter robs it of its appealing parsimony and blurs the distinction between it and the other models.

Of the other two models, the disconnection model also falls prey to objections (b), (c) and possibly (e). If simple disconnection of a perceptual module from a CAS that operates across multiple domains accounts for preserved implicit knowledge, it is difficult to see how preserved explicit knowledge can exist in a domain for which implicit knowledge is absent. Also, it is hard to see in light of the disconnection model how implicit and explicit knowledge can be qualitatively different from one another. Although the model does allow for information to accrue and become elaborated, enriched or even transformed when it is processed by the CAS, the information cannot be of a different type entirely once it enters consciousness.

An additional problem for disconnection models is evidence that semantic information can be accessed implicitly. According to many of these models (e.g. Schacter 1992a), semantics is the domain of the CAS and not the unconscious perceptual representation systems which may be disconnected from conscious awareness. Unlike the other problems, however, this one can be resolved by allowing for some limited, associative semantics to be part of perceptual modules that support implicit knowledge (see Fodor 1985, Moscovitch & Umiltà 1990, 1991).

Of the three models, the distinct knowledge model is not vulnerable to any of the above objections. Also, in reviewing the evidence, we did not encounter any findings that were inconsistent with the model, although it must be admitted that the findings often did not support this model over the others. What is crucial, however, is that the distinct knowledge model is the only one which can account for all of the types of findings listed in points (a)–(e).

Another factor in favour of the model is that it makes good biological sense to evolve a nervous system in which conscious and unconscious processes are mediated by different systems. One has no difficulty accepting that the neural substrates which control homeostasis are best served by operating independently of consciousness and that their output may never gain access to consciousness. Similarly, some processes we take to be cognitive may serve their function best without recourse to consciousness. In such cases, it makes sense to isolate these unconscious processes from those involved in consciousness so that they form functionally independent systems. The strongest evidence in favour of this view is that their functional and structural independence should also be observed in normal people under conditions that tap implicit and explicit knowledge selectively. Indeed, often this is the case (see Section 10.5 and further related examples in Milner & Goodale

1995; see also studies on implicit and explicit memory, e.g. Moscovitch et al. 1994).

The latter view helps to put the evaluation of the three models into perspective. The degraded representation model and the disconnection model describe what may occur under extreme, unnatural conditions such as when the nervous system is damaged or when perception and memory are weak or distorted. As such, they may indeed be valid models of the effects that such conditions sometimes have on conscious and unconscious processes; although even then, as we have seen, they fail to account for all of the data. On the other hand, the distinct knowledge model describes the cognitive characteristics and neural organization of conscious and unconscious processes that exist normally. Brain damage and other extreme conditions only reveal starkly what otherwise would be difficult to detect.

10.9.3 Implications for theories and research on perception and cognition

Discussions of consciousness currently abound in theories of perception, cognition and memory, and intensive research is being conducted to determine whether implicit or explicit knowledge underlies performance on experimental tasks (see Milner & Rugg 1991, Umiltà & Moscovitch 1994). It is disconcerting, therefore, to discover that few models on colour perception, reading and face-recognition involve consciousness. The information processing diagrams tracing the single or multiple routes to reading and face recognition or the neural network models that simulate these functions typically have no provisions for distinguishing implicit from explicit processes or representations. This is all the more surprising since some of those models are proposed by people who conduct research on implicit and explicit knowledge (e.g. Shallice 1988, Young 1994). Yet, if consciousness adds a vital dimension to perception and cognition, as our survey of the various syndromes indicates, then the models are at best incomplete or at worst seriously flawed. The incorporation of distinctions between conscious and unconscious processes into some models of memory (e.g. Tulving & Schacter 1990, Moscovitch 1992) bodes well for similar developments in other fields.

As yet, very little is known about the neuroanatomical substrates that underlie implicit and explicit knowledge in the various domains that were reviewed in this chapter. Functional neuroimaging studies involving positron emission tomography, functional magnetic resonance imaging and event-related potentials of normal people and of patients with preserved implicit but deficient explicit knowledge would provide an invaluable source of information. We fully expect a spate of such studies in the near future. With this in mind, we wish to end by advancing a hypothesis about the neuroanatomical basis of consciousness.

10.9.4 A hypothesis concerning the neural substrate of consciousness

The three models of consciousness discussed also have different implications for research on the neural substrate of consciousness. According to the degraded representation model, conscious and unconscious processes are mediated by the same neural mechanisms. For the other two models, however, consciousness is dependent on specific neural substrates that are distinct from those implicated in unconscious processes. The disconnection model is a serial processing model in the sense that neural mechanisms involved in unconscious processes project to those involved in consciousness. Moreover, it assumes that there is a dedicated neural system (CAS) that mediates conscious awareness across multiple domains. By contrast, the distinct knowledge model is more of a parallel processing model in which the neural substrates mediating conscious and unconscious processes are kept separate. Importantly, it does not propose that there is a dedicated system which mediates consciousness across different domains. Instead, those regions involved in the perceptual analyses that produce explicit knowledge also subserve conscious awareness for that knowledge.

The distinct knowledge model will direct the search for the neural basis of consciousness along the many regions that are involved in perceptual processes which lead to explicit knowledge in specific domains. In contrast, the disconnection model will direct the search towards a dedicated structure or a network of structures without which consciousness cannot exist in any domain. Neither course of investigation has yet been pursued systematically, but some recent observations encourage us to end with speculations about a strategy for identifying some of the structures that are involved in consciousness.

Let us take as the starting point the distinct knowledge model and the distinction between conscious and unconscious processes involved in pattern recognition (Milner & Goodale 1995). Regions in the dorsal stream (presumably areas LIP and 7a) are implicated in unconscious visual processes necessary for the guidance of action, whereas regions in the ventral stream mediate conscious processes necessary for object identification. In the monkey, the ventral stream has strong projections to the hippocampal formation and surrounding cortical structures (in particular, the parahippocampal gyrus), whereas projections from the dorsal stream to these areas are sparse (Suzuki & Amaral 1994). We assume that a similar situation will hold for humans. This neuroanatomical finding is significant because it is known that the hippocampal formation is necessary for the conscious recollection of past events. It is also known that only those events that were consciously apprehended or perceived at the time of their occurrence can lead to subsequent conscious recollection (for discussions, see Moscovitch 1995, Moscovitch et al. 1994). In other words, findings from memory research suggest that only knowledge that is consciously apprehended (i.e. only explicit knowledge) can feed into the hippocampus and, therefore, can be consciously recollected at a later time. *A working hypothesis, then, is that the regions necessary for consciousness are those which project to the hippocampal formation and surrounding cortex.* This hypothesis gains preliminary support from the findings cited earlier on the organization of the visual system. However, this hypothesis does not posit that the hippocampal formation is the repository of consciousness or the gateway to it. Rather, it posits that the hippocampal formation simply is a structure that requires "conscious input" for its operation and may, therefore, serve as a guide or pointer to those regions that are involved in consciousness.

Crick & Koch (1995) have proposed a similar hypothesis, but theirs focused on the frontal lobes, rather than the hippocampal formation, as the structure that serves as a marker for regions involved in consciousness. Although it may be the case that having projections to the frontal lobes is a characteristic of structures involved in consciousness, we do not think this is a sufficient condition. Regions in the dorsal pathway that support unconscious perception project to pre-motor regions of the frontal lobes (Milner & Goodale 1995). In addition, evidence is now accumulating that the frontal lobes contribute to performance on a variety of tests of unconscious memory (Winocur et al. 1996). Because projections to the frontal lobes are so widespread, Crick & Koch's frontal hypothesis may not be restrictive enough to exclude structures that are involved in unconscious perception only. Our hippocampal hypothesis may be more favourable in this regard. The exciting prospect, however, is not whether one or the other hypothesis is closer to capturing the truth (the likelihood is that both will be superseded by other better hypotheses), but that we are now approaching a stage where taking aim at a theory of consciousness based on sound psychological and neuroscientific data, principles and theory is a real possibility.

ACKNOWLEDGEMENTS

We thank Marlene Behrmann, Jeff Toth, Roberto Cabeza and Mick Rugg for their valuable comments on a previous draft of this chapter. This work was supported by funds from a Medical Research Council of Canada Grant to Gordon Winocur and M.M. S.K. was supported by a Women's Auxiliary Alzheimer Research Fellowship from the Baycrest Centre for Geriatric Care.

NOTE

1. There is another class of models which we will not discuss but which should be mentioned. These are interactionist models, which posit that consciousness arises as a result of interactions across various components or processes within a domain. At a neuroanatomical level, this means that consciousness depends on an interplay between multiple regions within a cortical processing stream, say within the visual system from V1 to inferotemporal cortex (Cowey & Stoerig, 1992). A variant of this theme is the idea that conscious awareness arises from the binding of disparate neural elements into an integrated pattern by an oscillating 40 Hz signal (Crick & Koch 1990, Singer 1993). Kinsbourne's integrated field theory (1988) can also be classified as an interactionist theory of consciousness (see also Dennett & Kinsbourne 1992, Marcel 1983).

REFERENCES

Aglioti, S., J. F. X. De Souza, M.A. Goodale 1995. Size-contrast illusions deceive the eye but not the hand. *Current Biology* **5**, 679–85.

Allport,A. 1988. What concept of consciousness? In *Consciousness in contemporary science*, A. J. Marcel & E. Bisiach (eds), 159–82. Oxford: Oxford University Press.

Allport, A. 1989. Visual attention. In *Foundations of cognitive science*, M. Posner (ed.), 1–82. Cambridge, MA: MIT Press.

Audet, T., D. Bub, A. R. Lecours 1991. Visual neglect and left-sided context effects. *Brain and Cognition* **16**, 11–28.

Barbur, J. L., K. H. Ruddock, V. A. Waterfield 1980. Human visual responses in the absence of the geniculo-calcarine projection. *Brain* **103**, 905–28.

Barbur, J. L., J. D. G. Watson, R. S. J. Frackowiak, S. Zeki 1993. Conscious visual perception without V1. *Brain* **116**, 1293–302.

Barbur, J. L.,A. J. Harlow, L. Weiskrantz 1994. Spatial and temporal response properties of residual vision in a case of hemianopia. *Philsophical Transactions of the Royal Society of London, Part B* **343**, 157–66.

Bauer, R. M. 1984.Autonomic recognition of names and faces in prosopagnosia: a neuropsychological application of the guilty knowledge test. *Neuropsychologia* **22**, 457–69.

Bauer, R. M. & M. Verfaellie 1988. Electrodermal recognition of familiar but not unfamiliar faces in prosopagnosia. *Brain and Cognition* **8**, 240–52.

Behrmann, M. 1994. Neglect dyslexia: attention and word recognition. In *The neuropsychology of high-level vision*, M. J. Farah & G. Ratcliff (eds), 173–214. Hillsdale, NJ: Lawrence Erlbaum Associates Inc.

Behrmann, M., S. E. Black, D. N. Bub 1990a. The evolution of pure alexia: a longitudinal study of recovery. *Brain and Language* **39**, 405–27.

Behrmann, M., M. Moscovitch, S. E. Black, M. Mozer. 1990b. Perceptual and conceptual mechanisms in neglect dyslexia. *Brain* **113**, 1163–83.

Berti, A. & G. Rizzolatti 1992. Visual processing without awareness: Evidence from unilateral neglect. *Journal of Cognitive Neuroscience* **4**, 345–51.

Berti,A., F. Frassinetti, C. Umiltà 1994. Nonconscious reading? Evidence from neglect dyslexia. *Cortex* **30**, 181–97.

Berti, A., A. Allport, J. Driver, Z. Dienes, J. Oxbury, S. Oxbury 1992. Levels of processing for visual stimuli in an "extinguished" field. *Neuropsychologia* **30**, 403–15.

Bisiach, E. & A. Berti 1994. Consciousness in dyschiria. In *The cognitive neurosciences*, M. S. Gazzaniga (ed.), 1331–40. Cambridge, MA: MIT Press.

Bisiach, E. & C. Luzzatti 1978. Unilateral neglect of representational space. *Cortex* **14**, 9–33.

Bisiach, E., C. Luzzatti, D. Perani 1979. Unilateral neglect, representational schema, and consciousness. *Brain* **102**, 609–18.

Bisiach, E. & M. L. Rusconi 1990. Break-down of perceptual awareness in unilateral neglect. *Cortex* **26**, 643–9.

Black, S. E. & M. Behrmann 1994. Localization in alexia. In *Localization and neuroimaging in neuropsychology*, A. Kertesz (ed.), 331–76. San Diego, CA: Academic Press.

Blythe, I. M., J. M. Bromley, C. Kennard, K. H. Rudduck 1986. Visual discrimination of target displacement remains after damage to the striate cortex in humans. *Nature* **20**, 619–21.

Blythe, I. M., C. Kennard, K. H. Ruddock 1987. Residual vision in patients with retrogeniculate lesions of the visual pathways. *Brain* **110**, 887–905.

Bruce, V. & G. W. Humphreys 1994. Recognizing objects and faces. *Visual Cognition* **1**, 1–80.

Bruyer, R., C. Laterre, X. Seron, P. Feyereisen, E. Strypstein, E. Pierrard, D. Rectem 1983. A case of prosopagnosia with some preserved covert remembrance of familiar faces. *Brain and Cognition* **2**, 257–84.

Bub, D. N. & M. Arguin 1995. Visual word activation in pure alexia. *Brain and Language* **49**, 77–103.

Bub, D. N., S. E. Black, J. Howell 1989. Word recognition and orthographic context effects in a letter-by-letter reader. *Brain and Language* **36**, 357–76.

Burton, A. M., A. W. Young, V. Bruce, R. A. Johnston, A. W. Ellis 1991. Understanding covert recognition. *Cognition* **39**, 129–66.

Campion, J., R. Latto, J. M. Smith 1983. Is blindsight an effect of scattered light, spared cortex, and near-threshold vision? *Behavioral and Brain Sciences* **6**, 423–48.

Carey, S. & S. Diamond 1994. Are faces perceived as configurations more by adults than by children? *Visual Cognition* **1**, 253–74.

Cohen, A., R. B. Ivry, R. D. Rafal, C. Kohn 1995. Activating response codes by stimuli in the neglected visual field. *Neuropsychology* **9**, 165–73.

Cohen, N. J. & L. R. Squire 1980. Preserved learning and retention of pattern-analyzing skill in amnesia: dissociation of knowing how and knowing that. *Science* **210**, 207–9.

Coltheart, M. 1980. Deep dyslexia: a right hemisphere hypothesis. In *Deep dyslexia*, M. Coltheart, K. Patterson, J. C. Marshall (eds), 326–80. London: Routledge & Kegan Paul.

Corbetta, M., C. A. Marzi, G. Tassinari, S. Aglioti 1990. Effectiveness of different task paradigms in revealing blindsight. *Brain* **113**, 603–16.

Coslett, H. B. & E. M. Saffran 1989. Evidence for preserved reading in "pure alexia". *Brain* **112**, 327–59.

Coslett, H. B. & E. M. Saffran 1994. Mechanisms of implicit reading in alexia. In *The neuropsychology of high-level vision*, M. J. Farah & G. Ratcliff (eds), 299–330. Hillsdale, NJ: Lawrence Erlbaum Associates Inc.

Cowey, A. & P. Stoerig 1992. Reflections on blindsight. In *The neuropsychology of consciousness*, A. D. Milner & M. D. Rugg (eds), 11–38. London: Academic Press.

Cowey, A. & P. Stoerig 1995. Blindsight in monkeys. *Nature* **373**, 247–9.

Crick, F. & C. Koch 1990. Towards a neurobiological theory of consciousness. *Seminars in Neuroscience* **2**, 263–75.

Crick, F. & C. Koch 1995. Are we aware of neural activity in primary visual cortex? *Nature* **375**, 121–3.

Damasio, A. R. & H. Damasio 1983. The anatomic basis of pure alexia. *Neurology* **33**, 73–83.

Damasio, H. & A. R. Damasio 1986. The anatomical substrate of prosopagnosia. In *The neuropsychology of face perception and facial expression*, R. Bruyer (ed.), 31–8. Hillsdale, NJ: Lawrence Erlbaum Associates Inc.

Damasio, A., T. Yamada, H. Damasio, J. Corbett, J. McKee 1980. Central achromatopsia: behavioural, anatomic, and physiological aspects. *Neurology* **30**, 1064–71.

Damasio, A. R., D. Tranel, H. Damasio 1991. Somatic markers and the guidance of behaviour: theory and preliminary testing. In *Frontal lobe function and dysfuntion*, H. S. Levin, H. M. Eisenberg, A. L. Benton (eds), 217–29. New York: Oxford University Press.

De Haan, E. H. F., A. W. Young, F. Newcombe 1987a. Face recognition without awareness. *Cognitive Neuropsychology* **4**, 385–415.

De Haan, E. H. F., A. W. Young, F. Newcombe 1987b. Faces interfere with name classification in a prosopagnosic patient. *Cortex* **23**, 309–16.

De Haan, E. H. F., A. W. Young, F. Newcombe 1991. Covert and overt recognition in prosopagnosia. *Brain* **114**, 2575–91.

De Haan, E. H. F., R. M. Bauer, K. W. Greve 1992. Behavioural and physiological evidence for covert face recognition in a prosopagnosic patient. *Cortex* **28**, 77–95.

Dennett, D. C. & M. Kinsbourne 1992. Time and the observer: the where and when of consciousness in the brain. *Behavioral and Brain Sciences* **15**, 183–247.

De Renzi, E. 1986a. Prosopagnosia in two patients with CT scan evidence of damage confined to the right hemisphere. *Neuropsychologia* **24**, 385–9.

De Renzi, E. 1986b. Current issues in prosopagnosia. In *Aspects of face processing*, H. D. Ilis, M. A. Jeeves, F. Newcombe, A. W. Young (eds), 243–52. Dordrecht: Martinus Nijhoff.

Driver, J., G. C. Baylis, R. D. Rafal 1992. Preserved figure–ground segregation and symmetry perception in visual neglect. *Nature* **360**, 73–5.

Eccles, J. C. 1973. *The understanding of the brain*. New York: McGraw-Hill.

Etcoff, N. L., R. Freeman, K. R. Cave 1991. Can we loose memories of faces? Content specificity and awareness in a prosopagnosic. *Journal of Cognitive Neuroscience* **3**, 25–41.

Farah, M. J. 1990. *Visual agnosia*. Cambridge, MA: MIT Press.

Farah, M. J. 1994. Visual perception and visual awareness after brain damage: a tutorial review. In *Attention and performance. XV. Conscious and unconscious information processing*, C. Umiltà & M. Moscovitch (eds), 37–75. Cambridge, MA: MIT Press.

Farah, M. J., M. A. Monheit, M. A. Wallace 1991. Unconscious perception of extinguished visual stimuli: reassessing the evidence. *Neuropsychologia* **29**, 949–58.

Farah, M. J., R. C. O'Reilly, S. P. Vecera 1993. Dissociated overt and covert recognition as an emergent property of a lesioned neural network. *Psychological Review* **100**, 571–88.

Fendrich, R., C. W. Wessinger, M. S. Gazzaniga 1992. Residual vision in a scotoma: implications for blindsight. *Science* **258**, 1489–91.

Fodor, J. A. 1985. Précis of the modularity of mind. *Behavioral and Brain Sciences* **8**, 1–42.

Forster, K. I., J. Booker, D. L. Schacter, C. Davis 1990. Masked repetition priming: lexical activation or novel memory trace. *Bulletin of the Psychonomic Society* **28**, 341–5.

Fuentes, L. J. & G. W. Humphreys 1996. On the processing of "extinguished" stimuli in unilateral neglect: an approach using negative priming. *Cognitive Neuropsychology* **13**, 111–36.

Gainotti, G., P. D'Erme, D. Monteleone, M. S. Silveri 1986. Mechanisms of unilateral patial neglect in relation to laterality of cerebral lesions. *Brain* **109**, 599–612.

Goodale, M. A. & A. D. Milner 1992. Separate visual pathways for perception and action. *Trends in Neuroscience* **15**, 20–5.

Goodale, M. A., A. D. Milner, L. S. Jakobson, D. P. Carey 1991. A neurological dissociation between perceiving objects and grasping them. *Nature* **349**, 154–6.

Goodale, M. A., J. P. Meenan, H. H. Bülthoff, D. A. Nicolle, K. J. Murphy, C. I. Acicot 1994a. Separate neural pathways for the visual analysis of object shape in perception and prehension. *Current Biology* **4**, 604–10.

Goodale, M. A., L. S. Jakobson, J. M. Keillor 1994b. Differences in the visual control of pantomimed and natural grasping movements. *Neuropsychologia* **32**, 1159–78.

Goodale, M. A., L. S. Jakobson, A. D. Milner, D. I. Perrett, P. J. Benson, J. K. Hietanen 1994c. The nature and limits of orientation and pattern processing supporting visuomotor control in a visual form agnosic. *Journal of Cognitive Neuroscience* **6**, 46–56.

Greve, K. W. & R. M. Bauer 1990. Implicit learning of new faces in prosopagnosia: an application of the mere-exposure paradigm. *Neuropsychologia* **28**, 1035–41.

Heide, W., E. Koenig, J. Dichgans 1990. Optokinetic nystagmus, self-motion sensation and their after-effects in patients with occipito-parietal lesions. *Clinical Vision Science* **5**, 145–56.

Heywood, C.A., B. Wilson, A. Cowey 1987. A case study of cortical colour "blindness" with relatively intact achromatic discrimination. *Journal of Neurology, Neurosurgery, and Psychiatry* **50**, 22–9.

Heywood, C. A., A. Cowey, F. Newcombe 1991. Chromatic discrimination in a cortically colour blind observer. *European Journal of Neuroscience* **3**, 802–12.

Heywood, C.A., A. Cowey, F. Newcombe 1994. On the role of parvocellular P and agnocellular M pathways in cerebral achromatopsia. *Brain* **117**, 245–54.

Howard, D. 1991. Letter-by-letter readers: evidence for parallel processing. In *Basic processes in reading. Visual word recognition*, D. Besner & G. W. Humphreys (eds), 34–76. Hillsdale, NJ: Lawrence Erlbaum Associates Inc.

Humphrey, G. K., M. A. Goodale, R. Gurnsey 1991. Orientation discrimination in a visual form agnosic: evidence from the McCollough effect. *Psychological Science* **2**, 331–5.

Humphreys, G. W., T. Troscianko, M. J. Riddoch, M. Boucart, N. Donnelly, G. F. A. Harding 1992. Covert processing in different visual recognition systems. In *The neuropsychology of consciousness*, A. D. Milner & M. D. Rugg (eds), 39–68. London: Academic Press.

Jacoby, L. L. 1991. A process dissociation framework: separating automatic from intentional uses of memory. *Journal of Memory and Language* **30**, 513–41.

Jacoby, L. L., J. P. Toth, A. P. Yonelinas 1993. Separating conscious and unconscious influences of memory: measuring recollection. *Journal of Experimental Psychology: General* **122**, 139–54.

Jakobson, L. S., Y. M. Archibald, D. P. Carey, M. A. Goodale 1991. A kinematic analysis of reaching and grasping movements in a patient recovering from optic ataxia. *Neuropsychologia* **29**, 803–9.

Karnath, H. O. 1988. Deficits of attention in acute and recovered visual hemineglect. *Neuropsychologia* **26**, 27–43.

Karnath, H. O. & W. Hartje 1987. Residual information processing in the neglected half-field. *Journal of Neurology* **234**, 180–4.

Kinsbourne, M. 1988. Integrated field theory of consciousness. In *Consciousness in contemporary science*, A. J. Marcel & E. Bisiach (eds), 239–56. Oxford: Oxford University Press.

Làdavas, E., R. Paladini, R. Cubelli 1993. Implicit associative priming in a patient with left visual neglect. *Neuropsychologia* **31**, 1307–20.

Làdavas, E., A. Petronio, C. Umiltà 1990. The deployment of visual attention in the intact field of hemineglect. *Cortex* **26**, 307–17.

Landis, T., M. Regard, A. Serrat 1980. Iconic reading in a case of alexia without agraphia caused by a brain tumor: a tachistoscopic study. *Brain and Language* **11**, 45–53.

Marcel, A. J. 1983. Conscious and unconscious perception: an approach to the relations between phenomenal experience and perceptual processes. *Cognitive Psychology* **15**, 238–300.

Marcel, A. J. 1993. Slippage in the unity of consciousness. In *Experimental and theoretical studies of consciousness. Ciba Foundation Symposium 174*, 168–86. Chichester: Wiley.

Marshall, J. C. & P. W. Halligan 1988. Blindsight and insight in visuo-spatial neglect. *Nature* **336**, 766–7.

Marzi, C. A., G. Tassinari, S. Aglioti, L. Lutzemberger 1986. Spatial summation across the vertical meridian in hemianopics: a test of blindsight. *Neuropsychologia* **24**, 749–58.

Marzi, C. A., N. Smania, M. C. Martini, G. Gambina, G. Tomelleri, A. Palamara, F. Allessandrini et al. 1996. Implicit redundant-targets effect in visual extinction. *Neuropsychologia* **34**, 9–22.

Mayes, A. R., R. Van Eijk, C. L. Isaac 1995. Assessment of familiarity and recollection in the false fame paradigm using a modified process dissociation procedure. *Journal of the International Neuropsychological Society* **1**, 469–82.

McCarthy, R. A. & E. K. Warrington 1990. *Cognitive neuropsychology. A clinical introduction*. San Diego, CA: Academic Press.

McGlinchey-Berroth, R., W. P. Milberg, M. Verfaellie, M. Alexander, P. T. Kilduff 1993. Semantic processing in the neglected visual field: evidence from a lexical decision task. *Cognitive Neuropsychology* **10**, 79–108.

McNeil, J. E. & E. K. Warrington 1991. Prosopagnosia: a reclassification. *Quarterly Journal of Experimental Psychology* **43A**, 267–87.

Meadows, J. C. 1974. Disturbed perception of colours associated with localized cerebral lesions. *Brain* **97**, 615–32.

Merikle, P. M., S. Joordens, J. Stolz 1995. Measuring the relative magnitude of unconscious influences. *Consciousness and Cognition* **4**, 422–39.

Mijovic-Prelec, D., L. M. Shin, C. Chabris, S. Kosslyn 1994. When does "no" really mean "yes"? A case study in unilateral visual neglect. *Neuropsychologia* **32**, 151–8.

Milner, A. D. 1995. Cerebral correlates of visual awareness. *Neuropsychologia* **33**, 1117–30.

Milner, A. D. & M. A. Goodale 1995. *The visual brain in action*. Oxford: Oxford University Press.

Milner, A. D. & M. D. Rugg (eds) 1992. *The neuropsychology of consciousness*. London: Academic Press.

Milner, A. D., D. I. Perret, R. S. Johnston, P. J. Benson, T. R. Jordan, D. W. Heeley, D. Bettucci et al. 1991. Perception and action in "visual form agnosia". *Brain* **114**, 405–28.

Milner, B. 1966. Amnesia following operation on the temporal lobe. In *Amnesia*, C. W. M. Whitty & O. L. Zangwill (eds), 109–33. London: Butterworth.

Mollon, J. D., F. Newcombe, P. G. Polden, G. Ratcliff 1980. On the presence of three cone mechanisms in a case of total achromatopsia. In *Colour vision deficiencies*, G. Verriest (ed.), 130–5. Bristol: A. Hilger.

Moscovitch, M. 1973. Language and the cerebral hemispheres: reaction-time studies and their implications for models of cerebral dominance. In *Communication and affect: language and thought*, P. Pliner, T. M. Alloway, L. Krames (eds), 89–126. New York: Academic Press.

Moscovitch, M. 1976. On the representation of language in the right hemisphere of right-handed people. *Brain and Language* **3**, 47–71.

Moscovitch, M. 1989. Confabulation and the frontal system: strategic versus associative retrieval in neuropsychological theories of memory. In *Varieties of memory and consciousness: essays in honor of Endel Tulving*, H. L. Roediger & F. I. M. Craik (eds), 133–60. Hillsdale, NJ: Lawrence Erlbaum Associates Inc.

Moscovitch, M. 1992. Memory and working-with-memory: a component process model based on modules and central systems. *Journal of Cognitive Neuroscience* **4**, 257–67.

Moscovitch, M. 1995. Recovered consciousness: a hypothesis concerning modularity and episodic memory. *Journal of Clinical and Experimental Neuropsychology* **17**, 276–90.

Moscovitch, M. & C. Umiltà 1990. Modularity and neuropsychology: implications for the organization of attention and memory in normal and brain-damaged people. In *Modular processes in dementia*, M. E. Schwartz (ed.), 1–59. Cambridge, MA: MIT Press.

Moscovitch, M. & C. Umiltà 1991. Conscious and nonconscious aspects of memory: a neuropsychological framework of modules and central systems. In *Perspectives on cognitive neuroscience*, H. J. Weingartner & R. G. Lister (eds), 229–66. Oxford: Oxford University Press.

Moscovitch, M., E. Vriezen, Y. Goshen-Gottstein 1993. Implicit tests of memory in patients with focal lesions or degenerative brain disorders. In *Handbook of neuropsychology*, vol. 8, F. Boller & J. Grafman (eds), 133–73. Amsterdam: Elsevier.

Moscovitch, M., Y. Goshen-Gottstein, E. Vriezen 1994. Memory without conscious recollection: a tutorial review from a neuropsychological perspective. In *Attention and performance. XV. Conscious and unconscious information processing*, M. Moscovitch & C. Umiltà (eds), 619–60. Cambridge, MA: MIT Press.

Mozer, M. C. & M. Behrmann 1990. On the interaction of selective attention and lexical knowledge: a connectionist account of neglect dyslexia. *Journal of Cognitive Neuroscience* **2**, 96–123.

Newcombe, F., A. W. Young, E. H. F. De Haan 1989. Prosopagnosia and object agnosia without covert recognition. *Neuropsychologia* **27**, 179–91.

Patterson, K. & J. Kay 1982. Letter-by-letter reading: psychological descriptions of a neurological syndrome. *Quarterly Journal of Experimental Psychology* **34A**, 411–41.

Perenin, M. T. 1991. Discrimination of motion direction in perimetrically blind fields. *EuroReport* **2**, 397–400.

Perenin, M. T. & M. Jeannerod 1975. Residual vision in cortically blind hemifields. *Neuropsychologia* **13**, 1–7.

Perenin, M. T. & M. Jeannerod 1978. Visual function within the hemianopic field following early cerebral hemidecortication in man. I. Spatial localization. *Neuropsychologia* **16**, 1–13.

Pizzamiglio, L., G. Antonucci, A. Francia 1984. Response of the cotically blind hemifields to a moving visual scene. *Cortex* **20**, 89–99.

Plaut, D. & T. Shallice 1993. Deep dyslexia: a case study of connectionist neuropsychology. *Cognitive Neuropsychology* **10**, 377–500.

Pöppel, E. 1986. Long-range colour-generating interactions across the retina. *Nature* **320**, 523–5.

Pöppel, E., R. Held, D. Frost 1973. Residual visual function after brain wounds involving the central visual pathways in man. *Nature* **243**, 295–6.

Ptito, A., M. Lassonde, F. Leporé, M. Ptito 1987. Visual discrimination in hemispherectomized patients. *Neuropsychologia* **25**, 869–79.

Ptito, A., F. Leporé, M. Ptito, M. Lassonde 1991. Target detection and movement discrimination in the blind field of hemispherectomized patients. *Brain* **114**, 497–512.

Rafal, R. D. 1994. Neglect. *Current Opinion in Neurobiology* **4**, 231–6.

Rafal, R., J. Smith, J. Krantz, A. Cohen, C. Brennan 1990. Extrageniculate vision in hemianopic humans: saccade inhibition by signals in the blind field. *Science* **250**, 118–21.

Reingold, E. M. & J. P. Toth 1996. Process dissociations versus task dissociations. In *Implicit cognition*, G. Underwood (ed.). Oxford: Oxford University Press.

Renault, B., J. L. Signoret, B. Debruille, F. Breton, F. Bolgert 1989. Brain potentials reveal covert facial recognition in prosopagnosia. *Neuropsychologia* **27**, 905–12.

Richardson-Klavehn, A. & R. A. Bjork 1988. Measures of memory. *Annual Review of Psychology* **39**, 475–543.

Rizzolatti, G., L. Riggio, B. M. Sheliga 1994. Space and selective attention. In *Attention and performance. XV. Conscious and unconscious information processing*, C. Umiltà & M. Moscovitch (eds), 231–65. Cambridge, MA: MIT Press.

Rock, I. 1983. *The logic of perception*. Cambridge, MA: MIT Press.

Saffran, E. M., L. C. Bogyo, M. F. Schwartz, O. S. M. Marin 1980. Does deep dyslexia reflect right-hemisphere reading? In *Deep dyslexia*, M. Coltheart, K. Patterson, J. C. Marshall (eds), 381–406. London: Routledge & Kegan Paul.

Schacter, D. L. 1989. On the relation between memory and consciousness: dissociable interactions and conscious experience. In *Varieties of memory and consciousness: essays in honour of Endel Tulving*, H. L. Roediger III & F. I. M. Craik (eds), 355–89. Hillsdale, NJ: Lawrence Erlbaum Associates Inc.

Schacter, D. L. 1990. Toward a cognitive neuropsychology of awareness: implicit knowledge and anosognosia. *Journal of Clinical and Experimental Neuropsychology* **12**, 155–78.

Schacter, D. L. 1992a. Implicit knowledge: new perspectives on unconscious processes. *Proceedings of the National Academy of Sciences, USA* **89**, 11113–17.

Schacter, D. L. 1992b. Priming and multiple memory systems: perceptual mechanisms of implicit memory. *Journal of Cognitive Neuroscience* **4**, 244–56.

Schacter, D. L., M. P. McAndrews, M. Moscovitch 1988. Dissociations between implicit and explicit knowledge in neuropsychological syndromes. In *Thought without language*, L. Weiskrantz (ed.), 242–78. Oxford: Oxford University Press.

Schacter, D. L., S. Z. Rapscak, A. B. Rubens, M. Tharan, J. Laguna 1990. Priming effects in a letter-by-letter reader depend on access to the word form system. *Neuropsychologia* **28**, 1079–94.

Schacter, D. L., E. Reiman, A. Uecker, M. R. Polster, L. S. Yung, L. A. Cooper 1995. Brain regions associated with retrieval of structurally coherent visual information. *Nature* **376**, 587–90.

Sergent, J. 1988. An investigation into perceptual completion in blind areas of the visual field. *Brain* **111**, 347–73.

Sergent, J. & M. Poncet 1990. From covert to overt recognition of faces in a prosopagnosic patient. *Brain* **113**, 989–1004.

Sergent, J. & J. L. Signoret 1992a. Functional and anatomical decomposition of face processing: evidence from prosopagnosia and PET study of normal subjects. *Philosophical Transactions of the Royal Society of London, Series B* **335**, 55–62.

Sergent, J. & J. L. Signoret 1992b. Implicit access to knowledge derived from unrecognized faces in prosopagnosia. *Cerebral Cortex* **2**, 389–400.

Sergent, J. & J. L. Signoret 1992c. Varieties of functional deficits in prosopagnosia. *Cerebral Cortex* **2**, 375–88.

Sergent, J. & J. G. Villemure 1989. Prosopagnosia in a right hemispherectomized patient. *Brain* **112**, 975–95.

Shallice, T. 1988. *From neuropsychology to mental structure*. Cambridge: Cambridge University Press.

Shallice, T. & E. Saffran 1986. Lexical processing in the absence of explicit word identification: evidence from a letter-by-letter reader. *Cognitive Neuropsychology* **3**, 429–58.

Singer, W. 1993. Synchronization of cortical activity and its putative role in information processing and learning. *Annual Review of Physiology* **55**, 349–74.

Singer, W., J. Zihl, E. Pöppel 1977. Subcortical control of visual thresholds in humans: evidence for modality specific and retinotopically organized mechanisms of selective attention. *Experimental Brain Research* **29**, 191–9.

Sperry, R. W., M. S. Gazzaniga, J. E. Bogen 1969. Interhemispheric relationships: the neocortical commissures syndromes of hemispheric disconnection. In *Handbook of Clinical Neurology* Vol. 4, P. J. Vinken & G. W. Bruyn (eds), 273–90. Amsterdam: North Holland.

Srinivas, K., S. D. Breedin, H. B. Coslett, E. M. Saffran (in press). Intact perceptual priming in a patient with damage to the anterior inferior temporal lobes. *Journal of Cognitive Neuroscience*.

Stoerig, P. 1987. Chromaticity and achromaticity: evidence of a functional differentiation in visual field defects. *Brain* **110**, 869–86.

Stoerig, P. & A. Cowey 1991. Increment-threshold spectral sensitivity in blindsight. *Brain* **114**, 1487–512.

Stoerig, P. & A. Cowey 1992. Wavelength discrimination in blindsight. *Brain* **115**, 425–44.

Stoerig, P., M. Hübner, E. Pöppel 1985. Signal detection analysis of residual vision in a field defect due to a post-geniculate lesion. *Neuropsychologia* **23**, 589–99.

Suzuki, W. A. & D. G. Amaral 1994. Perirhinal and parahippocampal cortices of the macaque monkey: cortical afferents. *Journal of Comparative Neurology* **350**, 497–533.

Taylor, D. A. 1977. Time course of context effects. *Journal of Experimental Psychology: General* **106**, 404–26.

Ter Braak, J. W. G., V. W. D. Schenk, A. G. M. Van Vliet 1971. Visual reactions in a case of long-lasting cortical blindness. *Journal of Neurology, Neurosurgery, and Psychiatry* **34**, 140–7.

Torjussen, T. 1976. Residual function in cortically blind hemifields. *Scandinavian Journal of Psychology* **17**, 320–2.

Torjussen, T. 1978. Visual processing in cortically blind hemifields. *Neuropsychologia* **16**, 15–21.

Toth, J. P., E. M. Reingold, L. L. Jacoby 1994. Toward a redefinition of implicit memory: process dissociations following elaborative processing and self-generation. *Journal of Experimental Psychology: Learning, Memory, and Cognition* **20**, 290–303.

Toth, J. P., B. Levine, D. T. Stuss, A. Oh, G. Winocur, N. Meiran 1995. Dissociation of processes underlying spatial S–R compatibility: evidence for the independent influence of what and where. *Consciousness and Cognition* **4**, 483–501.

Tranel, D. & A. R. Damasio 1985. Knowledge without awareness: an autonomic index of facial recognition by prosopagnosics. *Science* **228**, 1453–4.

Tranel, D. & A. R. Damasio 1988. Non-conscious face recognition in patients with face agnosia. *Behavioural Brain Research* **30**, 235–49.

Tranel, D., H. Damasio, A. R. Damasio 1995. Double dissociation between overt and covert face recognition. *Journal of Cognitive Neuroscience* **7**, 425–32.

Tulving, E. & D. L. Schacter 1990. Priming and human memory systems. *Science* **247**, 301–6.

Umiltà, C. & Moscovitch, M. (eds) 1994. *Attention and performance. XV. Conscious and unconscious information processing.* Cambridge, MA: MIT Press.

Ungerleider, L. G. & Mishkin, M. 1982. Two cortical visual systems. In *Analysis of visual behaviour*, D. J. Ingle & M. A. Goodale (eds), 549–86. Cambridge, MA: MIT Press.

Vallar, G. 1993. The anatomical basis of spatial neglect in humans. In *Unilateral neglect: clinical and experimental studies*, I. H. Robertson & J. C. Marshall (eds), 27–62. Hillsdale, NJ: Lawrence Erlbaum Associates Inc.

Verfaellie, M. & J. R. Treadwell 1993. Status of recognition memory in amnesia. *Neuropsychology* **7**, 5–13.

Victor, J. D., K. Maiese, R. Shapley, J. Sidtis, M. S. Gazzaniga 1989. Acquired central dyschromatopsia: analysis of a case with preservation of colour discrimination. *Clinical Vision Science* **4**, 183–96.

Volpe, B. T., J. Ledoux, M. S. Gazzaniga 1979. Information processing of visual stimuli in an "extinguished" field. *Nature* **282**, 722–4.

Wallace, M. A. 1994. Implicit perception in visual neglect: implications for theories of attention. In *The neuropsychology of high-level vision*, M. J. Farah & G. Ratcliff (eds), 359–70. Hillsdale, NJ: Lawrence Erlbaum Associates Inc..

Wallace, M. A. & M. J. Farah 1992. Savings in relearning as evidence for covert recognition in prosopagnosia. *Journal of Cognitive Neuroscience* **4**, 150–4.

Warrington, E. K. & T. Shallice 1980. Word-form dyslexia. *Brain* **103**, 99–112.

Warrington, E. K. & L. Weiskrantz 1970. The amnesic syndrome: consolidation or retrieval? *Nature* **228**, 628–30.

Weintraub, S. & M. M. Mesulam 1989. Neglect: hemispheric specialization, behavioural components and anatomical correlates. In *Handbook of neuropsychology* Vol. 2, F. Boller & J. Grafman (eds), 357–74. Amsterdam: Elsevier.

Weiskrantz, L. 1980. Varieties of residual experience. *Quarterly Journal of Experimental Psychology* **32**, 365–86.

Weiskrantz, L. 1986. *Blindsight: a case study and implications*. Oxford: Oxford University Press.

Weiskrantz, L. 1988. Some contributions of neuropsychology of vision and memory to the problem of consciousness. In *Consciousness in contemporary science*, A. J. Marcel & E. Bisiach (eds), 183–99. Oxford: Oxford University Press.

Weiskrantz, L. 1990. The Ferrier lecture. Outlooks for blindsight. *Proceedings of the Royal Society, London, Series B* **239**, 247–78.

Weiskrantz, L. 1995. Blindsight – not an island unto itself. *Current Directions in Psychological Science* **4**, 146–51.

Weiskrantz, L., J. L. Barbur, A. Sahraie 1995. Parameters affecting conscious versus unconscious visual discrimination with damage to the visual cortex V1. *Proceedings of the National Academy of Sciences, USA* **92**, 6122–6.

Winocur, G., M. Moscovitch, D. T. Stuss 1996. Explicit and implicit memory in the elderly: evidence for double dissociation involving medial temporal- and frontal-lobe functions. *Neuropsychology* **10**, 57–65.

Young, A. W. 1994. Conscious and non-conscious recognition of familiar faces. In *Attention and performance. XV. Conscious and unconscious information processing*, C. Umiltà & M. Moscovitch (eds), 153–78. Cambridge, MA: MIT Press.

Young, A. W. & E. H. F. De Haan 1988. Boundaries of covert recognition in prosopagnosia. *Cognitive Neuropsychology* **5**, 317–36.

Young, A. W., A. W. Ellis, B. M. Flude, K. H. McWeeny, D. C. Hay 1986. Face–name interference. *Journal of Experimental Psychology: Human Perception and Performance* **12**, 466–75.

Young, A. W., D. Hellawell, E. H. F. De Haan 1988. Cross-domain semantic priming in normal subjects and a prosopagnosic patient. *Quarterly Journal of Experimental Psychology* **40A**, 561–80.

Zeki, S. M. 1990. A century of cerebral achromatopsia. *Brain* **113**, 1721–77.

Zihl, J., F. Tretter, W. Singer 1980. Phasic electrodermal responses after visual stimulation in the cortically blind hemifield. *Behavioural Brain Research* **1**, 197–203.

Author index

Subject index